Wives and Husbands

New Directions in Native American Studies
Colin G. Calloway and K. Tsianina Lomawaima, General Editors

WIVES AND HUSBANDS

Gender and Age in
Southern Arapaho History

Loretta Fowler

University of Oklahoma Press : Norman

Also by Loretta Fowler

(ed. with Daniel M. Cobb) *Beyond Red Power: American Indian Politics and Activism Since 1900* (Santa Fe, N.M., 2007)

The Arapaho (Philadelphia, 2006; New York, 1989)

The Columbia Guide to American Indians of the Great Plains (New York, 2003)

Tribal Sovereignty and the Historical Imagination: Cheyenne-Arapaho Politics (Lincoln, Neb., 2002)

Shared Symbols, Contested Meanings: Gros Ventre Culture and History, 1778–1984 (Ithaca, N.Y., 1987)

Arapahoe Politics, 1851–1978: Symbols in Crises of Authority (Lincoln, Neb., 1982)

Publication of this book is made possible through the generosity of Edith Kinney Gaylord.

Library of Congress Cataloging-in-Publication Data

Fowler, Loretta, 1944–
    Wives and husbands : gender and age in Southern Arapaho history / Loretta Fowler.
        p.   cm. — (New directions in Native American studies ; v. 4)
    Includes bibliographical references and index.
    ISBN 978-0-8061-4116-9 (hardcover : alk. paper)
    1. Arapaho women—History. 2. Arapaho Indians—Social conditions. 3. Arapaho Indians—Kinship—History. 4. Arapaho Indians—Biography. 5. Indians of North America—First contact with Europeans—West (U.S.)—History. 6. Sex role—West (U.S.)—History. 7. Marriage—West (U.S.)—Ethnic relations. I Title.
    E99.A7F695 2010
    978.004'97354—dc22

2009051212

Wives and Husbands: Gender and Age in Southern Arapaho History is Volume 4 in the New Directions in Native American Studies series.

The paper in this book meets the guidelines for permanence and durability of the Committee on Production Guidelines for Book Longevity of the Council on Library Resources, Inc. ∞

For my mother,
Margaret Gilchrist Fowler

CONTENTS

Illustrations

Maps

Acknowledgments

The research for this book has spanned seventeen years. I am grateful to the National Endowment for the Humanities for supporting the research (RO-22497-92) and to the Newberry Library for a Lloyd Lewis/NEH Fellowship in 2001–02, when I wrote the first draft of this book. As I worked on this project, I benefited from conversations, comments, and suggestions from many colleagues, especially Patricia Albers, Brian Hosmer, Clara Sue Kidwell, Theda Perdue, and others who commented on papers that I presented at the American Society for Ethnohistory meetings, Paul A. Olson Seminars in Great Plains Studies (University of Nebraska), and Newberry Library, as well as my readers and editor, Alessandra Tamulevich, at the University of Oklahoma Press.

I had help locating documentary sources for this project from many archivists and librarians, especially John Aubrey at the Newberry Library, William Welge at the Oklahoma Historical Society, John Thiesen and James Lynch at the Mennonite Library and Archives, Barbara Rust at the Southwest Regional National Archives, and Armand Esai at The Field Museum. Wallace Hooper was my research assistant during 1993–94. In using sources with information on individuals, I followed National Archives guidelines.

This work would not have been possible without the contributions of Southern Arapahos who participated in recording personal observations and life stories. Truman Michelson hired Arapaho Jess Rowlodge to interview three Arapahos born in the 1850s—Bichea (Mrs. Fire), Red Woman (Mrs. White Bear), and

Medicine Grass. George Dorsey employed Arapaho Cleaver Warden to observe and interview Arapahos between 1901 and 1905. Dorsey's ethnographic work was an essential source for my interpretations. Finally, Julia Jordan, working for the Doris Duke Oral History Project at the University of Oklahoma, recorded many hours of interviews on a range of topics and life history material with Jess Rowlodge and Myrtle Lincoln in the late 1960s. I also want to thank the Southern Arapaho people for welcoming me into their community and sharing recollections with me. I especially want to express my thanks to Jim Warden and to three friends— Rose Tall Bear Birdshead, Imogene Lincoln Mosqueda, and Mary Mixed Hair Webber. Hardworking, generous, and courageous— like those women referenced in this book—they were my valued companions, consultants, and advisers during the years I worked in the Arapaho and Cheyenne community.

WIVES AND HUSBANDS

Introduction

Little Raven and his sister, Walking Backward, were born in the second decade of the nineteenth century, during a time when the Southern Arapahos were rich in horses and in control of eastern Colorado's buffalo range. As a young man, Little Raven had met the mountain men in Colorado, and he and his sister had sold buffalo robes to the traders. He and other warriors, with assistance from their wives, who made religious sacrifices on their behalf, fought men from other tribes to hold onto their hunting territory. With the arrival of gold miners in 1859, the Arapahos' circumstances began to deteriorate. When Colorado militia attacked a Cheyenne and Arapaho camp on Sand Creek in 1864, Little Raven's band was camped only a few miles away. His oldest sons joined war parties to retaliate, while Little Raven and Walking Backward, with their spouses and younger children, fled south. By this time, Little Raven was the leader of his band, and he, with the assistance of his wives and their families and his brothers' and sister's families, worked tirelessly to restore peace and obtain a safe haven for the Arapahos.

In 1870, the Arapahos settled on a reservation in what is now west-central Oklahoma, and Little Raven and his siblings continued to urge peaceful coexistence, while their older children worked at transitioning to an agricultural way of life and their younger children coped with boarding schools that tried to alienate them from their parents. By the 1890s, the Little Raven–Walking Backward family had been swept up in the Ghost Dance movement, convinced that a new world was imminent in which the buffalo would be numerous again and their deceased relatives would return to life. Little Raven and Walking Backward died before the beginning of the twentieth century, but their children and their children's children struggled to adjust to the monetization of their economy, loss of their reservation lands, and repression of their traditions.

Like the Little Raven–Walking Backward family, Arapahos who experienced the American encounter shared common problems and, depending on gender and other factors such as age, faced different kinds of challenges. These lived experiences were shaped by American domination while becoming the basis on which Arapahos reconfigured their world.

Recent analyses of postcolonial sociocultural transformations recognize the gendered dimension of cultural encounters. In Native North America, relatively egalitarian gender systems were common before the arrival of Europeans. Research in the field initially focused on how the encounter affected women, the central question being whether women's status declined or their material circumstances deteriorated. This work considered women in the aggregate, rather than exploring differentials.[1]

Scholars have addressed another important question: In what ways have women and men not only been affected by the encounter but also shaped that history? Early pioneering work focused on the development of the fur trade, specifically the formative role of Native women married to French and English men. More recent contributions explore the role of gender in forming the Cherokee Republic, women and men's contributions to developing regional economy in the Great Lakes area, and gender as a factor in Christian conversion and the indigenization of Christianity. Theda Perdue identified an important differential in her study of Cherokees—lower-class, or nonelite, women had different goals and strategies than elite women. When nineteenth-century Cherokee government was organized, the influence of nonelite women mitigated the views of elite men.[2]

Wives and Husbands is intended as a contribution to this growing literature on how gender systems are affected by and affect colonial encounters. It is a study of how gender figured in the sociocultural transformations in Arapaho life from the early nineteenth to the mid-twentieth centuries. Arapahos did not have class distinctions, and very few married Americans. Still, some Native women and men had more influence than others, or particular kinds of influence, as Arapahos dealt with American expansion and domination. I identify those groups and individuals who had key roles in the encounter, situate them in kinship and marital "partnerships," and explore how Arapaho ideas and practices of partnering shaped their history.

By "gender system" I mean a set of socioculturally constructed ideas, symbols, and behaviors that are based on perceived differences between men and women. This system, taken for granted as true, is crosscut by other dimensions of power and difference, so that a given society has different ways of attaining prestige and exercising power. At the time Arapahos began dealing with Americans, they had an egalitarian gender system grounded in patterns of complementary, or balanced, relations between women and men. The Arapaho gender system articulated with the age system, a set of socioculturally constructed ideas, symbols, and behaviors relating to age differences. Age categories—childhood, youth, maturity, and old age—were associated with differential prestige and perceived potentialities and limitations. Arapahos assigned governmental and ritual duties based largely on the age system, as manifested in a series of age-graded societies, or "lodges," realized in partnerships between women and men. An individual's status and role, then, depended on his or her position in both the gender and the age systems. Gender and age were encompassed by a larger body of religious conceptualizations and practices (a sociocultural framework) that was a charter for Arapaho life and was permeated by the reciprocity principle.[3]

This book is an account of economic, familial, political, and religious transformations in the lives of Arapahos after they engaged with Americans. The American encounter challenged the Arapahos' sociocultural framework as the colonial regime attempted to impose gender asymmetry where there was gender egalitarianism and to destroy the age-based prestige system that underlay Arapaho life. Implementation of the American assimilation programs exposed inconsistencies in them that encouraged resistance while from time to time privileging some groups based on gender or age (or education, associated with age). The interplay of external American forces with internal Arapaho gender- and age-based power relations revealed tensions between the sociocultural framework Arapahos had taken for granted and the world as lived experience. As Arapaho individuals and groups experienced different opportunities and advantages and coped with different constraints and disadvantages, they developed diverse strategies that created a sense of new alternatives available to all Arapahos.[4]

Over time, Arapahos reconfigured their world, reproducing the old sociocultural framework in some ways and changing it in others. This book explores how and why this happened and examines the way gender, always in interplay with age, shaped Arapaho history.

To account for these historical transformations in a systematic way, I use the framework of cohort analysis and life course study. The term "life course," or "life career," refers to a longitudinal view from birth to death of cohort members. A cohort is a group of people born within a particular time span whose experiences with historical events and circumstances distinguish them from their contemporaries. Cohorts have subsets of people who react to these common experiences in different ways. For example, women and men in a cohort experience and may react to events differently. We can think of a cohort in terms of historical age.

In contrast to historical age, social age (or career stage) is a timetable of the life course defined by people's expectations. The attainment of adulthood or maturity is a stage, for example. Arapahos had understandings of when each of the four stages of life began and ended and what roles were appropriate in each stage. When members of a cohort encounter a historical event, their reactions are influenced by their career stage. But life events can violate the expectations of social aging and can have different meanings for different cohorts, depending on what events the groups actually experienced and on how old they were when they experienced them. This, I argue, is what happened in the Arapaho case.[5]

In applying cohort analysis to the problem of historical age, I identified five cohorts (each named for a woman and a man in the cohort). Focusing on two Southern Arapaho bands, I followed life career patterns for each cohort based on its members' biographical information. This was a longitudinal study, spanning the mid-nineteenth century to 1936, in which I compared the cohorts in terms of how important events and new circumstances influenced lives and how Arapahos formulated and implemented strategies to cope with these conditions. I also made comparisons within each cohort: males and females; well-off and poor; high or low rank (in war, lodge organization, or marital status); and other appropriate measures (such as formal education) to identify which individuals exerted authority or influence. This approach allowed for an understanding of how ideas about gender and gender relations shaped the course of change.

The Little Raven and Walking Backward cohort's birth years spanned 1815–29. These people spent their childhood and youth during the Arapaho heyday, when Arapahos controlled their Colorado territory east of the Rockies. They learned age and gender roles that supported hunting and gathering, warfare, and the ceremonial lodge organization. Young men began their careers as warriors and ceremonial men, and as they matured, they defended Arapahos during the troubles in Colorado and negotiated treaties with the United States in the 1860s. The men's ranking system reflected war exploits, and the lodge organization was age graded so that individuals gained greater authority as they progressed through the lodges. Women, as wives of warriors, lodge men, and chiefs, shaped and shared in their husbands' careers and generally could establish their own careers and influence group decisions. Many of these women lived as co-wives in polygamous households where women had different ranks. In 1870, the men and women who had survived the wars and epidemics of this era arrived on the reservation as mature adults. During the 1870s and 1880s, they headed households, and several men led bands and negotiated with Indian agents when the federal government attempted to implement a "civilization" program. The priests of the lodge organization came from men and women in this group. Few had survived into the 1890s, when Arapahos encountered new religions—the Ghost Dance, peyote, and Christianity—and received allotments of land.

The members of Owl's and Left Hand's cohort were born between 1830 and 1845. They had been children during the time of Arapaho prosperity, but as youths or young adults, they suffered through the decline in Arapaho fortune. During their twenties and thirties, they defended against attacks from the U.S. Army and others. Men were ranked in relation to one another, and so were women. As warriors, men tried to earn coups (war honors) and began to rise in the ceremonial organization. Women, as wives of warriors and chiefs, contributed to and shared in their husbands' careers and established their own. In their households, women had differential statuses. The Owl–Left Hand cohort witnessed the treaty councils in Colorado and Kansas in the 1860s, but the older Little Raven–Walking Backward cohort had seniority in the treaty deliberations. Owl–Left Hand cohort members arrived on the reservation in 1870, when they were in their thirties or forties, and as they aged, they assumed responsibility for transitioning from a hunting way of life to agriculture and finding ways to influence federal policy. Federal agents relied on them to protect the agency and provide leadership for the "civilization" program. This cohort fervently embraced the Ghost Dance in the wake of increasing poverty and disease. In 1892 the surviving members received allotments of land. Those who lived into the twentieth century were elderly landowners at the head of the ceremonial organization.

The Medicine Grass–Bichea cohort's birth years spanned 1846–59. Prior to reservation settlement, as children they had lived in bands that hunted buffalo, engaged in warfare, and faced attacks from the U.S. Army. As youths in the 1860s and early 1870s, most boys would not yet have acquired a record of coups, at least from the perspective of their elders, but they could have accompanied war parties. Young men joined the boys' lodges in preparation for the ceremonial organization, and many began to proceed through the lodges as they matured, although the decline of the lodge organization prevented them from reaching the highest lodges. The girls would have witnessed and possibly participated in women's ceremonial lodges and helped their male relatives in war and ceremonial activity. The people in this cohort married as youths a few years before or at the time of reservation settlement, some polygamously, even though the Indian agents increasingly opposed these unions. On the reservation, they were too old to have been targeted for school, and they apprenticed themselves to the older cohorts economically, politically, and ritually. They had reached maturity in the 1890s, the time of the Ghost Dance, peyote movement, and land allotment. In the twentieth century, they had become senior leaders in the lodges and peyote ritual, and as elderly landowners, they provided major economic support for their households.

The Jessie Spread Hands and Little Raven, Jr., cohort's birth years spanned 1860 to 1879. Some members of this cohort were children in the 1860s, when the Arapahos still lived a nomadic existence and feared attack from enemies, but many spent their entire childhood on the reservation. This cohort's experiences contrasted sharply with those of the older ones. When these Arapahos reached their teenage years, federal officials targeted them for school, but only some actually attended. Those who avoided school (referred to as "camp Indians" by their contemporaries) apprenticed themselves to older people economically and ceremonially. The girls married, sometimes as co-wives, and contributed to and shared in their husbands' careers as they aged.

Those youths in this cohort who attended school on the reservation and then went to off-reservation boarding schools returned
to the reservation and unsuccessfully sought good jobs. In 1892,
the members of the Jessie Spread Hands–Little Raven, Jr., cohort
received allotments of land, but in the twentieth century, federal
officials found the "educated" *men* to be competent enough to have
the trust status of their land removed. While the camp Indians
retained their land, the educated men sold theirs. By the 1930s,
the members of this cohort had reached old age. Some men and
women had high political and ceremonial status, and those who
still had land provided economic support for their multigenera-
tional households.

The members of the Jess Rowlodge–Myrtle Lincoln cohort were
born between 1880 and 1899. As children and youths, all had
at least a few years at reservation boarding schools, and many
followed this by attending an off-reservation school, such as
Haskell. Many of the boys chose not to join the lodge organization. They and their wives embraced the peyote religion and led
in the formation of the Native American Church. Federal officials
considered this cohort to be educated, so the men and some of
the women born early enough to have received an allotment lost
the trust patent on their land, sold it, and worked for hire, often
for settlers. In the late 1920s and 1930s, when the members of this
largely landless cohort were in their thirties and forties, the Bureau
of Indian Affairs considered them mature enough and educated
enough for leadership positions and encouraged their participation in the elective, representative tribal government introduced
during the New Deal.

The organization of the book is chronological. Chapter 1 describes events in the nineteenth century, when the Arapahos were
in what is now Colorado, not yet on a reservation. Traders from
New Spain engaged in the slave and horse trade, American fur
trappers and traders brought new goods, then settlers arrived in
the 1840s and 1850s. All these changes encouraged intertribal
warfare as Arapahos struggled to hold on to their territory and
protect their families. They feared annihilation when American

troops entered their country in the late 1850s. The troubles of the 1860s forced Arapahos from their homeland and threatened to create a wedge between the older leaders, including Little Raven and Walking Backward, working for a permanent peace with the Americans, and the families of the younger warriors, including Left Hand, who wanted to defend their people, militarily if necessary. The outcome of these tensions was the Arapahos' conciliatory strategy toward the Americans, in contrast to the approach taken by their Cheyenne allies. This chapter considers how these difficulties affected women and men in different age groups and how the conciliatory strategy evolved; identifies *which* men and women successfully pushed for a strategy of conciliation; and explains how this new strategy worked to challenge the American colonial enterprise and to reconfigure Arapaho age and gender systems.

Chapter 2 opens in 1870, when Arapahos and Cheyennes settled on their reservation in what is now west-central Oklahoma. A few years later, the herds of buffalo were gone, intertribal warfare ended, and the tribes were dependent on the federal government for their food and clothing. They had to adapt to a federal "civilization" policy that applied sanctions against resistance to programs promoting agriculture, boarding school education, abandonment of religious ceremonies, and ending polygamous households. In 1892, federal officials allotted the tribes' reservation so that each person received acreage, and the remainder of the land was sold. In the face of hostility from the Arapahos' Cheyenne allies, the now fully mature Owl–Left Hand cohort attempted to initiate a new strategy that continued to promote alliance with local federal officials by accommodating to agriculture and education, while working to mitigate the repression of family and religious institutions. Their challenge was to convince younger cohorts to cooperate with the civilization strategy. By the 1890s, reeling from conditions on the reservation, the Arapahos embraced the Ghost Dance revitalization movement. In this chapter, I consider how these new challenges affected women and men of different age cohorts, identify the women and men who led the Arapahos in formulating the civilization strategy and religious revitalization, and explore how these innovations challenged both American domination and the Arapaho age hierarchy and contributed to the reconfiguration of the gender system.

Chapter 3 examines how Arapahos faced new challenges from the Bureau of Indian Affairs' assimilation policy during 1902–1936. In 1902 Congress provided for the sale of most of the allotments and subsequently directed the agency superintendents to oversee individuals' income from the sale and lease of their allotments. The Arapahos became engulfed by poverty and caught up in a money economy that encouraged individualism. Federal land policy discriminated on the basis of gender, age, and education. By the 1920s, the federal government actively promoted young, educated men for leadership positions in elective, representative tribal government and ignored the older leaders and the council form of government over which they presided. These tensions within the Arapaho community led to a new strategy of assertively countering federal policy, a reorientation of religious life toward peyotism, and by 1936 the Arapahos' acceptance of an elective, constitutional government. This chapter considers how these new difficulties affected the women and men in different cohorts, identifies which individuals and groups provided leadership for economic, political, and religious innovations, and examines how these innovations worked to challenge both American domination and Arapaho gender and age systems.

The concluding chapter summarizes my arguments that, first, cohort histories and the partnering of women and men in these cohorts provided the impetus for major transformations of Arapaho life that challenged American domination and the Arapaho age system. Second, partnering both reaffirmed the Arapaho gender system and transformed it as ideas and practices of gender were reworked over time. In this chapter, I also discuss how the Arapaho case suggests some new directions for research on the gendered dimension of cultural encounters in North America.

CHAPTER 1

RULES OF LIFE

Gender and Age before the Reservation, 1805–1869

Theodore Talbot, who traveled with the John Frémont expedition
in 1843, came upon an Arapaho camp where he saw old men
"haranging," men in their prime returning from hunting or talking
about camp business, and women bringing in water or wood,
cooking, or dressing hides. Youths attended the horse herds, and
younger boys practiced with weapons or played games to develop
strength or skill. The older girls assisted the women, and the
young ones played. Talbot's description corresponds to age and
gender roles that reflected and reinforced the Arapaho categories called "four hills of life": childhood, youth, maturity, and
old age. But Talbot had no inkling of Arapaho philosophy or
religious thought.[1]

In exploring gender and age, I use three kinds of information:
accounts by Americans, including Talbot, who met Arapahos under
various kinds of circumstances; accounts of ethnographers and
others who interviewed elderly Arapahos at the beginning of
the twentieth century; and Arapaho narratives. The first two kinds
of sources complement each other in some ways, but each has
advantages and limitations. Traders, explorers and travelers, army
officers, and federal officials identified leaders and reported on
witnessed events, describing political and economic relationships
between tribes and between Indians and whites. These accounts
were often ethnocentric, and they showed little understanding
of Arapaho behavior and thought. The anthropological studies
recorded memories of elderly people, who were influenced by

the topics introduced or the questions asked by the interviewer. These accounts have little information on specific events or personalities, but they reveal what the Americans' writings do not— details on kinship and family life, religious thought and symbolism, and social values. Narratives of Arapahos themselves complement the other sources, and I draw on these to provide more insight into the lived experience of Arapahos. Family wealth differentials and other differences had an effect on these experiences. And the personal stories can offset overgeneralizations in the documentary and ethnographic accounts.

This chapter offers a window into the nineteenth-century Arapaho culture of gender and age and explores how the entry of Americans into Arapaho country affected these beliefs and practices. What was the impact of increased intertribal warfare and of trade with Americans, and later American domination, on Arapaho men and women? Were individuals affected differently, depending on wealth, marital status, or other circumstances? Were there differential effects on the cohorts of Little Raven, Walking Backward, Left Hand, Owl, Medicine Grass, and Bichea? This chapter also examines how new ideas, strategies, and social arrangements emerged among Arapahos as they tried to deal with new challenges and identifies the Arapahos who led these transformations.

AFTER THE WHITE MEN CAME— IMPLEMENTING THE CONCILIATORY STRATEGY

Arapahos camped and hunted big game in the foothills and east of the Rocky Mountains in the early nineteenth century throughout what is now eastern Colorado and southeastern Wyoming. Trappers and traders from St. Louis and traders from Taos found them camped along the headwaters of the North and South Platte rivers, where Arapahos could hunt buffalo in the mountain parks in the winter. In the summer they went to the Arkansas River region, where sizable herds of buffalo could be found. The Arapahos had huge horse herds, and although they had to fight off war parties of Utes and Crows, this region between the upper Platte and Arkansas rivers was acknowledged as their territory by allied peoples.[2]

Traders came to Arapaho camps from Taos with grain, vegetables, metal tools, and blankets. Arapahos also wanted trade goods from the Americans working out of St. Louis, for these traders had a wider inventory of goods and sold guns and ammunition, unlike the Mexicans, who were restricted from selling guns by order of the King of Spain. For probably at least a generation before, Arapahos had attended trade fairs in the Black Hills, where Arikaras from the Missouri River brought products from their villages and some European trade goods. Before that, Arapahos probably traveled to the villages of the Hidatsas, Mandans, and Arikaras to trade meat, horses, and other products, such as prairie turnip flour, for the villagers' corn and tobacco. But the arrival of Cheyenne and Sioux bands on the Missouri River in the latter part of the eighteenth century interrupted this trade, and Cheyennes began to serve as intermediaries in the trade with Europeans. In 1795, when Spain controlled the trade out of St. Louis, Jean Baptiste Trudeau attempted to establish direct trade with Arapahos and other nomadic groups, such as Kiowas and Plains Apaches. With the Cheyennes as intermediaries, he went up the Cheyenne River, probably into the Black Hills, and met with Arapahos, who were eager to obtain trade goods directly from the traders. With the Louisiana Purchase of 1804, the United States gained control of the trade.[3]

In 1805 Arapahos sent a delegation to Santa Fe in an attempt to get regular access to the Taos market. A formal arrangement with Spanish officials would have offered some protection from abuse by independent traders and broken the Comanches' monopoly on trade there. Enemies of Arapahos (for example, Pawnees) had direct contact with American traders on the Missouri River at this time, so trade with the Spanish was attractive. In June 1805 two Arapaho leaders visited Santa Fe to ask for peace, alliance, and trade in northern Mexico for themselves and their allies.

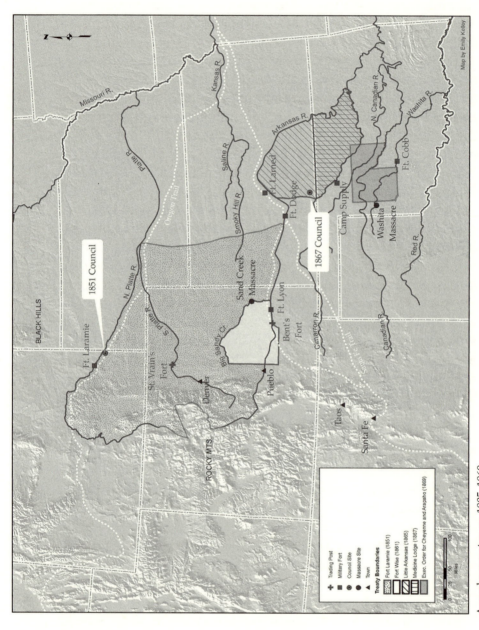

Arapaho country, ca. 1805–1869

They were welcomed, and a few days later, six Arapaho chiefs returned leading 130 people. They traded hides for gunpowder, blankets, and horses. Perhaps they were not able to make regular trips to Taos subsequently, because in 1807, a group of Arapahos and Cheyennes contacted a Spanish patrol on the upper Arkansas River and asked to visit Taos. In August Governor Real Alencaster welcomed an Arapaho delegation in Santa Fe and awarded medals and canes of office to three Arapaho chiefs as well as some Kiowa leaders. They received gifts of textiles, tobacco, mirrors, and metal tools.

Then in February 1809, a large delegation of Indians, including Kiowas, Plains Apaches, and Arapahos led by the Arapaho chief White Wolf arrived. White Wolf was recognized as the leader of all the nations in the delegation. He was received by Governor José Manrriquè, who gave White Wolf a Spanish flag, medal, and cane and promised that they could trade regularly at Taos. But the Mexican movement for independence prevented Spanish officials from developing the alliance, and independent Mexican traders continued to travel to camps on the Arkansas.[4]

The desire for trade led Arapahos to welcome at least some of the Americans who began to enter Arapaho country in 1812. Ezekiel Williams, employee of Manuel Lisa of the Missouri Fur Company, was sent to trap beaver on the Arkansas and Platte rivers. In the winter an Arapaho band provided Williams with "protection," and the leader of the band was his host. When the Americans traded with the Arapahos' enemies or disturbed the game, they provoked resentment and sometimes retaliation, but their trade goods were prized. In 1812, an Arapaho war party of twenty-three, who were in pursuit of some Crows who had raided their camp, met Robert Stuart and other employees of John Astor's Pacific Fur Company. They visited with them peacefully, asking for ammunition but settling for some meat from Stuart's group.[5]

During the 1820s, when Arapahos controlled the eastern Colorado area and had ample horses to trade, band leaders approached Americans, identified themselves as "Arapahos," took them to their camps, and supervised the trade. By this time several trappers

of various national origins were operating in Colorado. The United States sent an exploring expedition led by Major Stephen Long through Arapaho country in 1819–20. Edwin James wrote an account of the trip. He met Arapahos on the upper Arkansas River, where they presided over large camps of several tribes gathered for trade. Although they sometimes traded with Mexicans who came to the Arkansas River, they were at war with them, probably because of Mexican slave raids and because the Americans, then in conflict with Mexico, appeared the more promising allies. Arapaho leaders told James's party they were eager to trade. James identified the principal chief of the Arapahos as Bear Tooth, who was "head chief" of all the tribes trading on the Arkansas; the Cheyennes, still bringing trade goods from the Missouri River, were under his protection. Captain John Bell, with Long's expedition, also reported that Bear Tooth was chief over all the tribes gathered on the Arkansas (that is, while they were gathered on the Arkansas in the Arapaho homeland).[6]

Jacob Fowler traveled with a trading party along the Santa Fe Trail and into the Arapahos' Arkansas River country in 1821–22. He met Arapahos in November 1821, when they were in a Comanche camp. A man ran up and introduced himself as "Arapaho," shook hands, and indicated by signs that he and the approaching Arapaho band would host and protect Fowler's party. In fact, 300 lodges of Arapahos encircled the traders. In a camp of Cheyennes, Kiowas, Comanches, and Arapahos, Fowler and the others traded for buffalo robes, horses, and mules. The Arapahos complained that the gifts Long had promised them had not arrived from the president. They agreed to sell meat to the traders but asked them not to hunt because they would drive off the buffalo in the area. Fowler's party gave the Arapaho leader a medal and gifts, and they sold the men ammunition.[7]

Another military expedition encountered the Arapahos in July and August 1835. Colonel Henry Dodge's orders were to establish peace among Indians in the southern plains. Western expansion of the United States, resulting in population dislocations, caused other tribes to move farther into the plains region and compete with Arapahos as well as other groups already there. Warfare intensified. Dodge held a council with Arapahos and Cheyennes in August. Arapahos promised their friendship and agreed to help the Cheyennes make peace with other tribes, including the Comanches. Dodge engineered peace between the Pawnees and Arikaras (sedentary villagers), who lived farther east, and the nomadic Arapahos and Cheyennes. But it was short lived. Dodge noted that the Arapahos had long been friendly with Americans. "Captain" John Gantt, a guide for Dodge charged with bringing in all the Arapaho leaders, had built a small post to trade with them on the upper Arkansas and is credited with making a peace "treaty" with them, but he had gone out of business. In 1835 William Bent, eager to trade for buffalo robes, was attracting Arapahos to his post with knives, blankets, tobacco, and kettles. He and his partners Charles Bent and Céran St. Vrain had built a fort on the Arkansas in 1833.

At the council held at Bent's fort were 3,600 Arapahos (360 lodges), with 350 Gros Ventres who had allied with them, and 2,640 Cheyennes. Few had guns; guns were probably symbolic of leadership at this time, carried by senior, prominent warriors. Dodge noted that the Gros Ventres (the northernmost division of Arapaho-speaking peoples, most of whom lived in Montana and belonged to the Blackfeet Confederacy) periodically visited Arapahos on the Arkansas River. A band of 350 Gros Ventres were living permanently with the Arapahos. One of their two principal chiefs was Bear Tooth, so it is possible that Gros Ventres were with Arapahos when James encountered them, and that Arapahos relied on Gros Ventres for leadership because they had been trading for many years in Canada. The principal Arapaho chiefs were Old Raven, Buffalo Bull That Carries A Gun, Strong Bow, Black Dog, Mad Bear, and Buffalo Belly. Dodge gave the Arapahos gifts. Later, Charles Bent obtained presidential medals for Old Raven, Buffalo Belly, and Left Hand Soldier to fulfill a promise made by Dodge.

Dodge reported that Arapahos, who greatly outnumbered the Cheyennes, Kiowas, and Plains Apaches in the region, claimed the country between the South Platte and the Arkansas rivers. The Sioux were already on the North Platte, but Arapahos still hunted there. From all reports, the Arapahos were prospering, with many horses and mules, living in a country with plenty of buffalo and numerous herds of wild horses that could be caught and trained.[8]

In the years after their council with Col. Dodge, Arapahos faced new challenges. Increasing numbers of Teton Sioux moved into the North Platte country, and waves of immigrants traveling to Oregon began to disturb the buffalo herds on which Arapahos depended. Arapahos held control of the western part of their country in the headwaters of the South Platte and Arkansas rivers and established an uneasy friendship with the Sioux. They still outnumbered the Cheyennes, whom trader Rufus Sage described as guests on Arapaho land. For much of the year, Arapahos hunted in New Park, described by explorer John Frémont as a circular valley thirty miles wide, surrounded by mountains, with an abundance of water and grass, and in Old Park (near modern Denver), another place where buffalo congregated most of the year.

Arapahos were still prospering. Travelers who met them reported that they had beautifully decorated clothes, lots of meat, and many horses—"immense trains of pack-animals," according to Sage, who traveled through Arapaho country in 1842–43. Charles Pancoast commented in 1849 on the Arapahos' beautifully decorated buckskin clothing and their jewelry. According to Francis Parkman, a gentleman traveler, every year several thousand Arapahos went to Pueblo when the corn was ripe and took what they wanted. Arapahos took large numbers of buffalo robes, horses, and mules to traders at Fort Laramie, where the Bent and St. Vrain posts' rival, the American Fur Company, had a post. Although Bell noted in 1820 that Arapahos and Cheyennes had shown no interest in alcohol, Frémont, Talbot, Sage, Parkman, and the newly appointed Indian agent for the region, Thomas Fitzpatrick, all found that this rivalry had led to the distribution of alcohol, which traders diluted with water. Frémont gave the band he camped with a keg, which resulted in fighting among band members.

The occasional drunkenness in camp could result in violence and violation of the norms of Arapaho society.[9]

Arapahos tried to stay on friendly terms with Americans in the 1840s. Their leaders approached travelers, including E. Willard Smith in 1839; Frémont in 1842, 1843, and 1844; Talbot in 1843; Sage in 1842 and 1843; Lt. James Abert in 1847; Francis Parkman in 1846; and Lewis Garrard in 1847. The chiefs professed friendship and participated in smoking rituals to validate their peaceful intentions. When Arapahos encountered Sage in 1842, they told him they had kept the "peace treaty" with Americans, and the following year they identified themselves to him as "Amigos! Arapahos!" But there were tensions. Americans sold guns to the enemies of Arapahos and, because of careless hunting and the volume of immigrant traffic, Arapahos complained to the Office of Indian Affairs that the buffalo were decreasing and their range restricting. They tried to supervise hunters, including those with Frémont's and Sage's parties. When two American hunters were killed in Colorado, apparently counter to the wishes of Arapaho leaders, Arapahos offered to pay damages at Bent's Fort, according to Parkman.[10]

The military expedition of Col. S. W. Kearny addressed complaints against all the Indians along the trail when he came through the Arapaho country in 1845. Robberies of immigrants would be punished, he said, and he attempted to intimidate Indians with his howitzers. Lt. Abert, a member of the expedition, and Kearny acknowledged the damage done by the heavy immigrant travel: they counted 2,325 immigrants; 460 wagons; 7,000 cattle; and 400 horses and mules. The United States wanted to dissuade intertribal warfare as well because it posed a danger to the immigrants. But Arapahos had to fight the Pawnees and Utes to protect their hunting territory, and they had a longstanding ambivalence toward New Mexico. In fact, Charles Bent reported that they mobilized for war in 1841 because the Mexican officials refused to return a group of Arapaho captives sold to Mexicans by Utes. This was a matter of self-defense to the Arapahos, but after the United States won its war with Mexico in 1848, robberies on the Santa Fe Trail became a U.S. responsibility.

The Arapahos' Indian agent, Thomas Fitzpatrick, worked at getting their promise not to join with Comanches in attacking travelers on the trail. Fitzpatrick reported that the immigrants were promising Arapahos that the United States would compensate them for damages to their country, damages Arapahos had complained about to Garrard and others. And Arapahos regularly stopped wagon trains, such as Augustus Heslep's in 1849, to collect a toll. By this time Arapaho leaders had reputations among Americans as either hostile or friendly chiefs. Friendly chiefs, such as Beardy, approached the wagon trains and spoke with American officials. They carried documents from traders or American officials that supported their peaceful reputations. Fitzpatrick, following instructions from his superiors in Washington, began to arrange a treaty council between the Plains Indians and the United States.[11]

In 1851, at the request of the Indian Office, Fitzpatrick (with help from his father-in-law, trader John Poisal) arranged a treaty council below Fort Laramie on Horse Creek with Arapahos, Cheyennes, Sioux, and representatives of other tribes from the northern plains. The goal was to obtain the tribes' promise to allow travelers and troops to pass unmolested on the Oregon Trail. In return, the United States would pay reparations in annuity goods to the tribes for the damage to their economy. U.S. officials promised that no settlements, other than widely spaced military posts, would be built on the land assigned to the Arapahos and Cheyennes. With Poisal interpreting, Northern Arapaho chief Little Owl and Cut Nose and Big Man signed and agreed to serve as intermediary chiefs between the Arapahos and the U.S. government. An elderly man, "Authonishah," spoke to the Arapaho crowd, sanctioning the agreements and the selection of chiefs: "The whites want to be good to us; let us not be fools and refuse what they ask." He stressed that the treaty was supernaturally sanctioned: "The Great Spirit is over us, and sees all." A delegation of three Arapahos went east with Agent Fitzpatrick to see the large American towns: Storm, a Southern Arapaho, and two Northern Arapahos, Eagle Head and Friday.

Agent Fitzpatrick and his superior D. D. Mitchell reported that the Arapahos kept the peace in 1852 and 1853, even though the buffalo herds became so reduced that they were in want half the year. Contact with immigrants along the Oregon Trail brought population loss from smallpox, cholera, diphtheria, whooping cough, and measles. When the army provoked hostilities with the Sioux in 1854 and the Cheyennes in 1856–57, Arapahos moved away from the regions where there was fighting. They tried to compensate for the scarcity of game by continuing to collect tolls (in food, primarily) from travelers, Agent J. W. Whitfield (1854–55) reported. Medicine Grass, born in 1852, recalled that once when he was a boy, his band stopped a wagon train at a bridge crossing and refused to allow the train to pass until the band received flour, coffee, and bacon. But William Bent noted that Arapahos complained bitterly in 1858 and 1859 that immigrants established settlements in Colorado, where there were rumors of gold. Newspaperman Albert Richardson wrote that Arapahos declared themselves to be peaceful but ordered trespassing Americans to leave their territory.[12]

In 1859 hundreds of miners and settlers invaded the area around what is now Denver, spoiling hunting and camping grounds used by the Arapahos. Leaders attempted to maintain friendly relations. One of the miners, George Jackson, wrote that he frequently visited and traded with Arapaho chief Left Hand and his brother Neva, once giving Left Hand a bottle of "pain killer" for his ailing wife. Arapahos remained, camping part of the year amid or near the settlers, but their situation began to rapidly deteriorate. Their agent William Bent reported in 1859 and Agent S. G. Colley in 1863 that they were hungry much of the time. Denver had several saloons where Arapahos obtained whisky, and Richardson reported that in 1859, there were fights among Arapahos when they were intoxicated.[13]

Southern Arapaho leaders, deeply disturbed about the breakdown in social order and the deterioration of their economy, did what they could to remove Arapahos from settler influences and get guarantees that they could hunt unmolested. They wanted the U.S. government to compensate them for the violations of the treaty of 1851 and make a new agreement that the United States would uphold. In 1857 the principal chief of the Southern Arapahos was Little Raven, and he represented them in relations with the government. In 1860 Arapaho leaders insisted that, despite the provocations, Arapahos wanted peace. A treaty was signed in February 1861 by Little Raven, Storm, Big Mouth, Shavehead (possibly the leader of an Arapaho-Comanche band), and only a few Cheyenne leaders. They ceded the lands acknowledged as theirs and the Cheyennes' in 1851, except for a small area along the Arkansas River. At the time, the Arapahos thought that the Denver settlements would not be allowed to remain, but subsequently the Senate authorized the townsite. Later, as Colorado settler J. Saville reported, Left Hand, leader of the warriors, complained that he had not been there to interpret, and therefore the Arapahos did not understand what they were agreeing to.

When Agent Colley took a delegation to Washington, D.C., in 1863, Little Raven refused to go because Left Hand had not been included. Left Hand and his brother Neva had learned English as boys by associating with Americans. Left Hand's sister Snake Woman had married trader John Poisal, and one of their daughters, Margaret Poisal, married Thomas Fitzpatrick. It was this connection, especially the strong bond between brothers-in-law Left Hand and Poisal, that facilitated diplomacy between Americans and Arapahos. Left Hand was a trusted interpreter for Little Raven in important councils with Americans.[14]

The treaty council did little to solve the Arapahos' problems because settlers wanted to empty Colorado Territory of Indians. Arapaho men began to rob trespassers who killed buffalo. Settlers stole Arapaho stock and abused the women, and one of the settlers' leaders, John Chivington, made an unprovoked attack on a small camp of nine Arapaho lodges on the Platte in 1863, according to Saville. The Cheyennes also were retaliating against settlers and unprovoked attacks. Little Raven asked that the Arapahos be considered politically independent from the Cheyennes, but he was ignored. In October 1864, Left Hand and other leaders were fired upon when they approached Fort Larned carrying a white flag. These incidents culminated in Colorado officials sanctioning a surprise attack on a Cheyenne camp on Sand Creek (near Fort Lyon) in November 1864, even though these people, led by Black Kettle, a proponent of peace, had been told by officials to camp there. This attack became known as the Sand Creek Massacre. The victims were mostly Cheyennes but Little Raven subsequently stated that sixty-six Arapahos (thirty men, twenty women, and sixteen children) died there along with Left Hand, the leader of this band of eight lodges. Several Arapahos escaped and fled north to join the Northern Arapahos. One Arapaho boy was captured and exhibited in a circus, but Little Raven eventually succeeded in having him returned.[15]

In the aftermath of the Sand Creek Massacre, Little Raven led most of the Arapahos south of the Arkansas River, away from the Colorado settlers. By spring, the Cheyennes, Arapahos, and their allies were ready to retaliate for the massacre, and the warriors joined the Northern Arapahos in raiding the overland stage stations and some settlements throughout spring and summer. The massacre was "too bad to stand," Little Raven proclaimed to federal officials in 1865. The federal government persuaded Arapaho chiefs Little Raven, Storm, Big Mouth, and Spotted Wolf to sign a treaty of peace on October 14, 1865. This time the Arapahos insisted that their interpreter be Margaret Fitzpatrick Wilmott (sometimes written Wilmarth). Widowed in 1854, when Thomas Fitzpatrick died, she had subsequently remarried. The chiefs insisted on being paid for the land and the gold illegally taken by settlers and the right to hunt without being molested. The Treaty of the Little Arkansas provided for annuities for fifty years and specified a reservation for Cheyennes and Arapahos between the Arkansas and Cimarron rivers. They could hunt outside this area with a permit from the government. The Senate amended the treaty, providing that no land in Kansas would be included in the reservation. Some of the Cheyenne chiefs and the Arapaho chiefs Little Raven and Storm (Big Mouth had died) and other prominent Arapaho men agreed to the amendment in November 1866, which was translated to Arapahos by Mary Keith, Margaret's sister. But the Arapahos were not able to settle on the designated reservation.

At the treaty council, Little Raven spoke of the trauma Arapahos had experienced at the loss of their homeland and prosperity: "In old times we had nobody to annoy us"; Arapahos had their traders and their hunting grounds. It "will be a hard thing to leave the country that God gave" them on the Arkansas, he said. He expressed their disillusionment with the federal government, which had violated the sacred treaty by allowing trespass and the theft of their annuity goods. The only honest agent they had ever had was Fitzpatrick, he said. But Little Raven and the other leaders in his cohort believed that their only recourse was to establish a relationship of trust with officials from the Office of Indian Affairs (OIA) who sympathized with their plight, and who they hoped could overrule the army officers who had determined to annihilate all Indians, friendly or not.[16]

In response to a clash between some Cheyennes and settlers, in the spring of 1867 General Winfield Hancock led troops in a campaign against the Cheyennes and any other Indians he decided were hostile. The Southern Arapahos kept their distance, mostly staying south of the Arkansas River, and Yellow Bear, the Arapahos' war leader, went with Little Raven to talk with the general in April to profess their friendship and insist that Arapahos had not retaliated, even though Americans had broken the Treaty of 1865. Later that year, officials in Washington decided to attempt another peace treaty with Indians on both the southern and northern plains, where a war was being fought over the Powder River country. Arapahos worked with the army and the Indian Office to send messages to all the tribes of the southern plains. Arapahos also protected the American officials throughout the treaty negotiations.

The council was held on Medicine Lodge Creek in October 1867, and peace was concluded with Arapahos, Cheyennes, Kiowas, Comanches, and Plains Apaches. The Arapaho population now was smaller than the Cheyennes', and when Little Raven, who stressed that Arapahos had considered the 1865 treaty "sacred," insisted on being treated independently from the Cheyennes, he was ignored by the commissioners. Little Raven pleaded for a reservation in southern Colorado, but to achieve peace, chiefs Little Raven, Storm, Spotted Wolf, Yellow Bear, and Little Big Mouth (Big Mouth's son, subsequently known as Big Mouth), and other prominent men (including Powderface, Ice, and Tall Bear) signed the treaty, agreeing to a reservation between the Arkansas and Cimarron rivers, from which Americans were barred. The treaty also provided that the United States would establish an agency on the reservation with farmers, teachers, and other staff and a supply house; the Cheyennes and Arapahos agreed to send children to school. The tribes would receive annuities for thirty years; and hunting by the Cheyennes and Arapahos would be restricted to south of the Arkansas River.

Actually, the Cheyennes and Arapahos had been promised verbally that they could hunt between the Arkansas and South Platte rivers, and this was a major factor in their acquiescence; this promise was not reflected in the written version. The Arapahos' interpreter was Margaret Fitzpatrick Adams (remarried again), who sat next to the chiefs, dressed in a silk dress and elegantly decorated hat. Little Raven unsuccessfully tried to convince the federal government to hire her as the Arapahos' official interpreter. At this council, despite the hostile reaction of other tribes, Little Raven, in speaking for the Arapaho council, persisted with a conciliatory strategy. Despite Arapahos' disappointment with the OIA, the government was their best source of desperately needed supplies, including guns and ammunition. One of the treaty commissioners assured Little Raven, "we will never forget you."[17]

The treaty did not put an end to the Cheyennes' and Arapahos' troubles. According to their trader J. Butterworth, the sale of whisky to Indians at Fort Dodge led to drunkenness and then conflicts and bad judgment. Cheyennes continued to hunt in the Smoky Hill valley, which they believed they had a right to do. A Cheyenne war party of 200, joined by four Arapahos, including a son of Little Raven, went to raid the Pawnees and got into a conflict with some settlers on the Saline River in Kansas in August 1868. U.S. troops led by Colonel George Custer retaliated for these

and other depredations by attacking a Cheyenne village on the
Washita River in November 1868. They killed Chief Black Kettle
under a flag of truce, as well as several women and children. The
Arapaho camps were down river, and the warriors rode to the aid
of the Cheyennes, helping to kill all the members of one small
detachment. Custer withdrew with the remainder of the troops.

Little Raven, always working for peace, then led his people
south to the Red River and, by February 1869, back north to Fort
Cobb. There he convinced the army to escort them to Camp
Supply, where as "friendlies" they could have protection from the
army, receive rations, and hunt buffalo. In summer and fall of
1869 they hunted in the vicinity of Camp Supply. Finally, due in
some part to the representations of Little Raven, President Ulysses
Grant was persuaded to change the boundaries of the Arapaho
and Cheyenne reservation so that they would be farther from
enemies such as Osages and Pawnees and nearer good water,
forage, and the remaining buffalo. In May 1870, troops escorted
the Arapahos and a few Cheyennes to their reservation in Indian
Territory on the North Canadian River.[18]

LIFE CAREERS: THE ARAPAHO WAY

What was largely invisible to the Americans who traveled through
Arapaho country was the religious framework that supported
gender and age relations, as well as all behavior. Arapaho religion
called for respectful relationships between humans and the supernatural forces that generated and maintained life, including
animal and plant spirit beings. The survival of the Arapaho people
depended on fulfilling these religious duties. The link between
everyday behavior and concepts of creation or renewal of life
was impressed on peoples' minds when elders referred to origin
stories and directed ceremonies.[19]

Gender complementarity was a theme in the origin stories:
the male and female life principles both were sources of power,
and they worked together to produce life. The story of the earth's

creation involved the Pipe Being (male in essence) and Whirlwind Woman Being (female). The Pipe Being floated on an expanse of water, prayed for land, and sent the Turtle Being below the surface of the water to find land. Turtle emerged with mud under his feet and, when this dried, Pipe Being blew it in four directions to create land. Whirlwind Woman circled around, shaping the dust into an orb, increasing it to its present size. One could think of the puff of dirt as a seed and the female product the nurtured, larger orb. The Pipe Being instructed men on the use of the pipe. Whirlwind Woman gave instructions to women on their role in the renewal of life, creating the first food (berry) bag, first parfleche (a rawhide bag in which to store dried food), and first quilled tepee ornament. The Flat Pipe bundle (that belonged to the Arapaho people) contained objects that symbolized the Pipe Being's creation of earth and objects that symbolized the importance of female contributions (some regalia from the lodge of the Buffalo Women, including a moccasin containing quills that represented the women directors of quilling rituals). Nih'óóOoo (the Arapaho creator-trickster, sometimes equated with the Pipe Being) once challenged Whirlwind Woman in the making of whirlwinds. She defeated him, saying, "Such is my power." The story affirms that male and female powers are different and each is to be respected.[20]

The origin stories of the lodges reflect the understanding that the lodge organization required both male and female contributions. Arapahos received the "rules of life" when Buffalo Beings taught them the Offerings Lodge and the Buffalo Women's Lodge. These two ceremonies became the "foundation of law," that is, they were the original lodges. The latter was given to a *man and wife* by Buffalo Cow (also referred to as Old Woman), who selected the original Seven Old Men and Seven Old Women and gave them the duties and the "intellects to understand and reason." In addition, Cleaver Warden explained, both men and their wives had to receive the sacred paint of the lodges. According to Warden, the charter for this was the story of Blue Feather's marriage to Buffalo Cow. Blue Feather followed the trail of the Cow and found sinew and trimmings of rawhide she had discarded. Eventually, the trail led him to her tepee, where she was mending moccasins, and they married. Their marriage led to the Buffalo Beings agreeing to become food for humans. The age-graded lodges—Tomahawk, Spear, Lime Crazy, Dog, and Old Men—and the Buffalo Lodge had governmental functions that crosscut the Arapaho band organization and formed the basis of the councils that made political decisions. Generally, men's and women's activities had mythological referents that were symbolized in ceremonies and everyday activities that included hunting, digging roots, making fire, scalping enemies, courting, birthing, quilling, painting designs, and behavior toward relatives and elders generally.[21]

The age hierarchy was a reflection of the four hills of life concept, which equated the life course, the progress of the four seasons, the life force of the universe (the four directions or winds), and the Four Old Men and Four Old Women (representing priesthood). Age categories and associated behavior had supernatural sanction. The authority system of the ceremonial lodge organization (directed by the Seven Old Men) and the quilling rituals (directed by the Seven Old Women) represented the "natural" cycle of life. Individuals owed respect to parents, grandparents, mother's brothers, and father's sisters—all of whom had some measure of authority over their younger relatives (as did older siblings over younger ones). But older and younger relatives had reciprocal responsibilities, as did senior and junior ceremonial participants. In the life course progression through the four hills—childhood, youth, maturity, and old age—Arapaho women and men struggled to live in a "good way," to earn prestige, to acquire authority in households or camps, to acquire supernatural help, and in some cases, to influence the course of history.[22]

The tumultuous conditions of the nineteenth century affected each of the four age groups, and I consider, for each group, how economic contributions, family responsibilities, and, where appropriate, political influence and religious activity interrelated. I also argue that overlaying the Arapaho age categories and associated roles were cohort histories that figured into the conciliatory strategy that Arapahos adopted.

Childhood: Protection and Instruction

Motivated by a perilous world, adults committed to elaborate ceremonies to protect and instruct children and youths. Pregnancy was usually welcomed, and parents desired both boys and girls. A child had an extended group of relatives considered to be close and potential helpmates. Children lived with their father, mother or mothers (if the father married sisters), children of his father and mothers, and possibly a grandparent or younger brother or sister of a parent. Nearby were the tepees of a child's father's brothers or father's father or the lodges of his mother's relatives. All these people were committed to helping the child grow up well. A child's achievements were celebrated publicly. Parents who had the means would have feasts and invite important guests (prominent warriors or elderly people) to recognize a first tooth, first walk, first words, or a boy's first successful hunt for a small animal, such as a rabbit. As a girl approached maturity, she wore a special leather belt (where tools were attached) that signified women's work. The family tried to celebrate these landmarks, even if they could afford only to have a grandparent pray for the child at a family meal. A family might have their children's ears pierced at a public gathering, usually by a prominent warrior. But not every child had his or her ears pierced. As Bird White Bear told Fred Eggan, some families could not afford it; usually only "higher ups" were able to sponsor this ceremony. A family would give away a good horse to a prominent warrior who pierced a boy's or girl's ears. This act was designed to protect and help the child succeed in life. Alfred Kroeber explained that in the ear piercing ritual, the ears were pierced with a sewing awl, which symbolized a spear; the hole represented a wound. The ear ornaments symbolized dripping blood. The piercing allowed the child to escape injury (for it has already happened symbolically) and grow up well.[23]

Orphans were less likely to receive special ceremonial recognition, even though relatives cared for them. If a child's parent died, his or her situation might worsen if a stepparent were not attentive (although ideally, a stepparent should be kind). And there could be conflict between co-wives who were not related. The animosity might affect children's circumstances. Inez Hilger also noted that Arapaho parents might have a favored child, who received more in the way of honors or material goods than the other children. But even families that did not have considerable wealth tried to help their children through prayer.[24]

As children grew up, they learned adult roles through observation and play. Both boys and girls had opportunities to excel, and families that had the means continued to honor their children. Parents frequently asked elderly people to pray for their children, and these elders (usually "grandparents" from both the mother's and father's families) advised children, commented on good and bad behavior in the camp, and told stories designed to teach Arapaho values as well as instruct about the world around them. Children learned that reputation was all-important. Good behavior earned as much respect as outstanding achievements did.[25]

Girls played with toys that represented a woman's duties in the lodge and camp. Dolls represented adults in the family, and there were toy meat racks where girls could dry bits of meat given them by their mothers and toy tepees with furnishings and bags for storing things. George Dorsey found one doll that had symbols of a girl's relatives—her mother used the doll to instruct the child about her responsibilities to kin. A girl's grandmother might make toy pouches, back rests, spoons, and parfleches. Girls had stick horses and toy travoises as they played at moving camp. Athletic games for girls helped them develop strength and agility (ball games or swimming competitions, for example).[26]

Truman Michelson recorded the life stories of two women. One was Bichea, born in 1852, the daughter of Black Deer and Spotted Woman, and the eldest daughter in a large and wealthy family. She had several ponies and a saddle of her own as a child. A Sioux man pierced her ears, after which her father gave him his best riding horse, several packs of buffalo robes, and a silver bridle. She had many toy dolls, tepees, bags, and robes with which to practice women's work, and her mother let her practice slicing meat. Bichea had two brothers and a younger sister. Red Woman was born in 1851 to a moderately well-off Northern Arapaho family that eventually settled on the reservation in Oklahoma. Her father, Red Pipe, was prosperous enough to have more than one wife. Red Woman's mother, Plenty Killer, was the "boss" wife, whose other children included Rabbit Run, Red Woman's younger brother. Red Woman had siblings from Red Pipe's other wives as well. She had toys to practice women's work but did not mention to Michelson that she received the special honor of an ear piercing ceremony. Red Woman described how, after she learned to ride, she chased buffalo calves, tossing ropes over their heads.[27]

Boys practiced marksmanship with toy bows and arrows and hunted small animals and birds. They could hit a silver half-dollar at sixty or seventy yards. In play, boys pretended to be sons or husbands going to hunt on mud ponies or going to war against mud dolls. They might organize a war party to steal meat from a rack. Boys had miniature shields with which they played war, and they had pretend dances with toy drums. They learned to braid rope from rawhide, ride, shoot, and care for horses, first by observation, then by supervision. Boys played athletic games and games of dexterity (darts, javelin, and cup and pin).[28]

A child usually received a pony when quite young. Truman Michelson interviewed Medicine Grass, born in 1852, whose father was Storm and mother Thunder Woman. He had two older brothers and five sisters, children of Storm and another wife, who was probably the boss wife. Medicine Grass recalled that his sister (probably the oldest) rode a pony, but he had to walk when he was a small boy. Not all children had ponies. Families that were well off gave ponies to children to reward them for achievements or good behavior. A child's mother's brother was apt to do this and to take a special interest in the child's comportment. A woman might give a pony to her eldest son or her daughter.

Parents also honored their children by agreeing to their joining a sacred lodge. The Buffalo Lodge chose two little girls to receive honors (that is, carry particular regalia) during their ceremony. The parents had to make substantial gifts to the ritual authorities of the lodge, so the children were generally selected from wealthy families. Two little boys were similarly selected for the Spear Lodge. The clothing children wore in the sacred lodge ceremonies reflected their family's means and reminded them of religious teachings.

The designs that were quilled and beaded on moccasins, leggings, and navel cord bags represented prayers made on behalf of the children who wore them. Wealthy families could provide more clothing and more elaborately decorated garments. The designs were also symbolic of Arapaho ideas about the life force and creation, and they reminded children of how older Arapahos guided and helped them with prayer as well as material things. For example, a child's moccasins often had horizontal lines of quill embroidery or beads on the front that represented paths through life and a symbol of danger, such as a zigzag line representing a snake. The prayer symbolism here was that danger would be avoided as the child went through life. Children's moccasins also might have symbols of the old people's sweat lodge, which were a prayer for long life. A child's leggings might have the Arapaho symbol for the life force or symbols of abundance (water, game), all of which were prayers for long life and prosperity.[29]

Children during these times experienced the trauma of cholera, smallpox, and measles epidemics that killed Arapahos by the hundreds. They had to be careful when they played, lest they be taken captive by enemy warriors. Perhaps Arapahos tattooed their children in hopes of identifying them if they were captured: boys had three horizontal dots on the chest, and girls had one dot in the center of the forehead. In the 1860s, Arapaho children were directly involved in massacres, including those at Sand Creek and Washita River. Red Woman told Michelson that when she heard the shooting at Washita, she grabbed her two-year-old brother White Hawk and her own baby, jumped with them on her horse, and fled.[30]

What of the children of American trappers and traders? We know something about the childhoods of John Poisal's, Thomas Fitzpatrick's, and Kit Carson's Arapaho children. Poisal was born in 1810 in Kentucky and was trapping and trading in Arapaho country at least by 1831. He and his Arapaho wife, Snake Woman, had two sons, Robert (born in 1838) and John (born in 1850), and three daughters, Margaret (born in 1834), Mary (born in 1845), and Matilda (born in 1845). On their way east to Washington, D.C., with the Indian delegation selected at the treaty of 1851, Agent Fitzpatrick (Margaret's husband) and missionary Father Pierre De Smet stopped at St. Mary's Mission School (a Catholic boarding school for Indians, located in what is now Potawatomi County, eastern Kansas). The Jesuits gave them a reception, and the delegation members danced for their hosts. Fitzpatrick took the delegation on a tour of the Indian farms in the area, and he presumably left Robert and his sister Mary at the school. These two children were in attendance there in 1853. In 1854 John Poisal, Sr., arrived at the school in September and took his children (unnamed) with him to Westport (now part of greater Kansas City), a traders' community. He returned a few days later. Robert was confirmed at St. Mary's in 1856.

By 1860, Poisal and Snake Woman had their sons and daughters Mary and Matilda with them in the Denver area, where Poisal traded. Margaret, or Walking Woman, married Fitzpatrick probably in 1849. Their son Andrew Jackson (Jack), who eventually took his father's Indian name (Crippled Arm) was born in 1850, and their daughter Virginia (Jenny) in 1854, the year Fitzpatrick died. In 1860 Margaret lived in Leavenworth, Kansas, with her second husband, L. J. Wilmarth, and her two children. She and Wilmarth had taken the children with them to the Denver area in 1860 to live with her parents for a time, but Andrew entered St. Mary's Mission School October 17, 1866, and left November 9, 1867. Virginia was at the school during the same period. Fees in the amount of sixty dollars were paid for these children, who apparently attended school elsewhere before they arrived at St. Mary's.[31]

Kit Carson married an Arapaho girl in 1835. Their daughter, Adaline, was born in 1837. She must have learned something of women's work from her mother or other Indian women, because when her father took her to Westport, Missouri, in 1843, after her mother's death, she dug up vines to get roots to eat. Carson replaced her buckskin clothing with a dress made "in as fine good as could be bought" and took her to his relatives in Missouri, where she was reared like other white girls, although she probably experienced the frontier prejudice against Indians. She attended rural public and perhaps boarding schools in Missouri.[32]

Youth: The Right Path

An Arapaho child took on more responsibility in the teenage years, and the brother-sister relationship took on major importance. Brothers and sisters helped each other and, upon maturity, each other's children. Boys organized as a company of age cohorts who would go through men's lodge ceremonies together, and after puberty, most girls married.

Boys would begin to wear a blanket in public and a loincloth of some sort. Family relationships were central to the development of adult roles. Arapaho boys and girls considered their father's brothers to be their fathers also, and their mother's sisters, their mothers. All the children of their parents and their parents' siblings were brothers and sisters. All their mother's brothers and father's sisters also were important, especially because they had obligations to these youths. "Grandparents" included the siblings of their parents' parents. Relationships with older family members and ceremonial kin (from lodge membership) took on special significance. Elderly people continued to stress the importance of a good reputation, and youths would assist the elderly by bringing them a drink of water, for example, in return for their blessings or prayers. Older relatives took responsibility for a youth's health, either paying for medical treatment or making a formal vow or

prayer for his health. A boy's mother's brother played an important role in supervising, encouraging, and advising. If a youth's
father was dead, the mother's brother played a central role. Brothers
formed very close bonds, playing with, working with, and protecting each other.[33]

Arapahos particularly encouraged respect relations between
brothers and sisters. When Row Of Lodges, born in 1837, was
about twelve, the husbands of his older sisters mentored him
because he was an orphan. They took him with them on a long
trip toward the Missouri River, where they encountered a camp
of Hidatsas with their lodges in rows. To encourage him in his
future endeavors, they gave him the name Row Of Lodges because
he had shown fortitude during the trip. Brothers had an obligation to enter a respect relationship with their sisters by sending
children as messengers instead of speaking directly to them and
by referring to them by a kinship term. When a sister showed
him attention or helped him in some way (by bringing him a
special food or making him moccasins, for example), a brother was
supposed to give her a substantial present. Fulfilling one's duty
to kin helped establish a good reputation, and notable generosity
brought additional prestige.[34]

When a boy reached his teenage years, his economic contribution to the household became more important. As Talbot observed,
herding the family's horses was a youth's responsibility. Although
youths were not allowed to participate in a communal buffalo
hunt, a youth's father usually taught him to handle horses,
butcher, and hunt other large game. His father or grandfather
usually made his arrows. When he succeeded in killing his first
game animal, such as an elk or a buffalo he had stalked, his family
would honor him with a feast to which important people came,
or a relative might give him a horse or give someone else a horse
in his honor. Medicine Grass's father, Storm, in whose band he
lived, taught him to make bows and arrows and care for the
pony he got when he was a youth. It was a wild horse (particularly good for hunting because it did not fear buffalo and was
long winded), and he broke it himself. As a youth, he began to

hunt buffalo under his father's supervision, at first concentrating on calves. Once, after hunting a bear with other youths (including Rabbit Run and Flint), he shared his kill with all the boys in the party. When eventually his mother's brother took him on a buffalo hunt and killed thirteen buffalo, they took three and notified the others in their camp to take the rest of the meat. They claimed the hides, Medicine Grass explained, because they needed them to repair tepee covers.[35]

The youth's father or grandfather, or sometimes his mother's brother, usually helped him establish himself as a warrior. If the father was prominent enough to lead a war expedition, he might allow his son to go along. Or a youth might volunteer to accompany a war party as a servant or helper and gradually gain experience that way. Youths rarely attempted a vision quest to obtain a spirit helper to protect them and make them successful. Those who had a relative who owned a bundle (indicative of a relationship with a spirit helper) could ask the relative to gradually transfer some of the powers and teach the proper way to establish a relationship with the spirit. If a youth did have a vision, he asked an old man to interpret it for him.[36]

Youths born in the 1830s and early 1840s (members of the Left Hand cohort) had many opportunities to meet family expectations for a career in war. Powderface was born in 1836 and spent much of his youth in the Black Hills, being mentored by his father, a renowned warrior. His father and his father's fellow war chiefs encouraged him to become an outstanding warrior. When Powderface was seventeen, his father gave him his own shield (transferred his war medicine) and sent him on a raid against Pawnees. He returned with six scalps, which he gave to his father. The "old chiefs" then made him the head of a group of warriors (probably gave him a high degree in the Tomahawk Lodge).

On the other hand, Left Hand (not the man killed at Sand Creek) was an orphan. Born in 1839 in the Oklahoma panhandle, he was raised by his grandparents after his mother, Hairy Face, died when he was small. His father, Crooked Foot, was killed on a buffalo hunt and did not have the opportunity to mentor him.

Left Hand recalled that as a youth he learned from his grand-parents how to go on the warpath, and they encouraged him to become a great warrior in battles with Utes and Pawnees. By the age of twenty-three, he had an outstanding record as a warrior and became a leader of war parties. He said that the old people had helped him with his war medicine, especially in the treat-ment of wounds. He had a high rank in the Tomahawk Lodge. He stated that it was his aim in life to make his name "great among [his] people."

Other youths, born later, had only a few years before reserva-tion settlement to acquire war experience, and some had more opportunity than others. Sitting Bull's brother Arrow (a member of the Left Hand cohort) took him to war against the Pawnees when Sitting Bull was very young—not quite a teenager. When the Pawnees were coming toward them, he told Sitting Bull, "Let your horse go." Every arrow missed him. He had to do this four times, and every time the enemy missed him. Arrow said, "You're going to be a man or going to get killed." Arrow mentored Sitting Bull (born in 1853—a member of Medicine Grass's cohort) and presumably transferred protection to him from his own spirit helper. But Medicine Grass's father would not allow him to go with his older brother on a Cheyenne war party. This was a time when Storm was a chief committed by treaty to peace. In conse-quence, Medicine Grass told Michelson, he was still considered a boy (not a mature man) when he was sixteen. He was on the scene at the Washita Massacre but did not engage in combat. He and a friend came upon the site of the slaughter, and Medicine Grass struck a dead soldier. They found a severed hand, carried it for a while, then threw it away.[37]

Early in their teenage years, boys of approximately the same age formed a group and selected an older man to be their cere-monial "elder brother" (he would be a Tomahawk Man). They tried to convince this man to take an offered pipe, which would obligate him to help them. Once organized, they became the Kit Fox Lodge and held periodic dances, and they were sent on errands by the older men. Arapahos regarded their dances as a service because these events kept the people's spirits up, according to Cleaver Warden's interviews. No ritual secrets or privileges were associated with the Kit Fox Lodge, but youths had to be members if they expected to work their way up the series of age-graded lodges and achieve their people's respect. Not to participate meant that a youth could not mature; he might age chronologically, but he could not become a man socially. As a lodge member, a youth learned to cooperate with other youths who might not be kinsmen, and he received physical training. They raced, swam, walked long distances and slept on the ground, carried heavy objects, ran errands from camp to camp, and had wrestling competitions. They participated in shooting contests with a bow and arrow and in other competitions to prepare for war.

In a few years, all the Kit Fox comrades went through the Star ceremony with their elder brother's help. They announced publicly that they were ready for war parties; in fact, they probably had some kind of war experience at this point. Sometimes youths surreptitiously went in small groups to try to steal horses. They had some new duties in the camp, but still no religious knowledge was conveyed or ceremonial status earned in the Star Lodge. During the Offerings or Sacrifice Lodge, both the Kit Foxes and the Stars had duties, such as participating in sham battles and going on errands.[38]

It was possible, though rare, that a youth vowed to fast in the Sacrifice Lodge (virtually an annual event) in return for supernatural help, particularly in war. In such a case, the youth's father might also vow to participate in order to encourage his son. In the Offerings Lodge, in which men of all ages fulfilled their vows, a participant gained ritual knowledge and, even if too young to have entered the first of the men's lodges, began a career in the ceremonial organization. After he made his vow, he had to select a ceremonial "grandfather" to instruct him in the ceremony. The relationship with the grandfather was lifelong. They were supposed to support each other and never enter into any kind of conflict. Sisters, mothers, and father's sisters also provided essential support for youths' ceremonial participation.[39]

Youths also began to court girls. Most did not marry until they were considered mature men. In courting, youths usually covered themselves with a blanket and waited on trails for girls to pass by on their way to gather wood or get water. They tried to interest a girl in talking briefly with them. Or at night they might adjust the girl's family's tepee flaps so that smoke would get into the tepee and the girl would go out to fix the flaps, during which a brief conversation could be held. Reputation mattered, however, and older relatives discouraged youths from trying to seduce married women. Reputation would also suffer if any kind of coercion were used in trying to talk to a girl. If, for example, a youth had sexual contact with a resisting girl or untied the "rope" she wore under her clothes to prevent sexual intercourse, he was disgraced, and the girl's family pressured his family to hold the marriage ceremony. Youths tried to build reputations as good warriors so that they could attract girls and eventually be considered good potential husbands by girls' families.[40]

Girls reached the status of maturity sooner than boys, after the start of menses. A girl in this condition was regarded as infused with supernatural power (*beeteet*—she has the life force). This power was uncontrollable by her, so she avoided vulnerable people, such as sick people or participants in a religious ceremony. After the start of their menstrual periods, some girls tied a cloth or a blanket around their middle, and some wore a rope or cord to prevent intercourse. As youths, girls continued to receive direction and mentoring from old people, whom they waited on to obtain blessings. A girl's father's sister took great responsibility for instructing her in the importance of reputation. The father's sister also gave the girl gifts to honor and reward her. Grandparents and parents took responsibility for a girl's health. Her relationship with her older brothers or brothers near her own age assumed great importance as well. A respect relationship was in force so that she avoided being near her brother and did not speak to him directly. Her duty was to do favors for him, such as cooking him a special food or making him moccasins. He should reciprocate for these actions by giving her a substantial gift. If he gave her a horse, she would mount it and ride around the camp praising him.[41]

Mothers and grandmothers taught girls to cook; dry meat, roots and berries; and sew hide clothing. Girls assisted other women in tanning hides. By observing and assisting, they learned how to put up and take down tepees and how to transport the household goods on a travois or packhorse. Girls also helped gather edible roots and berries, learning about plant foods and medicines in the process, and they fetched kindling and water for their household. Girls demonstrated that they would be good wives by trying to show the camp that they were good workers and had good dispositions. As they grew up, they might acquire horses from brothers or inherit horses from family members. They could make gifts of their horses to their relatives, which would bring them respect.[42]

As a teenager, a girl might have dreams suggesting that she should orient herself to some sort of religious activity. Older women helped interpret the dreams. Occasionally, a girl began to sit with old women when they did ceremonial quillwork, and in this way, she began a ceremonial career. In the one case of this that Warden mentioned, the girl's mother had a high ceremonial office and was encouraging her daughter to pursue high ceremonial rank: Firewood began to "work in quills when fifteen and was induced to work and honor herself and her relatives through the stimulus offered by her mother who was a famous worker [in quills]." A girl could make a prayer vow to sacrifice something in return for a relative's recovery from illness or a male relative's safe return from battle. In the event that a relative made a vow to participate in the Offerings Lodge or one of the men's or the women's ceremonial lodges, a girl could help by contributing labor or property. All these efforts were respected.[43]

Michelson learned from Bichea that when she was a youth, her relatives, who were prominent people, helped her to acquire the knowledge that brought prominence as an adult. At ten, she was closely supervised. By fourteen, she was able to tan hides and bead clothing. Her mother and father's sister were quill workers, and she practiced under their supervision, presumably making only token "payments." Her mother was a doctor, from whom she learned the use of plants for curing. Michelson's interviews of Red Woman also revealed how she learned women's work. Her mother taught her to slice and dry meat and gather roots and berries and dry them. She learned to tan hides by watching her mother.[44]

Girls, as well as boys, dealt with fear of disease and enemy attacks. Girls were particularly vulnerable to capture. The story of "Mrs. North" illustrates the kind of bravery and ingenuity Arapahos encouraged. She was out picking chokecherries with three other girls when a Ute war party came upon them. The three other girls managed to escape, but she was taken prisoner. In the Ute camp for three years, she had to work for the household of her captor—chopping wood, butchering, and cooking. At night she was tied to an old woman of the household. But eventually the old woman "pitied" her and made provisions and two horses available. She fled, enduring great hardship and evading a search party. Eventually she made her way to a stagecoach station and a man there, "Mr. North," returned her to the Arapahos ("friendlies" at this time). In the Arapaho camp, they were holding the Offerings Lodge, and her brother and uncle had made a vow that as a result of their sacrifice, she would return from captivity.[45]

Girls were advised to be very careful during the courtship period, and mothers or grandmothers watched the girls carefully. Some, if not all, girls wore a "rope" that tied their legs together when they were not under supervision. They were instructed to refuse to elope with a suitor, and instead marry a man of whom the family approved. If a man tried to take liberties when a girl was in a public place and behaving properly, he risked being attacked by a group of women. Ideally, a girl would not go for water or into the brush without a chaperone. Going alone with a man to a place outside the camp would put a girl at risk, and she was held accountable, not the man. Bichea's mother accompanied her to the brush when she went to relieve herself and to public ceremonies at night. She told Bichea "not to glance around in public places, not to laugh out loud, not to peep at young men whenever they were near our tepee, and not to respond to the flashes of mirrors held by young men at a distance, as these indications would govern young men's opinions of the character of a girl." [46]

In reality, girls and women played a more active role in courtship. Despite her mother's attentions, Bichea received a ring from an admirer. Red Woman told Michelson that boys courted her when she went for water, and she met boys secretly. Both these women had prestigious gift-exchange marriages. Drawings by Arapaho men often included courting scenes—usually a man standing by a woman with an ax (which she was using to chop wood). The women appear to be assertive in relation to the men. Warden saw one pair of leggings that had a design that represented men waiting in the trees to court women—he pointed out that the design was a "women's jest." In other words, they found men obsessed with courting women ridiculous. Women did not see themselves as subordinate in these encounters. [47]

The Poisals, living in the Denver vicinity, experienced the fear of attack by settlers and miners. In fact, the family was attacked at least once. After Robert's time (and possibly John's) at St. Mary's School, he joined his parents in Colorado and worked with his father as a trader and teamster. A speaker of Arapaho, English, and Spanish, he interpreted for Arapahos and others. John also lived with his parents in Colorado. When his father died about 1861, he apparently stayed with his mother and her Arapaho relatives. He was present during or immediately after the fight on the Washita River in 1868, when he was eighteen. He apparently obtained some kind of employment with the army at least occasionally. Jack Fitzpatrick and his sister, Jenny, lived with their mother, Margaret, and her American husband in Leavenworth, Kansas. After attending St. Mary's as a teenager, Jack returned to stay with or near his Arapaho relatives. He was with John Poisal at the Washita fight. In 1860, Mary, or Small Woman, married Ben Keith, an American, and remained associated with the Arapahos. By 1864 Matilda was also married to a white man by the name of Pepperdin. According to Janet Lecompte, Mary and her mother were at Sand Creek when the camp was attacked. Her husband may have been out hunting with the Arapaho men at this time. These children, then, experienced the violence in Colorado as did other Arapaho youths.[48]

In Missouri, Adaline Carson, very well educated, was visited regularly by her father, and in 1851 he took her to New Mexico, where he had married a Mexican woman. Along the way she was terrified by hostile Cheyennes. Once in New Mexico, Kit and his business associate, a trapper by the name of Louis Simmons, agreed on a marriage between Simmons and Adaline. Simmons, described as "grizzled," was more than twice her age. She never had any association with Arapahos.[49]

Maturity: Warfare, Polygamy, and Rank

Marriage

For women, marriage usually occurred soon after menses and was the start of adulthood. Men married when they could support a household. Marriage was very important to building and maintaining reputation. A person could get a bad reputation by mistreating a spouse or refusing to behave cooperatively and congenially with in-laws, as well as with kinspeople. There were two types of marriage: gift exchange and elopement. Gift exchange was prestigious. Elopement could be a legitimate marriage, but it did not bring the parties as much respect as gift-exchange marriage.

In a gift-exchange marriage, the would-be groom might initiate the negotiations. A young man seeking to marry for the first time could choose his prospective bride through courtship or by merely observing her, or a girl's oldest brother might approach a young man and suggest the arrangement. In either case, the young man would go to his parents and discuss the girl's character and her parents' record of helping others. If they agreed, a female relative (sometimes an old woman) was sent to the girl's family with as many horses as the family could afford. The young man would solicit horses from his male relatives. The bride-to-be's brother would make the final decision, and if he agreed to the union, he would distribute the horses among the men in the family. The girl's family asked her to consent. She usually did so readily to fulfill her duty to her older brother and show her affection for him; sometimes, she was pressured to consent. Of course, she also could have been courted and could have subsequently encouraged her suitor and convinced her brother. The groom-to-be's family would send as many presents as the women in the family could collect: bedding, clothes, moccasins, and food in parfleches. The bride's brother's wife distributed these gifts among the women of the bride's family. Then the bride's female relatives (especially the mother and father's sister) provided a tepee and gifts, including clothing, moccasins, bedding, and other household items, and the men in the family (especially brothers and father's brothers) contributed horses. Each should contribute the number of horses he received from the groom. Then the groom and his family were invited to a feast where they received the women's gifts and the horses. They took an amount equal to what they contributed. So the gift exchange was supposed to be an equal exchange between families. At the feast the bride and groom ate together, and old people prayed for them. A rich family might have a ceremonial priest preside; they would give him gifts in return. This completed the marriage ceremony.[50]

Bichea told Michelson that in 1866, her first husband, Fire Log, had sent his mother, two sisters, and father's sister to ask her brother and her mother's brother to consent to marriage with her. She had not met him. Her brother came to talk to her and stressed that the marriage would be good for their parents and that they approved. Her mother talked to her to ask what she thought of the idea. Bichea agreed because she did not want to hurt her brother's feelings—she would express her support for him this way. Her husband's family brought eight horses, and her family returned eight. The horses were laden with robes, Mexican blankets, quivers, bows and arrows, guns, and saddles. Red Woman married her first husband, Flying Crow, a warrior, when she was fifteen. Presumably this was a gift-exchange marriage.[51]

There were alternative forms of a gift-exchange marriage. If a young man were marrying a high-ranking leader's daughter, he might live in the girl's camp and work for her father for a time. A chief might allow a young man without much wealth to work for him in lieu of the actual gift exchange. The girl's family would have a feast and invite the groom to officially acknowledge the union. Sometimes a father was ambitious for his son to marry the daughter of a high-ranking leader. He would give gifts and horses to the leader or chief. The chief would hold the wedding feast and provide household gifts but would not return horses. Arapahos regarded this as a great honor to the chief.[52]

Arapahos also practiced alliance marriages. Chiefs often married women from other tribes and might arrange a marriage of a relative to a person from another tribe. This was considered very honorable and would have involved gift exchange of some sort. Several Arapahos married Plains Apaches during the time that a group of Apaches were adopted in an Arapaho council. After that, the Apaches camped with Arapahos in the camp circle. Little Raven had a Comanche wife for a time, probably to strengthen the Arapaho alliance with Comanches, into whose territory they had moved. Little Raven's brother Trunk also married a woman who was part Comanche. In fact, Arapahos told Kroeber how this kind of marriage was important to establishing peace among Arapahos themselves. Before Arapahos began to congregate between the Platte and Arkansas rivers, they lived in five north-to-south divisions. There was a quarrel between the two northernmost divisions that was resolved when the ritual leader from one married a woman from another. This unified the divisions. And two Arapaho bands—the Blackfeet (a band of Blackfeet and Gros Ventre to which Row Of Lodges belonged) and the Bad Faces (Little Raven's band) intermarried to reinforce their social bond.[53]

In an elopement marriage, a young man would convince a girl to leave with him. They would go to his mother's or father's

parents or his father's sister's or mother's brother's camp. The
women in his family would collect gifts and have a feast for the
men in the family to persuade them to contribute horses. Members
of the family of the would-be groom would take the gifts to the
girl's family. The girl's family would make a return; all parties
were supposed to be satisfied with what they got, but the groom's
family tried to make the best present that they could. The girl's
family held a feast and sometimes invited an old woman to advise
the couple; she would urge both families to accept each other.
The couple left the feast legitimately married. The girl's parents
and brothers had the option of rejecting the would-be groom
and taking their daughter and sister back. Hilger noted that the
elopement was recognized and tolerated but not preferred. The
girl who chose to elope might be abandoned by the man, which
would be disastrous for her reputation. Her family would try to
pressure his family to go through the marriage ceremony. If a girl
in these circumstances should become pregnant when unmarried,
she would not be wanted as a wife, and the child would be considered fatherless, although her parents or other relatives probably
would care for them. Neither the young woman nor the man
involved would be respected, according to Hilger.[54]

After a couple were married for some time, the husband might
ask for one or more of the bride's sisters as co-wives. If her family
was satisfied with him, they agreed. There might not be another
gift exchange because the initial exchange was between families.
But it would be prestigious if some gifts were exchanged. These
plural marriages usually involved older men in their prime.
In the early 1860s, Owl, the daughter of Little Raven's brother
Trunk, first married Bear Robe (a warrior in Little Raven's cohort)
as her older sister's co-wife. A girl could refuse to become a
co-wife, and according to Kroeber, often her wishes were honored.
Apparently, pressure could be applied to persuade a reluctant girl.
In the 1870s, Salt, a Northern Arapaho, was a teenager when her
brother was killed in battle. Her uncle agreed to her marrying a
man already married to her sisters. She was to be the fourth wife.
She told Hilger that if her brother had been alive, he would not

have agreed because he "thought much" of her (and would have preferred a more prestigious marriage). She ran away, but her new husband's sisters brought her back by force, and she had to be persuaded by men in her family to accept her husband. Salt's experience aside, probably women more readily objected to a co-wife who was not a sister.[55]

Arapaho men might take female captives when they went on war expeditions. It is likely that these women were considered concubines and that their captor had complete control over them. Female captives were part of the booty of war parties. Road Traveler, born in 1831, took two Sioux women captive. His granddaughter characterized captives as women who worked for the household. The reports of Americans also make reference to this practice of taking female captives. In 1812 Stuart met an Arapaho war party from a camp on the South Platte pursuing Crows who had stolen some Arapaho women. It was probably captive women (although the record does not say one way or the other) whom Captain Bell, with James's expedition in 1820, saw Arapahos bringing into James's camp to spend the night in return for some tobacco or vermillion. The brother of the principal chief Bear Tooth brought a woman for this purpose. Only one case on record shows how a captive woman was treated by Arapahos. A Ute woman was held prisoner by Arapahos for years and offered by her captor to other men, then sold to a Cheyenne man. After he died, his wife took her to Camp Cantonment and offered her to soldiers for money. If a captive girl were to be adopted by an Arapaho family, her status would change and she could be married. Similarly, Arapahos would adopt children they captured and raise them as Arapahos.[56]

A few Arapaho women had American husbands. In the 1830s Kit Carson and John Poisal, trappers and traders, married Arapaho women, presumably according to Arapaho custom, although the gift exchange was probably modified to be more narrowly configured. At the 1865 treaty council, Little Raven referred to Carson as "raised with Arapahos," probably because he was very young when he met them. He may have been sponsored by an Arapaho family that made gifts on his behalf. Carson's Arapaho wife, whose wifely skills he praised, died a few years after their marriage. Subsequently, he married a Cheyenne woman; they soon separated.[57]

John Poisal married Snake Woman about 1833 and remained with her and her Arapaho relatives all his life. She was a Blackfeet captive, adopted into Left Hand's family when she was a small child. Poisal, born in Kentucky in 1810, had come as a teenager to Colorado with the St. Louis traders and traded between Santa Fe and Missouri in the 1830s. He worked with John Gantt and William Bent in the Arkansas River trade with Arapahos and was often in the company of Left Hand. He worked for the American officials, acting as interpreter in their dealings with Comanches in 1855–56. In 1857 he had a camp at the mouth of Cherry Creek, where he raised cattle and horses. His in-laws relied on him. On one occasion in the winter of 1857–58, a Cheyenne war party led by Snake Woman's relative Ice received a cow and a loan of two horses from Poisal. In 1860 he was living at the junction of Cherry Creek and the South Platte, when his family was attacked by drunken Americans. He defended Snake Woman from sexual attack, endangering his own life.[58]

John Poisal's daughter Margaret, who was married to Thomas Fitzpatrick from 1849 to 1854, traveled with Fitzpatrick to Washington, D.C., and throughout the plains as he performed his duties as agent to the Arapahos and Cheyennes; she was his legal heir, inheriting over ten thousand dollars and two lots and houses in Westport. Fitzpatrick was prosperous, and Margaret had many luxuries. Her second husband, L. J. Wilmott, born in 1823 in Ohio, lived with her in Leavenworth, where in 1860 he was a "gardener" worth over one thousand dollars. At John Poisal's urging, he moved his family to Colorado to try to take advantage of the gold rush. There the census lists him as worth twenty thousand dollars. He may have controlled Margaret's property at that time. When Margaret was at the Medicine Lodge treaty council, she was married to her third husband. She told a *Chicago Tribune* reporter, who described her as well educated in an eastern seminary, that she had been wealthy, living in "great style," when she had resided in Leavenworth. She lost her husband and became poor, she said. At the time of the council, she was living on lands given her by Arapahos. Reportedly, she along with the treaty commissioners and Indian leaders drank alcohol to excess. Ben Keith, married to Mary, another of Poisal's daughters, remained with her and her Arapaho relatives all his life. The Carson and Poisal cases are probably exceptional. There is no record of how many Arapaho women were deserted by American men, although reservation records reveal several children with "unknown" fathers described as having Indian and "white" heritage.[59]

Intensive warfare that resulted from slave raids, competition with other tribes over territory, and the need for trade with Americans led to high casualties among warriors. Polygamous marriage and, I would argue, its increasing frequency helped Arapahos cope with the population imbalance between women and men. The emergence of the boss wife (who directed work in the household) and the ranking of women in households (with captives ranked lowest) provided for the organization of labor in families, especially large, wealthy families. Disease and enemy attacks took their toll on both women and men. Good relations between in-laws facilitated the replacement of husbands with husbands' brothers, and wives with wives' sisters. In this way, Arapahos developed marriage customs and household organizations to accommodate the difficult circumstances in which they lived.

Women

After her marriage, a woman played a central role in her household's economy. A woman's labor was viewed as equivalent to and in exchange for a man's. She prepared the family's food and distributed it. It was her duty to dry as much food as the family needed for the times when the hunt was poor or plants not available. Her duties included moving the family's tepee and household goods. She often worked with a group of women from her household, particularly when gathering plants or tanning hides to use for manufacturing clothing, tepees, and blankets. In 1843–44,

Frémont noted complementary subsistence activity by men and women: men hunting and women digging for roots. He also saw women riding their horses to the hunting grounds to help butcher and transport meat back to camp. Father De Smet noted in 1851 that women were working in groups removing stones from plums to prepare the skins for drying. Warden's notes indicate that it was a wife's duty to make the fire in the tepee, but her husband had to be present. His presence was necessary because he protected the tepee even though she owned it. This was a symbolic exchange of male and female labor and reflected an incident in an origin story: fire was made in a woman's lodge with stone and wood because the Pipe (male power) made light when the earth was created. Similarly, women's tools and the items they made had origin story referents and religious significance. For example, parfleche designs had been originated by the actions of Whirlwind Woman, a female spirit being.[60]

A wife owned the tepee, all the furnishings, the food she collected, and the food her husband or sons brought into the tepee. She owned horses she received as a child, youth, and married woman, and she owned the clothing and other household items she made. A woman's scraper, used on hides and in digging roots, might have marks on it that stood for her "degrees," or accomplishments in ritual matters (for example, the number of times she participated in a particular ceremonial lodge). Women kept a record of the robes and other quilled articles they made, the hides they dressed, and the number of times they received paints in the Dog Lodge. Red Woman took great pride in the number of tepees, robes, leggings, and bed rests she made. And she tanned hides for trading purposes. Kroeber noted that sometimes women's beadwork designs referred to geographical territories Arapahos used and events at particular places, so their work also included recordkeeping for their family or band. Women were honored for and took pride in being industrious, skillful workers.[61]

Travelers reported that men and women owned property independently and traded separately. James's expedition in 1820 on the Arkansas River obtained horses, mules, and rawhide rope from Arapaho men and purchased dried meat, dried berry cakes, and salt from Arapaho women. James carried trade goods for both men and women. Women particularly wanted awls to make their work easier as well as items such as combs, mirrors, paint, and beads. Men wanted guns and ammunition, tobacco, knives, and blankets. At Bent's Fort, women and men traded robes separately in the 1830s and 1840s. Income from the buffalo robes was probably divided in some way between the hunter and his wife (or possibly his mother or sister). Profits from robes tanned by captives probably went to the owner of the captives. In 1859 Richardson reported that Arapaho women made beaded moccasins and sold them for sugar in the Denver area. Both men and women accepted goods delivered to Arapahos from federal officials in fulfillment of treaty obligations. When the goods were distributed at the 1867 treaty council, the chiefs came forward to receive them accompanied by women (probably their wives); the women led the packhorses away.[62]

A woman built a reputation for good character not only by industry but also by how she treated her relatives. Ideally, she gave gifts to her brother, his wife, and his children. Often, she took responsibility for obtaining the cradle for her brother's child; this required feasting old women with the ceremonial knowledge for cradle making. She would also be respected if she gave colts from her horses to her children, younger brother, or other relatives. Women decorated garments with quill or bead designs that conveyed prayers, usually for the wearer's good health. She could make extra moccasins, leggings, pillows, beaded bags, painted parfleches, and other clothing or household items to contribute to relatives who were arranging marriages or participating in religious ceremonies. After marriage, much of her time was spent ornamenting garments with prayer designs for her husband. She was also expected to show generosity to her in-laws by giving gifts—making moccasins for her father-in-law, for example. Daughters-in-law also received gifts from their husband's parents. Arapahos respected a woman who got along with her mother-in-law.[63]

George Dorsey was told a story with this theme: an Arapaho woman (the "Mrs. North" referred to above) was captured by a Ute and worked for a household chopping wood and slicing meat. But, after she formed a bond with her captor's mother (probably a "mother-in-law"), she helped her escape. Hilger noted an instance in which sharp criticism of a daughter-in-law (in this case by her father-in-law) moved the woman to suicide. A sister's rejection could move her brother to suicide. Another woman, Big Head, living with the Northern Arapahos, asked her brother to loan her a horse for a travois when they were moving camp. He refused, saying he was saving it for a buffalo hunt. As Jess Rowlodge told the story, "In them days, you know, if your brother refuse you of anything that you requested him, it was a kind of disgrace—a bad feeling." So she decided to leave and go south to the Southern Arapahos where her sister was married to Chief Yellow Bear. She said, "He can take that bay mare for his sister the rest of his life." After she reached her sister's camp, she became a co-wife.[64]

When a woman became pregnant, she showed her good character by protecting the unborn child through observing food taboos and by making quilled articles (if she were ceremonially qualified) for others as a prayer sacrifice to protect her child. She made a bag for the child's navel cord, the designs for which were prayers for the child to have a long and successful life. She used her property to make gifts to others in return for their piercing her child's ears or praying for or curing her child, and she could make a religious vow, for example, to sponsor a ceremony, or make a prayer sacrifice for her child. A woman was respected for spacing her children; women nursed a child for four or more years, thus making a new pregnancy unlikely. Arapahos viewed the spacing of children as a matter of restraint and sacrifice for the health of the child. The great effort expended on property and body sacrifice on behalf of children was possibly a response to the high mortality rate of the mid-nineteenth century, when epidemics killed many children. And sacrifice also helped protect a child from enemies. Walking Backward, Little Raven's sister, who was born in 1821,

would have made sacrifices for her two daughters, Sweat House
and Howling Woman, who lived to adulthood. Their father was
Gummy Head, whom she married sometime in the 1830s.[65]

A woman was supposed to cooperate with co-wives, if any. A
man's first wife usually was the head of the household (the "boss"
wife), directing the other women in their work and serving as
his political and ceremonial partner. If a man had a very young
wife, his mother might take this role. Captain Lemuel Ford, who
was with Dodge's expedition in 1835, noted that Arapaho men
had from one to four wives. After several more years of intertribal warfare, Agent J. W. Whitfield reported in 1855 that Arapaho women outnumbered men by fifty percent, and in 1861
Agent Albert Boone wrote that the Arapahos, who numbered
244 tepees, had 486 women and 312 men. This disparity contributed to the custom of polygamous marriages. What was plural
marriage like for the women involved? Of course, co-wives
could share the work of the household, and if the co-wives were
sisters, they were used to cooperating. Also, women nursed children for several years, and husbands ideally avoided them during
this time. Polygamy facilitated this arrangement.[66]

Some wives had no children. In fact, women could obtain sterility
medicine from a specialist before or after marriage. Why would
a woman want to avoid having children? Perhaps it was a response
to a difficult personal situation or a means to allow her to go on
war parties or travel with her husband. Oscar Lewis's research
on Blackfeet women offers another explanation. He describes
rivalry and jealousy as women jockeyed for position within a
household, with the boss wife trying to maintain position, and
lower-ranked wives trying to displace her. Boss wives ("chief"
or "sit-by" wives, in Lewis's terms) were desirable sexual partners,
that is, sexually aggressive women. Without children, a woman
could devote herself to her relationship with her husband.[67]

For women not in the boss position, there were probably fewer
opportunities for a career in the ceremonial realm, although if a
man were married to two sisters, one might assist the other and
share in her ceremonial status. If a man were a chief, the boss

wife was the "chief wife" and ceremonial partner, and her sister might assist her and learn these duties. But if there were several wives, the younger or lower-ranked ones might not be able to improve their positions. This was clearly in Salt's mind when she resisted marriage as a fourth wife. Competition among women who were not sisters could occur. In any case, women in a household were ranked. Even in a monogamous household, the wife directed the work of other women (divorced and widowed women, unmarried girls, and perhaps a captive), and there were status differentials between these women. Most women became widows at some point, at least for a time. In other words, women's rank could change over time, as could men's. Married women, particularly those married to the same man for a long time, had considerable respect from other Arapahos. Warden noted that the leggings of mature women who were widows or divorcees bore ornamentation different from the leggings of women married to a man for a long time. In the latter instance, the wife had two white lines down the front of her leggings, representing the paths of husband and wife who successfully endured hardship. Single women had one white line on their leggings. Of course, women could also have political and ceremonial ranking outside the household.[68]

A wife was expected to be loyal to her husband. Ideally, she had the right to veto additional wives (and she probably encouraged her sisters becoming co-wives), but as a practical matter, her husband might resent her for opposing a co-wife. If a woman's husband neglected her or he or a co-wife mistreated her, a woman might convince her brother to take her back to her parents. If she wanted to marry another man, she might run away with him. Sometimes her husband accepted her decision (and other people encouraged him to do so), but she might be forced to return, and then no one would intervene if she were mistreated. In one case (which apparently was unusual) known to Pumpkin (from Owl's cohort), a married woman paid attention to another man. Her husband slashed her nose and ear. Arapahos then sang a song about him, ridiculing his loss of control. Pumpkin said that he was embarrassed every time he heard the song. If a woman were widowed, she might live with her parents and postpone remarriage, and she had more influence in the choice of a new husband. Michelson learned from Red Woman that, when she was sixteen, her first husband was killed by Pawnees during her first year of marriage. After that, she and her baby returned to her parents for several years.[69]

A wife had a great deal to do with her husband's success in warfare and in developing a reputation for leadership. If he were prominent, she helped him maintain his position. A wife might accompany her husband hunting or on a war expedition. Parkman observed the chief of an Arapaho band hunting buffalo in the company of his wife, who gave him water. Members of James's party observed an Arapaho war party against the Pawnees. There were eight men and one woman, who was the wife of the leader. The woman discovered the members of the expedition and alerted the others. If a wife remained in the camp, she prayed for her husband's success and sometimes made property or body sacrifices (such as wearing special face paint or having a finger joint removed) to gain supernatural help for him in battle. Arapahos believed that burying the joint substituted for the wounding or death of the husband. When the husband returned from battle with trophies (for example, scalps), his wife (or if he were unmarried, his mother, sister, or other female relative) would dance carrying the trophy to call attention to his achievement.[70]

Sitting Bull told the story of a woman whose son was killed in battle. When a war party went out, she said she would go, and she took her dog. Pawnee warriors came close to their party and wounded an Arapaho. The "old lady" yelled during the fighting, encouraging the men, who told her to go into a makeshift fortification they had made while under siege. But she said she wanted to die the way her son had. The dog ran out when the enemy charged and drove them back. After night came, she and her dog left, and the Pawnees gave up. The war party went home and on the way found her and her dog sitting on a hill. Jess Rowlodge (Owl's son, born in 1884) knew an old woman (probably from Bichea's cohort) who insisted on going on a war party with her husband soon after they married. She engaged with some army troops and earned a coup. If a woman encountered an enemy with her husband or on her own, she could achieve a "coup," that is, do something brave that she would be recognized and honored for later. In fact, a woman who pierced an enemy could count coup (proclaim it publicly) when making tepee decorations with an awl. Walking Backward earned this honor. A woman who had a coup could also pierce a child's ears at the Offerings Lodge. After Big Head left her brother's camp, she and another woman, both widows, went south, drifting from place to place. They came to a ranch owned by a Mexican, and he told them that a Cheyenne and Arapaho war party out against the Utes was nearby. They camped, worried about the Ute war party. They slept with their knives ready; then one night while Big Head was awake, a Ute jumped in the tepee, and she killed him with her knife. Thereafter, the women traveled with the Arapahos and Cheyennes to the Arapaho camp in the south. She took the name Night Killer as recognition of her bravery, of her coup.[71]

Red Woman's experience at the Washita fight can also be mentioned in this context. She and her family were traveling to the camp on the Washita River, when she thought she saw troops in the distance. She told her father not to camp among the Cheyennes, which he wanted to do. "I insisted on moving further along." That night she and her mother went to a dance, then early in the morning she awoke to shots. She grabbed her baby, younger brother, saddle, and got them on her horse. The family fled south, spending several sleepless nights worried about pursuit. "It was awful," she said. Her experience shows not only her bravery under fire, but also the respect her father had for her judgment. Medicine Grass also recalled that women alerted his group to the presence of enemies, and once his mother's dream warned them of an imminent attack.[72]

In politics, women expressed their opinions and exerted pressure on men (sometimes by ridicule). A prominent man or a band leader relied on his wife: an industrious woman accumulated extra food and household goods that her husband could give away to others or she could give away on his behalf to gain a reputation for generosity and leadership ability. Women played a key role in gift-exchange marriages and could initiate these matches. Walking Backward's daughter Sweat House married Chief Bird Chief. This was a prestigious marriage that would have involved a large exchange of presents between the prominent Bird Chief and Little Raven families. The marriage strengthened the alliance of these two chiefs. A story told by Arapahos may reflect the pressure men felt from the exhortations of women, as well as their recognition of the female principle in the life force: seven men on the warpath heard something following them—a woman's genitalia. They fought over it and unsuccessfully tried to stop it from following them.[73]

Female leaders joined with male leaders to participate in important events. E. Williard Smith, on the emigrant trail in 1839, noted that an Arapaho delegation that met with him to discuss the train's passage included twenty-two men and three women (presumably wives of principal chiefs). In another instance, trying to stave off trouble from trespassing Americans in Colorado, the principal chiefs of the Arapahos (and the Cheyennes, Kiowas, and Comanches) asked Agent Boone to take a delegation to Washington to discuss the problems in the region. Arapahos wanted to send three men and one woman. Events at the Medicine Lodge treaty in 1867 also exemplify women's political influence. The Arapaho "warriors" sat facing the commissioners from Washington, and standing behind them were the old men and behind them, the "wives of some of the warriors." The presence of all these people was important to Arapahos. During the proceedings, Kaws stole some horses from the Arapahos, and the warriors left in pursuit. Little Raven had to tell the commissioners that negotiations had to wait until their return. He complained that the delay was the fault of Arapaho women. Presumably, their exhortations forced the men's departure, and they, like other Arapahos, wanted all the important people present to deal with the commissioners.[74]

Religious devotion was a central theme in women's lives. In many religious ceremonies, a woman and a man acted in partnership;

the participation of both was necessary and both simultaneously had ceremonial career achievements. Women could also act independently to acquire ritual authority. Even women who did not acquire prominent status in the religious realm built and maintained a good reputation by religious devotion within the family context.

A wife helped her husband in religious ceremonies; in fact, his ceremonial career depended on or was linked to his wife's participation. Warden noted, "A man may have no inclination to enter into true manhood [lodge advancement], while his wife may be an ambitious one." As a result of joint participation in the Offerings Lodge, the age-graded lodges, and doctoring, wives (and their husbands) earned degrees of ritual authority. As Warden put it, the women had to acquire the "womanhood" through proper channels (earning the right to do something) before obtaining "excellence as advisors among their companions." Men who vowed to participate in the Offerings Lodge (a four-day dramatization of the creation story and a means to acquire supernatural assistance), needed their wives' help. A young unmarried man would probably rely on his sister-in-law or relative of a friend. The vower or supplicant had to provide food for his "grandfather" or instructor in the ceremony and give the man and his wife gifts. The grandfather painted the supplicant each day, and the supplicant's wife brought the water and sage (used to apply the paint) into the Offerings Lodge. When the supplicant, who fasted the entire four days, danced and prayed, his wife encouraged him by remaining near the lodge and singing or dancing. The wives of the grandfathers provided food and gifts for the supplicant, or "grandson," on the last day. The man who initially pledged to sponsor the Offerings Lodge was called the Lodge Maker. He and his wife played central roles in the three-day preliminary rite as well as in the four-day ritual. His grandfather and his grandfather's wife also played special roles. The Lodge Maker's wife offered her body to supernatural beings, received power from the grandfather (who represented them), then passed that power to her husband. She fasted and wore the paint of the lodge just as her husband did.[75]

Men in the Star Lodge eventually (usually by their twenties) entered the first of the series of sacred lodges, the Tomahawk Lodge. As they aged they progressively joined the Spear Lodge, Lime Crazy Lodge, and Dog Lodge. The men's wives played crucial roles in these lodges and acquired the same ceremonial knowledge, or degree, as their husbands did when participating in the ceremonies. In the Tomahawk and Spear lodges, the wives took responsibility for providing food and gifts to the instructors, or "grandfathers," and their wives. They stood behind the men, encouraging them at certain points in the ritual. The wives of the grandfathers made the regalia that the inductees wore. In the Lime Crazy and Dog lodges, the wives of the novices additionally made a body sacrifice, that is, they offered their bodies to supernatural beings, received power from their husband's grandfather, and passed that power to their husbands. The wives as well as their husbands wore paint (a form of body sacrifice). In the Lime Crazy Lodge, the grandsons walked across burning coals as part of the ritual. The "elder brothers" of the men went with their wives to the grandparents and learned how to build the fire. The grandfathers instructed the elder brothers, and the grandmothers taught the wives. In the Dog Lodge, the grandfathers provided the paint for the ceremony and the grandmothers, the food. The grandfathers painted the men, and the grandmothers painted the men's wives. The grandfathers and grandmothers jointly had the authority to pass on the knowledge of the lodge. If a grandfather did not have a wife, a substitute who had gone through the ceremony with her husband could help him. Dog Lodge people selected the chiefs from their number to represent the Arapahos in councils. The wives ("chief wives") of these men also shared in their prominence.[76]

Women could vow to participate in or sponsor the Buffalo Lodge. Although the main participants in this lodge were women, here, as in the other lodge ceremonies, the participation of women *and* men was required. Most of what we know about the Buffalo Lodge comes from the memories of Arapahos who spoke to Kroeber and Warden, but in 1862 twenty-five soldiers sent by the governor of Colorado to intimidate Indians along the South Platte came across Cut Nose's camp of seventy lodges of Arapahos having an Offerings Lodge and a Buffalo Lodge. About forty women in the Buffalo Lodge were dressed as buffaloes, and the soldiers viewed with fascination the "White Woman" (the sponsor of the ceremony, wearing white face paint and representing a white buffalo) and the two little girl "calves." According to Kroeber, Arapahos regarded the Buffalo Lodge as equivalent to the combined Tomahawk, Spear, Lime Crazy, and Dog lodges in terms of the symbolism, powers, and degrees of ritual authority available to the participants. For example, the paint of one of the women holding a degree (that is, wearing particular regalia) was the same design as that worn by one of the degree-holders in the Tomahawk Lodge. Warden said it represented the "same idea and purpose." A woman who pledged to sponsor the ceremony went with her husband, who carried a pipe, to persuade other women to participate. The husband encouraged his wife to become a Buffalo Woman, and his support for his wife built his "qualities as a man," according to Warden. Husbands received paint every day, just as the wives did, and the men's paint reminded them to "look out for the wants and needs" of their wives. Young unmarried men had to stay away from the lodge at certain times. The women had "grandmothers" to instruct them, and these women *and their husbands* made the regalia that the participants wore.

Participants in the lodge made a property sacrifice, and the pledger, a body sacrifice as well, and they received, in the process, prestige, blessings, and added ceremonial rank and qualifications. Mostly young married women pledged the Buffalo Lodge, but older women probably attained the degrees by wearing the honorary regalia. The two mothers of the little girls chosen to wear regalia as "calves" went through the ceremony with their daughters. The ceremony was held in a tepee in the center of the camp, and everyone in the camp helped build it. The women's families had to cook for and give gifts to the elderly ritual authorities, just as the men's families did in the other lodges. Men contributed horses and arrows, and women gave horses, bags, moccasins, and meat. Ideally, the sisters of the participants offered material and emotional support. The pledger could be assisted by other women in collecting the gifts, which gave the helpers honor but did not entitle them to the ritual authority that the pledger gained from the ceremony. The greater the prestige, the greater the expense. During the four-day ceremony, the pledger fasted and prayed. She could not move unless her family contributed property. Similarly, the calves had to remain still unless their families made gifts. The pledger and other participants chose calves from wealthy families, some of whom tried to hide their children.[77]

Arapahos believed that this lodge originated when buffalo spirit beings pitied humans (a poor husband and wife) and instructed a couple on how to perform the ritual. Also part of the origin story for this lodge was the rescue of the wife from captivity by the digging of a gopher spirit helper. The Buffalo Lodge dramatized the actions of the spirit beings, brought success in hunting buffalo, and was a prayer for prosperity and the survival of the people. As discussed above, the lodge symbolism paralleled that of the Seven Old Women, who gave rules of life. Notably, four pegs at the base of the center poles in the lodge represented the Four Old Women, according to Warden. The paint and the regalia worn by all the participants symbolized buffalo: cows, steers, calves, and bulls. Two men, representing hunters, stalked two of the cows, counted coup on them, and one hunter shot one of the Buffalo Women, who had a piece of tallow. She was "butchered" and the tallow distributed to make the paint for the lodge. The woman chosen for this ceremony was a chief's or prominent warrior's wife, and considerable property had to be contributed for the honor. Warden explained that this lodge reenacted the story of Blue Feather, who was trampled by Buffalo Beings, then resurrected; thus, the lodge had a "saving" role—it renewed life and prosperity. As the pledger and her husband walked through the camp, people touched her in order to have a long life. The White Woman (pledger of the lodge) and the woman wearing the "owner of the tent poles" regalia had to keep food and behavior taboos after the ceremony. The pledger and perhaps others in this lodge probably had influence politically; for example, they would have been consulted about or could have initiated collective hunts.[78]

Women also had ceremonial careers independently of their husbands'. They could acquire degrees in quilling and become doctors (medicine women). Certain items had to be quilled in a religious ceremony, and women made vows to do this. A vow required payment of the expenses of the ritual by feeding and giving gifts to the elderly women authorities (the Seven Old Women), who directed the work on tepee ornaments, tepee doors, tepee pins, tepee linings, leanbacks or beds, pillows, buffalo skin blankets, robes, and cradles. Women made religious vows to make a quilled object to help a relative in war or illness or to ensure a safe delivery of a child. Warden noted that women tried to attain degrees of quillwork on various objects and to be leaders in tepee rituals: "Thus she is known by her work, by her tepee, and by the appearance of her tepee." One woman of great renown was Firewood, who had a record of sixty cradles, fourteen buffalo robes, five ornamented tepees, ten calf robes, and one buffalo lean- back cover. Hides used for the tepee cover were dressed without ceremony, but when the skins were cut and sewn together and decorated with quilled designs, a ceremony had to take place, and only certain women had the right to cut and sew hides for a tepee. Thus, not all women had quill-decorated tepees, and only certain women had renown for their ability to cut, sew, and do the work of ornamenting a tepee. Little Raven's mother Backward was one of the Seven Old Women, and she mentored her daughter Walking Backward and probably her granddaughter Owl in quillwork. Eventually, quills became difficult to get, and Arapahos substi- tuted beads in these designs.

There were at least seven kinds of tepee designs. Each repre- sented a different degree. Ornaments on a tepee consisted of five disks and usually eighteen pairs of pendants with buffalo hair on them. A tepee was named according to the symbolism on the disks and pendants. The symbolism of each was a prayer for prosperity, long life, and fertility, alluding to supernatural beings in the origin stories. Arapahos also equated the shape of the tepee with a woman's breast. When the ornaments were attached to the tepee, the sponsor who made the vow provided a feast for the Seven Old Women, and they marked the places of attachment, just as they had marked out the designs. One common design on disks was alternatively colored concentric circles with four radii. The circles represented the wind created at the time the earth was first made, personified as Whirlwind Woman, who worked at quilling as she circled over the earth. She made the first tepee ornament to represent her work at the time of creation. One large disk was placed at the top of the back of the tent; four disks were attached to the sides at the four cardinal directions. Pendants were attached in two vertical rows at the front of the tepee and on the two flaps. Designs similar to those on the tepee were used on other objects, such as robes, blankets, and pillows. Whirlwind Woman also originated the painted designs on rawhide bags.[79]

There were two styles of tepee doors, one made of painted rawhide and one of quilled buffalo skin. Each style represented a degree. The shape of the quilled door symbolized the life force (the life symbol, as Kroeber called it). This shape corresponded to the cleared space in the tepee. The hides used for linings could be tanned by any woman, but decoration required ceremonially validated knowledge. Tepee linings were decorated with geometric designs or drawings of a man's exploits. A married woman would give the old women a feast, and they would supervise the ritual of making the lining. Buffalo hide covers for pillows were decorated with symbols of creation, old age, and food. The ornamentation differed for a leanback and pillow, depending on whether it was made for a man, woman, or child.[80]

Quilled robes were usually made for men. Each of at least seven kinds of quilled robe designs for men represented a degree. The Seven Old Women supervised the work on these in a ceremony like that for tepee ornamentation. A robe decorated with one hundred parallel lines of quillwork, which a woman made only for a prominent chief, brought the greatest prestige to the quill worker. A twenty-line robe was less prestigious. These lines represented buffalo paths (prosperity and success), long life, and the four eons of existence since the time of creation. When a woman made a quilled item for a man, he was obligated to give her a horse. Quilled robes for women often had decoration symbolizing women's work as well as the life force. Warden noted that one old Southern Arapaho woman made thirty robes, one for every member of her family, and received a horse for each. Firewood, a Northern Arapaho, made vows to make robes to help her brothers and others: she made one for a brother who was ill, and another for a brother on a war party. Firewood was recognized for "good deeds," according to Warden, and her brothers gave her horses. In the case of brothers on a war party, she received captured horses. Painted robes, as well as quilled ones, were made for women, with symbolism for long life, prosperity, and success; it is likely that these too were made after a vow and under the supervision of the Seven Old Women, but Kroeber and Dorsey were silent on this subject.[81]

Warden found that Arapahos had several cradle designs, each representing a degree. Kroeber recorded the meaning of the symbolism on the cradles that were decorated with quilled designs. In one case, the designs at once represented the child in infancy and old age (a prayer for a long life), and included a tepee that the grown-up child would inhabit. A design stood simultaneously for a tepee disk and the child's head, for example. Warden described a cradle with a design symbolizing progress through all the lodges to old age. Probably not every child had a quill-decorated cradle. Such a cradle brought prestige to the donor and the child and his or her family.[82]

Women also dreamed and received messages from spirit beings to embark on a career as a doctor. Occasionally, a woman would fast for this power. In a woman's dream, the spirit might advise her to "purchase" power by apprenticeship to a successful doctor. In the latter case, over time she would provide gifts to the doctor in return for instruction. Women started this work in middle age and probably became noted doctors in old age. More typically, a woman could learn to doctor from her mother or from her husband. A woman's power came from plants (herbs, bark, roots, leaves, and seeds) that she used as tonics, poultices, and smudges. Women doctors specialized in women's health—fertility, sterility, miscarriage prevention, and childbirth.[83]

Occasionally, a woman would pledge to "make" the Offerings Lodge. If she had no husband, she could get a substitute. In Dorsey's version of the Mrs. North story, she vowed to sponsor an Offerings Lodge if she returned safely to her people. She planned to ask her brother to serve as Lodge Maker on her behalf. A women made this kind of vow usually to help a relative, but it also brought a woman ritual authority. A woman who acquired paints in the Dog Lodge could use this authority to perform a sacred ritual duty in the Offerings Lodge. Warden noted that when a woman had eighty knots on the Dog Lodge paint bag, she had the privilege of cutting the center pole of the Offerings Lodge. There were several ritual acts that only women could qualify to perform during the course of the Offerings Lodge ceremony.[84]

Even for women who did not pursue a "career" in ceremonialism, religious devotion was the mark of good character. Through property or body sacrifice, a woman ideally tried to help her family. She might help a sister, brother, or husband participate in a lodge ceremony, or she might help a brother or brother's child with property sacrifices. She made quilled and beaded clothing, including moccasins and leggings, for family members, and embroidered symbols of her prayer for their well-being, success (for example, in hunting), and good character. She might dream or "hard-think" the designs. Often the designs represented those first made by Whirlwind Woman; they came in a dream from the spirit world and thus were a promise of protection. A mother could tie cloth or clothing to the Offerings Lodge center pole as a sacrifice for her children's health or take gifts to old people to pray for her children. She could use her property or horses to pay for a doctor's cure.[85]

Men depended on women in their efforts to become successful in provisioning their households, in war and politics, and in attaining high ceremonial rank. Women's control of food was instrumental in protecting and helping others. Women's relations with men helped them gain influence, status, and property, as did their ingenuity in initiating trade with Americans and skillfully managing their households' resources. The complex of property and body sacrifices wives and husbands (and often women and men kin) made for each other created mutual obligations supported by public pressure and supernatural sanction. Women also had reciprocal obligations to each other based on kinship, marriage, and ceremonial participation. These exchanges mitigated inequalities among people and helped foster cooperation. It also seems likely that such obligations became more extensive and elaborate during these years of heightened insecurity in the mid-nineteenth century.

As we have seen, the expulsion of the Southern Arapahos from Colorado and the very real threat of their extermination by Americans led to the conciliatory strategy advocated by Arapaho leaders. Who were the women who provided leadership during its formation and implementation? By the early 1860s if not before, many married couples from the Little Raven–Walking Backward cohort had risen to the Dog Lodge. With the support of the old people, these senior lodge members had the authority to sway public opinion and affect behavior. Those particularly wealthy in horses had large households and the ability to use economic incentives to influence others. Little Raven and other chiefs and prominent, wealthy men in his cohort represented Arapaho views at the treaty councils of the 1860s, and they had influence at councils in the Arapaho camps. So did their wives (boss wives), who were women of the Dog and Buffalo lodges who managed large, prosperous households. These women would have expressed their views about hunting and gathering territories, trade, war, and peace within households and within the large camps. Some accompanied their husbands in dealings with settlers and American officials. What women said to their husbands did not appear in the record, but, as Little Raven explained in 1867, a treaty could not be made without their participation. How did a man become a "prominent" leader? His success at providing for others, his war record, and his ceremonial rank figured in his life career and he needed the help of women for all these accomplishments.

Men

Like women, men had responsibility for the health and safety of others. Their work was a dangerous and high-energy activity. Work figured in a man's status both in his acquisition of wealth (primarily horses and food) and his exploits in battle—activities that also contributed to a man's place in the lodge ranking system. Men hunted for their relatives and cared for the horses of their households. A husband looked after his wife's ponies, but they belonged to her. Men had responsibility for equipment related to horses, such as ropes and saddles, as well as tools for hunting and warfare. Men protected the camp. They were sentinels and went on revenge war parties to retaliate for enemy attacks. They went on horse-stealing expeditions, where they might also take captives. How well a man could provide for his family greatly depended on the size of his horse herd. Some men had considerably more horses than others. Of course, older men with large horse herds would lend horses to younger or poorer men, and their wives always shared meat from the hunts with needy people. This is how families earned a reputation for generosity and leadership. Hides were not widely shared, though. Women prepared many for trade and used others for gifts, primarily to husbands and relatives. Arapahos also traded extra horses.[86]

These wealth differences were reflected not only in disparity in the size of horse herds but also in the size of tepees. Some tepees had only twenty poles and covers of fifteen buffalo skins; others had thirty poles and twenty skin covers. In 1843 Talbot observed that some Arapaho men rode fine American horses, while others had "shaggy" ponies or mules, and he noted that tepees varied in size, comfort, and elaborateness of decoration. Beardy, a leading chief in 1846, occupied a huge, well-appointed tepee, the most luxurious that Abert had seen. Garrard saw that Beardy's tepee was the largest in the camp he visited. Agent Albert Boone reported in 1861 that when the Arapahos went on a buffalo hunt, a few families had too few horses to participate. Poor men were considered "no account" and were at a disadvantage in marriage negotiations and in efforts to build a political or ceremonial career.[87]

How a man treated his family was also central to the judgments people made about his character. Men were supposed to be generous with their siblings and reward sisters for any special attention by giving them a horse or a tepee. If he gave a tepee, it was left standing when the camp circle broke up; then, in the sight of all, the new owners would take it down. If a man's sister vowed to sponsor the Offerings Lodge, her brother was expected to participate as the Lodge Maker. In the case of Mrs. North, her brother did serve as Lodge Maker, according to Jess Rowlodge. People respected a man for helping his sister's children, and he took particular responsibility for his sister's sons. Men were respected for providing horses and meat for elderly parents. When a relative made a vow to participate in a religious ceremony, a man earned the respect of others when he fulfilled his obligation to help his kin by contributing horses toward property sacrifices. Fathers might offer grown sons special support by accompanying them through a ceremony; for example, if a young man vowed to participate in the Offerings Lodge, his father might also participate. A brother might marry his brother's widow, which was not required but was greatly respected because it continued his family's initial bond and obligation to his sister-in-law's family.[88]

Men had pipes made of black stone, and they used these when they prayed for their family's well-being. These pipes, kept in bags with quilled "life" designs, symbolized paths through life. A man's duties included daily prayers for his family, that their paths be good, safe, and long lived. Warden explained that the offering of a pipe replicated Pipe Being's calling on animals to dive for earth when the world was created, and as such, activated the life force. Men's pipe ritual was comparable to women's ornamentation of clothing, with quilled and beaded designs as prayer symbolism.[89]

When a man married, he took on new obligations. He had to provide for his wife, including getting the trade goods she wanted. Thus, traders reported large trade in beads, knives, and other women's tools, pots, and cloth. A man was supposed to make frequent gifts to his in-laws. He had a duty to help his wife's brothers, and they exchanged gifts. When his wife became pregnant, he was expected to respect certain food taboos and to be careful not to upset her—a custom that served to reinforce in his mind his duties to his wife, whose pregnancy could go badly if he did not follow these customs. People expected him to provide property for ceremonies to ensure his children's health—if he were wealthy enough, horses to the people who named his children, pierced their ears, and doctored them. A good hunter could afford lavish feasts to celebrate his child's first steps, words, and other accomplishments. When a couple married, the relative wealth of the families of the bride and groom was the main factor in where they resided. If the groom or his family was well off, the couple would likely live near or in the band of the groom's family. If the bride's family was wealthier, the groom would live with her family, at least for a time, and he would hunt for his mother-in-law and help his father-in-law with men's work. Arapahos told Michelson that in patrilocal residence, the bride was a servant, and in matrilocal residence the groom was a servant, terms which reflected status differentials between the two families.[90]

Divorce was common. Sometimes the husband agreed that his wife could leave when he took a co-wife she disliked. Occasionally a woman's family allowed her to return home if her husband did not support her or mistreated her. According to Warden, when a man's wife left him for another man, his character was tested. He was supposed to take it "coolly" and ask his older brother or other relative to handle the matter. The husband's relatives would demand a payment for damages from the paramour's family. The paramour should then ask an old man (usually the husband's ceremonial "grandfather") to take a pipe to the offended husband's family and offer horses. The old man would attempt to persuade the husband to accept the offer by advising him that people would "say hard things" about him if he refused to settle the matter peacefully. "Don't disgrace yourself," he would say. People in the camp waited outside the tepee while the matter was discussed. The elder brother of the husband should accept the offer, praise the husband, and smoke with the old man. The people in the crowd then thanked all parties. The pipe smoking settled the trouble, and the husband felt "new" and was relieved from "sorrows." The husband could keep the children, but the runaway wife could have a relationship with the children and was not disgraced. The wife felt "proud," that is, relieved that she had improved her circumstances.[91]

The husband may have been away on war parties too much, or she may have disliked him even though she married him to please her brother. Smoking the pipe amounted to a legal divorce. If the husband and brother refused to smoke, they could take the wife back and keep the horses. In this case, everyone was disgraced, and the wife might experience abuse. Pumpkin's story— of the mocking song Arapahos sung about the jealous husband who slashed his wife's face—indicates that individuals who took revenge faced ridicule. Arapahos told Eggan that a high-ranking, prominent man should ignore his wife's misbehavior and show little interest in receiving damages upon her desertion. The smoking-the-pipe ritual was used in any kind of family trouble— slander, theft, threats—to restore harmony in the family.[92]

Row Of Lodges, chosen as an intermediary chief about 1867, had a reputation for living up to his family responsibilities, according to his stepson. When the Arapahos still resided in Colorado, several worked for ranches and businesses trying to find a way to coexist with Americans. Row Of Lodges's sister married a "Mexican" rancher, and two of her brothers went to work for him cutting hay. Row Of Lodges apparently became apprehensive (perhaps because of the growing hostility to Indians in Colorado) and went to the ranch and got them all to leave with him. Big Mouth, the son of Chief Big Mouth, had a good reputation as a warrior but, in 1866, when an American trader brought whisky to an Indian camp, he became inebriated and struck his father with a piece of wood, killing him, which affected Big Mouth's reputation in later years.[93]

Going to war was an important vehicle for a man to advance his "career." When he went on a war expedition, he might ask his ceremonial "elder brother" (in the lodge organization) for help, and he would go on the expedition with his lodgemates or his brothers, men he could count on for support. An experienced man with a successful war record led a war party. His achievements indicated that he had a powerful spirit helper (that is, a supernatural being who helped him in return for rituals of respect). When James's party met an Arapaho war party in 1820, the leader carried a "medicine bag" (with objects representing his spirit helper) that he used to pray for the party's success. In 1847 traveler George Ruxton met a party of twenty-one warriors, all of whom were younger than thirty, except for their older leader Coho, or Lame Leg. Medicine Grass went with a war party led by Row Of Lodges and Powderface (both members of the Left Hand cohort) in the late 1860s. One of the younger warriors was Scabby Bull (from Medicine Grass's cohort). Hilger was told that after a man had two or three successful war expeditions, he was regarded to have good character and to be acceptable as a husband.[94]

A war party would ask women relatives to sing for them and make moccasins for them to use on the expedition. In fact, Dorsey was told that it was "necessary" to have women sing for the war party. If the party returned with booty or trophies (such as scalps), and particularly if no member of the party was killed, there would be a celebration in camp. The warriors would ride to the center of the camp, where relatives of men who had taken scalps would give away horses in their honor. The warriors' wives, sisters, father's sisters, or brother's daughters would carry their trophies or sing their praises at a victory dance. After accomplishing something brave, a man might take a new name publicly to remind people of his feat. These names could later be transferred to relatives, which brought honor to the donor.[95]

If a warrior accomplished something that Arapahos considered a ranked deed of bravery, such as touching an enemy, taking a scalp, or stealing a picketed horse next to an enemy lodge, that coup would be a factor in his career. Coups were associated with particular regalia in the lodges so that only a man who had accomplished a particular coup could serve as a grandfather to men who were awarded the associated honorary regalia. At the Offerings Lodge, certain kinds of coups entitled the owner to perform particular acts within the lodge. Left Hand and Row Of Lodges had this distinction. A prominent warrior, if he could afford it, would have his tepee lining painted through the efforts of his wife. She would feast the Seven Old Women to supervise the ornamentation representing his war deeds or the vision experiences that brought him protection in battle from a spirit helper. Men wore clothing decorated according to their rank. They told about their war exploits publicly, especially during ceremonies. Left Hand told the story of how he and Bull Thunder (a member of his cohort) and an Apache companion were on scouting duty, on foot in Ute country. Left Hand encountered a Ute warrior, struggled with him, and took his scalp. Then Bull Thunder and the Apache tapped him while he was still alive. "That was a sign that you were a man if you did that," Hilger was told.[96]

A man tried to obtain war medicine from a very successful warrior if he could. Often this medicine was associated with a shield (symbolizing a spirit helper). Arapahos owned several famous shields that were copied and transferred. Spread Hands obtained the Thunderbird shield from his father after he had success in battle against Pawnees, Utes, and Navajos. Scabby Bull obtained the shield from Spread Hands, his older brother and a member of Left Hand's cohort, when he was twenty years old. First Scabby Bull had to prove himself worthy by success in several military engagements and learning how to care for the shield. When he owned the shield, he had miraculous escapes from death: the feather pendants were shot off the shield, and although a bullet struck it, he was not injured. Twice his horse was shot from under him, and twice his horse gave out and his companions rescued him. He was wounded once in the arm, and he recovered. The shield also protected him from storms. Body paint, lance decoration, horse decorations, and a headdress were associated with the shield. He used the headdress as a pillow when on the warpath, and in his dreams he received instructions on how to avoid danger. At times he sacrificed skin to the Thunderbird spirit being. When he returned from battle, he made a property sacrifice of his booty to Spread Hands, and he was careful to follow the rules associated with the shield. Others who owned this shield included White Buffalo, Sitting Bull, and Black Horse. Other famous shields included the Bear shield and the Water Monster shield, which was owned by Left Hand.[97]

War exploits were largely the province of men in the Little Raven and Left Hand cohorts. Men in Little Raven's cohort had thirty years or more battle experience by the 1850s and had war records from many intertribal engagements. By the early 1860s, they and their wives would have risen to the Lime Crazy or Dog Lodge. This group included Little Raven, Trunk, Yellow Bear, Old Sun, Red Pipe, Bird Chief (another hero of the Washita fight) and Tall Bear.

Although he was a warrior, Little Raven also had a career as an intermediary chief; he represented the wishes of the Arapaho council in meetings with Americans and sometimes other tribes. Little Raven's ceremonial partner was probably Short Woman, one of three sisters who were co-wives. His brother Trunk, who was a renowned warrior and lodge leader, supported him in council. In the 1850s Trunk had at least five wives, three of whom were sisters (including Owl's mother). Chief Yellow Bear, another intermediary chief, was the brother of three of Little Raven's wives, Short Woman, Beaver Woman, and Good Woman. Short Woman's sisters probably assisted her in ceremonial duties. Yellow Bear's wives were Grass Woman (boss wife), Big Head (known for her coup), and Woman Going In. These men all had great authority over the Left Hand cohort because of their status in the lodges. In fact, even after Little Raven and the other chiefs selected Left Hand and some other members of his cohort as successors to their positions as intermediary chiefs, Little Raven and the others came out of "retirement" to sign the treaty of Medicine Lodge in lieu of the younger men.

The men of Left Hand's cohort were accomplished warriors who had fought the Americans and others in an attempt to hold on to their homeland. They would have reached the Spear Lodge at least by the early 1860s and the Lime Crazy or possibly the Dog Lodge by the late 1860s. Powderface was renowned for his bravery in intertribal warfare. Not until the Americans began to trespass in the Arkansas River country and destroy the game did he go to war against them. He killed and scalped five. Then the Arapahos made peace (1865). After the peace was broken, he killed six Americans. He recounted that in all his engagements with American men, he had fifty-five horses shot while he was riding them, and he was wounded four times. Powderface married before or by 1867.

Left Hand had an outstanding record as a leader of war parties by twenty-three years. He held a high degree in the Tomahawk Lodge and had the support of elderly men who prayed for him (in return for his property sacrifices). He married Bear Woman (whose mother was Cheyenne) when he was about twenty-one and she was about twelve, and around the same time married Singing Woman. Singing Woman was probably the boss wife. When the Americans began to build settlements in Colorado and introduce whisky, the Arapahos suffered. When settlers tried to take the Arapaho homeland, he led war parties against the trespassers and the U.S. troops who had attacked Arapahos. He witnessed the Arapaho position getting progressively weaker as they were "driven from one place to another." Left Hand realized they could not win militarily, so he supported Little Raven and the other chiefs who made a treaty and secured a reservation.

Row Of Lodges was another renowned warrior. He married several of Little Raven's and Trunk's daughters. Big Mouth also had war honors, including those gained when he led Arapaho warriors against Colonel George Custer's troops at the Washita Massacre. He had several wives. Others in the Left Hand cohort included Spread Hands, Road Traveler, White Buffalo, Arrow, and Heap Of Bears (Little Raven's son).

Men in Medicine Grass's cohort chose elder brothers from the Left Hand cohort. Some, like Scabby Bull, Sitting Bull, and White Owl, had considerable war experience and probably were Tomahawk Men by the late 1860s. Others, including Medicine Grass and Little Left Hand, had less battle experience. The policy of conciliation created obstacles for young men. Some slipped away from the Southern Arapahos and joined warriors from other tribes, which helped the chiefs demonstrate their peaceful intent while giving the most frustrated men an outlet. Sitting Bull and a few others from the Medicine Grass cohort went to Wyoming and joined the Northern Arapaho in the 1860s. There they engaged militarily with Americans. In 1868, when a Cheyenne war party of two hundred went north, four Arapaho warriors went with them, including one of Little Raven's sons. They attacked settlers on the Saline River in Kansas. Realizing the younger men's dilemma, Little Raven tried to get permission for the young warriors to raid the Utes in 1869. For the most part, though, Little Raven and the other members of his cohort prevented Arapaho warriors from endangering their conciliatory strategy.[98]

A man with a good war record who was prosperous, generous, and of a good disposition would emerge as the leader or one of the leaders in a band. There could be several chiefs in a band. A young man with an outstanding record was referred to as "young man chief," and older, established warriors were "big chiefs." In other words, chiefs were loosely ranked. Leaders of the men's lodges—the elder brothers or headmen—were chosen for their reputation and wealth and for their having a "good wife," one who also had a reputation for generosity. Chiefs were expected to give horses away and provide feasts during councils or visits from traders or other outsiders. When a chief was formally recognized, he had to commit himself to "take pity on" or help poor people and orphans, to avoid disagreements and conflict (to respect the pipe), and to tolerate criticism. His wife was also instructed to be generous; in other words, the selection of a chief was actually the selection of a marital unit. Councils brought together most of the adults in a band or several bands. Some spokesmen had more authority than others because of their reputations. With the help of the lodge men, band leaders could enforce rules, but policy decisions were made by a band or interband council. Dorsey reported that men's rank or influence was reflected in their dress: a warrior's shirt was decorated according to his achievements in war. Middle-aged men wore shirts on ordinary occasions that differed from the shirts of young men. Some chiefs, including Little Raven, emerged as political intermediaries in the nineteenth century, representing their people in dealings with Americans. They expressed the consensus of councils. Intermediary leadership grew in importance during these troubled times.[99]

Arapaho leaders helped James's expedition and Fowler's party in 1821. The principal chief (probably a representative of several bands in the region) greeted Fowler and his fellow traders, offered them protection, and supervised the trade. Arapahos surrounded the traders with their camps. The leader of Fowler's party gave the chief a presidential medal and gifts, and the chief's brothers escorted the traders while they were in Arapaho country. Bear Tooth, the principal chief of the Arapahos, acted as host to James's party, and Arapaho lodge men policed the crowd. The chief distributed the traders' gifts to the other Arapaho men. Arapaho chiefs also hosted Frémont. When he encountered them in 1843, he was feasted and participated in a smoking ritual, which sanctified the proceedings and amounted to a sacred oath binding Arapahos to their promises. The two principal chiefs Roman Nose (Big Nose) and Cut Nose hosted a feast and a council between Frémont's and Talbot's group and the leading Arapaho men. They smoked and exchanged gifts. When Parkman encountered Arapahos, he was escorted to the chief's lodge, where he was feasted and gifts were exchanged. Garrard's party was hosted by Beardy, who smoked with them. Of course, the wives of the chiefs and lodge men provided the food for the feast, and Arapahos regarded their participation as essential.[100]

These intermediaries acted to facilitate trade or peace but did not make agreements with the federal government on behalf of their people. Agent Fitzpatrick reported that Arapaho delegates would not agree to the proposals he presented on behalf of federal officials in 1847: they insisted on returning to the main camp for a proper council. At the 1851 treaty council, where the United States recognized Arapaho intermediary chiefs for the first time, the commissioners feasted and smoked with the principal chiefs, each of whom received gifts to symbolize his role as an intermediary. Intermediary chiefs also got a document or "certificate of character," as Percival Lowe, a witness to the council, put it, that testified to the confidence the United States government had in the bearer. The chiefs also distributed the gifts the commissioners brought for the tribes. Chiefs presented their documents to wagon trains and other travelers when they solicited tolls, and then distributed what the travelers gave. Settlers in Denver reported having councils with Arapahos where they smoked, and Thomas Wildman noted that the chiefs could physically prevent Indians from "bothering" settlers in Denver. In fact, Chief Spotted Wolf (with the lodge men's assistance) compelled men in his band to return stolen oxen to the army in 1861. The record also indicated that these chiefs had to work to keep the support of their followers. At the 1867 treaty council, Little Raven felt obligated to delay negotiating until the return of the important warriors from a retaliatory raid.[101]

A man's career in life was shaped by his ceremonial participation, which was supported by his war exploits and his family relations. When the camps moved, the men rode with their fellow lodge members. Warden described participation in these lodges as "steps of manhood," necessary to full maturity. Warden noted that persons who significantly misbehaved might have to repeat a lodge ceremony (be demoted, so to speak). Individuals might also vow to sponsor the dance again (after they had joined the lodge) as a prayer sacrifice. James Mooney was told that if a man did not join (which happened occasionally), he was never respected or included in councils. Kroeber learned that fellow lodge members could force a reluctant member to advance to the next lodge in the series. Warden noted that the primary purpose of the lodge ceremonies was "war inspiration." In fact, men used their lodge regalia in battle. The Tomahawk, Spear, Lime Crazy, and Dog lodges also performed political functions, advanced men's ceremonial knowledge, and reassured the Arapaho people in general. The Tomahawk Men and Spear Men announced the council's rules for a communal hunt and for war parties, and they enforced the rules. Individuals or parties who began hunting before the signal or who went on a war party against the council's wishes would be attacked by these lodge men. Their property could be destroyed, and they could be beaten. If they were submissive and repentant, the punishment would be lighter than if they were defiant.[102]

Little Left Hand told Michelson that when he was young, he went buffalo hunting against orders and as a result his possessions, including his saddle and war trophies, were destroyed; he was submissive, so he was spared further punishment. They could have shot his horses and beaten him. These lodge men also kept order in the camp, especially when several bands were assembled, and they supervised the movement of the camps.[103]

The Lime Crazy Men had the power to use supernatural sanctions to control behavior in camp; they tried to prevent violence among Arapahos. The chiefs were selected from the Dog Lodge. Their ceremonies (as well as those of the junior Tomahawks and Spears) drew virtually all Arapahos, not only because of familial obligations, but also because the ritual performance was impressive and because men and women entertained as clowns during the lull in the singing and dancing. Thus, the year-round authority of the senior lodges was ceremonially reinforced periodically.[104]

Medicine Grass witnessed the Tomahawk Lodge in the 1860s. It was held when a member of the Star Lodge vowed to sponsor the ceremony. Such a pledge was made in return for supernatural assistance to avert danger or recover from illness. Often, recovery of a sick relative or wife was the object of the vow. The pledger's fellow Star Men were obligated to participate in the lodge ceremony. An individual might get a substitute in special circumstances but would have to participate in the ceremony at a later time in order to advance. The Star Men would petition their elder brothers (who would be Lime Crazy Men) to help them secure grandfathers for the ceremony (the grandfathers could be from any of the higher lodges, that is, any men who had been through the Tomahawk ceremony). These elder brothers had obligations to help the incoming Tomahawk Men by donating property subsequent to the ceremony as well as during it; and they could require the Tomahawk Men to perform certain services for them. With the help of wives or women relatives, the Tomahawk Men made gifts of food and property to the grandfathers throughout the seven-day ceremony.

Subsequent to the ceremony, the grandsons and grandfathers were obligated to have harmonious relations or suffer supernatural sanctions. It is for this reason that when a man threatened violence, his relatives sent for his ceremonial grandfather. In fact, if a man subverted the authority of older relatives or wealthier men, he could avoid punishment or retaliation by getting his grandfather to intercede. The first three days, the grandfathers and their wives produced the regalia that the men would wear when they participated in the Tomahawk Lodge, including honorary regalia given to a few men singled out by the elder brothers for their bravery. The subsequent four days were given over to dancing with the regalia and races between the Tomahawk dancers, who were divided into two groups. According to Kroeber, Arapahos referred to the Tomahawk Men as "unreal"—complete, culturally conditioned men (rather than men in the natural state). The ceremony made them men instead of youths. In fact, in the origin story for this lodge, a buffalo spirit took pity on a social outcast, who was redeemed by the gift of the lodge.[105]

The honorary regalia consisted of four weapons (each carried by one of the chosen recipients) shaped like tomahawks that the grandfathers rubbed with dog root, which was a protective substance. The owners of these clubs received protection in battle (and prayed for protection by dancing with the objects) and were expected to perform special acts of bravery with the weapons. Tomahawk Lodge symbolism was also a reflection on the sexual maturity of these men. The root most associated in symbolism with the lodge was the "cockleburr," which was linked with the sex act in origin stories. Painted designs that represented a buffalo wallow were also representative of the sex act.[106]

The symbolism of this lodge (paint, decoration on headdresses, belts, and so on, as well as the weapons carried) generally reflected on creation and the guidelines given to Arapahos by supernatural beings. For example, certain colors stood for the Four Old Men and the Sun and Moon. The race run on each of four days symbolized traversing the four hills of life. The competition represented the reciprocal relations that Arapahos had been instructed to respect: alternation of summer and winter (the earth's cycles), the duties of men and women, and the act of giving to others and receiving from them in return. The Tomahawk Men were dressed to represent male and female buffalo: the lodge symbolism was also a prayer for the people's prosperity because buffalo brought life. Sweetgrass root was used, which was a prayer for the vegetation that supported the buffalo as well as the people.[107]

The Spear Lodge was held when a member of the Tomahawk Lodge pledged to sponsor it in return for supernatural aid; his fellow lodge members were supposed to participate with him. As in the Tomahawk Lodge, the men persuaded their elder brothers (who should be Dog Men) to secure ceremonial grandfathers for them. The regalia were made the first three days, then the men danced and raced on the subsequent four days. With the help of their wives, they fed and gave gifts to their grandfathers, and the grandfathers reciprocated. The elder brothers selected recipients of the honorary regalia. These nine men were supposed to have shown unusual bravery in war. Two boys, comparable to the little girls in the Buffalo Lodge, also received regalia. Their families had the means to accumulate many gifts.[108]

The symbolism of the regalia, all but one of which were lances, referred to thunder (the power to make a deadly strike). The highest honor went to a club with thunder symbolism and symbolism that referred to an elk who leads his herd. The man who was chosen for this regalia urged the others to keep dancing. All the dancers wore belts with symbols of animal spirits that bestowed special powers. Horsehair symbolized a strong advance against the enemy, and crow feathers represented swiftness. Lances had otter fur that signified softness so that injury would be avoided. These weapons were used in war and had been treated by the grandfathers to ward off harm. Those with honorary regalia had a responsibility to stick their lance in the ground during battle and not retreat unless a companion removed it, thus inspiring the others in his party. Arapahos encouraged bravery but apparently did not support recklessness. Warden noted that at one time, regalia of a high degree were supposed to be rolled into the breast-work of the enemy and followed by the warrior who owned it. But a consensus developed among fathers and other relatives of the warriors that the custom was "too hard," so it was stopped. During this time, Arapahos were experiencing high casualties from war and disease, which could have been a factor in the challenge made on behalf of the junior men to the senior lodge authorities. In addition to references to war, the symbolism on all the Spear Men's regalia represented a prayer for a long and good life (a straight path).[109]

The entire camp received a blessing from the ceremony, and people prayed during the ritual for the growth of children, old age, and protection from storms. The design of the regalia symbolized creation and the rules of conduct that accompanied it. Fertility (the birth of numerous children) was also associated with the Spear Lodge through rain symbols and use of the cockleburr root. This lodge promoted controlled sexuality and the birth of healthy children.[110]

The Lime Crazy Lodge was pledged by a member of the Spear Lodge, and his fellow lodge members joined him. The elder brothers (and their wives) were necessarily old. The would-be Lime Crazies selected grandfathers and grandmothers from the Dog Lodge or even the Old Men's Lodge. Grandfathers and grandmothers made the regalia the first three days and taught the details of the fire ritual to the elder brothers and their wives. The last four days involved a performance by the new Lime Crazy Men designed to instill awe. They behaved in a "backwards" manner. They

annoyed other people in the camp and shot arrows that paralyzed
an animal or person. They walked across red hot coals. Grandfathers transferred a "crazy root" to the Lime Crazy Men's wives
in a ritual in which the wives exposed themselves to supernatural
forces (represented by the grandfathers). Dog root was also transferred, which prevented the men from tiring. This lodge (particularly the crazy root) gave its members the power to cure, control
people's behavior by supernatural sanction, prevent game from
fleeing, and control the movements of enemies.[111]

The symbolism of the regalia was a reflection on creation and on
the foolishness of ignoring the rules of conduct that were associated
with creation. The chaos that ensued during the lodge reinforced the commitment to good behavior. One man had honorary
regalia, and the regalia for all were primarily a cape, owl feather
headdress, and a bow and four arrows, all of which had crazy
root attached.[112]

Medicine Grass witnessed the Dog Lodge in the 1860s. The
Lime Crazy Men vowed to participate in this ceremony after one
member made a pledge to sponsor it. According to Warden, some
of the Lime Crazy Men could not afford to enter the Dog Lodge
because it was particularly expensive. Old men served as elder
brothers and grandfathers, and the wives of all the men played key
roles in this lodge as well as the Lime Crazy Lodge. The regalia
were made the first three days, and then the dancing took place at
intervals during the next four days. The Dog Men solicited gifts
from people in the camp during this time, and the gifts were
widely distributed. The ceremony revolved around the transfer
of paint and dog and "main" roots, the latter transferred from the
grandfathers to the wives of the Dog Men and the paint from
grandfathers and grandmothers to the Dog Men and their wives.
These transfers were accompanied by gifts made to the grandfather
and grandmother. In fact, the body sacrifice of the Dog Man's wife
was also considered his sacrifice. Warden stressed that men needed
the aid of their wives to be "gifted with all the powers or privileges" of this lodge. The paint designs were applied to the face
and body each day, and each design was represented by a knot

in a string that the grandfather had; when he applied paint he untied his knot, and the Dog Man made a knot in his string. In this way, the right to the design was transferred. The number of knots represented the number of times the grandfather was painted when he went through the ceremony.[113]

The five men selected for honorary regalia wore leggings with scalps and other symbols of coups attached; one wore a special shirt, and four wore scarves representing ropes. All the dancers represented dogs, who gave power in battle, for example, to be nimble and quick. The dog was considered to be an animal spirit that had greatly helped Arapahos in earlier times, reviving warriors who were wounded. Dog Men carried rattles and eagle bone whistles, rather than weapons. The dog root could be used in ceremonies, for example, when the root was spit (as the first earth was blown in the four directions) on regalia in other ceremonies and on weapons for war. This root prevented weakness. "Main" root gave quietude or wisdom; men bit on it in battle. And it helped them in making good decisions in households and councils. The Dog Men might rarely accompany a war party to give direction, and they were expected to play a major role if their camp experienced an attack. The Dog Men's role was to stake down their long scarves and not retreat until a comrade pulled them free. Eagle down on the scarf protected the wearer from being wounded. Their bravery inspired bravery in others and helped the camp's defense. The men with scarves also had headdresses with blue beads, which represented invulnerability and smoke that made them invisible. In general, the regalia symbolized the four hills of life, the Seven Old Men, and the four seasons—in other words, progress through the life course. The Dog Lodge was a prayer for the future life of the people.[114]

Men also built their careers in the Offerings Lodge. Pledging the lodge brought great status for a man and his wife, and subsequently they were members of the Rabbit Lodge, the priesthood that directed the Offerings Lodge. Other men also could vow to participate in the four-day rite that followed the three-day Rabbit Lodge. Men obtained grandfathers who mentored them and applied paint designs during the ceremony, and some of these designs carried more weight than others, requiring more sacrifice and bringing more prestige and authority. Men could also vow to fast in the Rabbit Lodge while wearing the paint design that the pledger or Lodge Maker wore, which was very respected and which qualified a man as a Rabbit Man. The Offerings Lodge was both a property and a body sacrifice, made to obtain help from the supernatural. Men could vow to fast or be "pierced" with a point attached to a thong that they pulled out while dancing, tearing away the skin. Piercing substituted for, and thus prevented, being pierced by an enemy. Another kind of body sacrifice that a man could vow in order to help a relative, usually in cases of illness, was to cut off strips of skin and bury them. This act would forestall the death (that is, the burial) of a relative, and it attracted attention from the supernatural world, as all acts of sacrifice did. These religious acts on behalf of other people were regarded as examples of respect and love for others, not merely as prestigious.[115]

Men also attempted to acquire a supernatural helper to assist them in war, doctoring, or other activities, such as divination (location, prediction) and weather control. Men could apprentice to learn herbal cure, as women did, but they also doctored through physiotherapy, psychotherapy, and bloodletting. A man could fast several times, trying to attract the pity of a spirit helper, or he might have a dream or vision when he was awake. He would obtain advice from older people in these endeavors, asking an old man when to begin fasting for power. Or a man could have a dream that instructed him to apprentice himself to an established doctor and make payments until he was accomplished or, if his father was a medicine man, ask him for instruction. To retain the confidence of the teacher, a man had to show good character, that he would not abuse the power (for example, by using it to hurt other Arapahos) and would live by the rules given by the spirit helper. Most men had such power, although in varying degrees.[116]

Little Raven's life illustrated many factors important to the pursuit of a career. For example, family position and wealth certainly helped a man or a woman advance in the ceremonial organization and earn other markers of success. Little Raven was one of the most prominent men of his generation. He belonged to a prosperous family, which contributed to his success, and his wives shared in and contributed to his accomplishments. Little Raven was born about 1815. As a child he would have received many prayers, encouragement, and blessings from prominent warriors and elders during the rituals associated with childhood. His father was Raven, a warrior with a great reputation, a high-ranking priest in his advanced years (probably one of the Seven Old Men), and quite possibly the principal chief referred to by Dodge in 1835.[117]

One of Little Raven's sons told Mooney how as a youth, Little Raven acquired a Thunderbird shield, which helped him be successful in war. His father had owned the shield and gave Little Raven "lessons" in how to use it in battle, helping him understand the "rules for life" associated with the shield. Once, when Little Raven was on a war party against the Utes and his horse tired, the power of the shield protected him; it stopped arrows and prevented guns from shooting, so he intimidated the Utes with his medicine power, and he escaped. This shield lit his path at night when he became lost on a war expedition, and it protected him from injury during storms. Little Raven's mother, Backward, was one of the Seven Old Women who held many degrees in quillwork and would have earned the lodge degrees of her husband. She made prayer sacrifices on behalf of Little Raven as he progressed through the Kit Fox and Star lodges as a youth and beyond. He had two sisters besides Walking Backward, who would have made prayer offerings for his success in battle and his health generally. He also had several brothers, one of whom was Trunk, a renowned warrior, a band leader in his own right, prosperous, and a steadfast supporter of Little Raven's political career. All his relatives would have contributed property for his religious sacrifices as he progressed through the lodges and became a doctor. His high-ranking parents surely mentored him as he pursued his career.

As a mature man he progressed through the Tomahawk, Spear, Lime Crazy, and Dog lodges with the help of his wives and their families, as well as his sisters and brothers. Little Raven had at least five wives in the 1850s: Yellow Hair, his first; Nebaissa; then three sisters of Yellow Bear—Short Woman, Good Woman, and Beaver Woman. These women had different statuses within his household, and he and Yellow Hair eventually divorced, which probably resulted in Short Woman becoming boss wife. Little Raven was chosen principal chief in the mid-1850s and became the main intermediary chief for the Southern Arapahos during the 1860s. He was supported in the chieftainship by his wives, Trunk and his other brothers, Walking Backward and his other sisters, and by his brother-in-law Yellow Bear (born in 1822), the "war chief" (highest-ranking warrior and Dog Man) of the Arapahos. These two prominent extended families bolstered each other's status and supported each other economically. Little Raven's life also illustrates how gender complementarity was central to an individual's progress through the life course. The aid of his mother, sisters, and later his wives was crucial to his advancement, as his aid was to theirs.[118]

In the early nineteenth century, men pursued war to try to hold their territory. After mid-century, they began to lose territory and political independence. Many Americans wanted them and other Natives expelled from the West. The turbulent times of the mid-nineteenth century affected the men's cohorts differently. Little Raven's cohort had to face the intensification of warfare as young men, and their parents made changes in the requirements of the lodges to prevent needless loss of life. By the time of the treaty councils of the 1860s, they held the senior lodge positions, and the intermediary chiefs came from their ranks. With the support of elderly people, they and their wives took responsibility for formulating and implementing the conciliatory strategy. The men in Left Hand's cohort held lodge positions junior to those of Little Raven's cohort. They deferred to the older men and embraced the course of conciliation, which was counter to the duties they had initially accepted as lodge men, to aggressively fight enemies, and to their own aspirations for coups. Most of the men of Medicine Grass's cohort could not follow in the footsteps of their older brothers and fathers, so the conciliatory strategy curtailed their military careers even more. In their difficulties, all these men relied on the help and prayers of relatives and in-laws, many of them women.

Old People: Supporting the Rules of Life

Arapahos depended on protective ceremonies led by old people, many of whom headed the lodge organization. Old people were respected for their longevity, a sign of a successful relationship with supernatural forces. For this reason, children often received the names of elderly persons. Old men had symbols of their ceremonial careers painted on their families' tepees. Old women had symbols of their accomplishments on their tools. When old men and women painted themselves, they used red paint, which represented the Arapaho people, the earth, and the rules by which Arapahos were supposed to live. The wearing of red paint symbolized for all to see that old people helped the Arapahos survive. Old people had the duty to comfort mourners, give names to children and teach them Arapaho values, and attend feasts for children's accomplishments and for marriages. After a person died, old men would paint with red on the forehead, hair, hands, and body of the deceased's relatives. Arapahos thought that very old men and women were reborn in infants; they actualized the four hills of life through the cycle or regeneration of life. Elderly survival of epidemics and enemy attacks brought about by American expansion was a supernatural blessing and gave them great influence.[119]

What of the well-being of the elderly in general? Despite the great respect old age brought an Arapaho, old people with no close relatives might be allowed to stay behind when the camp moved if they could not keep up; presumably wealthy families would be able to transport even "distant" relatives. About 1842, Rufus Sage saw old Arapahos being transported by travois (which could have prolonged life and improved health generally), but he had heard of situations where the elderly had to walk and try to keep up with the moving camp. The family's wealth in horses clearly was a factor. When Medicine Grass was a boy in the late 1850s, an old woman who was the mother of one of the men in his band walked while holding on to a travois in which her grandchildren rode. She was almost blind. One day her son went hunting and, when the pony tied to the back of the travois bolted, she lost her hold on the travois and became separated from the group. Her daughter-in-law chased after the pony. The old lady did not return to camp, and even though a search party led by her son looked for her all night, she was never found. They found her trail as far as the bank of a creek. Medicine Grass also knew of one old man who, tired of his infirmities, decided to die in battle. He left with a war party and rode in among the enemy. It seems that old people were cared for to the best of their family's means and that they tried to contribute to the household as best they could.[120]

Old men were distinguished from younger Arapahos by behavior and dress as well as special rights and privileges. Elderly men (and women) dressed more simply and in more subdued colors than young people. Old men wore their hair in a distinctive style (in a roll over the forehead) and used red paint daily. In Arapaho origin stories, tobacco was given by supernatural beings to old men, and they were charged with handling pipes. Eggan was told that old men used pipes and youths did not pray with a pipe. Certainly, old men with proper ceremonial rank supervised the use of pipes in tribal ceremonies. According to Kroeber, eagle wing fans were used by old men (to shade their eyes, fan themselves, brush dust off, and drive away flies) on behalf of the people, and this right was validated in an origin story. The eagle was a vehicle of prayer. Some old men were approached by young men to make their arrows ceremonially; the arrows were blessed and given an identification mark so that these old men could settle disputes about whose arrow brought down a game animal. This arrow ceremony was also associated with an origin story. All old men might give advice to younger people, and some old men held ceremonial positions that gave them great authority. Clearly, certain old men had to be consulted about important matters. At the 1851 treaty council, an elderly Arapaho man (possibly one of the Seven Old

Men) made a speech to the Arapahos before the treaty was signed. And at the 1865 treaty council, Little Raven noted that he would report on the proceedings to "our old men"; presumably they had a role in preparing Little Raven's remarks to the commissioners. As noted above, old people were prominently in attendance at the 1867 treaty council. These old people could facilitate consensus by expressing support for intermediary chiefs. They also helped control conflict within the camps by resolving quarrels between men and, in matters of divorce, men and women.[121]

Old men who had gone through the Dog Lodge could vow the Old Men's, or Red Granite (paint), Lodge, if their wives had already joined the Buffalo Lodge. This group of old men (probably a segment of the surviving old men, because joining this lodge was expensive) would vow the lodge after one Dog Man pledged to sponsor it. Wearing red robes, they sang for four nights, learning ritual duties from the Seven Old Men. The incoming Old Men gave gifts for the instruction. Sometimes the Old Men danced, imitating prairie chickens (symbolically associated with the stars) while the Seven Old Men sang for them. Their face paint represented the four hills of life or Four Old Men. They received the right to give the dog root and its powers to others.[122]

The Seven Old Men were chosen from the ranks of the Old Men's Lodge and they directed all the lodge ceremonies, including the Buffalo Lodge and the Offerings Lodge. They directed painting and smoking in particular. And they chewed and spit dog root on objects and bodies, which symbolized the creation of the world and had the power of life. When they spit the root they promoted kind speech and prevented illness and bad luck. When the Arapahos camped together, the Seven had a sweat lodge in the center of the camp circle. Arapahos viewed them to be almost sacred, according to Warden: they had ceased to perspire, so they had returned to dust, or origin. These men were bound to talk kindly and think positive, peaceful thoughts. Arapahos might make property sacrifices to them in return for prayers for long life. Every day the Seven painted themselves red and went into a sweat lodge with their bundles and fasted, sitting perfectly still, while they prayed for the people. They might bring a person into the sweat lodge for a blessing; in fact, members of the Seven often brought their sons inside.

These Seven wore headdresses with a stone attached by a red string. Women from all the camps brought them food to distribute. Each man was the custodian of a sacred buffalo-skin bag. The bag represented the mountain from where the first buffalo came; it symbolized the life of the people. The bags contained all the roots and paint pigments (with certain paints and stones for making incense that represented all the animal species) that the Arapahos needed to survive, as well as a rattle (painted to represent the sun and moon) and buffalo tail, which were used in the sweat lodge, and a bear claw (symbolizing old age, that is, an old man's long nails). Their prayers could make things grow and reproduce.[123]

Old women's activities, such as creating designs on the objects they made, manufacturing tent pegs, and helping deliver babies, also had reference to origin myths. Clothing of elderly women often had designs representing the paths of their grandchildren— prayers for these children to reach old age. Certain old women (midwives) had the medicine power that enabled them to take charge of delivering babies, as well as women's reproductive health generally. These midwives supervised pregnant women's diet and exercise throughout their pregnancy to make for an easy and safe delivery. After the birth, they tended to a woman until she healed. Old women had much the same kind of prestige and authority as old men: they were invited to feasts for children and marriage, and very old women could name children.[124]

The highest ritual positions held by women were in the Seven Old Women organization, a companion to the Seven Old Men, and positions in the Rabbit Lodge (associated with the Offerings Lodge). Each of the Seven Old Women had made property and body (fasts) sacrifices to obtain one of the sacred bags passed down through time from one old woman to another. If a custodian died, the other six would select a successor. These women supervised the application of designs on and construction of tepees, backrests, tepee doors and linings, buffalo-skin pillows, robes, and cradle boards. Arapahos made property sacrifices to this group in return for prayers. The women's face paint—five dots—represented the Four Old Men (or perhaps the Four Old Women—the record is unclear on this point) and the Pipe spirit being (the tribal medicine bundle). The contents of the sacred bags were comparable to the Seven Old Men's bags—paint, stones (paint cups), and incense (pounded roots) used to animate objects with the life force and protect the owner—with the addition of tools needed for sewing and a leather object representing the spirit of the bag. Some women had positions of authority in the Rabbit Lodge, which was held three days before the beginning of the Offerings Lodge.[125]

Old women—after menopause, no longer required to avoid attending ceremonies—as well as old men were prominent in all the ceremonial lodges, including the Offerings Lodge. This lodge was described from memory to Kroeber, and Dorsey spoke to Arapahos about past Offerings Lodges as well as observing the ceremony himself. Rufus Sage reported that he saw one in 1842. He described a three-day fast before a center pole and buffalo skull, where the dancers were "washed" (painted each day) and pierced, and where property sacrifices were made.[126]

The Offerings Lodge required a vow: a person had a dream or experienced some crisis in life, then vowed to sponsor (pay the expenses of) the lodge to fulfill the dream or the vow made to secure help from supernatural forces. The sponsor and his wife, known as Lodge Maker and Lodge Maker's Wife, had to enlist the aid of others to acquire the food and property required. They could call on the Lodge Maker's lodge brothers and their wives or on their relatives. The Lodge Maker had to secure a grandfather to instruct and take care of him during the ceremony. All their lives, grandfather and grandson had duties to each other. Grandsons showed respect, and grandfathers helped them through crises. Food exchange symbolized the relationship. Other men could vow to dance and fast in the lodge, and they also got grandfathers, but more was required of the Lodge Maker. He fasted in the three-day Rabbit Lodge preparatory to the four-day Offerings Lodge ceremony, in which the dancers also participated. The Lodge Maker had to acquire the help of the Old Men and Women, who would direct the lodge, and the materials needed for the altar. His wife also fasted during the Rabbit Lodge.

The activities in the Rabbit Lodge and during the construction of the Offerings Lodge (a separate structure) were a dramatization of the events and symbols of creation. One of the Seven Old Men impersonated the Sun and was the chief priest. Wives of these Seven also helped supervise the women's ritual acts during the ceremony. One old woman (referred to as the Peacemaker) represented Moon, or Night Old Woman. This woman had to initiate ritual actions by speaking, and she was bound to never speak unpleasantly to anyone. Sun and Moon generated and renewed the life force, and the two impersonators were regarded as equivalent. These two priests also directed the other Arapaho lodges. They drew on the life force and became one with it. The Keeper of the Sacred Pipe and his wife also had to bring the Pipe to the ceremony. Another old man directed aspects of the ceremonies, and he represented the first Arapaho man praying. This male Director was the counterpart of a Woman Director who impersonated the human wife of Moon (and the first Arapaho woman). The grandfather of the Lodge Maker represented the forces of creation Above and his wife represented the forces of creation from Earth. This connection between sky and earth symbolized all life. These six individuals (and the Pipe Keeper) were Rabbit priests. Qualifying for these positions normally took a lifetime, and therefore the Rabbit priests were elderly. For example, the Male Director qualified by being a Lodge Maker several times or painting the center pole several times and apprenticing himself to Rabbit priests. Women could begin to qualify after menopause. Each of these old people had apprentices who were learning the rituals of the lodge through sacrifice of body and property and by working under supervision.[127]

This Offerings Lodge ceremony recreated the origin story: after a deluge, Pipe Being was floating on top of the water thinking "hard" and weeping to show sincerity. This became a charter for the act of prayer. He called in the four directions to the four corners of the universe (or the Four Old Men) for help. The Turtle Being came to his aid, diving below the water to bring up mud. The mud was put on the Pipe and blown (or spit) in four directions to create the earth. Pipe Being aided by Whirlwind Woman blew life into the mud. The Rabbit priests reproduced these acts of creation or animation when they prayed with a pipe, offered food in four directions, and spit on objects. The Sun, Moon, Star, Animal and Plant Beings were created and agreed to sacrifice themselves to help humans. These beings were symbolized in the lodge by the use of pelts, feathers, trees, scrubs, sticks, and various designs. Parts of the buffalo were particularly important because the buffalo provided all that Arapahos needed to survive. The Pipe Being then went into the Sky world and became Man Above. Its physical representation on earth was the tribal medicine bundle, the Flat, or Sacred, Pipe, which went north with the Northern Arapahos in the 1860s. It had symbolic representation in the form of a stone in the custody of the Southern Arapahos.

In another Arapaho origin story, Sun and Moon were brothers when Sun married Frog Woman and Moon married a human woman and a Buffalo Woman. Frog Woman jumped on Moon, and he was transformed into Night Old Woman. Thereafter, Moon's human wife gave birth. This act was a charter for conception and birth. Other stories refer to gifts received from Buffalo beings (cows and steers) and to the actions of Moon's human wife, who dug a hole in the Sky and descended to Earth. Arapahos recreated these events in the Offerings Lodge ceremonies; for example, the digging of Moon's human wife was replicated by the Woman Director, who dug sods and the ditch for the altar.

During the Rabbit Lodge, by painting the objects used in the ceremonies, the priests animated them. These objects were a buffalo hide, buffalo skull, drum and rattle made from buffalo parts, rawhide lariat, buffalo robe for the Lodge Maker, apron for the Lodge Maker's Wife, a badger skin (representing the world Below), and a digging stick. The first day, the old people started making the ritual objects. The second day, they went into a sweat lodge with the Lodge Maker and wife to pray for help, and they painted the Lodge Maker and his wife. The old women prepared the digging stick and rawhide lariat and dressed the Lodge Maker's wife. The old men dressed the Lodge Maker. The third day, a qualified old woman went to chop the center pole down. The Lodge Maker and his wife painted the poles, and the priests brought the ritual objects into the Offerings Lodge and subsequently built the altar. The grandfather, representing the powers of creation, transferred power to the Lodge Maker's Wife (who offered herself to the powers represented by the grandfather).

In the Rabbit and Offerings lodges, males and females had to cooperate. The men used a pipe to bless the work of women: carving the digging stick, cutting the rawhide lariat (used to tie objects to the center pole), cutting out two sods (representing male and female), digging the ditch used for the altar, and cutting the cedar tree used for the center pole of the Offerings Lodge. The men painted designs on the pole to which the buffalo hide and digging stick were tied. The designs on all objects represented creation (or the life force), a good path (a long and good life for all the people), and male and female connection and cooperation. The sticks that helped form the altar (the ditch, sods, tree border, and buffalo skull on a mound of dirt) and the digging stick symbolized all the Arapaho households. The center pole represented at once Man Above and the human woman descending from the Sky to the Earth. The survival and prosperity of the Arapaho people depended on the lodge rituals directed with authority by certain old men and women and on the everyday prayers of old men and women in general. The Offerings Lodge ceremony, directed by old people, expressed and reinforced the age hierarchy with its mitigating reciprocities as well as gender complementarity.[128]

American expansion challenged Arapahos in the nineteenth century, making the world a more dangerous place. By the late 1850s they had lost control of their best hunting territory and begun to lose political independence. With their survival as a people at stake, they developed a conciliatory strategy toward the Americans, cultivating them as allies and attempting to counter efforts to expel them from the region altogether. The men and women who led this conciliatory strategy belonged to the Little Raven and Walking Backward cohort because these were the people who had senior lodge status and thus considerable authority backed by elderly ritual authorities. For example, they served as grandparents to grandchildren in junior lodges, helping to generate consensus and cooperation. The most prominent among them, the chiefs and chiefs' wives, also had considerable wealth in food, horses, and property in general that they used to motivate others to cooperate. Despite tensions between the older cohort and the Left Hand and Owl cohort, the latter were persuaded to curb their ambitions for achievements in war and raiding and support the conciliatory strategy.

Women played no small part in this. The casualties of war contributed to the expansion of polygamy and the increased development of a ranking system for women within households, polygamous or not. The boss wife gained political leverage with her husband by successfully managing the household and its resources, and she maintained authority and influence in relation to the other women in the household. Boss wives likely joined the Buffalo Lodge and had other kinds of ceremonial degrees as well as partnering their husbands ceremonially. These women, and especially chiefs' wives, could influence not only council decisions through their husbands, but also junior women outside their households. These junior women could make their views known to male relatives as well as their husbands, who depended on them in many ways. They could affect the formation of war parties, either by encouraging or restraining them. As granddaughters in the lodge organization, they experienced the same pressures toward cooperation with senior lodge people as their husbands did. Reciprocities between women and men, especially wives and husbands, were the basis for successful life careers and for the implementation of the conciliatory strategy.

The Arapahos moved to the reservation in 1870. How did the members of the Little Raven and Walking Backward cohort fare?

How did the members of the Owl and Left Hand cohort—for example, Left Hand, Row Of Lodges, and Owl—adjust? Warfare ended, and the federal government tried to destroy the ceremonial organization. So what became of the careers of Medicine Grass's cohort (Scabby Bull and several of Little Raven's sons, for example) and the women in Bichea's cohort, most of whom were married to the men in the Medicine Grass or Left Hand cohorts after arrival on the reservation? What new challenges awaited the children born in the 1860s, who would grow up on the reservation? We have seen how Arapahos adapted to the crises of the latter part of the nineteenth century. How did they deal with reservation life?

Margaret Poisal Adams with Arapaho chiefs at the Medicine Lodge Creek treaty council, 1867. Margaret (1834 to ca. 1884) was the interpreter for Little Raven and the other chiefs. She was also the Arapahos' interpreter at the 1865 treaty council. The participants are smoking a pipe to sanctify the proceedings. From a sketch by Theodore R. Davis, *Harper's Weekly*, 29 June 1867, p. 405. Courtesy of National Anthropological Archives, Smithsonian Institution (55,949).

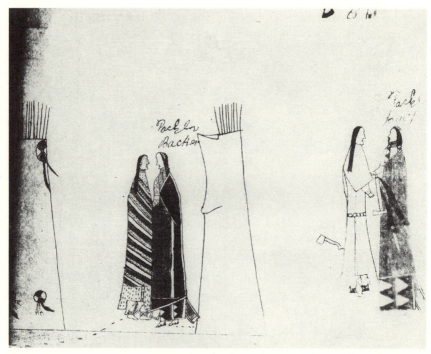

Drawing of courtship scenes by the Arapaho warrior, Packer, ca. 1876. In one scene, a man wraps his blanket around the girl he is courting, and they talk privately. In the other, a man approaches a woman out chopping wood with the intention of courting her. Probably the latter is married, widowed, or divorced and thus appears more assertive than the other girl. Packer (1851–1893) was accused of killing an agency employee, so in 1875 he was sent (along with one other Arapaho, White Bear) to a prison at Ft. Marion, Florida. There, he received some educational instruction and encouragement to draw. These prisoners also received pictographic messages from their families. At the time he was sent away, Packer's wife Blue left him. After he returned in 1878, he remarried and, after this wife died, married one more time. Courtesy of Hampton University Archives.

Quilled buffalo robe, 1873, Southern Arapaho. This is the 100th Robe design, which was the highest degree in women's robe work. Only a high-ranking warrior or chief had the right to wear such a robe, which had 100 rows of quilled design. The design was a prayer for the long life and prosperity of the wearer: the lines represented life paths and also buffalo trails. Courtesy of The Field Museum (CSA17053).

Black Wolf and daughter, ca. 1875. Black Wolf (1846–1893), from the Blackfeet band, served on the agency police force and became an intermediary chief in the 1880s. His daughter Ethel attended the Arapaho School, Haskell (1884–87), Carlisle (1889–90), and Chilocco (1890–91). Ethel (or Walks on Road; 1867–1930) was Black Wolf's oldest child, and here, she wears an expensive, elaborately decorated dress. Black Wolf holds his pipe and pipe bag. Ethel's mother was Trunk's daughter Walking Straight, probably the boss wife in Black Wolf's polygamous household. After Chilocco, Ethel worked at the Arapaho School for a short time, then returned to camp and in 1896 married James R. Hutchinson, divorced, then married Willie Meeks (1872–1936). Photo by Henry Stevenson Art Gallery, El Reno, Arthur R. Bastian Collection. Courtesy of Research Division of the Oklahoma Historical Society (20245.1).

Mennonite missionary Henry R. Voth with school girls, 1893. Voth was at the Mennonite school at Darlington Agency from 1883 to 1890, then was stationed at Cantonment from 1891 to 1893. The Mennonite missionaries' school had fewer students and was less regimented than the government school, and it placed more emphasis on religious teaching. Photo by James Mooney. Courtesy of National Anthropological Archives, Smithsonian Institution (213-a).

Jessie Spread Hands at Carlisle Indian School. Jessie (1867–1946) attended Carlisle from 1880 to 1883 and 1885 to 1894. The dress she is wearing was made by students, probably by Jessie herself. At the time she went to Carlisle, her father Spread Hands was living at Cantonment, as was her brother Henry Sage, but her mother had died. After she returned to the agency, she worked briefly at the Arapaho School, then, against the Indian agent's wishes, married Bringing Good (1857–1935) in 1896. They were members of the Lime Crazy Lodge and a chief couple in the Cantonment area. Jessie was married to Bringing Good until his death, after which she lived with her son's family. She had seven children, two of whom lived to maturity. Photo by John N. Choate. Courtesy of Cumberland County Historical Society, Carlisle, PA (PA-CH2-88f).

Boys' work detail, Seger School, ca. 1900. The boys, wearing school uniforms, are cleaning up the school yard. They spent half of each day working to keep the government boarding school operating. Campbell Collection. Courtesy of Western History Collections, University of Oklahoma (1840).

Powderface and wife, November 1873. This photograph was taken when Chief Powderface and his wife Red Woman went to Washington, D.C., as part of a delegation of chiefs. Powderface (1836–1886) was the highest ranking chief on this delegation. Red Woman, born about 1844, died a year or two after Powderface was found dead on a hunting trail, apparently frozen to death. Reportedly they had been devoted to each other during their long marriage. Photo by Alexander Gardner. Courtesy of National Anthropological Archives, Smithsonian Institution (181).

Arapaho delegates, Washington, D.C., 1891. This delegation tried to persuade federal officials to keep the promises made by the Jerome Commission, which negotiated allotment and sale of surplus land on the reservation. Standing, *left to right*, wearing the peace medals received by chiefs: Row Of Lodges (1837–1904), Black Wolf (1846–1893), and the interpreter, Carlisle alumnus Jesse Bent (1863–1923). Seated, *left to right*: Scabby Bull (1848–1903); Black Coyote (1854–1911), who after Sitting Bull was the most important Ghost Dance leader; Woman Going In (Mrs. Left Hand); and Left Hand (1839–1911). Left Hand was the principal chief at this time and because of his stature, his wife accompanied the delegation. Photo by C. M. Bell. Courtesy of Research Division of the Oklahoma Historical Society (9471).

Old Crow praising a long-married couple, 1901. Old Crow (1828–1904), one of the Seven Old Men, took this opportunity on the occasion of the Offerings Lodge to publicly praise all the couples who had long, stable marriages. Those couples provided leadership and served as role models. The couple here are Black Bull (1831–1902), a Dog Man, and his wife Yellow Woman (1852–1926), a Dog Woman and a woman with high rank in the Offerings Lodge. After Black Bull died, she married Spotted Corn, a high-ranking ceremonial authority. Eight of her nine children were dead by 1902. Photo by George A. Dorsey. Courtesy of National Anthropological Archives, Smithsonian Institution (T10096).

Old Crow announcing the gift of a pony by Little Raven, Jr., and his wife, 1901. Little Raven, Jr. (1861–1938) and his wife Jenny Bringing Good (1881–1915) are making a property sacrifice on behalf of the child Jenny is carrying in a shawl on her back. Old Crow, one of the Seven Old Men, speaks for them, which gives special import to the occasion. Little Raven, Jr., married Jenny in 1898. The marriage was a long, stable one. Jenny was the daughter of White Eyed Woman, a widow, who was the sister of Black Horse. Jenny had four children who lived to maturity and six who died when they were small. This couple held the chieftainship in the early twentieth century, and during the years of their marriage, they rose in the Offerings Lodge ceremonial organization. Photo by George A. Dorsey. Courtesy of The Field Museum (CSA10110).

Mrs. Bears Lariat and Mrs. Charcoal chopping down the tree for the center pole, Offerings Lodge, 1902. The right to perform this ritual act was earned by the prayer sacrifices of these women, who held Rabbit Lodge status. Mrs. Bears Lariat was Mouse (1857–1925), a daughter of Trunk. She had been a co-wife with her sister, a daughter of Little Raven. Mrs. Charcoal was substituting for Yellow Woman, indisposed at the time. Photo by George A. Dorsey. Courtesy of The Field Museum (CSA1483).

CHAPTER 2

SEEING SIGNS AND WONDERS

Cohorts, Civilization, and New Religions, 1870–1901

In the early spring of 1884, the Arapahos had been on their reservation fourteen years. Bands still camped together and moved to sheltered areas in the winter and to more open grassland in the spring, when prominent people decided they would break camp, and the crier announced it. Laughing and talking, women began taking down the tepee poles and tying them to their horses. They rolled up the covers and, along with their household utensils, laid them on their travoises. The small children hung in skin sacks from saddles or rested on a travois. The older children and the women mounted their horses loaded with saddlebags, and the household began moving in line with others while the men of the Spear Lodge supervised. Women guided the horses pulling travoises and herded packs of barking dogs running alongside or pulling smaller travoises. Teenage boys riding their ponies had charge of the families' stock. The men of the families rode together. Arapaho bands traveled this way from one campsite to another. In fact, camp life was much as it had been before reservation settlement.[1]

But times were more difficult. The large buffalo herds had disappeared by the late 1870s. The agency was at Darlington, a small settlement of three traders' stores, a hotel and stable, three schools for Indians, and the government buildings, including the federal agent's residence, workshops, and a commissary. Fort Reno was two miles to the southwest. The agency could not provide sufficient help to Arapahos trying to adjust to reservation life, for the government had not furnished the supplies and aid promised at the treaty of 1867. Agency policy affected children and adults and men and women differently. The age cohorts faced different kinds of challenges and had different opportunities.[2]

The agents tried to place as many children as possible in boarding schools, where they could be weaned away from Arapaho values. The Jessie Spread Hands and Little Raven, Jr., cohort also had to cope with the possibility of attendance at off-reservation boarding schools, where long absences from home could make children more vulnerable to alienation from their families. The Little Raven–Walking Backward and Owl–Left Hand cohorts arrived on the reservation with herds of horses and high positions in the lodge organization, and they could use their resources to transition into agriculture and freighting. But the Medicine Grass cohort and their wives (mainly from Bichea's cohort) came as very young people—the men had little or no war experience or property and belonged to the junior lodges. In these times, they could not rely on war and horse raids to improve their position. The agents also attempted to abolish polygamous marriage, which threatened many women in the Bichea and Jessie Spread Hands cohorts with loss of position within the households and camps.

The Arapahos met the challenges of reservation life by developing and implementing a "civilization strategy." They cooperated with the agents in accepting new kinds of work and schools, but they did so on their own terms and used their apparent cooperation to attain better treatment, particularly in comparison to the Cheyennes, many of whom openly defied the agents. As examples of "progressive" Indians, Arapahos dissuaded agents from completely suppressing polygamy and the lodge organization. The efforts of the older cohorts to implement the civilization strategy and retain communal work and sharing (rather than adopting the individualism promoted by the agents) shaped the way Arapaho society changed. This chapter details the way this change occurred through the efforts of both women and men and identifies the leaders of the civilization strategy as relatively prosperous senior lodge men and their wives. By 1889 the Arapahos suffered destruction of their ranching economy, ration reduction, and a high mortality rate, yet the government dismissed their complaints. When their reservation was allotted in 1892, Arapahos lost the means of self-support and were exposed to a predatory population of settlers. The Medicine Grass cohort and their wives, who followed the lead of the older cohorts in accepting the civilization strategy, changed the direction of Arapaho religious life in providing the leadership for new religions that brought hope for a better future.

Doing What They Were Told: School Boys and Girls

John Seger, superintendent of the government school in the 1870s, was determined to retrieve some runaways from a Cheyenne camp. As he saddled his horse, he was approached by two of the older schoolboys, Arapahos Dan Tucker and Neatha Seger. They advised against his going because they knew it would be dangerous. When he insisted, they got on their horses and went with him. In the camp, when he was threatened, they stood beside him, with their guns ready. The Cheyennes challenged them: why were they defending the white man who was abusive to them? Dan and Neatha replied that as Arapahos, they had been taught by their seniors to do what they were told, and they had been told to cooperate with Seger. These boys probably saved Seger's life. They were atypical of Arapahos because, for one thing, they were still attending school as youths. But their commitment to Arapaho values was typical of Arapaho children in the 1870s through the 1890s, a time when the assimilation program of the federal government was targeting children through recruitment into boarding school.[3]

How were children brought up during these reservation years? Their older relatives advised them about proper behavior and reinforced these lectures with rituals in which elderly people prayed for them, praised their good behavior, and gave advice on how to live a good life. Cleaver Warden noted that grandparents assumed responsibility for the character development of their

grandchildren, regularly telling them stories at night that reinforced social values. Missionary S. S. Haury commented that
Arapahos inculcated religion into the child from infancy. Arapahos
stressed that adults did not whip children; rather, they encouraged them and lectured.[4]

   Although the reservation years were poor ones, and some families could have only modest rituals, parents had feasts when their
children first walked, and often had their children's ears pierced.
Naming ceremonies were still held; sometimes an elderly relative
named the child without much ceremony, but the name was still
regarded as a protective prayer and a charter for good behavior.
Jess Rowlodge, born in 1884, noted that when his ears were pierced,
his father gave two ponies. His parents, Owl and Row Of Lodges
(actually his stepfather, who married Owl after she left Jess's
father Bear Robe), also sacrificed a shell (which they tied to the
buffalo head on the center pole of the Offerings Lodge) as a
blessing for him when he was small. He had a beaded cradle,
which was given to another child in the family when he was too
old for it. Women may have begun to pass cradles down rather
than sponsoring expensive ceremonies to make new ones. Jess's
mother's sister's husband named the boy Mystical Magpie after
this man's war experience, when a magpie spirit helper led his
party to the enemy and to victory. The name was a prayer for
similar success in Jess's life.[5]

   When a boy killed his first small game, he was recognized for
his skill and hard work. Arnold Woolworth, born in 1862, told
Inez Hilger that his parents praised him when he killed his first
rabbit. The boys hunted squirrels, rabbits, and birds. Sometimes
boys cooked and ate squirrel and told their "buffalo story" as if
they were old hunters. Jess Rowlodge fished, caught small animals
(such as beaver), and shot prairie chickens with a bow and arrow
(the bow made by his father). His mother, Owl, kept a record of
his animal kills. Crazy Wolf (who became known as Myrtle Lincoln), born in 1888, recalled playing with dolls made of cow bone
wrapped in rags, sardine cans (representing wagons), weeds that
she used to make toy arbors, and stick horses. Myrtle was not

from a chief's family; rather, her mother, Blind Woman, was the daughter of Sleeping Wolf (the brother of Road Traveler's wives), who died in 1878, when Blind Woman was eleven. Blind Woman became a co-wife of Bad Man. After Myrtle was orphaned in 1901, Pumpkin (widow of Road Traveler) took care of her. Ponca Woman (later Annie Pedro), born in 1881, noted that her brothers brought her rabbits to slice that they had hunted with bows and arrows, and she played with rag dolls, toy tepees, and bone animals.[6]

Games encouraged both boys and girls to develop stamina and physical skills. In the 1870s and 1880s, when Arapahos were operating freight trains and fording rivers, as well as moving camp frequently, horseback riding and swimming continued to be important. Children played games such as mud ball, swimming on their backs with a ball of mud between their toes. Some boys were chosen by their older male relatives to be errand boys for the lodges; this responsibility also prepared them to assume the duties of mature men.[7]

The first school was opened at the agency at Darlington in 1871. This was a day school, and seventeen Arapaho and eight Cheyenne children were enrolled. The following year the Mission School, with John Seger in charge, was opened, and it became a government boarding school in 1875. Most of the Arapaho children who attended came from Big Mouth's band, which had settled near the agency. Nineteen Arapaho boys and twenty-four girls shared the school with twenty Cheyennes, who were angry at having to attend the same school. In 1876 Agent John D. Miles noted that the school had places for seventy-eight (only about 11 percent of the tribes' children).[8]

By 1880 there were two boarding schools, one for each tribe. The following year, the Arapaho school had 120 students, who stayed on average about one year. The Mennonites opened a small school at Darlington in 1881 and one at Cantonment in the old military barracks in 1883. They taught a smaller number of students and treated them like family members, according to observers. By 1887 most school-age Arapaho children were enrolled in school, although attendance could be sporadic, and not all the children boarded. Sixty-three boys and the same number of girls attended the Arapaho school in the first quarter of 1898, and the Mennonites' school had about twenty boys and twenty girls. Arapaho children attended the school at Cantonment as well.[9]

Jess Rowlodge was five years old when he arrived at the Arapaho school. He was probably dressed in buckskin leggings, a g-string, and a long cloth shirt when he was issued school clothes and shoes. He did not know how to button clothing or lace shoes. Annie Pedro arrived in 1886 at the age of five, having come from a camp of tepees, where she had slept on a willow bed. The children were given English names; usually surnames were those of agency employees or famous Americans or others (for example, Christopher Columbus). Chiefs' children, such as Jess, usually took their father's name as a surname: Row Of Lodges's son became Jess Rowlodge. At the Arapaho school the focus of classroom work was teaching English. Students spent much of their time working. In 1881 the small children weeded, hoed, and planted seeds for vegetables and melons in the school garden. Carl Sweezy told Althea Bass that Arapaho children understood the importance of plants, so they did not resent gardening. The boys chopped wood, cleaned the yard, drove teams, plowed and planted corn, milked cows, and cared for the school's stock. They also had to do military drills, marching daily. The girls sewed, washed, and ironed clothes; did bed chamber and dining room work; and helped cook. Josie Poisal described her work at the Arapaho school thus: "We eat mulberries in the garden. . . . In the morning and in the evening we saw wood. . . . Our corn is all long and we are done hoeing the corn. . . . When we were done hoeing the corn Mr. Sprunger gave us candies and cookies."[10]

Employees (police, for example) were generally required to send children to school. Policeman Black Wolf sent his daughter Ethel. The chiefs sent some of their children to impress federal officials with their willingness to embrace "civilization" goals or to influence federal policy (for example, tying enrollment to permission for a delegation). As Jess Rowlodge put it, tribal chiefs had

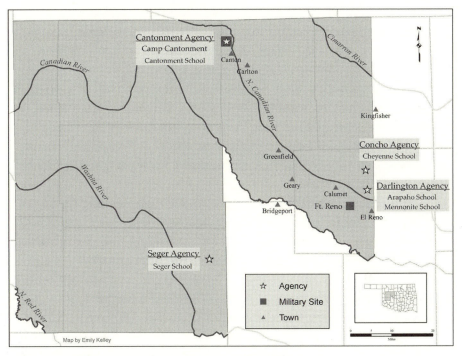

Agencies, military posts, schools, and towns, 1870–1936

to show an example by sending their children to school. Several children from Little Raven's band attended the Arapaho school in the 1870s and 1880s, even though their camps were some distance from the agency. Little Raven sent his youngest daughter, Anna, as well as other children in his band: Harry Raven (his grandson), Cleaver Warden (an orphan), Edwin Glenn, Jessie and Sarah Scabby Bull, Henry Lincoln, Lydia Harrington (an orphan), Alice Road Traveler, and Bessie, Grant, and Matthew (Red Woman's children and Red Pipe's grandchildren). Little Raven's brother-in-law Yellow Bear sent his two daughters, Belle and Minnie, as well as Jenny Arrow, Percy and Leslie Scabby Horse, Willie Meeks (an orphan), Leah Road Traveler, and Chase Harrington (an orphan). Left Hand sent his sons Grant and Ernest and other children, including Mrs. North's children Henry, Mary, and Theodore. Generally, orphans received more years of school than the others and rarely went back to camp during the summer. Poor families often agreed to send children because they believed they would be fed and clothed.[11]

New rituals developed to encourage and help children cope with school conditions. A hair-cutting ceremony was often held. It followed the procedures used in ear piercing so that when a warrior cut a child's hair, the ceremony took away the potential harm of the school haircut. And sometimes a "whipping" ritual was held to fortify children psychologically for the corporal punishment that they sometimes faced.[12]

The census of 1881 indicates that many families had children living with them who were described as "nephews," "nieces," stepchildren, or "cousins." All could be considered orphans. Both Dan Tucker and Neatha Seger were orphans. So was Carl Sweezy, who was born in 1881. He was taken to the Mennonite school at Darlington because his mother died when he was small. According to Sweezy, the Mennonites treated children with "Christian kindness."[13]

Parents came to expect their children to learn English so that the children could translate and read and write for them. Fluency in English, as much as gathering and hunting, became children's work. New skills related to farming also became helpful to the children's families. The superintendent of the Arapaho school reported in 1881 that parents wanted their children home in the summer and at other times so that they could help with the corn: they were "more expert than camp Indians." Schoolgirls probably helped their mothers sew. And when the children left school, they usually received a cow or two to take with them. Parents often rewarded children who were in school by giving them ponies. In fact, the census of 1881 shows that usually children who had several ponies, as opposed to one or none, were in school. In 1900 Agent John Seger at Colony noted that most white boys in the community did not have a pony much less a saddle, while every Indian boy in school had a pony, and many had saddles costing ten to twenty-five dollars.[14]

In school, the children learned new games, some from white children at the agency, such as prisoner's base and drop-the-handkerchief, and some in imitation of the activities they observed at the agency, such as "making cord wood." They made clay cows as well as horses when they played "camp life." The school personnel rewarded children who spoke English, and in the early years teachers avoided corporal punishment. Superintendent Seger reported that the Arapaho school encouraged English by reward not punishment: boys who used English received advancement in "military rank," and children who spoke English could participate in games as well as musical and literary exercises. A Christmas celebration brought the children treats and toys, and they looked forward to it. Boys became enthusiastic baseball players.[15]

But camp life was still the foremost influence in children's lives, even those who attended school. In 1881 and 1882, children ran away from the Arapaho school during the Arapahos' religious ceremonies because they considered it "a religious duty" to attend. Children left the school to attend the Offerings Lodge, to be doctored by medicine men, to visit relatives generally (relatives also visited them), and in the 1890s, they left to attend Ghost Dance ceremonies. Children left school at the beginning of the summer and stayed in camp until fall. The Arapaho school released children for Thanksgiving and days when the agency issued rations and beef, and even weekends. Arapaho children continued to speak Arapaho while learning English. Missionary Henry Voth reported in 1886 that Arapaho children spoke their language in play and sleeping rooms. And in the Arapaho school, children were not prohibited from speaking Arapaho.[16]

In the 1890s, school policy became more repressive in the four boarding schools (three for Arapahos—the Arapaho school, the Mennonite school at Darlington, and the Mennonite school at Cantonment). By 1895, the school superintendent was curtailing visits to camp. There was an English-only policy at the Arapaho school, according to an inspection report in 1897. Even so, children left without permission to attend the Ghost Dance ceremonies and left school to go hunting with their families or to visit with relatives.

Runaways were dealt with harshly: in 1900, one was confined in jail for two days and hobbled for sixteen. Corporal punishment was used at the Arapaho school until the chiefs protested in council in 1895—children were whipped until they could not "stand it," an unacceptable punishment, chiefs thought. As a result of their complaints, federal officials promised to end the practice.[17]

Conditions in the schools encouraged runaways and nonattendance. The Arapaho school was terribly overcrowded. In 1882 Agent Miles noted that Arapaho children came to school healthy but soon sickened and died. Often, if allowed to return to camp, they recovered. The Arapaho school had been built on low ground in the midst of pools of stagnant water where mosquitoes collected, and poor construction of the buildings permitted cold and damp drafts. Inspections evaluated sanitary conditions at the school as low. In 1892 there was a malaria epidemic at the Arapaho school, followed by an epidemic of influenza and whooping cough in 1893. Inspector Frank Armstrong described the living conditions in 1886 as like the "bunk of the dirtiest deck hand on a third class Mississippi River steamboat." The water supply was polluted: river water contained open sewage from Fort Reno, and there was an open drain at the school. In 1896, when the Arapaho school had an enrollment of about 132, up to 35 children were in the school hospital. By 1901 the Arapaho school was in disrepair, very dirty, and lacking in supplies and clothing for the children. Tuberculosis was widespread. The boarding schools were enrolling sick children to achieve maximum enrollment, even though they could not properly care for them all. Despite the high absentee rate and the general unwillingness to remain in school for a long period, missionary J. S. Krehbiel was able to report in 1894 that in nearly every camp, several Arapaho children spoke English. A few of these children went on to off-reservation schools as teenagers or occasionally at a younger age.[18]

EXALTED IDEAS: CAMP YOUTHS AND EDUCATED ARAPAHOS

Nellie Morrison was the ideal Arapaho girl from the federal government's point of view. Her father was James Morrison, a white man and an agency employee, and her mother was the daughter of Chief Big Mouth. Born in 1869, as a child she was sent by her father to Lawrence, Kansas, where she lived with the family of Indian Office employee John Miles during most of her childhood. Brought up and educated with Miles's daughter, her dream was to become a teacher and return to the reservation to work with Arapaho children. But when she returned, she only managed to secure a position as a seamstress in the Cheyenne school, even though she graduated from the University of Kansas with a first-grade teacher's certificate. But Agent Charles Ashley, impressed by her "refinement," secured a position for her as a teacher at the Arapaho school in 1889 at $600 per year. She held the position for only a short time before she died of tuberculosis at the age of twenty-one.[19]

Similarly, as we shall see, Dan Tucker was the ideal Arapaho youth. Both Nellie and Dan were "educated" Arapahos who attended school off the reservation. Dan went to Carlisle Indian School in Pennsylvania. Educated youths like Nellie and Dan represented a small minority of Arapaho youths during the 1870s and 1880s. How did the lives of these youths, who spent some years in schools off the reservation, compare with those who remained on the reservation? When they reached maturity, did these two groups have different life careers in terms of marriage, economic activity, and political or ceremonial roles and status?

Arapahos born in the early 1860s, like Little Raven, Jr., and Dan Tucker, were teenagers in the mid-1870s. And those born in the 1870s were youths in the late 1880s. This group—the Jessie Spread Hands–Little Raven, Jr., cohort—faced challenges on the reservation. So did a few from the cohort of Jess Rowlodge and Myrtle Lincoln, who were born in the 1880s. Boys could not achieve reputations for war exploits or wealth as their older siblings and parents had. In their twenties and often their thirties, the males were still considered "boys." So this "youth" category was redefined (expanded) for boys. Girls still became mature women when they married, but boarding school could complicate this road to maturity. For example, girls might postpone marriage. Some youths were considered too old to attend school, and some (camp Indians) went to school only a year or two, then returned to camp life. The "educated" group attended off-reservation boarding schools for several years.

Camp Indians continued to learn the values associated with a good life through the lectures of their elders and through their work experiences. Hilger noted that the brother-sister respect relationship was maintained. Generally, behavior that reflected respect for others, especially senior relatives and old people, was expected, and youths would be ostracized if they deviated, a frustrated Agent A. E. Woodson reported. Youths continued to hunt for their families, and these boys had charge of the families' stock. Jess Rowlodge described how his father, Row Of Lodges, lectured and trained him on how to behave, be industrious, and help people. He stressed that his father was proud of him when, as a fourteen-year-old, he gave his fine pony, saddle, and bridle to a friend on foot. Families also expected youths to help them mow and rake hay and to instruct older relatives in farming.[20]

Myrtle Lincoln also received frequent lectures on the importance of industry and circumspect behavior. Jess Rowlodge noted that when girls (or some girls) reached puberty, they began to wear a thick leather belt that symbolized their readiness for women's work; perhaps the rope worn under clothing at night had been discarded in the early reservation years. The girls also tried to live up to Arapaho values. Hilger mentioned one sacrificing a finger joint so that her brother would be released from jail. In camp, teenage girls did tasks such as carrying water from streams and bringing kindling to the camp. Skills learned in school were also part of girls' work. Grace Powderface (born in 1881), the daughter of Chief Powderface's son Clarence and Cedar Woman, washed dishes, cooked, made bread, and sewed at home after she left school. Her mother urged her to show respect to her relatives by making them bread, clothing, and moccasins.[21]

Even though warfare was no longer an avenue to prestige, boys could start a career in the ceremonial organization, and their families expected them to do so. Many of these youths organized as Kit Foxes and subsequently Stars. These groups were no longer trained or encouraged in warfare but still had duties during the Offerings Lodge, and their social duties assumed major importance. Warden noted that the lodge ceremonies had a "strong 'will power' to correct past deeds and to teach young people in better attainments." But, as Arnold Woolworth told Hilger, not all joined with their age peers. He did, and so did his fellow boarding school alumnus Henry North, both of whom were in the Little Raven, Jr., cohort. Straight Crazy and his wife Curley Hair (from the Jessie Spread Hands–Little Raven, Jr., cohort) made the Lodge Maker vow in the 1901 Offerings Lodge. Camp Indian Straight Crazy had had a vision in which he was instructed to make the sacrifice to recover from depression. He had attempted suicide but recovered after he completed the vow, according to Jess Rowlodge. Others in the Little Raven, Jr., cohort completed vows to participate in the 1901 and 1902 lodges.[22]

Jess Rowlodge joined both societies. He joined the Foxes when he was sixteen. As a member, he learned to be industrious, endure hardship, and develop "the good qualities of manhood." Old men sat with the initiates, teaching them the songs and dance associated with the group. And they and the elder brothers (those who had completed the Star ceremony and were about to be or already were Tomahawk Men) lectured the new Foxes on their duties. They should learn to butcher, hunt, make arrows, handle horses, and bring food and other help to the needy. The Foxes would dance at tribal gatherings. Jess later moved up to the Star society. Parents would give away property to show respect and ask for a blessing for their sons. Jess also noted that some youths began to train as doctors, particularly if they had older male relatives who were doctors. Some girls began to train for a ceremonial career as well. Myrtle Lincoln began to receive training in midwifery from her grandmother Pumpkin.[23]

Horses were still a status symbol. Not all teenage boys had horses, and only a few had several. Boys raced their horses to show off, Sweezy told Bass. Collectively, girls owned more horses than boys did, perhaps because brothers gave horses to their sisters in return for gifts such as moccasins. The 1881 census shows that a little less than half the camp youths had no horses; about one-fourth had one, and one-fourth had two to ten. Males who were "orphans" (living not with their fathers but with a stepfather or relatives) had no horse or just one horse. In contrast, Little Raven's son Little Raven, Jr., had ten horses. Little Raven's stepson had only one. His daughter Anna had eight, while most teenage girls had only one unless they were the daughters of important chiefs. Girls who owned no horses were generally orphans.[24]

Youths in the Reservation Schools

What impact did school attendance on the reservation for a year or more have on Arapaho youths? Instruction in farming allowed boys to help their families make a transition to an agricultural way of life. Jess Rowlodge maintained that the school boys taught older Arapahos to farm. In the 1880s, Agent Miles began issuing cattle from the school herd to students and tried to help school graduates get a start in freighting. The cattle that these girls and boys accumulated brought them social status and a way to demonstrate respect for relatives and make an economic contribution to their families. In 1878 Seger noted that the students pointed out their individually owned cattle with pride. Inspector John McNeil reported that the school owned 56 animals, and fifty-five pupils owned 155 in 1878. In 1881, those youths who owned cattle were all at the Arapaho school, where, in the 1870s, John Seger had implemented a policy of paying the older children for their work. Older boys cut and hauled wood for the Mennonite mission and the agency, assisted in butchering, cared for agency stock, and plowed and planted the 120-acre school farm. The boys got half the corn crop to sell. They bought a few things like clothing but primarily purchased cattle, which they owned individually. Each youth had his or her own brand, and when they left school, they took their cattle.[25]

Girls could make shirts and beaded items to sell to the trader to buy things for themselves; often their families gave them cattle. Girls could help family members by making garments for them,

Woodson reported. Annie Pedro recalled making beaded belts on a loom, beaded necklaces, and baby moccasins in school. The matron sold these items and gave the girls some of the money. The Mennonites at Cantonment school were paying the older students six to eight dollars a month for their work, Haury reported in 1883. In 1882 the Mennonites began taking older boys to the Mennonite community in Kansas to work on farms during the summer. By 1890 the Mennonites paid the large boys thirty dollars for a summer's work. Some youths worked for settlers during the summers, taking advantage of what they had learned and bringing income back to their families.[26]

Jess Rowlodge joined oat- and wheat-threshing crews in 1897. He worked as a cowboy in 1898 and 1899, when he and other Arapahos herded cattle, using their own horses. After that, he worked as a clerk in a store, owned by his Sunday School teacher at the Arapaho school, for seventy-five dollars a month. He used his income to help his parents. Annie Pedro, whose father was one of the Indian police at Darlington, learned to cook American style in school and worked as a cook for an agency employee.[27]

Seger's experiment and youths' observation that adults were paid for their work at the agency shaped the youths' attitude toward their work. Miles reported in 1878 that the schoolboys would not sell him their corn under market price. By 1883 Inspector James Haworth reported that the Cheyenne pupils argued that they should be paid for all the work they did at their school—clearly a widespread sentiment at all the reservation schools. The Mennonites also found that students resisted working without pay.[28]

Despite the new skills learned, youths still were subject to the advice and pressure of older relatives to live up to Arapaho values. Attendance at ceremonies and gatherings continued even in the 1890s, when the school authorities tried to coerce nonattendance. The Mennonite authorities reported in 1891 that three large girls ran away to camp to participate in Ghost Dances. They came back from camp with camp clothes on, "defiant, still singing the songs." Boys ran away to attend the Offerings Lodge and other events, such as Omaha Dances. The Mennonites punished all by locking them in a dark closet for several hours. Agent Woodson complained in 1896 that "educated Indians are absorbed back" into camp life. Missionary Mary Jayne noted that the drummers at the Ghost Dance hand games were young, educated men and that these educated men participated in peyote ritual.[29]

Probably the most serious problem that school attendance caused for youths was the lack of supervision of the girls. Myrtle Lincoln stressed that parents were upset that girls and boys played together, presumably brothers and sisters included. Clearly reputations were damaged. Carlisle alumnus John Williams refused to marry Arrow's daughter, despite pressure from his father, because she had been involved with another boy at Halstead. In 1889 Inspector Edmund Mallet brought attention to the problem by reporting that a boy and girl were found together in bed at the Arapaho school. The same situation prevailed at the Cantonment school. In 1890 Agent Ashley complained that Arapaho scouts would come to the school at night and "interfere" with girls. Woodson insisted that the commander at Fort Reno put two youths in the guard house for thirty days for entering the girls' dormitory at night for "improper purposes," and he asked the commander to prevent his men from coming to the school. Girls were also vulnerable to school staff. Woodson, pressured by outraged parents, tried to force the resignation of the Arapaho school superintendent for molesting Indian girls.[30]

School attendance facilitated a few elopements. Usually, the couple was forced to legally marry. When Bichea's daughter became involved with another student, the families treated the incident like an elopement. Girls also occasionally tried to avoid an arranged marriage by appealing to school officials to keep them in school. The officials were glad to oblige. As missionary Haury put it, "In order to Christianize and civilize the Indians we must try to educate and lift up the women from her most miserable state; we must try to effect a Christian family, and to build up a Christian home." School officials believed that if girls married "educated" Indians, they would avoid the corruptions of camp life.[31]

Youths in Off-Reservation Schools

A minority of youths in the Jessie Spread Hands–Little Raven, Jr., cohort went to boarding schools off the reservation. The first group of Arapahos went to Carlisle in 1879—six boys and three girls. In 1882 sixteen boys and one girl left for the Mennonite College, and in 1884 nineteen boys and five girls went to Haskell Institute. In 1885, forty-five Arapaho boys and twenty-eight girls were at off-reservation schools. At Carlisle Indian School in Pennsylvania, boys learned trades including blacksmith, wagon maker, carpenter, shoemaker, tailor, tinner, harness maker, printer, and baker, as well as farm work. Girls learned housekeeping, doing the domestic work at the school, including cleaning the teachers' rooms. Carlisle was prestigious in part because chiefs sent many of their children there and visited Carlisle from time to time. The boys there made wagons for chiefs; Left Hand received one in 1882. The school had military-style discipline, with students organized into companies headed by student leaders (including Grant Left Hand), and provided "outing" experiences in which children lived with American families and worked outside the school.

Some of the children, including Anna Little Raven and Mary North, wrote letters home expressing satisfaction with the training. The latter was particularly happy to learn to sew on a machine. Minnie Yellow Bear accepted her duty as a chief's daughter: "You [Yellow Bear] sent me to this Carlisle to learn so I have to [learn English]." She reported that some Arapaho girls resisted talking English when they did not have to do so. John Williams took the same position. As the son of Chief Bull Thunder, he wrote his father that he tried to learn to read and speak English and train for a trade. Dan Tucker was in the band at Carlisle and worked on two wagons for Arapaho chiefs. He was happy at the school, he said and, in a letter to Agent John Miles, referred to Arapahos as "ignorant." In contrast, Anna wrote that Jessie Spread Hands did not like being at the school.[32]

Henry North, the son of "Mrs. North" and Mr. North (who brought his children to the reservation in 1875 after his wife died), was optimistic about how his life and the circumstances of Arapahos would be improved by education. He worked on a farm in Pennsylvania in the summer, learning to handle stock and plow and harrow. He was paid for his work. At Carlisle he learned printing and was the printer of the school newspaper. He wrote, "I think if I keep working at this trade, that I will be able to establish more printing at Indian Territory. So the White people can hear more about the Indians." He (and other boys who learned trades) would be disappointed.[33]

Girls went to the country on "outings" to do domestic work. Jessie Spread Hands worked for a woman in the summer of 1888 who described her as very industrious, studying in her off hours. In 1890 Jessie postponed returning home in order to work for the family of a Doctor Haines. Girls earned $1.50 per week from these outings. Lydia Harrington went to work in the home of Commissioner of Indian Affairs Thomas Morgan in 1890.[34]

Halstead (also known as the Mennonite College) was operated near Newton, Kansas, as a family farm by Mennonites. Boys learned to farm and lived the country life, riding horses and hunting rabbits with a bow and arrow, according to Walker Road Traveler. Girls learned housework and also probably other farm work, such as care of chickens. Halstead stressed religious indoctrination, as well as farm work and use of English. Walker resisted the pressure against speaking Arapaho. Chase Harrington was unsure if the returned Halstead students had the "right" to attend the Offerings Lodge on the reservation, but many did. Arapaho students might be placed with Mennonite families in the area to work on farms.[35]

Haskell Institute was not as well regarded by parents as Carlisle and Halstead, and youths went reluctantly when the Arapahos were pressured to send students to the new school, which was established in Lawrence, Kansas, in 1884, with support from the local community. The school had a farm and dairy where boys worked. Girls worked in the kitchen, dining room, and laundry, and did general housework. At first, classroom work centered on English. The focus of the school was "discipline," or good "work habits," so more time was spent working than in the classroom. In fact, the students maintained and built much of the school. Gradually, Haskell introduced training in trades for older boys. As at Carlisle, students were organized into companies, with some pupils acting as drill officers and disciplinarians. In 1887 parents refused to send their children to Haskell. Agent Ashley wrote in 1891 that Arapaho parents considered Haskell a death trap and did not want their children there. The outing system was established in 1891, and in the late 1890s the course of study was revised to offer advanced "commercial" courses that eventually became popular with some boys and girls, especially within the Jess Rowlodge–Myrtle Lincoln cohort.[36]

Arapaho chiefs continued to use their influence to persuade parents to send their children to these schools because they viewed it as a treaty obligation. Frank Henderson, an orphan from Bull Thunder's camp, wrote to Agent Miles that Bull Thunder told him to "try hard" at Carlisle. This obligation weighed heavily on the chiefs. Black Coyote insisted that he sent his boy Harry Mann to Carlisle so that others would send their children. He was promised that Harry could return after one year, but four years had passed. Parents worried about their children's health at these schools, where many became ill. Chief Powderface and his wife felt great concern for their son Clarence, who had been at Carlisle one year and was not in good health. Powderface promised to send three other children from his band if Clarence could come home. At Carlisle, Clarence learned how to operate threshing machines when he went on an outing.[37]

The Poisal family also sent children to school. In 1882 Johnny Poisal (John's son) died at Halstead. Not until 1889 did Poisal send another child there. Children from this family went to Haskell in 1889 and later, probably for more advanced training than they could get on the reservation. Mary Keith and her husband, as well as John Poisal, sent children to Haskell. Some of the Shields children (whose parents were Josephine Keith and her American husband) went to Haskell in 1890. Jenny Fitzpatrick (Margaret's daughter), who was married to an American, sent her daughter

Maggie to St. Mary's Academy in Leavenworth in 1885, but her son Henry Meagher went to the Arapaho school and, when he was nineteen, to Haskell.[38]

Federal officials encouraged the youths who went to off-reservation boarding schools to believe that they could get jobs and make good livings when they returned to the reservation. Orphans especially sought new opportunities. Several boys, regarded as too old for Carlisle, sold their ponies and cows to raise the money to pay their expenses at the school so that they could learn trades: Theodore North, Jah Seger, Neatha Seger, and Arnold Woolworth. Jock Bull Bear and Jesse Bent, both nineteen, also made this choice. Ben Come Up Hill was twenty-two and married when he chose to go to Carlisle in 1886. When students returned to the reservation, their expectations of good jobs often went unfulfilled.[39]

The agents' expectations were also not met, and they blamed the students. In 1887 Agent G. D. Williams reported that seventy-six Cheyennes and Arapahos had returned from Carlisle and were living on the reservation. Of the fifty-five males, eight farmed, twelve served as scouts, three were agency employees, one worked at a trading company, and thirty-one had returned to "blanket life." Of the females, three were legally married and living on farms, three were in "civilized" life (employed, usually at a school), and fifteen had returned to "blanket life" (married, Indian custom). Carlisle students had been encouraged to think they could obtain good-paying jobs in the trades they learned or at the agency in some capacity, but there were not enough jobs for all of them, and the pay was lower than non-Natives received for the same kind of work. The agents thought that the returned students had unrealistic expectations—they should have realized they could not be paid as much as non-Natives. Agent J. M. Lee criticized them for having "exalted ideas." If they complained, they risked being fired.[40]

When Dan Tucker returned to the reservation, he was touted as a successful example of assimilation and described as "the best of the Carlisle Indians." By 1885 he had risen to head blacksmith with supervisory duties over Arapaho apprentices. His complaints about his salary led the agent to want to fire him, but because he "stood too well with the Indian Department," he kept his job. In 1895, his continued complaints led to his firing. Peter Arrow, Arrow's son, returned from Halstead after two years. He had aspirations of joining the police force, but the Mennonites offered him a job making brooms. Disappointed in him, the missionaries reported that he quit after four days and returned to camp, where he worked alongside his family members.[41]

These students' experiences at off-reservation boarding schools ultimately failed to destroy their commitment to Arapaho community life. When they were at school, they corresponded with family members. Their parents sent them moccasins and leggings and bows and arrows. So they were not isolated from camp influences, as the federal government had hoped. At Carlisle, they apparently held on to basic beliefs about their responsibility for renewing life: Jock Bull Bear, at Carlisle from 1881–84, wrote that he and other Arapaho boys "greeted" the thunder in the spring, praying for the grass to grow. Arapahos at home also held ceremonies at the first sign of spring.[42]

When they returned from Carlisle, many became interpreters for chiefs and for Arapaho councils and delegations. In 1894, when most were in their late twenties or thirties, thirteen signed their names alongside the names of camp Indians petitioning the Indian Office to correct fraudulent practices arising from the Jerome Commission agreement. Carlisle alumnus Paul Boynton (White Eyed Antelope's son) refused an agent's order when he was a policeman in 1895. Most returned students attended the Offerings Lodge, and some made a vow in the 1901 Offerings Lodge (including Anna Pedro's brother Dan Dyer, Bichea's son Dan Webster, and Arnold Woolworth). In the 1890s, this first generation of Carlisle, Halstead, and Haskell alumni participated, and some became part of the Ghost Dance leadership. They participated in peyote ritual as well. Paul Boynton served on the Cheyenne Sun Dance committee in 1896 (he was of Arapaho-Cheyenne ancestry). Probably all or almost all joined the Foxes and Stars.[43]

After Francis Lee (an orphan) returned from Carlisle, he told Voth that his people and their practices demanded that he engage in their social customs, and that if he did not live in camp and participate in Arapaho community life, his ponies would be shot. Carlisle boys also complained that even if they could get jobs with minimal salaries, their relatives "begged" every cent from them. They shared to avoid being called "stingy like the White people." These returned students pointed out that their fellow Arapahos ridiculed them because the federal government did not help them any more than they helped the camp Indians. Henry North wrote, "Sometimes I feel like giving up." Harry Bates, who went to Halstead when he was sixteen and stayed from 1886 to 1889, was regarded by the Mennonites as a success. But in 1890, he reportedly had "fallen back" into the Indian dances. When missionary Rudolf Petter visited him in 1893, although Bates was farming, and his wife (Trunk's daughter Blanche, who had received some education from the Mennonites on the reservation) was raising chickens, they wore "Indian clothes," and they refused to move away from the Arapaho camps and closer to the mission.[44]

Girls rejected the agents' initiatives against marriage with camp Indians. Bessie Red Pipe (who attended White Indian Industrial School in Iowa) refused to stay at the Arapaho school, where she was employed. She returned to camp, where her family began negotiations over an Indian custom marriage. She declined their first choice, then married Lester Rising Bear, who returned to camp life after he came back from Carlisle. Jessie Spread Hands, whose mother died when she was small, was the daughter of Spread Hands. She attended Carlisle from 1880 to 1886 and 1891 to 1892, then returned to work at Cantonment school as assistant matron. From there, she eloped with camp Indian and former police officer Bringing Good, defying the agency officials. Lulu Blind tried to leave Haskell by outmaneuvering federal officials. When she was at Carlisle, officials there became convinced that she was blind in one eye and epileptic; she returned home in 1890 after less than a year there. She was sent to Haskell in 1891 and subsequently returned "paralytic and incurable," but the agency doctor found her healthy. She was hired at the Arapaho school, where she subsequently disappointed school officials.[45]

The youths faced new challenges to their values when federal officials pressured or compelled them to practice American customs, and they often resisted the best way they could. Yet some new circumstances could be perceived as opportunities, either to pursue traditional goals or to avoid constraints built into the Arapaho social order. A few girls who returned to the reservation obtained jobs at the schools rather than returning to camp right away. Minnie Yellow Bear worked as a laundress at the Arapaho school for thirty dollars a month. Some girls used the schools as a way to avoid a marriage. Lulu Blind's family engineered a marriage with White Shirt, a camp Indian who was her brother-in-law, but Lulu refused to leave the school to live with him. Later, she agreed to marry Circle, a chief. Boys sometimes took advantage of the agents' power over Arapahos to improve their situation. Enos Fire, an orphan under the guardianship of Chief Scabby Bull, appealed to the agent to get the annuity money that the chief was collecting as his guardian. When Henry North's in-laws pressured him (perhaps to help them economically, because he was employed, or because they disapproved of his behavior toward his wife and children), Henry complained, and agent Woodson threatened Henry's wife's uncle with jail.[46]

The youths hired as scouts, several of whom were alumni of off-reservation boarding schools, lived at Fort Reno in their own camp. They had relatively good salaries and access to trade goods that many other Arapahos did not have. Not being subject to direct supervision from their relatives, they engaged in behavior of which older Arapahos disapproved. A few unmarried women lived first with one then the other, and the scouts were able to obtain liquor easily. Several tried to force themselves on women in the camp near the post or trespassed into school compounds to try to seduce the girls. At the time of the 1890 council with federal officials, when Arapahos discussed allotment, four or five of these young scouts actually opposed the chiefs' views.[47]

Camp and Educated Youths Compared

How do the life careers of camp youths and off-reservation educated youths compare in the 1880s and 1890s? At Cantonment,
thirty-nine boys were born between 1860 and 1879, and thirty-
seven lived to maturity. Those born before 1875 were youths in
the 1870s and 1880s and were targeted for off-reservation schools.
Those born after 1874 were youths in the 1890s, when the federal
government was promoting the reservation boarding schools.
Twenty boys stayed on the reservation, including Little Raven,
Jr., Hoof, Lime, Singing Man, Mixed Hair, Red Man, and White
Shirt—all born before 1875. Of the seventeen educated boys, four
had gone to Carlisle, six attended Halstead, four went to Haskell,
one attended Chilocco, and one went to White Institute in Iowa.
Haskell students included James R. Hutchinson and Ira Sankey,
and William Meeks went to Chilocco. The boys who attended
Halstead in Kansas were Harry Bates (a stepson of Spotted Wolf),
Edwin Glenn (Coming On Horseback's son), Chase Harrington
(a stepson of Spread Hands), Henry Lincoln (Birdshead's son),
Ben Road Traveler (Road Traveler's son), and Leslie Scabby Horse
(whose mother separated from his father, Scabby Horse). Those
who went to Carlisle were Francis Lee (an orphan), Frank Harrington (a stepson of Spread Hands), John Williams (Bull Thunder's
son), and Dan Tucker (an orphan, whose father was an unnamed
white man). Only two of the boys born between 1875 and 1879
went to school off the reservation—one went to Halstead, and
one attended Haskell.[48]

In Left Hand's band, there were 24 youths born between 1860
and 1879. Of the seventeen born between 1860 and 1874, seven
remained camp Indians, including Circle (Left Hand's oldest son),
Cut Nose, Lone Man, and Straight Crazy. Six went to Carlisle, 2
attended Haskell, 1 went to Halstead, and 1 went to Chilocco.
At Carlisle were Ben Come Up Hill (orphaned son of Trunk);
Left Hand's sons Grant, Ernest, and Robert; Arnold Woolworth,
and Neatha Seger. Neatha was an orphan whose father was an
unknown white man. Arnold, related to Row Of Lodges, also

was an orphan. Charles Campbell and Whitt Matthews both went to Haskell. Of those born between 1875 and 1879, Henry Rowlodge (Row Of Lodges's son) went to Carlisle and two boys attended Halstead.

Most youths married by Indian custom in the late 1880s and 1890s, and they married camp girls for the most part. Some married brothers' widows or married sisters as co-wives. Educated youth Francis Lee's Indian custom marriage was arranged. He married a woman who had been married to his brother. John Williams married a camp girl by Indian custom, having previously rejected family pressure to marry another girl because she had not been chaste. The exception to the pattern was Dan Tucker. In a legal ceremony, he married a white woman who was employed at a government school on the reservation. The youths from Left Hand's group also married camp girls by Indian custom, except Grant, who married a Cheyenne camp girl. Many of these youths, as well as the camp Indians, joined the Fox and Star societies. Families urged Indian custom marriage to a camp girl in part because such a marriage helped a man's ceremonial career.

The educated youths were more likely than the camp youths to have agency salaried jobs, such as butcher or farmer. The four boys from Cantonment who went to Carlisle all received good jobs. Dan Tucker was hired as a butcher when he returned, and Francis Lee, a nephew of Chief Powderface, became a scout. Scouting was a valued occupation because a young man could live a life close to that of a warrior, camping with the other scouts, and it paid well. Frank Harrington became a policeman, and John Williams worked at the Arapaho school. Some camp youths were scouts, particularly the sons of chiefs, such as Circle Left Hand. Grant Left Hand worked at the trader's store. Camp youths, and some of the educated youths (particularly Halstead graduates and those out of favor with the agent) worked as freighters with older relatives or worked on a family "farm," putting up hay or helping with the cornfield.

At Cantonment, fifty-two girls were born between 1860 and 1879. Forty-four were camp girls, and eight (all born before

1875) attended off-reservation boarding schools. Jenny Arrow (Arrow's daughter) and Nellie Bighead (Big Head's daughter) attended Halstead. Lydia Harrington (a stepdaughter of Spread Hands), Anna Raven (Chief Little Raven's daughter), Minnie Yellow Bear (Chief Yellow Bear's daughter), and Jessie Spread Hands (Spread Hands's daughter) attended Carlisle. Ethel Black Wolf (Black Wolf's daughter) went to Haskell, then Carlisle, as did Tabitha Carroll (Horseback's daughter). Tabitha's sister Belle (born in 1878) went to Carlisle also. These girls, and the ones who attended school only on the reservation, no doubt realized that they could do women's work in the camp, where their labor was valued and potentially brought them authority and influence, or they could do women's work for the Office of Indian Affairs (OIA), as school employees, and be treated as subordinates.

All who lived to maturity married by Indian custom. Lydia was a co-wife to Deaf, Little Raven's son. Anna returned from Carlisle, worked briefly at the school at Cantonment, then married a mature, prominent man with warrior status. They were divorced, and she married camp youth White Shirt. Jessie worked at the Arapaho school, then married the warrior Bringing Good when she was twenty-nine. Minnie married James R. Hutchinson, who had attended Haskell and who was in the men's lodge organization. He was the orphaned son of Chief Cut Finger. Nellie Bighead was married to Deaf as a co-wife. At the age of twenty-nine, Ethel became James R. Hutchinson's second wife after Minnie died. Belle and Tabitha died unmarried. The school girls tended to delay marriage. Among Left Hand's Arapahos, one girl out of seventeen born between 1860 and 1874 went to Halstead. Subsequently, the federal agent forced her to legally marry a white man with whom she was living.

The educated youths, who spent several years in off-reservation schools, faced intense pressure to alienate themselves from the Arapaho way of life. But although the members of the Jessie Spread Hands and Little Raven, Jr., cohort could take alternative paths during their teenage years, by the turn of the century, the paths taken by the camp Indians and by many educated Arapahos had converged. The latter re-identified themselves as camp Indians because of the experiences they had after returning from the off-reservation schools. They had discovered what the camp Indians had learned in or about the reservation schools—that the civilization ideology promoted by Americans did not reflect reality. They could not get the jobs they had been promised or pay equal to that received by Americans. In addition, the girls realized that their "domestic" labor did not earn them respect from Americans, and that American men might sexually exploit them. These youths came to challenge American ideas about age and gender by making a place for themselves within Arapaho households, camps, and the ceremonial organization.

Youths' circumstances changed after the Arapahos settled on the reservation. Boys could not use war experience as a way to progress through the ceremonial hierarchy. The end of buffalo hunting also potentially limited youths' opportunities to contribute to their households. In fact, the age category "youth" came to characterize not only the teenage years but also the twenties and even the thirties. But, the members of the Jessie Spread Hands and Little Raven, Jr., cohort took on new roles that redefined the kinds of responsibilities youths had. Drawing on their experience in reservation schools, the boys became expert in farming with machinery, and the girls learned to make clothing on sewing machines. These skills helped Arapahos transition from a dependence on hunting to an agricultural economy. And most boys entered the ceremonial organization as Foxes and Stars. The older cohorts redesigned the lodge system to accommodate them. The focus became service to the community, not warfare. By making Indian custom marriages, the girls assumed responsibility to a wide network of kin and began to partner husbands ceremonially, as well as economically and politically. Some took husbands from the Little Raven, Jr., cohort, and others married older men.

OF CONTEMPLATIVE DISPOSITION:
MEN EMBRACE NEW WORK AND NEW RELIGIONS

Little Left Hand had been on a few war parties as a teenager, before he came to the reservation at the age of nineteen. But he was eager to establish a reputation for bravery and took every opportunity to go out against the Arapahos' enemies, even after the chiefs promised the federal government that they would curtail these war parties. In the early 1870s, he and his friend Little Chief heard that a war party was going out against the Pawnees. They each took their best horse and an additional pack animal on a lead and traveled north from Arapaho camps near the agency to join the party. The Spear Men were in pursuit, and if they caught the party, they would destroy their property and attack them physically. But Little Left Hand was willing to take the risk. Without war exploits, he did not believe he could be influential in men's councils, and a war record would make a favorable impression on the families of prospective brides, as well as on the girls themselves.

The Spear Men did not catch the war party, but by the time Little Left Hand was a few miles north of the South Canadian, he encountered the warriors returning from a successful attack. They had a Pawnee scalp on a pole. They invited Little Left Hand to join them in their triumphant return, probably because the Pawnees could be nearby and an extra man with a gun would improve their chances. They rode into camp and were celebrated with a victory dance. Two girls singled out Little Left Hand for attention, but he tried to keep a low profile out of fear of the Spear Men. From his perspective, the adventure was not a total success because he had not had contact with the enemy.[49]

Medicine Grass did not achieve such distinction on his first war party, led by Row Of Lodges and Powderface. He went along to help, but it was Scabby Bull who scouted ahead and killed a herder. Young men in the Medicine Grass cohort, like Little Left Hand (born in the 1850s), were at a disadvantage in relation to the men who came to the reservation in their maturity. These mature men from the Little Raven and Left Hand cohorts had war records, the largest horse herds, and the major responsibility for helping Arapahos adjust to reservation life. Prestige and influence aside, all men had responsibilities to the people in their camp and band.[50]

Provisioning Households: New Kinds of Work

To support their households, men hunted, raised cattle, freighted, grew corn and hay, and worked for store credit when they could. Men were expected to hunt. They went after buffalo as long as herds frequented the reservation or its adjacent grassland. The buffalo began to be scarce in the late 1870s. Then, only the men with good horses, who were well trained and strong enough for an arduous hunt, went. Medicine Grass describes how he and his friend Theok Raven (Little Raven's son) went hunting near the Cimarron River. Medicine Grass had a "chasing pony," and they found a herd of elk and killed several. Men hunted with their bands, and in the 1870s Little Raven's cohort, including Tall Bear and Bird Chief, generally led the hunting bands. The younger, main war chiefs Left Hand and Powderface, as well as Big Mouth, also led bands.[51]

Beginning in the late 1870s, the Arapahos could not find enough buffalo to justify a tribal hunt. Then deer, quail, turkey, and prairie chicken replaced the buffalo as the object of smaller groups' hunting expeditions. The bands continued to camp together while several men went out after game. According to Jess Rowlodge, there was still plenty of game in the 1880s—the treetops along the rivers were "black with turkeys," he said. And they fished in the rivers and streams. After 1892, when thousands of settlers moved into the area and outnumbered the Cheyennes and Arapahos ten to one, the game gradually disappeared.[52]

The federal government met its treaty obligation by issuing beef every two weeks to compensate for the decline of game. Agency personnel released steers from corrals, and as the leader of the "beef band" directed, men from the bands would chase down and kill the steers allotted to their band. Jess Rowlodge explained that families would take turns receiving the choice parts of the animal, and the beef band leader would take the hide. This beef was a major source, if not the main source, of meat during the 1880s and 1890s. Even in the 1870s, when Arapahos were on their fall hunt, they sent young men to the agency to bring back cattle to feed the camp. Yellow Bear, Bird Chief, and Tall Bear led beef bands in 1880. Little Raven was listed as a member of his oldest son Heap Of Bears's band then. Most of the members of Little Raven's cohort had reached old age and were exercising leadership in religious matters, so the Left Hand cohort provided most of the beef band leaders in 1880: Left Hand, Powderface, Big Mouth, White Eyed Antelope, Bull Thunder, and Row Of Lodges. Two policemen—Black Wolf and Black Coyote—and an army scout, Scabby Bull, led bands, although they were in the Medicine Grass cohort. They attracted followers partly because of the resources their positions brought them. By 1887, more men in the Medicine Grass cohort led bands, as those in Left Hand's cohort aged or died. For example, Little Raven's son Deaf took over their band after his older brother died.[53]

Agent Miles began to issue cattle to Cheyenne and Arapaho men in 1877. Then it became men's responsibility to protect their cattle, as well as to hunt. Arapaho chiefs began purchasing cattle and building herds to supplement the beef issue when necessary. Powderface had begun his herd before 1877, purchasing cattle for one hundred dollars, using the money he got from his buffalo robes in 1876. Miles reported that Arapahos had 186 cattle in addition to 2,185 horses and 73 mules in 1878. Of course, a few prominent men still owned most of the cattle. In 1880 Agent Miles reported that Left Hand, Powderface, and Yellow Bear had sizable herds with superior bulls. Powderface had 107 head of cattle that year. In 1881 Arapahos still held the great majority of cattle issued to them and had increased the size of their herds. In 1881 the families of Little Raven, Yellow Bear, and Bird Chief, and those of the younger Left Hand, Powderface, Big Mouth, and White Eyed Antelope had the largest herds. These herds were larger than the Cheyennes'. Several men would combine their cattle into one herd that they all took care of, but individuals marked their cattle. The cattle owned by women and children were put with the men's cattle. Poor relatives helped with the work. The *Cheyenne Transporter* reported that Indians marked their cattle with their "own peculiar devices" (not necessarily a branding iron), and that they knew each other's brands.[54]

The agent leased most of the reservation grazing land to American ranchers in 1883. Jess Rowlodge explained that Arapahos would corral their cattle at night to try to prevent them from mixing in with the ranchers' stock, but when the leases were canceled in 1886, most of the Indian stock was removed (and stolen) by the American ranchers.[55]

Arapahos needed cash or goods at the traders' stores. They bought clothes (largely men's garments), household tools (including women's tools), and some food, as well as luxury goods (most for their wives). Men earned money in several ways. The traders bought buffalo robes and the skins of small animals, which Arapahos used for food as well as fur: bear, beaver, wild cat, raccoon, wolf, badger, skunk, and deer. Traders also bought corn grown by Arapahos. But, for the most part, Arapahos relied on freighting to acquire goods. Agent Miles launched the Arapahos and Cheyennes into the freighting business. He bought wagons and gave them to leading men, who gradually paid for them out of the profits of their transport business. In 1877 wagons went to Little Raven (whose son Deaf drove), Bird Chief (whose driver was Black Coyote), Yellow Bear (who used Scabby Bull as a driver), Tall Bear, and Spotted Wolf. Also, Left Hand, Big Mouth, Powderface, and Row Of Lodges received wagons (Black Wolf drove for Row Of Lodges). Freighting was of major importance, but only about half the men could acquire a wagon and team. Horse ownership was key in freighting as it was in hunting. In 1878, a property survey showed that the large herds belonged to Little Raven, Yellow Bear, Big Mouth, Left Hand, Powderface, and Row Of Lodges. Little Raven had eighty horses (and ninety-six in 1881). Left Hand and Big Mouth also had mules, more useful for freighting than horses.[56]

The *Cheyenne Transformer* reported that Indian freighters were more resourceful than white freighters, successful even in the worst weather. Sweezy told Bass that they were used to camp life and bad weather and had large numbers of horses. They could cover about thirty miles a day. The trip from the agency to Wichita was 165 miles, to Caldwell, 110. Each man bought his own canvas-covered wagon and used his own four-horse team. Drivers rode on other horses at the sides of the team to guide it. They decorated their horses but did not use bridles and lines. The pay was one hundred dollars per one hundred pounds, and Arapahos divided the money among the heads of families that took part. In 1887 agent G. D. Williams reported that the Indians did most of the freighting for the agency.[57]

The agents hired a few laborers to make brick, cut hay, chop and haul wood, work on fences, and carry mail. On their own volition, Arapahos cut and hauled fence posts to Kansas, where they sold them. A few men were employed in the prestigious jobs of policeman and scout. Police received guns, badges, five dollars a month, and a double ration in 1881. The police retrieved stolen stock, settled conflicts, and removed trespassers and their stock. The agents also hired interpreters. In 1876, out of 360 Arapaho men, 50 were employed as laborers. The rest freighted and sold labor and produce to missionaries, traders, and settlers in Kansas. Military commanders hired Arapahos to track down deserters. At Camp Cantonment, "the Indians invariably [brought] the culprits back." In 1887 Agent Williams hired twenty-two men (mostly Arapahos) as clerks, carpenters, blacksmiths, teamsters, and herders, as well as other part-time employees.[58]

Arapahos had gardens worked primarily by women, and many had little patches of corn. Prominent families had the largest farms, where they used machinery in the fields. In 1883 inspector Robert Gardner identified the men with the largest cultivated plots (twenty-five acres): Little Raven, Powderface, Bird Chief, and Left Hand. In 1885, Left Hand had forty acres in cultivation, the largest Arapaho farm. Little Raven cultivated fifty acres in 1886. He grew enough corn to sell half of it to ranchers. He gave the rest away to his followers. Men also learned to cut hay and store it for their stock in the winter. The agency distributed seed and lent equipment (plows, mowing machines) to Arapahos, and sometimes an employee would give instruction, but schoolboys took a major role in this farm work. In addition to owning horses and cattle, some Arapahos took an interest in chickens, and a few had hogs. Jess Rowlodge described how Row Of Lodges cut hay in his large field. He invited people to a feast, and they all worked cooperatively to cut and stack the hay. He raised horses on the open range and sold some to American buyers. Row Of Lodges had corn and a vegetable garden with potatoes, pumpkins, and onions, as well as fruit trees. He learned to farm primarily from his relatives the Poisals. He was an orphan, whose father was Gros Ventre–Blackfeet. He was raised by his aunts, one of whom was Snake Woman, who had married John Poisal. She and her children Robert, John, and Mary Keith settled southeast of the agency in the same area as Row Of Lodges.[59]

The Poisal family came to the reservation in 1870 because they could not succeed at ranching in Colorado, according to Jess Rowlodge. At the agency they began to prosper. John was hired as a laborer in 1873, and he, Robert, and Ben Keith formed a band along with some of their Arapaho relatives. Jack Fitzpatrick was in this band. By 1875 Robert had started to build a herd of cattle, and Yellow Bear wanted John as an interpreter. They were making a place for themselves in Arapaho society. Arapahos routinely came to the Poisals and asked for steers—Agent Miles thought the Arapahos took advantage of them. By 1876 Robert and John had a seventy-five-acre farm southeast of the agency and had so many cattle that the agent borrowed from them when he was short of cattle for the issue, and Pawnees raided their herd. In 1877 Robert and John had a freight wagon. In 1878 the Poisal brothers had a cattle herd of 260, and by 1881 Robert's herd had increased to 564 and John's to 680. Jack owned 50. They were prosperous and respected by other ranchers and Americans in the agency vicinity, and they raised cattle commercially. The Poisal brothers and Jack Fitzpatrick married Arapaho women.

In 1882, a Creek bandit murdered Robert while he was taking Jenny Fitzpatrick Meagher's daughter Maggie to the Sacred Heart Mission School in the Creek Nation in eastern Oklahoma. The Arapahos tried to kill the man, but he escaped. Later, a group of cowboys caught and lynched him. John continued to operate his ranch, and in 1887 the agent decided to stop issuing rations to his family. Poisal protested, standing on his treaty rights as an Arapaho. In 1892, John was allotted west of Geary. He was head of a beef band in the mid-1890s, and in the 1890s, he, like the other Arapahos, suffered a great economic reversal following the allotment of the reservation.[60]

The 1890s brought increased poverty for all Arapahos, largely because in 1892, the federal government gave each tribal member an allotment of land and sold the "surplus" reservation land to settlers. Row Of Lodges could not raise horses for sale because settlers had fenced the range, but he still sold hay, garden vegetables, and chickens to Americans. Most of the cattle owned by Arapahos were stolen during the cattle-leasing years between 1883 and 1886. Outlaws raided their horse herds. On one occasion in 1892, Bringing Good went in pursuit and suffered a wound in the process. The federal government disbanded the scouts in 1894. In the 1890s, only a few members of the Owl–Left Hand cohort still had enough resources to support camps on allotment clusters: Left Hand, White Eyed Antelope, and Row Of Lodges in the area where Left Hand's band had settled. The members of the Medicine Grass–Bichea cohort did most of the freighting. Some of these men headed beef bands, and some had police positions.[61]

But by 1897 much of the freighting was done by the Indian police, and the development of the railroad made long-distance freighting unnecessary. Rations were reduced during these years. In 1902 the government farmer in Calumet (a settlement southeast of Left Hand's band), where Black Coyote and Bird Chief's sons camped, reported that most Indians lived on the annual payment (the fifteen-dollar annual interest on the money for the land ceded when the reservation was opened to settlement) and money from leasing some of their allotments to settlers. Ninety percent were "partially" self-supporting, that is, they did a little farming and worked for wages when they could. Only ten percent were "self-supporting," that is, not dependent on rations.[62]

Influencing Council Decisions: The Senior Lodge Men

Arapahos had to transition from hunting to agriculture, and they had to find a way to defend their valued institutions despite their dependence on the federal government. Arapaho leaders adopted a civilization strategy to cope with reservation life. What characteristics, aside from the ability to provide for others, did these leaders have?

Men who aspired to earn a reputation for leadership qualities, who wanted to have influence within a band or in relations with federal officials, had to use their prosperity to help others and host political meetings. As Sweezy told Bass, band leaders advised people and cared for the needy. Federal officials and other Arapahos recognized a leader's potential in these terms. On the reservation, prosperity depended on management skills—on raising cattle, freighting, selling hay, and so on. Allotments had to be managed as well. Heads of bands personally selected allotments for family members and followers so that they could have access to a large block of land with native grass for pasture and soil suitable for farming. The women insisted on allotments near wood and water. Row Of Lodges chose adjoining allotments for himself, his wife and children, and other relatives, including an orphan, an aunt and her family, his sister, and other widowed aunts. Band leaders also received resources from agency personnel in the 1870s and 1880s and redistributed them—food and hides and annuity goods (cloth, kettles, and needles, for example, which were dispensed once a year).[63]

A few band leaders were council or intermediary chiefs (men who dealt directly with local and national federal officials in formal councils). Cleaver Warden noted that Arapahos had a ceremony for the installation of these chiefs. A chief (after consultation with other chiefs) would select a successor when he desired to "retire."

Both the incumbent and the new chief would give away property to those in attendance, to the "poorest," according to Warden. The new chief received a pipe from the retiring chief, a symbol of peacemaking and consensus building. They held a smoking ritual, which had been part of the treaty councils in the previous century, and this ceremony sanctified the selection of the new chief.[64]

As Rowlodge pointed out, a chief's military record was not as important as his care of the elderly, the sick, and needy children. He was expected to use his income and surplus resources for "common purposes." Row Of Lodges took responsibility for his niece and her husband, another niece and her children, and his wife's widowed sister. Left Hand also took care of several families. Drawing on his cattle herd and a large garden, he killed a steer and provided food each week for the people who camped around him, according to Rowlodge. He had a large house with a living room, kitchen, visitors' room, and sleeping rooms so that he could fulfill the hosting duties once conducted in a large tepee while convincing the agent of his commitment to "civilization." Ranchers whose herds trespassed on reservation land paid a toll in cattle to intermediary chiefs; this continued to some extent during and after the years ranchers leased the range. The chiefs' cattle herds (smaller after 1886) made it possible for them to be generous to the needy.[65]

Prosperous, generous leaders counted on their kin and in-laws for help in providing for others. In return for this help, men had to meet expectations of respect and sacrifice. Men should respect others by sharing food and property, displaying humility and tolerance, and making property and body sacrifices for others. Husbands followed pregnancy taboos and made property and body sacrifices for their children and other relatives. Despite threats from federal agents, Black Coyote followed instructions in a dream to sacrifice pieces of his skin (removing and burying them) for the health of his children. He had seventy scars arranged in symbolic patterns on his chest and arms. Indian custom marriage obligated men to consult relatives and to maintain good relations with their in-laws. During the 1902 Offerings Lodge, Two Babies and his wife Shaved Head made an offering in the Rabbit Lodge for their child's recovery, and Little Raven, Jr., and his wife Jenny gave away a horse as a property sacrifice for their child.

Husbands sought good relations with their in-laws. Medicine Grass had first married a girl from the Old Sun family, but they separated. Another wife died. Then, in his forties, he married two of Big Mouth's daughters, which was a union of two prominent families and showed mutual respect. Arnold Woolworth (from the Little Raven, Jr., cohort) chose his wife based on his observation that she (a camp girl) was a good worker and knew how to do beadwork, but he committed himself to an Indian custom wedding that obligated him to his in-laws. Black Coyote and his wife Singing Woman, worried about their relations with their daughter-in-law's family, made a property sacrifice in the 1902 Rabbit Lodge as part of their prayer for good relations. Husbands were supposed to treat their wives with respect and not show jealousy. Scabby Bull, showing the temperament expected of a chief, ignored his wife Good Looking's elopement with another man, even though he was the wronged party.[66]

Property and family support helped individuals become leaders, but lodge membership was a necessary qualification. Arapahos made important decisions in large councils, where influential men and women made their opinions known, sometimes by speaking and sometimes by having others speak for them. Generally, the spokespeople were senior men and probably some of their wives from the senior ceremonial lodges, the Lime Crazy and Dog.

During the 1880s and 1890s, lodge ceremonies took place several times, so men in the Left Hand and Medicine Grass cohorts could have progressed through the series as far as the Dog Lodge. Arapahos held a Spear Lodge in about 1888 and inducted largely men from the Medicine Grass cohort, but Two Lances (born in 1861) joined as well. It is clear that not all members of a lodge moved up to the next with their lodge mates, and that some men advanced earlier than their fellow lodge members. Men may have delayed because of the expense, or because they were away from the reservation when their lodge mates advanced, or because they lost interest once they could not pursue a warrior career. Possibly some skipped a step in the series because they stood out in some way or were substituting for an older family member. In any case, a Lime Crazy Lodge took place in 1892, and many members of the Medicine Grass cohort joined, including Hail from Left Hand's district and Deaf from Cantonment. Other members of this cohort (for example, Lizard, who was born in 1851) already were Lime Crazy Men. Arapahos held the last Dog Lodge, vowed by Cedar-tree (1853–95), about 1894. Some members of the Medicine Grass cohort probably joined as well as some from Left Hand's cohort.

Before Arapahos settled on the reservation, being a lodge man was essential to a successful career as a warrior, but during reservation times, men joined for religious reasons (to help themselves or a family member), because of family pressure, or because they had ambitions politically or in the ceremonial hierarchy (or all these reasons). The ceremonial lodges reinforced Arapaho ideas about gender and age. Warden concluded that the ceremonies offset "adversity," not only for the men who vowed to sponsor them as a prayer offering, but for all Arapahos. Clown performances helped hold the attention of the crowd, as did the public dancing and the races between the lodge men.

Warden concluded that each lodge conveyed spiritual knowledge and understanding as well as "temporal" (material) blessings. The Tomahawk Lodge was the "beginning of knowledge." In fact, Arapahos regarded the Tomahawk and Spear lodges as "small societies," without the more significant ritual authority gained in the Lime Crazy and Dog lodges (the use of sacred roots, for example). But men in the Tomahawk and Spear lodges began to learn to use pipes in ceremonies, one of the important male ceremonial obligations. Once a man participated in the Tomahawk ceremony, he was qualified to be a ceremonial grandfather to would-be Tomahawk Men and an elder brother to the boys in the Fox society. Warden noted that the Spear Lodge helped men keep their family on "the right path." The Spear Men had primary responsibility for maintaining social order through policing. The senior Lime Crazy and Dog men and their wives mentored the "small societies" and had authority to treat illness in some instances. The Lime Crazy Lodge used supernatural authority to try to enforce social control, and the Dog Men became important primarily for the conduct of the Offerings Lodge.[67]

The Lime Crazy and Dog men were the elder brothers, or headmen, of the Spear and Tomahawk men, because ideally the headmen for a lodge were chosen from two societies above that of the lodge. For example, when a man vowed the Tomahawk Lodge, he and his lodge mates tried to recruit men from the Lime Crazy Lodge as headmen. These senior lodges, acting as headmen and grandfathers, had political influence over the junior lodge men. The mutual obligations between lodge men and their elder brothers (headmen) and the grandson-grandfather relationship "preserved peace," in Warden's terms. The wives of these men, with their contributions of food, helped maintain the relationship between the men.[68]

The headmen of the Spear and Tomahawk lodges had a role in supervising war parties that went out against Osages, Pawnees, Poncas, Utes, and other enemy tribes in the 1870s. These leaders, Yellow Bear in particular, were referred to as "war chiefs." The agents noted the departure of several war parties between 1871 and 1874, but the lodge organization (probably the Spear Men) stopped several war parties, including one that was on the way to join the Cheyenne and Comanche warriors at the Battle of Adobe Walls. Men with reputations as warriors continued to use their exploits to influence others. Jess Rowlodge told how White Owl and his elder brother Row Of Lodges competed against each other in recounting war deeds and other successes.[69]

In addition to policing the camp and the buffalo hunt, the Spear Men carried out the decisions of the chiefs' council. As Little Left Hand said, they could and did destroy property, shoot horses, and assault men who violated council orders. In Little Left Hand's case, they caught him hunting contrary to their orders, and they destroyed his saddle so he could not transport meat; they stopped short of assaulting him because he was submissive. They could destroy the family lodge, which was the wife's property, an additional sanction on men's behavior since wives would want to prevent this kind of retaliation. The senior lodge men, intent on reassuring federal officials that Arapahos were dependable allies during a time when military skirmishes occurred between Indians and whites, sent the Spear and probably the Tomahawk men to protect agency employees during 1874–75 when some of the Cheyenne men were in revolt. The Spear Men likely were the "soldiers" sent by the chiefs to enforce school attendance in 1884. As late as 1896, the agent reported that Arapaho chiefs could make and enforce policy.[70]

The agents on the reservation hired some of the warriors as police in 1878. Carl Sweezy's father was a policeman. His painted war shield stood by the family tepee, and his personal medicine bundle was on the west side of the lodge near his bed and backrest. In the early 1880s, Bears Lariat, Black Coyote, and Killing With a Stick served as police and also belonged to the lodge organization. They apparently took orders from the Arapaho council, not the agent. They would not "fight their own," complained Agent D. B. Dyer. Arapaho police had the responsibility to prevent gatherings of which agents disapproved, but led by Black Coyote, they managed to reassure the agents during the Ghost Dance years. In 1895, however, Little Left Hand, a lodge man, refused an order from the agent and subsequently lost his position as policeman. By the 1890s, these police had the responsibility to maintain order in the camps.[71]

The headmen could mobilize the junior lodges to work on behalf of Arapaho households, and they molded the opinions of their juniors while serving as spokesmen for them in councils. The headmen gave advice, and they discussed with the lodge men the issues Arapahos dealt with on the reservation. Arapahos viewed this relationship as a reciprocal one. The lodge men could ask their headmen for help, usually of a material nature, and the headmen could recruit their lodge men to help with work. Warden noted that headmen should be generous and have plenty of property and a "good wife." Clearly, the wife's support was essential to fulfilling the men's responsibilities.

Lime Crazy and Dog men, grandfathers of the junior lodge men, had already gone through the junior lodges. These men painted the lodge men during the Spear and Tomahawk ceremonies and smoked with them as part of a mentoring process. Warden noted that grandfathers prayed for their grandsons, for example, asking for protection from "bad people" (presumably settlers and officials). Food and property was exchanged between the grandfathers' wives and the lodge men's wives. Arapahos had a strict rule that the two men (grandson and grandfather) could not be in conflict or competition. If a lodge man got in trouble or was socially disruptive, his grandfather could restore him to his senses or settle his trouble (for example, adultery) by using his ceremonial pipe to symbolically intimidate a disruptive or stubborn person. Grandfathers of the junior lodge men could generate consensus through their influence over the junior men.[72]

While the senior lodge men had great influence in council, those with credentials in the Rabbit Lodge as well as the medicine men, or "doctors," also had influence, and most of the senior lodge men also qualified to participate in the Rabbit Lodge. Arapahos had great respect for the Lodge Maker and for others making sacrifices that earned them degrees in the lodge. The Lodge Maker and his wife took an important step toward a ceremonial career in the Rabbit Lodge when they vowed to sponsor the Offerings Lodge. They not only fasted during the three-day Rabbit Lodge (when preparations for the ceremony took place) and during the subsequent four-day painting and dancing, but the couple also sacrificed to the Four Old Men, spirit beings symbolically represented by the Lodge Maker's grandfather. The wife offered herself (by exposure) to the grandfather. The Lodge Maker and his wife also made property sacrifices, which amounted to five hundred dollars at the turn of the century. The grandfather's authority over the grandson and his respect relationship with him continued for life.[73]

In 1899 Alfred Kroeber learned that middle-aged and older men still used personal medicine power. Noted doctors in the Left Hand cohort included Blindy and Lumpmouth. Several members of the Medicine Grass cohort had organized themselves into "clans" of doctors. Men apprenticed themselves to doctors who had fasted for power to cure and had obtained powerful spirit helpers. Power was mostly used for doctoring, although some had received power to affect the health and speed of horses or to assist hunters. Men agreed to sell Kroeber medicine objects that symbolized war power but refused to give up medicine for curing. They fasted on Coyote Hill (near Black Coyote's camp) and in the Red Hills in Geary, as well as on Buffalo Mountain in Cantonment. The supplicants left stone offerings where they tried to attract spirit helpers. Apprentices paid doctors for their lessons.

One man who was successful in receiving a vision in the 1890s told Kroeber that he received power to call rain and to see into the future from his spirit helper Turtle. He also received advice: "Do not speak evil of people. You will have no difficulties hereafter. Everything will be pleasant." So at least this spirit helper was working to help the supplicant adjust to reservation life. Warden described Blackman's vision quest, probably in the 1880s. Blackman was born in 1856 (a member of Medicine Grass's cohort), and as a young man was skeptical of "medicine men." Then he saw his dying uncle cured by one. Blackman's father gave the doctor a horse, six other gifts, and food that the doctor offered to his spirit helpers. The doctor used his medicine root for spittle and to brew tea for the patient. He removed the illness by "sucking it out." Afterward, the food was distributed to people in the doctor's camp. Blackman decided to try to acquire doctoring power, so he fasted for four days and received help from the spirit of a crystal stone of the sort used in the sweat lodge and Rabbit Lodge. He then went to an old man for help in interpreting the vision and continuing the process of becoming a good doctor. According to Jess Rowlodge, Blackman trained Little Left Hand and Young Bull (both from the Medicine Grass cohort) to call on the Beaver Spirit.

A man who wanted to become a doctor would go to the leader of the "clan" to which he wanted to belong and sit with them when they fasted and when they cured, learning the rituals, restrictions, and songs. In Cantonment, Deaf fasted for power and later trained other members of the Medicine Grass cohort to cure. Jess Rowlodge recalled that Deaf doctored all kinds of sickness—pneumonia, fever, and stomach problems. Each spring, the head of the doctors (for example, Deaf in Cantonment) called them all together, and they took the bundles into a sweat lodge, prayed, and renewed their powers. Each participant would receive some of the revitalized herbs. In this way, they maintained their relationship with their spirit helpers by showing respect for the powers they were given. These clans were Beaver, Lizard (specializing in curing poisonous bites from reptiles), Horse, and Thunderbird. Myrtle Lincoln also named Big Head as a doctor in Cantonment who specialized in pregnancy and early childhood ailments. He received the traditional seven gifts as a fee, as did the other doctors.[74]

Identification of the men with influence—the prosperous, senior lodge men—shows the central importance of cohort membership in leadership roles. The wealthiest members of the Little Raven cohort (for example, Little Raven, Yellow Bear, and Tall Bear) and of the Left Hand cohort (for example, Left Hand, Row Of Lodges, and Bull Thunder) arrived on the reservation with enough horses to support buffalo hunts and freight trains in the 1870s. They attracted dependents and followers to herd stock, help them farm, and drive wagons in the 1880s. Their wives controlled the household food and its distribution, managed the work of the household, and owned stock—all of which strengthened their husbands' (and other male relatives') positions. Little Raven and Tall Bear had become Dog Men at least by 1870, and after that they became priests of the Seven Old Men group. Left Hand, Row Of Lodges, and Bull Thunder were Dog Men at least by the 1880s, and Bull Thunder became a priest. Their prominence allowed them to institute the civilization strategy. As the members of the older cohort died, Left Hand's cohort assumed more responsibility. Some members of the Medicine Grass cohort had become Lime Crazy Men by the 1890s and continued to implement the civilization policy—for example, at Cantonment, Henry Sage (Spread Hands's son), employed as a policeman; Deaf (Little Raven's son), paid a doctor; and Sitting Bull (Scabby Bull's brother), made wealthy from his Ghost Dance followers.

A few of these men became intermediary chiefs. In the 1870s, Little Raven, Spotted Wolf, and Bird Chief (all signatory to the treaty of 1867 and members of the Little Raven cohort) and Powderface and Left Hand, prominent war chiefs of the Left Hand cohort, served as chiefs. In the 1880s, Little Raven and Tall Bear had outlived the other men of their cohort and were still called upon to talk to federal officials. For example, when a nervous new agent tried to summon troops to intimidate the Cheyennes in 1885, Little Raven reassured the troops that there was no danger. Also, Left Hand, White Eyed Antelope and Row Of Lodges had chief positions in the 1880s. Although it was unusual, so did Scabby Bull and Black Wolf (born in the late 1840s and members of the Medicine Grass cohort).[75]

A look at the circumstances of a few chiefs shows the interplay between having a prosperous family, senior lodge status, and chieftainship. Little Raven's large family was the most prosperous in the Cantonment area, and he was a senior lodge man. His brother Trunk was also well off, and their sister had a ceremonial office. Little Raven's eldest son with his wife Blood Woman was Heap Of Bears, a band leader. Little Raven and Yellow Hair (1816–1900) had one son, Deaf, and a daughter, Singing Woman. Deaf married Singing In Water, one of Yellow Bear's sister's daughters, and, when she died, her sister. Singing Woman married Ice, a band headman and prominent warrior; then, widowed, she married her brother's brother-in-law from the Yellow Bear band. Little Raven also married three of Yellow Bear's sisters. With Short Woman, he had a daughter, Sitting Down, who married Row Of Lodges. With Beaver, Little Raven had a daughter, Curley, who also married Row Of Lodges. The third sister, Good Woman, was the mother of Anna (who went to Carlisle), Theok Raven, and Little Raven, Jr. Theok married a daughter of Bull Going Down (from the Yellow Bear band), whose sisters were married to Little Raven's brother Trunk.[76]

Trunk had four wives, three of them sisters. His son Knocking Face married a daughter of Yellow Bear, and his son Coal Of Fire married into the Scabby Bull band, which, after Little Raven's, became the most prominent band at Cantonment. Walking Straight, one of Trunk's daughters, married headman Black Wolf, and another daughter, Owl, married Row Of Lodges. Two others, Good Looking and Traveler, married Scabby Bull. Scabby Bull's brothers were Spread Hands, Sitting Bull, and Arrow, and his two sisters married Road Traveler. So Little Raven had marital alliances with Yellow Bear, Row Of Lodges, Scabby Bull, and Black Wolf. Of the fifteen lodge men in Cantonment, thirteen were members of the Little Raven–Trunk and Scabby Bull families.[77]

Left Hand was also from a prominent family. He was a lodge man, who had been awarded a degree in the Tomahawk Lodge when he was young, and who became a senior lodge man shortly after settling on the reservation. His sister Hairy (Mrs. Old Sun) and her husband Old Sun (one of the Seven Old Men) were important ceremonial authorities. Brother and sister would have helped each other, and Old Sun's children, by Mrs. Old Sun and other wives who died before the 1890s, also had a mutually supportive relationship with Left Hand. Of these, White Eyed Antelope and Hail (the son of Mrs. Old Sun's sister, Lone Woman) were senior lodge men and authorities in the Offerings Lodge. Old Sun's daughter Bushyhead married Hawkan, who had high rank in the Rabbit Lodge. Left Hand's son Circle was in the lodge organization.[78]

Scabby Bull, a member of the Medicine Grass cohort, was in Yellow Bear's band in 1874. He demonstrated such bravery when he assisted the army in a fight with Northern Cheyennes who had left the agency in 1879 that he became increasingly prominent on the reservation. By 1882 he spoke in council with the older men and was a spokesman at the council with the Jerome Commission in 1890 (when reservation land was ceded). A lodge man, he had married into the Little Raven family. By 1894 he was named as one of the three Arapaho chiefs at Cantonment.[79]

Black Coyote (also a member of the Medicine Grass cohort) rose to membership in the Lime Crazy Lodge with his wife Singing Woman and became chief in the Calumet district in the 1890s. His rise was remarkable because he achieved prominence without the aid of a prosperous family. His father was a Kiowa who separated from Black Coyote's mother, a Northern Arapaho. His siblings resided with either the Northern Arapahos or Kiowas. The family of two of his wives does not seem to have been particularly prominent. In 1881 he was a man of modest means, personally owning four horses, six cows, and a wagon. His household property included only seven horses, seven cows, and two dogs. He became a policeman and rose to a leadership position, perhaps because, though young, he had a war record. He had been on a war party as a youth, working as a helper doing chores for the older men. When they encountered Pawnees, he struck one before the enemy could shoot and stole his horse. This exploit gave him status beyond his years because he subsequently pierced children's ears at tribal gatherings. James Mooney described him as "a man of contemplative disposition, much given to speculate on the unseen world .... With a natural predisposition to religious things, it is the dream of his life to be a great priest and medicine man." He was respected for his religiosity as well as his war experience.[80]

The Civilization Strategy

The senior lodge men and the chiefs of the Little Raven and Left Hand cohorts, with the help of their wives, focused on developing and implementing the civilization strategy that was an offshoot of their conciliatory strategy of prereservation years. The economic resources and lodge status of all the men in these cohorts worked to generate cooperation and support for the civilization strategy from the Medicine Grass cohort. The strategy had its roots in the treaty of 1867, at which time the Arapahos believed that they promised to turn to crops for subsistence rather than game and to support schools in return for adequate rations and supplies and protection of their land base. After they had the support of prominent Arapahos, the chiefs went as delegates to complain to federal officials that the federal government had not protected them from trespass and property theft by Americans. To gain a favorable reception, chiefs tried to impress the agents with their leadership in farming and stock raising, and they took responsibility for supporting schools, enrolling one or more of their children to encourage other parents.

Arapahos did not view their commitment to agriculture and schools as part of a willingness to abandon their understandings about the world and their values. They continued working cooperatively and sharing food, as well as sponsoring ceremonies that reinforced respect relations between Arapahos and supernatural forces. This resistance to the Indian Office's assimilation policy was based on religious faith, but it may have helped the resistance effort that other Americans criticized and otherwise countered the agents' orders. The society of cavalry officers at Fort Reno was a receptive audience for Indian scouts to celebrate horsemanship and bravery in encounters with criminals and trespassers. Fort Reno also sponsored horse races at which Indian riders excelled and where horse-doctoring power remained relevant. The military officers also openly criticized the Indian Office, accusing them of incompetence and corruption. The army sometimes supplemented the rations issued by the Indian Office.

Although missionaries had little success converting the Arapahos, they taught the values of Christianity. The behavior of many agents and school employees, who represented themselves as Christians, suggested hypocrisy to Arapahos and to the missionaries with whom they visited. Mary Jayne, Baptist missionary, wrote that Arapahos viewed Agent Woodson as "not a Christian." They became indifferent to his instructions to desist from gathering in camp. In fact, Arapaho delegates used Woodson's behavior against him in Washington. The new agent, George Stouch, allowed them to dance "to their heart's content," wrote Jayne. The Baptist missionaries attended Arapaho dances and gatherings, which suggested approval, and the Indian Office was inconsistent about the assimilation policy. The agents encouraged the Arapahos to show the "savage life" at state fairs in Kansas and at the Omaha Exposition in 1898. Arapaho participation at the exposition rewarded them in the form of a permit for a dance.[81]

The Arapahos and Cheyennes viewed the 1890 attempt of the Jerome Commission to coerce them to accept allotment, which began in 1891, and the sale of lands not allotted as a violation of the treaty. Using fraud and coercion, the commission succeeded. Left Hand was able to persuade the commission to agree that Arapaho leaders could select the location of the allotments (in consultation with other Arapahos), each Arapaho would receive 160 acres, the interest on the payment (deposited in the Treasury) for the land would be 5 not 4 percent, and the price per acre would be more than initially offered (although still below market value). Commissioners also guaranteed that Arapahos would get adequate rations, but these rations were reduced, and Arapahos faced the prospect of the government distributing their trust funds per capita. During the 1890s the chiefs struggled unsuccessfully against the ration policy and successfully against the distribution of their funds. The men of the Medicine Grass cohort, who were apprenticed to the older men in economic pursuits and junior to them in the ceremonial lodge organization, signed the agreement along with the senior men.[82]

These men of the Medicine Grass cohort, mature by the 1890s, realized that they were not going to prosper, and despite Arapaho religious devotion, conditions would continue to worsen. The agents tried to wean them away from the senior lodge men by offering agency jobs, but virtually all found another source of hope—new religions.[83]

New Religions and the Medicine Grass Cohort

The introduction of the Ghost Dance was a new vehicle for prayer in the 1890s, when many Arapahos began to lose faith that the lodge ceremonies could help them prosper. Word came to the Northern Arapahos of a new religion led by a prophet in Nevada, and when the Southern Arapahos heard of this, Black Coyote and another Arapaho named Washee went to Wyoming to get more information. Sitting Bull, living among the Northern Arapahos, had made a pilgrimage and was a convert. In the spring of 1890, Black Coyote visited the prophet and by late summer was leading Ghost Dance ceremonies among the Southern Arapahos. Sitting

Bull arrived in the fall of 1890 and began to attract huge crowds. Two more delegations went in 1891 (one led by Black Coyote), and in fall 1892, Sitting Bull and his wife Dropping Lip visited the prophet.[84]

For Arapahos, the Ghost Dance was not only a ceremony designed to transform the world and end their poverty. It also was a vehicle for them to perpetuate their traditions in their new circumstances. Kroeber noted that symbolism from lodge regalia was incorporated into the Ghost Dance regalia: a quirt similar to the clubs carried by the Tomahawk Men with the two highest degrees; the staff and headdress of the Spear Lodge; and the whistle used in the Dog Lodge. Regalia were individualized, that is, persons received dreams that directed how they dressed or what they carried. The quilled hoops on Buffalo Lodge regalia were also seen on clothing worn by Ghost Dancers. Kroeber observed that medicine men would brush their personal medicine objects against sick people and children at these Ghost Dances, believing that their power was enhanced by the Ghost Dance visions. The Ghost Dance visions seemed to be irrefutable evidence of prosperity to come. Ceremonies lasted four days and were held two or three times a week during the peak years, according to James Mooney, who observed the Arapahos several times between 1890 and 1893.[85]

Sitting Bull was the most prominent Ghost Dance leader, and Black Coyote was next in importance. They were in their early forties. Sitting Bull was a Southern Arapaho, born in 1853, who joined the Northern Arapahos as one of Sharp Nose's scouts in 1876. These scouts helped the army in return for guarantees of a reservation in Wyoming. He was on the Northern Arapahos' reservation when he heard of Wovoka and visited him in 1889. In September 1890 he came south to join the Southern Arapahos, possibly because there was such great interest in the Ghost Dance there. He had two sisters and an older brother, Arrow, at Cantonment, and Scabby Bull, also at Cantonment, was a half-brother (brothers in the Arapaho view). Scabby Bull was also known as Sitting Bull then, so he changed his name. Sitting Bull had married three daughters of a Northern Arapaho man. When he came south, he still had two wives, and his mother-in-law Eagle Feather was with her daughters. One, Big Nose, died in 1891 and the other, Dropping Lip, had several children who survived to adulthood. Jess Rowlodge maintained that Sitting Bull acquired 1,500 horses from followers, which he sold to buy a hotel at Darlington (later sold for a loss). Black Coyote was captain of the Indian police and deputy sheriff of Canadian County. By the time of Mooney's visit, he was prosperous, owning considerable property in wagons and stock. He had three wives, one of whom he divorced in 1893, and the two others, Singing Woman and Big Woman, sisters.[86]

Sitting Bull, who hypnotized people with a feather or a black handkerchief, sending hundreds of them into trance, provided headdresses and shirts for seven men (and seven women), whom he authorized to lead Ghost Dance ceremonies. He received property sacrifices from them. The Ghost Dance leadership, based on the names provided by Jess Rowlodge and Myrtle Lincoln, came from the Medicine Grass cohort: in addition to Sitting Bull and Black Coyote, Cut Finger, Jr. (married to Buffalo Fat) and Hail (married to Cross Killer) in the Darlington jurisdiction, and Heap Of Crows (married to Killing Across) at Cantonment. Accompanying Black Coyote on an 1891 delegation was Red Wolf, policeman and member of the Medicine Grass cohort.

Kroeber noted that in 1899, young men were more interested in the Ghost Dance than in the age-graded lodges, although participation in both was not uncommon. Young men could become leaders in the Ghost Dance, especially in interactions with other tribes and in their success at composing songs that were incorporated into the ceremonies. The 1891 delegations included men in the Little Raven, Jr., cohort: Little Raven, Jr., Arnold Woolworth, Grant Left Hand, and Casper Edson (Carlisle alumnus, who was a scribe for the delegates). Clearly, at least some young men in their twenties and thirties aspired to prestige and influence, even though they had no war exploits. Kroeber noted that several young men who had not been to war pierced children's ears and cut their hair at public gatherings. They had to get older men to count coup for them. The property received from the children's families would have been shared between the two men. Presumably, these young men who were asked to pierce ears were boarding school alumni who had returned safely, or men who had dreams or visions about ear piercing. But Kroeber does not explore this point.

Older men, including Left Hand, Row Of Lodges, Bull Thunder, and Goat Chief (Annie Pedro's father, who was also a policeman and a member of Left Hand's cohort) attended and supported the Ghost Dances but did not provide leadership, so the Ghost Dance was a vehicle for the Medicine Grass cohort especially to attain ritual authority outside the lodge organization. Arapahos made many visits to other tribes in Oklahoma during the late 1890s, proselytizing and exchanging ideas and ritual forms.[87]

When Sitting Bull's prophesy of the new world did not materialize, the Arapahos continued to pray for help, turning to new kinds of rituals inspired by visions, namely the Ghost Dance hand game and the Crow Dance. Kroeber noted that the hand game was directed by someone whose leadership was validated in a vision received when he fasted on a hill. Or an individual could apprentice to a bundle owner. A person in need would vow to sponsor a hand game ritual, that is, make a sacrifice of food and property to accompany a prayer for help with illness or some other crisis. As Myrtle Lincoln said, they used it as "a way of prayer." The directors of these ceremonies had hand game bundles, the content of which was inspired by their visions. Hand game songs could also express support for the Arapaho way of life; for example, one song was about Blackman's fasting for power.

Before the ritual began, the director would pray for a successful outcome. The game was played with a "button" and several different kinds of sticks, the symbolism of which represented prayer for abundance and generation of life. A bundle owner might include Christian symbolism as well as traditional symbolism. The players were divided into two groups, one associated with the sponsor. Each side had feathered sticks used to point to the button that was being concealed by the other side. Counter sticks were used to tally the score during the course of play. The success of the sponsor's prayer was linked to his or her side winning the game. The director was expected to facilitate the outcome. Again, men who owned bundles and provided the leadership for the hand game rituals in Cantonment came from the Medicine Grass cohort (Young Bear, for example) and two camp Indians from Little Raven, Jr.'s cohort (Mixed Hair and Striking).[88]

Kroeber observed a Crow Dance in September 1899. According to Mooney, this ceremony was introduced through a dream by Grant Left Hand, in his thirties in the 1890s and a member of the Stars. The ceremony had become very popular with young people by the time Kroeber arrived. Northern Arapahos, who also had a Crow Dance ceremony, were in attendance, helping the Southern Arapaho conduct the ceremony that Kroeber witnessed. The regalia were inspired by individual visions or dreams, but much of the symbolism was derived from the lodge regalia: whips similar to Tomahawk Lodge clubs and fans similar to Spear Lodge head-dresses. A feathered stick carried in the Crow Dance was stuck in the ground between dances, like a lodge man's staff. The symbolism represented prayer for abundance and health. The Kit Fox Men and Star Men participated in a Crow Dance at the Offerings Lodge in 1901, according to Dorsey.[89]

In the mid-1880s, peyote ritual was introduced to the Arapahos when some individuals, who probably sought cures, learned about peyote ritual from Comanches, Plains Apaches, and Kiowas. Quannah Parker, Comanche principal chief, led meetings among the Southern Arapahos about 1884. After returning from Carlisle, Jock Bull Bear, at the age of twenty-two, began learning the ritual from him. Arapahos also attended Apache meetings, and one, Medicine Bird of the Medicine Grass cohort, "changed things in the tepee," according to Jess Rowlodge, that is, he organized a uniquely Arapaho ritual in 1888 that others accepted.

As a youth of about eighteen, Medicine Bird was a good hunter and a Star Man. He asked to borrow his brother's horse to go hunting, and his brother refused. Very offended—in fact, he said his brother could consider the horse his brother—he went south and lived with the Plains Apaches. While there he married an

Apache girl, whose former suitor was jealous and used bad medicine, or sorcery, against him. Ill, he went to a peyote meeting and was cured. At that point, he converted. Later, he returned to the Arapahos, married an Arapaho woman, and started the Arapaho "peyote way."

Middle-aged members of the Medicine Grass cohort adopted his way and directed rituals: from Cantonment (Medicine Bird's community), Osage, Young Bear, White Rabbit, Bringing Good, Heap Of Crows, and Broken Rib among them. Several camp Indians and educated men from the Little Raven, Jr., cohort also followed Medicine Bird. Support built during the 1890s as belief in the Ghost Dance prophesies waned. The peyote meetings were easy to conceal from the agents, especially with cooperation from the police. The large intertribal Ghost Dances also brought the Arapahos together with peyotists from other tribes, helping to convert people.[90]

As in the Crow Dance and the hand game rituals, leaders of peyote rituals conducted ceremonies following their own visions or dreams. In other words, these rituals were individualized and did not require long, expensive apprenticeships as in the Offerings Lodge. Leaders could modify procedures over time if their visions authorized this. Peyotism was compatible with Arapaho ideals about prayer and ritual, though. Carl Sweezy told Bass that, for him, peyote ritual took the place of the traditional ceremonial rituals, but as a peyotist he fasted, meditated, had visions, and fulfilled vows through participation. The peyote plant was viewed as a spirit helper. There was a common procedure according to Kroeber, who witnessed two peyote ceremonies. First, the leader selected the site for the peyote tepee or tent; then after it was erected, he made the drum and selected a fire tender or fire chief who started the fire. The leader made a crescent-shaped altar out of earth and put sage on the ground where the participants sat. The participants entered the tepee and sat around the fire; then they had a ceremonial smoke. With the other men's help, the leader made a line on the altar that represented the path by which prayers traveled to the peyote spirit. The leader used cedar incense to smudge his drum, rattle, fan, staff, and the peyote plant he carried in a pouch. He then distributed four pieces of peyote to each man, and they consumed them.

The leader took his rattle and sang four songs, while the man on his left drummed for him, then passed the drum and rattle to the man on his left. Each man sang four songs and passed the drum and rattle. The singing continued around the circle, with the songs referring to the peyote spirit or the bird messengers that conveyed prayers to spirits. Participants had visions during the night. At midnight the leader's wife, the only woman present when Kroeber attended, went out and returned with a jar of water. They all drank four swallows and continued singing. At sunrise, the woman went out and returned with four ceremonially prepared foods. The drum was dismantled and passed around. There was another meal at noon, everyone eating with the same spoon.

The leader's peyote regalia (rattle, fan, staff, pouch, headdress, wristband), comparable to a medicine bundle, had designs symbolizing prayers for abundance and health. These designs employed color symbolism or combinations of feathers to represent a prayer wish for something specific or the peyote spirit itself. Some leaders also incorporated Christian symbols. Before dispersing, the men probably would exchange or give as gifts some of their peyote regalia. This gift giving helped create "community," that is "peace and good-feelings" among peyote participants. Some peyote meetings were held specifically to cure people. In curing rituals, the tepee could symbolize the sweat lodge used in traditional curing. So a relative might vow to sponsor the meeting in return for a cure. Jess Rowlodge noted that the elderly people who supported the Ghost Dance did not look favorably on peyotism. But many of the young members of the Little Raven, Jr., cohort (in their twenties) converted.[91]

The men of the Medicine Grass cohort and their wives—economic and ritual partners—continued to implement the strategy of accommodation designed by their seniors but also changed the direction of religious life. They and other Arapahos ceased to rely exclusively on the lodge organization for supernatural assistance. The male leaders of the revitalization movements in the 1890s belonged to the Medicine Grass cohort. Some of the men in the Little Raven, Jr., cohort followed their lead.

THE CONFIDENCE OF ALL HER HUSBANDS:
WOMEN'S NEW ECONOMIC AND CEREMONIAL PARTNERSHIPS

When Bichea spoke about her life, she emphasized that she was proud that she had the confidence of all her husbands. As a wife who was trusted, she had unlimited liberty to visit relatives and "chums" and to attend any tribal gathering, such as a women's dart game or football game. The role of a hard-working and trusted wife who was also a generous kinswoman brought a woman a good reputation. On the reservation, women found new ways of respecting kinspeople and working industriously and expertly. Like the men in the senior cohorts, the women in the Walking Backward and Owl cohorts took on new responsibilities, especially gardening and agriculture. Active politically, the senior lodge women supported Arapaho resistance to the Indian Office's ban on Indian custom marriage and polygamy. As partners to the senior lodge men and intermediary chiefs, they played a part in the Arapahos' acceptance of allotment and the implementation of the civilization strategy. The wives of the men in the Medicine Grass cohort partnered with them in establishing the Ghost Dance and peyote religions.[92]

Provisioning Households

Women's work expanded to include gardening, commercial farming, freighting, and wage work. They continued to gather roots and berries and found minerals for paint and dye. Some dug medicinal or sacred roots, first praying and tugging on the root four times. Myrtle Lincoln described how women gathered wild potatoes, wild onions, grapes, plums, soapweed (for soap and gravy), walnuts, elm bark (for tea), and salt from Salt Creek. The customary association of women and plants extended to the vegetable gardens introduced by agency personnel. Myrtle helped her grandmother Pumpkin with their small vegetable garden, planting seeds and watering it with water from the river. Women also had small plots where they grew corn. Myrtle noted that Arapahos considered these gardens "women's job," even though men might help if they "felt like it." Myrtle's grandmother used her digging stick to plant "squaw" or "spotted" corn, and she watered it twice a day while it grew. Women used both bone and metal hoes to tend the corn. They built willow reed fences around their corn plots to keep out animals. When it was time to shell the corn, women worked in groups.[93]

Jess Rowlodge's parents had a larger corn field (probably "yellow corn," also planted by settlers), and they worked it together using a plow. Row Of Lodges obtained the Baptist missionary's help preparing land for cotton, and he and his wife Owl had help from other Arapahos picking the cotton. They invited them to a feast. These communal work parties depended on the preparation of food by women.[94]

Until the beginning of beef issues on-the-block (already butchered), women had responsibility for helping to butcher buffalo, then cattle after about 1876. At beef issues, they followed the men who killed the cattle and then loaded the meat on their travoises. As in prereservation times, they dried, preserved, and cooked meat and the plant food they gathered. Women made and ornamented canvas tepees by the mid-1870s, but they still made the furnishings, such as bed rests and wind screens, from willows and reeds. Women continued to tan buffalo and deer hides and make containers, cradles, men's pipe bags, and toys for their daughters. Still in charge of the household's food, they began making small hide bags to hold the family's ration tickets. These bags had beaded designs representing prayers for abundance. Making moccasins remained important work, but the annual issue of manufactured clothing and dress goods by the federal government lessened the need to make all the family's garments from hides. At first, women relied on school girls to sew shirts and dresses. Women also chopped wood for the household. Baptist missionary Mary Jayne tried to teach Arapaho women to quilt, using material donated to the mission, but while some young women made quilt tops of their own design (presumably to substitute for buffalo robes as bedding), older women like Woman Going In (Mrs. Left Hand) had no interest.[95]

Women of this era still had the responsibility for moving camp: taking down the tepees, loading pack horses and wagons, driving pack horses and dogs along the route, and setting up the tepees at the new location. When Arapaho bands began freighting between the agency and destinations in Kansas, women performed essential duties on the freight train—they established and dismantled camps along the route and performed the household duties during the trip. They also might help drive the teams. Being able to work largely defined mature womanhood. Myrtle's husband's sister Cross Eyed had some sort of mental disability and could do little— she could not sew or "do anything," and no one would marry her, Myrtle said.[96]

Women's work was as important as men's work to the support of the household, and they owned the products of their labor and shared in the profits from joint labor with their husbands. In the 1870s the tanned buffalo robes the Arapahos sold to the trader were the property of the man who killed the animal and the woman who tanned the hide. In 1873 a group of Arapaho women, all wives of chiefs, including Big Mouth, Tall Bear, and Cut Finger, insisted that Agent Miles prevent the men from trading robes for whisky. That winter the women refused to dress any more hides until Miles could guarantee that all the robes would be traded for family subsistence. The price of these robes depended on the quality of the tanning. The trader also paid women to tan the hides brought in by American hunters, giving them two dollars per hide.[97]

In 1882 men received $484 for selling horses and $154 for transporting lumber, and women sold moccasins for $90. Men collected $348 from freighting and $286 for chopping wood, activities that women participated in as well and for which they were entitled to a share of the money. After the disappearance of the buffalo, women tanned deer hides for sale. Jess Rowlodge noted that his mother and other Arapaho women sold fur caps they made from beaver and otter, and they made rawhide ropes to sell to cowboys. They traded with other tribes as well, selling saddles and salt, according to Myrtle Lincoln. Women also worked at military posts, probably doing laundry. Colonel Richard Dodge, at Camp Cantonment, noted that women came to the post daily to beg for food or work, as well as to buy from the trader. "Everyday some Indian women are in the post area begging for food or work. They behave themselves well, don't go into men's quarters. At night virtuous women are in their own camps." Myrtle remembered going there with older women to trade for food.[98]

In the 1890s, women still sold handiwork, such as coin purses, napkin rings, chatelaine bags, lamp mats, ladies' belts, and moccasins and received money from tanning beef issue hides, which were used to make shoe soles. Some women, including Mrs. Birdshead and Mrs. Henry Sage (Coming Up) from Canton, and Long Hair (Mrs. Little Left Hand) from Greenfield freighted, probably using their husbands' equipment but possibly their own wagons. When the beef issue was largely discontinued, both men and women worked in settlers' corn fields to earn money.[99]

In their adaptations to new economic opportunities, women as well as men did things on their own terms—working in groups and sharing products and profits from their cooperative labor. This was all to the dismay of at least some federal officials who had tried to make farming and freighting exclusively men's work.

Defending Marriage

Women's work was a primary means of fulfilling their obligations to kin and in-laws. But during the reservation years, the Arapaho family became a target of Indian Office "civilization" policy. Women as well as men resisted this policy. Arapahos expected women to make food and property sacrifices for relatives, as well as to show generosity generally. Hilger found that Arapahos still observed respect relations—that is, avoidance of certain relatives such as siblings of the opposite sex and parents-in-law. Myrtle Lincoln noted that gift exchanges between in-laws showed love for one's own relatives—for example, a sister demonstrated respect for a brother when she treated his wife well. Jess Rowlodge pointed out that his mother, Owl, provided for some relatives when they could not provide for themselves. Red Woman (Wacht, in Pratt), Powderface's wife, who according to Richard Pratt had great pride in Powderface's career, made a buffalo robe and beaded moccasins and leggings for him (with prayer-thought designs). Women also tried to make prayer sacrifices for relatives by donating food and property during religious ceremonies, such as the Offerings Lodge, Ghost Dance, Ghost Dance hand game, and peyote rituals. Food and property sacrifices on behalf of relatives probably had to be more modest during the reservation years, as poverty gradually engulfed Arapahos, but they still made them. Women also made body sacrifices for relatives. Bichea sacrificed her left little finger so that her sister would recover from an illness. Her father expressed to her his immense gratitude and praised her, she told Michelson.[100]

Women dedicated themselves to protecting their children, who faced all sorts of dangers. Child mortality on the reservation remained high during the late nineteenth century. Women continued to make prayer sacrifices in the form of navel amulets and cradle boards, and they prepared the feasts for important events in their children's lives. Women kept food taboos when they became pregnant and spaced their children. They tried to treat minor illnesses in the family, trading with women throughout the plains area for medicines. Southern Arapahos used the mail service to send wild pumpkin root used as a purgative, seeds of a plant found in the hills used as an ingredient in nearly every medical preparation, and quinine weed, which neutralized snake poison. In the return mail from the northern plains, they received bear root for wounds and cuts, sweet root for nursing mothers, and long root as a general cure.[101]

An honorable marriage was very important to a woman's reputation, and it marked a woman as "mature" and initiated a potential life partnership with a man. But reservation life created obstacles.

The federal government issued directives against polygamy and tried to dissuade Indian custom marriage, which was an expression between two families of social alliance, commitment, and support. The practice of a man marrying sisters or a man marrying his brother's widow was another means to maintain this bond between families and between children and their older relatives on both the mother's and father's sides of the family.

Bichea had been married to four men. Her first husband was Fire Log, whom she married by Indian custom in 1869 when she was about eighteen. She was proud that he never scolded or hit her. They had a son, Lump Forehead—his school name was Daniel Webster. After Fire Log died, she returned to her father's household for two years. Then her family urged her to marry Red Breast. She wanted to remain single for her "boy's sake" (because she feared a stepfather would neglect him), but a male relative persuaded her to relent. She married Red Breast in about 1873. He worked one year for her parents, herding, hunting, and getting wood; thereafter, they had an Indian custom marriage and exchanged three horses. Red Breast treated her son well, and she had a daughter, Molly, and two other children with him and acted properly by avoiding him for two years after the birth of each child. After he died, she returned to her father's household determined to remain single. Then in 1884, her "brother" convinced her to marry Man Ahead, several years younger than she. She had a child with him but left him two years later because she objected to his plans to marry a second wife. Later, in 1889, while again living with her parents, she agreed to marry Fire, who was born in 1859. She had a son with Fire. Fire never scolded or mistreated her, her point to Michelson being that she was a good worker and a virtuous, trusted wife.

Red Woman also had four husbands. Her first died in battle and left her with a baby daughter. About eight years later, she and her sister married Spotted Corn (from Medicine Grass's cohort), but he divorced them shortly thereafter to marry someone else. She took her baby son with her to her third husband, White Bear (Old Sun's son). This was a stable marriage, lasting from 1878 until he died in 1891. Arapahos referred to her as Mrs. White Bear. From the Medicine Grass cohort, White Bear apparently had some military experience. Described as a warrior, he was sent as a prisoner to Fort Marion in 1875. According to Jess Rowlodge, White Bear's younger brother had tried to kill the son of an agency employee, and rather than let the youth be sent away, White Bear took his place. When White Bear returned from the east, Agent Miles felt disappointment that he then succumbed to camp influences. White Bear married Red Woman, and Agent Miles appointed him as a policeman. So he and Red Woman were fairly prosperous during their marriage, and she had two more children. After his death, she waited four years, then married again in 1895 and eventually became known as Mrs. Warpath, but this marriage lasted only eight years. While Bichea, who remained married to Fire for thirty years, rose with him in the ceremonial organization, Red Woman did not have that opportunity.

Owl, married to Bear Robe as a co-wife, left him shortly after Jess was born and went to Row Of Lodges, who was married to her sister. The agents on the reservation in the 1870s and 1880s ignored polygamous marriages of chiefs like Row Of Lodges to retain their support for the civilization program. Owl's sister was the chief wife, but she soon died, and Owl assumed that position. So with her divorce from Bear Robe, Owl improved her position.[102]

Despite serious efforts, the agents could not suppress Indian custom marriage. As late as 1889, missionary Henry Voth admitted that even young, educated people still married Indian custom. Perhaps the increased poverty encouraged more grooms to work for their father-in-law rather than presenting many horses and other gifts, which would then have to be returned. But wealthier families still exchanged horses decorated commensurate with the wealth and position of the participants, according to Agent Ashley in 1890. Ashley reported that the prominent chiefs selected by the agent as a Court of Indian Offenses refused to punish Indian custom marriage—what the agents referred to as the "purchase of women." In 1896, even though by then territorial law required legal marriage so as to conform to American custom,

Indian custom marriage was still prevalent, and Woodson was particularly bent on stopping it. When he was informed of a case, he generally had the parties arrested. He would suspend their sentences (presumably to labor in confinement at the agency) if they married legally. Gradually, young Arapahos came to accept legal marriage, although gift exchange usually still occurred.[103]

With Indian custom marriage, families clearly remained involved in their members' marriages, monitoring the behavior of the parties. The agents often saw this involvement as an incentive to divorce, which they sought to prevent. Agents complained that mothers (that is, female relatives) supported their daughters' efforts to divorce and return to their parents households for "trivial causes," such as failure to share with the wife's relatives (that is, stinginess). In Bichea's case, her family supported her decision at least in part because she argued that the woman chosen by her husband for his second wife was too closely connected by kinship and thus inappropriate. Women enforced "good" behavior through such actions.[104]

Arapahos regarded polygamy as necessary, given the disparity between the numbers of men and women. In 1876, Agent Miles reported that Arapahos had 353 men and 546 women. On the census of 1881, twenty Arapaho men had more than one wife, and many women in the household were listed as sisters-in-law. Arapahos had the custom of a sister entering into the household of a married sister and then after several years marrying her sister's husband. Of course, women listed as sisters-in-law could have actually been wives whose status was hidden from the enumerator. In 1888 Agent Williams counted 285 males over the age of eighteen and 364 females over the age of fourteen.[105]

The chiefs on the Court of Indian Offenses refused to punish polygamists even in the 1890s. All the agent could do was try to force young people, particularly educated Indians, to live monogamously; but even in this, he sometimes failed, as we saw from the marital histories of youths who went to off-reservation boarding schools. Little Raven, Jr., insisted to agency personnel that he needed to marry Jenny Bringing Good because his other wife was sick and could not do the work of the household. Agent Woodson reported that fifty men still had more than one wife in 1897. Sometimes parties remained married surreptitiously, as in the case of Long Hair. She told Hilger that when she was fourteen, her mother died and her mother's sister sent her to Lime's household. Lime was married to her older sister Spotted Woman. She did not realize that she was married. She lived in her sister's tepee and did not want anything to do with Lime, she told Hilger. Eventually, she became pregnant. Her childless sister (the chief wife) ran the household and raised all Long Hair's five children, while Long Hair did beadwork. Not only was polygamy practical but it could also work to the advantage of women. On the other hand, sometimes co-wives did not get along. Usually conflict occurred when co-wives were not relatives, but James Scabby Horse told missionaries that his mother, Wind, "always [got] angry" at her husband over his marriage to her sister, a co-wife.[106]

The census of 1881 showed the rank of women within households, listing wives as "housekeepers" and other women as wood carriers, water carriers, and wood choppers. In a polygamous household, the wives were referred to as wife "number one," "number two," and so on. These terms reflected the fact that one wife was the boss wife, who directed the work of the others and probably was her husband's companion in the ceremonies. The title of "housekeeper" outranked the status of "wood carrier" and "water carrier," and presumably a wood carrier was considered more mature than a water carrier since carrying heavy pieces of wood was restricted to mature women, and unmarried girls were not allowed to perform this work. "Wood chopper" status (held by mature rather than young women) probably indicated that the woman earned money chopping wood, which would have given her considerable independence in the household.[107]

Married women, whether in a monogamous or polygamous household, had an economic advantage. Those of mature age had more horses than divorced and widowed women. There were 165 married women on the 1881 census, and about one-fifth had no horses. Almost all women had dogs, which they used to transport belongings. Most married women had one or two horses. About one-fourth of the married women had four or more horses—these were the ones who were clearly wealthy by Arapaho standards. Among these were six women with ten horses; four of the women were from Chief Little Raven's household—his two wives and his two divorced daughters (who benefited from his wealth). Most divorced and widowed women were living in the households of male relatives or in-laws. Nineteen households were headed by women, half of whom were divorced, and half widowed. One-third of these had no horses, and the average was one horse. None had more than two. The ages of the women heads of household ranged from fourteen to forty-six. Clearly these female-headed households were among the poorest. The households headed by women were also considerably smaller, which made the work load heavier than in the large male-headed households that included several unattached women whose work was listed as water carrier, wood carrier, or wood chopper.[108]

The agents' campaign against polygamy could have affected women adversely. It certainly increased the number of unmarried women among the Arapahos. A woman taken as a co-wife by White Hawk (born in 1866) in 1899 was forced to leave his camp when the agent threatened to send White Hawk to "the pen." An orphan born in 1881, she went from camp to camp, finally arriving at Scabby Bull's camp, where her child was born. Rumors circulated that the baby was a "night baby," that is, one whose father did not recognize him because there was no legal marriage. She died not too long after the baby was born. In a polygamous household, plural wives (wife number two, for example) could apprentice to the chief wife and eventually move up in the hierarchy. Without this opportunity, their options were limited.[109]

Women who demonstrated a pattern of illicit sexual relations faced a grim future. They could be the sole support of several children, struggling to survive by whatever means possible. The presence of Fort Reno and Camp Cantonment encouraged prostitution, presumably among those few women who were unmarried and from very poor households or women who were considered unmarriageable (because of bad behavior or perhaps some disability). Colonel Dodge noted that Indian men (and probably women, occasionally) would bring women to the vicinity of the posts at night and prostitute them to white officers, African American soldiers, and Indian scouts. The woman received a share of the fee. A few women set up camps in the vicinity of military establishments. In another case, a woman had lived successively with several Arapaho scouts at Fort Reno. None of them would subsequently acknowledge a marriage with her or accept her child as his own. There is one case in the record of a woman dying from these contacts; she was murdered by a soldier. It is quite possible that the policy against polygamy contributed to prostitution.[110]

Women who were unmarried tried to challenge their circumstances, taking advantage of the agents' disapproval of Arapaho marital customs. Agents, who viewed men as abusers, justified interfering as a means of protecting women. Some widows tried to improve their circumstances by challenging inheritance norms. Prior to settling on the reservation, when a husband died, his relatives (usually his brothers and sometimes sisters) took his property. If they chose to be generous (and they should be), they would give something to the widow and children. But the agents were promoting Western notions of family, and they often supported a widow's attempt to keep her husband's property. Killing Ahead, widow of Theok Raven, asked to have title to the Cantonment hospital building, which her husband had inherited from his father, Chief Little Raven, who had received the building as a gift from the government. Yellowhair's widow asked the agent to prevent his relatives from taking his property. In an exceptional case, Packer indicated that he wanted his ex-wife to have his horse after his impending death, rather than his brother.[111]

Agents also began to divert money from men to women considered "unmarried," that is, co-wives. The first wife's (or boss wife's) share and her children's share of the interest payment from the land sale of 1892 went to her husband. Arapahos expected a husband to purchase what his wife and children needed—food and clothing, especially. Agents began to pay other wives their money, rather than allowing their husbands to receipt for it. These "plural wives" eventually began to lease their allotments themselves (under the agents' supervision), collecting the lease money. Widows and legally divorced women collected their and their children's shares. For example, when Mixed Hair divorced Buffalo Fat in 1892 (and eloped with Scabby Bull's wife, Good Looking), Buffalo Fat insisted to the agent that their son's interest money should go to her. In this way, women hoped to protect the interests of their children, who might be neglected by a stepparent. In 1897, Bichea collected the money of her young daughter, Molly (known as Molly Candy), in place of Molly's stepfather Fire.[112]

The Indian Office did not succeed in ending Indian custom and polygamous marriages. Wives, including the boss wife in polygamous households, remained essential economic, political, and ceremonial partners to their husbands. But unmarried women— widows and divorcees—and possibly plural wives began to use Indian Office regulations to challenge their subordinate position (or the disadvantaged position of their children) within households.

Partners in Politics

In political life, women as well as men had to be consulted and their participation and support obtained, not only for the implementation of the civilization strategy but also for the continued fusion of political and ceremonial leadership that facilitated the cooperation of Arapahos. The senior lodge women and the wives of the intermediary chiefs played key roles in the political process.

Women had input in council decisions, primarily by expressing their views to each other and to their husbands. The "government farmers," that is, agency employees hired to live among the bands, ostensibly to give instruction in farming, reported to the agents about Arapaho behavior. One, J. Witcher, wrote that Arapaho women—presumably the prominent senior lodge women— made their views known to the men when they held council. The women's views generally prevailed, according to Witcher.[113]

The Buffalo Lodge women would have had considerable influence. Once oriented toward successful hunts, the lodge now took place as the result of a religious vow for recovery from illness, protection from trouble, and success in one's career. The participants still followed restrictions, or taboos, the violation of which produced blindness, deafness, or "skin sores." According to Warden, as the women with degrees walked through the camp, people touched them to attain long life. The last ceremony took place about 1888 near Left Hand's camp. One of the women who received regalia of a high degree gave her grandmother four horses, two cows, and other property. Pumpkin (Myrtle Lincoln's grandmother and the wife of Road Traveler), Coming Up (married to Henry Sage), Bitchea (Mrs. White Eyed Antelope), and Singing Woman (Black Horse's wife)—all wives of lodge men—became members. Their achievement added to the stature of their husbands. Like the Buffalo Lodge women, who potentially helped their husbands' ceremonial careers, women like Owl and Powderface's wife Red Woman, who made quilled tepee ornaments or clothing, also helped the men in their families and potentially had input in family decisions and political activity.[114]

What happened to the Poisal women, so important in prereservation days as liaisons? Snake Woman came to the agency with her sons Robert and John, and daughter Mary, but there is less information about her other children, Matilda and Margaret. Snake Woman died about 1889. Mary Keith and her husband came to the agency soon after it was established. In 1875 a clash with troops was narrowly averted when an Arapaho woman who spoke English negotiated with the army officers in charge. This woman was probably Mary Keith, but she is not mentioned by name. Mary's son Albert described her as an educated woman who dressed like a white woman. Mary's oldest daughter, Josephine, attended St. Mary's Academy and married Peter Shields, a white man working at the agency. Matilda Poisal's daughter Minnie Pepperdin was at the agency—presumably her mother died before or during the 1870s, because John Poisal, her guardian, sent her to the Arapaho school in 1880. She apparently died before the allotment of land.

Margaret Poisal Adams's daughter Jenny came with her husband, an Irish immigrant named John Meagher. Inspector William Pollock described Jenny as a "fine appearing lady" who had never lived with Indians before she came to the agency. She worked at the Arapaho school in the 1880s. Her second husband was also a white man. Jenny's daughter Maggie had married a white man and moved to Fort Smith, Arkansas, by 1896. Margaret Fitzpatrick Wilmott Adams is not listed on the agency rolls or censuses, but in 1877 her daughter Jenny reported that she lived with her. Perhaps later she lived in Colorado or Kansas. In 1883 Margaret went with the Arapaho delegation to Washington, D.C., as their interpreter. John Williams, the agency employee in charge of the delegation, mentions "Mrs. Adams" as dressed like a white woman, in proud possession of a gold watch and other jewelry, but with a drinking problem. Powderface expressed disgust with her intoxication, and Arapahos do not seem to have relied on her services as an interpreter after this. She probably died before 1892 because she was not allotted, and her brother John's probate indicated that she had died before allotment. Youths who learned English in school took on the task of interpreting, so the Poisals became less important in this regard.[115]

It is clear that Arapaho chiefs considered women to be important constituents who had to be persuaded to cooperate. For example, Chief Yellow Bear attended the General Council of Indian Territory in Okmulgee in 1875, where he stated that he would try to persuade *both* the men and women to cooperate with the federal government's civilization program. Jess Rowlodge had recollections of instances when women influenced either their husband's behavior or the course of events. Once, in 1901, the Arapaho Offerings Lodge was delayed because one woman from the Little Raven family refused to send her six-year-old daughter to school because she thought she was still too young. The agent denied the Arapahos permission for the ceremony until the child was brought to school. Little Raven, Jr., a man with ceremonial standing then and the girl's mother's brother, tried and failed to persuade his sister. It was not until December that she relented and the ceremony took place. On that same occasion, another woman refused to allow the men to use her tepee for a council lodge.

In explaining how the Arapahos were persuaded to agree to the cession of land proposed by the Jerome Commission in 1890, Jess Rowlodge told how Arapaho chiefs and their wives (including Row Of Lodges and Owl) visited Sitting Bull, the Ghost Dance leader, to ask his advice. When he told them that the new world would come soon and the cession money could be used to buy presents for their dead relatives who would become alive again, they decided to accept allotments. Jess made clear that both his father and mother concurred. The agreement of both men and women seems to have been an important part of reaching consensus. Left Hand took into account the women's insistence on allotments near wood and water when he met with the Jerome Commission.[116]

Much of the work of generating consensus and cooperation fell to the senior lodge men and their wives. Bichea and Fire successively belonged to the Tomahawk, Spear, and Lime Crazy lodges. He became a headman for a junior lodge. Through these achievements, Bichea mentored and instructed other women. Fire was a grandfather in the Offerings Lodge, and Bichea, a grandmother. This accomplishment gave them influence. Fire was also a doctor, and because of that, Bichea said, she was respected. Bichea remarked that these were the best years of her life, for as a mature woman, she went through all the tribe's lodges in accordance with her husband's ranks. The wives of the men of Left Hand's cohort and some of the men in Medicine Grass's cohort similarly had influence. In the Cantonment area, the senior lodge women included Bitchea (Mrs. Rabbit Run), Singing In Water (Mrs. Deaf), Coming Up (then her sister Red Mouth, wives of Henry Sage), and Dropping Lip (Mrs. Sitting Bull), and in Left Hand's band, Woman (Mrs. Gun) and Cross Killer (Mrs. Hail).[117]

The chiefs assumed major responsibility for generating consensus in councils and for implementing decisions. An Arapaho intermediary chief considered his wife to be a political helpmate. She had to manage the entertaining of prominent people and the distribution of food and supplies to needy followers. She also traveled with him and advised him when they went on delegations to confer with the local agent. The most prominent chiefs would try to take their wives with them when they went to Washington, D.C., although the Indian Office rarely approved such requests. Powderface took his wife on the delegation of 1873. In 1884, Left Hand's wife Woman Going In went east with him. Richard Pratt, superintendent of Carlisle Indian School, asked Left Hand and Powderface to bring their wives to Carlisle because he thought they could influence Arapahos to send more girls to the school. When the delegates met with officials in Washington, the men wore special suits of clothing that they had received from the officials on prior visits (pants and vests, for example), and the women wore special clothing as well. When she met the secretary of the interior, Left Hand's wife wore a dress like ones worn by white women. In 1891, when Arapaho chiefs went to Washington to discuss allotment, Left Hand, now principal chief, took his wife Woman Going In.[118]

A chief's wife had a position of prominence. When Left Hand, married to Bear Woman (the mother of his sons Circle, Grant, Robert, and two others who lived to maturity), married Yellow Bear's widow Woman Going In as a co-wife in 1884, Bear Woman was outraged that he chose Woman Going In to go to Washington that year. In essence, he had demoted her from the position of chief wife. Woman Going In told agency personnel, "I went to Washington with the old man, and when we came home at our house, she [Bear Woman] would not look at us, and that was the time they separated." But Bear Woman retained her position as Dog Woman and had influence through her sons in the years to come. Chiefs' wives in Cantonment were Striking In Night (Mrs. Bull Thunder), Bitchea (Mrs. Rabbit Run), and Traveler (Mrs. Scabby Bull), and in Left Hand's band, Bitchea (Mrs. White Eyed Antelope) and Owl (Mrs. Row Of Lodges).[119]

Women had ceremonial careers that potentially helped them influence others. Arapaho women successfully resisted the agents' efforts to have agency physicians attend to childbirth. Midwifery continued, and several women had medicine power to treat pregnancy, nursing mothers, and infants. Myrtle Lincoln's grandmother Pumpkin (born in 1848 and married to Road Traveler) and Striking Night (born in 1858 and married to Big Head) worked as midwives. Jess Rowlodge's mother-in-law Big Woman (born in 1872 and married to Lumpmouth) and her sister Bad Teeth, born in 1862, doctored. The latter was married to a medicine man, Strong Bull, who taught her, and they both belonged to a doctor's society. Several women worked with their husbands as doctors for all sorts of ailments. These midwives and doctors may have had influence with women. But it was possible for a woman to lose status. Road Traveler was a fairly prosperous band leader who, upset over his health, committed suicide about 1890. Thereafter, Pumpkin became poor.[120]

Women participated in the reorganization and reorientation of the lodge ceremonies, including the Offerings Lodge, and resisted the Office of Indian Affairs's efforts to suppress it. The wives of the men who participated through body and property sacrifice supported their husbands by making some of their regalia (such as moccasins), preparing the food offerings, and accumulating property to give as gifts to their husbands' ceremonial grandfathers. They also encouraged them from outside the lodge, singing and otherwise participating. Women made vows to sponsor the ceremony or to fast in the lodge, and often their brothers (as well as husbands) advanced their sisters' ceremonial careers as the women helped them. Jess Rowlodge's mother, Owl, fasted in the Offerings Lodge for four days as a prayer for her recovery from illness—a great sacrifice, Arapahos thought. Her brother and mother's brother had vowed their participation to help her, and her brother had been pierced. She recovered as a result of the vows, she believed. In 1879, Shaved Head's brothers had vowed to participate in the Offerings Lodge, and one of their friends had pledged to be Lodge

Maker. The friend had no wife, so in support of her brothers, Shaved Head (Medicine Grass's sister and later Mrs. Two Babies) agreed to substitute as the Lodge Maker's wife. The widow of a Lodge Maker, Mrs. Old Camp, was also a substitute for the Lodge Maker's wife in 1901. The wives of the grandfathers and the Lodge Maker had ceremonial authority from this lodge.

In Cantonment, Singing Woman's husband Black Horse had been a Lodge Maker, and she a Lodge Maker's wife. Rabbit Run and his wife Bitchea assisted a grandfather in the 1901 Offerings Lodge. In Left Hand's band, Cross Killer (Mrs. Hail) and Blackfeet Woman (Mrs. White Owl) were grandmothers in this lodge. Some women had earned the right to perform acts only women could do, such as digging earth for the altar and cutting the central pole. Mouse, Trunk's daughter and Bears Lariat's wife, who was born in 1857, had the right to cut the center pole of the lodge. She also was a grandmother in the lodges. Yellow Woman, born in 1852, also had this right. Shoshone Woman (Mrs. Lizard), born in 1857, had the right to cut the rawhide used in the ceremony, and she was also a grandmother. She had been asked to be the grandmother of the Lodge Maker in 1901 because she had had this role when her husband Old Horse was alive, but her second husband, Lizard, had not participated, so as a husband-wife Lodge Maker team they could not qualify. During the 1901 Offerings Lodge, three women received instruction in women's duties so that they would have authority to conduct Offerings Lodge rituals in the future: Shoshone Woman (aforementioned), Singing Woman (married to Black Coyote), and Grass Singing, the youngest wife of the Offerings Lodge director Hawkan.[121]

Arapahos referred to men and women who had lodge positions as "ceremonial people." It was not unusual for ceremonial people to pursue various other routes (such as the Ghost Dance or peyote) to secure help from the Creator. Ceremonial people tended to marry other ceremonial people if they lost a spouse to divorce or death. In this way, neither the man nor the woman suffered a setback in his or her ceremonial career.

During the Offerings Lodge, couples made offerings to the Sacred Wheel to accompany prayers. The wheel used in the Offerings

Lodge was an important medicine bundle and tribal symbol for the Southern Arapahos. This wheel had been neglected for some time after reservation settlement, but in the general mood of revitalization that accompanied the Ghost Dance movement, it was restored and refurbished by Charles Campbell and his wife Singing After. Both were members of the Jessie Spread Hands–Little Raven, Jr., cohort, and the wheel had been in the custody of Singing After's father Heap Of Hair before he died. Singing After was trying to advance her ceremonial career, and she became increasingly important in the twentieth century.[122]

The senior lodge women who were leaders often had Offerings Lodge degrees as well by the turn of the century. These accomplishments may have increased their influence. In the 1870s Good Woman, wife of Chief Little Raven, had Dog Lodge status and subsequently attained the priesthood with him. Bitchea, the wife of Chief White Eyed Antelope, was a Buffalo Lodge Woman and joined the Dog Lodge with her husband. They achieved the priesthood. Black Coyote and his wife Singing Woman joined the Lime Crazy Lodge and were trying to acquire degrees in the Offerings Lodge. Coming Up, married to Henry Sage (a grandfather in the Offerings Lodge), had joined the Buffalo Lodge, and she and Henry had become Lime Crazy Lodge members. At the turn of the century, the important Rabbit Lodge women were Shaved Head (Mrs. Two Babies, a chief at Colony in 1894); Mouse (Mrs. Bears Lariat), who had attained the Dog Lodge; and Yellow Woman (Mrs. Black Bull), also a woman of the Dog Lodge. These senior lodge women and the wives of the chiefs worked to help their husbands convince others to accept the civilization strategy and to support the ceremonial organization. They had influence especially with the wives of the junior lodge men and the men who were Offerings Lodge participants. And the wives influenced their husbands.[123]

Women and New Religions

Women as well as men began to question whether the prayer sacrifices of the lodge organization would end their suffering. Their support of the Ghost Dance and peyote revitalization movements assured that these new religions took hold among Arapahos. Women assumed key roles in religious leadership in the 1890s and beyond, playing an important part in the Arapahos' acceptance of new religions.

Sitting Bull understood the place of women in Arapaho ceremonial life. He selected seven men and women as Ghost Dance leaders. He gave shirts to the men and buckskin dresses (painted with stars to represent the spirit world) to the women. Each received a feather as a symbol of authority, and women were authorized to wear the eagle feather in their hair. After the receipt of this right, they presented gifts to Sitting Bull, which were viewed as property sacrifices. Night Striker, the wife of Chief Spotted Wolf's son chief White Snake, had one of these dresses, according to Jess Rowlodge. Sitting Bull probably chose prominent senior lodge women. Missionaries reported that at the Ghost Dances, men painted their wives' faces as well as their own.

Women in general helped shape the Arapaho Ghost Dance religion by their composition of songs and by the many visions they had while in trance. Sitting Bull used an eagle feather when he hypnotized women and induced visions. Women painted symbols of their visions on their dresses. These visions contributed to revitalizing and infusing with new meaning many aspects of Arapaho tradition, including the hand game. One woman composed a song about her vision of her dead child playing with a hummer (similar to a bull roarer), which she sang to induce more visions: "My children, my children, I am about to hum." Women composed many of the Ghost Dance songs. One of the women renowned for her songs was Little Woman, Grant Left Hand's Cheyenne wife, whose first child died soon after birth and whose son died at age four. She and Grant were devastated by his death and, in trance, played with him in the spirit world.

Mooney attributed the Arapaho fervor for the Ghost Dance (in contrast to the Cheyennes' skepticism) to personality—to their penchant for "continually seeing signs and wonders." But women's participation and leadership should be viewed in historical context. The high infant and child mortality throughout the reservation years spurred women, especially young women of child-bearing age, to seek visions of their children in the spirit world. On the 1900 U.S. Census, women living in the Greenfield area (where Left Hand's band settled) were asked how many children they gave birth to and how many of these survived. Grant Left Hand's second wife, Kate, gave birth to three children, none of whom survived. Two of Owl's (Mrs. Row Of Lodges) six children survived. Woman Going In (Mrs. Left Hand) had two daughters who did not live to maturity. The heirship records reveal that at Cantonment, women had from no children to ten children. Four was the average. Half of the children born did not live to maturity. Dropping Lip (Sitting Bull's wife) had eleven children; five lived to maturity.

Married couples often, if not always, shared leadership in the Ghost Dance movement. When Sitting Bull and three other Arapahos went to visit Wovoka in October 1892, Dropping Lip went along on the delegation. When Mooney made his study of the Ghost Dance among the Arapahos in 1890, he visited the camp of Left Hand after returning from a visit to Wovoka. In the tepee Left Hand and other prominent men sat on one side, and Left Hand's wife and the other men's wives were on the other side. Mooney had brought back nuts and other objects from Wovoka's homeland, and these objects had religious associations with Wovoka himself. The men and women each took Mooney's hand and prayed, and the Arapahos divided the nuts among both the men and women. Men and women leaders rehearsed Ghost Dance songs in Black Coyote's large tepee. Jess Rowlodge identified some of the couples who were leaders in the new religion—mostly men of the Medicine Grass cohort and their wives: Cross Killer and her husband, Hail, and Buffalo Fat and her husband, Cut Finger. A younger couple, Cut Nose and his wife Big Heart, also were leaders.[124]

The Ghost Dance hand game had widespread participation during and after the 1890s. The hand game ceremony could be sponsored by a woman making a property sacrifice to accompany a prayer. In addition, sticks were given to several women who then provided food for the ceremony. This gift would be considered a property sacrifice as well. During the hand game ritual, individuals could make gifts of property to others; these gifts also were property sacrifices that accompanied prayers. The missionary Mary Jayne witnessed several hand games and noted the prevalence of women making these gifts. For example, Hide In The Night, wife of the lodge man Bald Head and member of Bichea's cohort, gave a horse to Mrs. Bear Track and her mother (both Cheyenne women). The recipients prayed for Hide In The Night. Warden noted that each side in the hand game had two representative leaders, a man and a woman. The hand game leaders received instructions in visions so that the procedures and regalia varied from leader to leader. Based on these messages from the spirit helpers, they made their hand game bundle, which contained the "buttons," headdresses for participants, and at least three kinds of sticks (pointers, red and black counters, and sticks symbolic of gifts or food). Commonly, symbolism referred to Whirlwind Woman and to prayers for health and abundance. Kroeber observed Ghost Dance hand games in 1899, but while he mentions the participation of women, he does not report women leaders.[125]

Arapaho men organized the Crow Dance during the 1890s. Grant Left Hand first experienced a vision in which he was instructed to organize the dance. Women were key participants in this ceremony. Kroeber observed a Crow Dance in September 1899 on the North Canadian River. The women sat together on the east side of the circular arena. Four women acted as servants, running errands for the participants. The women danced and were painted with the symbols of the ceremony, just as the men were. Property was given away during the dance, and women as well as men contributed it. Women and men sponsored the Crow Dances by making a property sacrifice of food and other items.[126]

The peyote religion took hold among the Arapahos during the 1890s. Kroeber observed two ceremonies in 1899. In each, one woman, the wife of the ceremony's leader, participated. It was her responsibility to prepare the four foods for the participants in a ritually proper manner and to bring in a jar of water at midnight.

She brought in the food at sunrise. Her dress had designs symbolic of prayer for health and prosperity, which is generally the goal of the ritual itself. Warden, a peyote leader, noted that other women could take part, unless they were menstruating. He stressed that the food for the ceremony had to be cooked by "contented" women—that is, women thinking good thoughts. Warden also pointed out that both the man who vowed the ceremony and his wife selected the site for the peyote ritual. Then the wife took her hoe and made lines from west to east and south to north, then scraped out a circle on the ground on which the peyote tepee would sit. This spot was identical to the spot, or "foundation" symbol, made on the ground inside the ceremonial lodges. When the leader's wife brought in the water, he linked her act to the origin of the "sex of humanity," according to Warden (in other words, to the Offerings Lodge symbolism of the first conception). As in the other Arapaho ceremonies, women could sponsor a peyote ceremony, or "meeting," to help relatives in need. In the peyote religion, as in the lodge ceremonies, the wives of the leaders ("peyote chiefs") were ceremonial partners. Junior lodge men from the Medicine Grass cohort and their wives provided leadership— for example, Cut Finger and his wife Buffalo Fat.[127]

An Old Man of Importance: The Old People Sanctify Change

Little Raven made an impression on the camp, especially on the children. Carl Sweezy told Bass that Little Raven went about advising and encouraging, walking slowly, wearing a fine robe as "an old man of importance" does. Little Raven was still called upon to speak with federal officials in times of trouble because they had confidence in him. But his primary role was that of one of the seven priests of the ceremonial order—the seven venerable priests of the sweat lodge, as they were referred to in a Ghost Dance song. He and the other elderly men and women at the head of the ceremonial organization directed the tribal religious ceremonies and had great influence and authority because of the sacrifices they had made to achieve their positions. In general, reservation life buttressed the importance of old people to Arapaho households, and the elderly ceremonial authorities helped the senior lodge men generate support for council decisions.[128]

Kroeber made clear that families relied on old people for prayers. Arapahos particularly respected people who lived to old age because their prayer sacrifices presumably had brought them health and prosperity. Families asked old men and women to preside over and pray at family ceremonies such as first word, naming, marriage, and funeral. Elderly people received gifts of food and perhaps property, which they later redistributed. In their redistribution of the gifts, they provided a model for the good way of life that would bring abundance and health. Honoring these old people with gifts was a property sacrifice that would bring a blessing on the family. Relatives encouraged young people to do kindnesses for old people, for example, to bring them drinks of water. When a young man wanted arrows, the best way was to invite old men to eat while they made arrows for him. When there were disputes, the parties sometimes asked old men to settle the conflict. In their storytelling, old people educated their grandchildren about Arapaho values. Old men and women set themselves apart physically from other Arapahos with paint and clothing. Old women wore their hair loose, while younger women braided theirs. Old men used eagle-wing fans as a means of praying for blessings for all Arapahos. This right and duty had sanction in an origin story.[129]

By the 1880s, the hard times of the 1860s had taken their toll. The census of 1881 shows few old people: nine men age sixty and above and twenty-four women. Actually, thirteen additional women in their fifties also could be considered "old," because postmenopausal status allowed them to be present at all the ceremonies. Most of the old men were renowned for some kind of medicine power. Three were listed as "Doctors." These men had great power from spirit helpers and used their powers to cure; find people, property, or animals; or affect the weather. Sometimes their wives partnered them in this work. Old Sun (a "Medicine Man" on the census) and Little Raven were priests, two of the seven priests who directed all the lodge ceremonies. Another old man was a "Horseracer," that is, a man with power from a spirit helper to make horses swift. Another was a "Pipemaker." He would have had to make sacrifices to learn this craft. Another was a prosperous freighter, and the ninth, a farmer of little means. Except for the wealthy Little Raven, these men's households owned from two to thirteen horses. On the reservation, old people received rations of food every two weeks, and also because of their small number, Arapahos held them in particularly high regard.

In 1892 five old men lived in Canton and one in Greenfield; in 1901, five and four respectively. Kroeber met several old men who were doctors in 1899. Blindy (1842–1909), a Dog Man and a widower, was not active politically. Blind all his life, he was greatly respected because he had committed to memory the history of the Arapahos going back sixty years, and he had been Lodge Maker several times.[130]

Many of the old women also held high status in the ceremonial realm. Sixty percent on the 1881 census were either "Midwives"— which involved a special kind of medicine power—or "Rootdiggers." Rootdiggers were women who knew how to make sacred incenses and rubs for various ceremonies. Only elderly women had this occupation. Two of the women described as rootdiggers actually belonged to the Seven Old Women priesthood: Large Head and Thread Woman. Other old women were "Housekeepers." If married, they shared in their husbands' ceremonial status. A few unmarried ones were apparently poor women without ceremonial authority; they were described as "Woodcarriers," a job usually given to younger women attached to large households. Many women in their fifties had husbands; all but one of the women over age sixty were widowed or separated. They lived in households with their grandchildren, children, or nieces. By 1887 Walking Backward was a widow living in her granddaughter Warrior Woman's camp and caring for a young grandson. Warrior Woman's husband was Wolf Chief, a leader among the warriors, and Walking Backward was one of the old women who supervised the ornamentation of tepees. In 1892 there were eight old women at Canton and five at Greenfield; in 1901, seven and five respectively.[131]

The age-graded lodge organization operated during the 1870s and 1880s probably much as it used to, although Arapahos began to have difficulty perpetuating the priesthood. The last Old Men's Lodge (which prepared men for the priesthood) was vowed in 1874. Those who were inducted sat immovable, fasting for four days and nights. As these old men died, most of their positions went unfilled. Young Man Bear (born in 1828) was in the Old Men's Lodge. Row Of Lodges also belonged, but he died before he could be considered for the priesthood; he injured his hand hauling lumber and died from blood poisoning in 1904. The surviving old men continued to direct ceremonies or serve as ceremonial grandfathers during the inductions of men into the lodges. These old men and the priests attended councils, their presence signaling support for the political work of the senior lodge men, with whom they had reciprocal supportive relationships.[132]

The priesthood positions (the Seven Old Men) could not all be filled. The names of some priests have been recorded: Bird Chief, who died in 1884; Big Robe, who died in 1888 at the age of ninety; Little Raven, who died 15 February 1890; Old Sun, who died about 1890; Crier, who directed the last Dog Lodge about 1894 and died shortly after (he was so feeble at age seventy-two, he had to be carried in a blanket from place to place in the lodge); and Red Woman's father, Red Pipe (listed as a doctor on the 1881 census), who died in 1898 at the age of sixty-nine. Although the last time the Seven Old Men held their ceremony was in 1878, Old Crow and Tall Bear became priests about 1888, and about 1901 old men chose White Eyed Antelope and Mountain. Each of the Seven Old Men had a sacred bag containing a rattle (for singing), buffalo tail, paint, stones (for incense), and other objects used in ceremonies. These men painted with red paint daily. Arapahos were in awe of them. Myrtle Lincoln commented that the priests prayed for rain, and it rained. Jess Rowlodge maintained that the priests cured people with the bundles. Kroeber wrote that in 1899, all seven of the bundles kept by the Seven Old Men still existed. Dorsey noted that by the end of the century, the Old Men's Lodge and Seven Old Men had combined. In their struggle to perpetuate the Arapaho ceremonies, the old priests made adjustments, approving innovations by right of their positions. Warden explained that in the reservation context, priests did not need to be very old but must have offered the appropriate sacrifices and gone through the apprenticeships. These old people succeeded in preventing missionaries from making inroads with Arapaho adults.[133]

In Kroeber's discussion of the age-graded lodge ceremonies, "old men" sat in one place in the lodges and "old women" in another. Old women as well as men sang during the ceremonies. These old people probably included or actually were the old men priests, their wives, and the old women priests, but Kroeber is not clear on this point. The wives of Little Raven (Good Woman, or Mrs. Little Raven) and Old Sun (Hairy, or Mrs. Old Sun) outlived both and participated in the direction of ceremonies. Mrs. Old Sun became the custodian of the "straight pipe" used in the Offerings Lodge and the stones that represented the Flat Pipe, the tribe's medicine bundle kept by the Northern Arapahos. She also qualified as a Peacemaker. Big Robe's wife Long Claws died in 1901, and before she died, she tried to pass on the knowledge of the priesthood to her sister and son, but this did not count as a succession.[134]

Kroeber names the Seven Old Women who were apparently alive in 1870: Backward (Little Raven's mother), River Woman, Big or Large Head, Thread Woman 1, Thread Woman 2, Sorelegs, and Flying Woman. Backward transferred her bundle to Cedar Woman, who spoke with Kroeber in 1900. When the bag was transferred, Cedar Woman provided food, clothing, and horses that the older woman subsequently redistributed. Cedar Woman fasted for four days. After this body and property sacrifice, she received instruction. These old women conducted ceremonies during which tepee covers, buffalo robes, and cradles were decorated. Their bags contained leaves and roots for incense and rubs or spittle, stones used for burning incense, paint, and implements of bone for marking and sewing. Their face paint symbolized creation. These bags were the equivalent of the men's seven bags. The women permitted certain adaptations—shredded corn shucks and beads for quills, and canvas for buffalo-hide tepees.

Cedar Woman described to Kroeber a ceremony used to make a robe. Yellow Woman (Mrs. Black Bull) vowed to make a robe for Bird In Tree. She took her dressed buffalo hide to Cedar Woman with a property sacrifice. The other six old women came and ate some of the food; then it was distributed among the people. Incense and whipping sticks were used to animate the hide with the life force. Cedar Woman spit root medicine on the marking bones and incensed or smudged it. She then directed and supervised Yellow Woman, who marked lines (representing paths) on the robe that were to be embroidered with porcupine quills. Yellow Woman used dog root in her mouth to wet the bone with saliva. Cedar Woman applied medicine to her hands with spittle and gave her the red, yellow, white, and black quills (which represented creation). It took a month to complete the robe. When it was finished, Yellow Woman again feasted the old women, and the robe was set up to resemble a buffalo, smudged, and touched to animate it with the life force (to protect Bird In Tree). The recipient and robe were smudged, and Bird In Tree gave Yellow Woman his best horse.[135]

Arapahos had a similar ceremony when tepee or tent ornaments were made. Apparently, as time passed, all seven women did not have to be present for these ceremonies; one could supervise. Kroeber witnessed a ceremony to ornament a canvas tent. A middle-aged woman brought a piece of skin with a large beaded circular tepee ornament and four smaller ones on it, cow tails, and quilled pendants with hoops on the end. The woman probably obtained the ornaments from a relative and needed ritual sanction to attach them to her tent. Cedar Woman presided over the ceremony; one other of the "Seven" came, as did other old women. Men were normally excluded, but Kroeber's presence was tolerated. Cedar Woman took medicine from her sacred bag and chewed it, put the substance on the woman's hands, head, and chest (heart), and into her mouth. The food, brought by the owner of the tent, was offered to the directors and to the tent poles (to their spiritual essence), then eaten by the old women. The remaining food was distributed to the people. Cedar Woman made an incense and prayed for the tent occupants. The tent cover was brought in and "animated." Cedar Woman then supervised the sewing of the ornaments on the tent cover. Finally, the tent owner took the completed cover and tied it to her tent frame.[136]

Walking Backward (Backward's daughter and Little Raven's sister, who lived from 1821–1898) directed a tepee ceremony, according to Jess Rowlodge. His mother, Owl (Walking Backward's brother's daughter), was in the group of five or six women who worked on Mixed Hair's ceremonial tepee. He killed a steer and gave them a feast. Rowlodge explained that Walking Backward had been on the warpath and achieved a "coup." She had to hit the tepee and pray—just as she overcame the enemy, her ritual act would overcome any defect in or trouble for the tepee and its occupants. It is clear that after buffalo hunting was no longer possible, the women's ceremonies that protected the family continued, albeit focused on canvas tents and reservation life, rather than buffalo-hide tepees and the dangers of the hunt and war. Annie Pedro identified Big Face, married to the doctor and lodge man Black Bear, as qualified to work on a tepee. She was Chief Powderface's sister. Annie said that people had to be quiet when these women worked.[137]

Women also made cradles under the supervision of the Seven. One or more, joined by other old women, would supervise the work of the woman making the cradle and would smudge it. The cradle maker or the relative sponsoring the ceremony provided a property sacrifice. The old women in the tepee or tent where the work was being done ate the food brought by the sponsor and took some home to redistribute. The old women said prayers for the child to have a long life. As time passed, Arapahos transferred some cradles from relative to relative. A ceremony may have been held to bless the new cradle and pray for the child. Old women who had been present at ceremonies directed by the Seven could have presided. There is no record of whether the Seven transferred their bundles to younger women, other than the case of Back-ward's transfer to Cedar Woman.[138]

The Offerings Lodge had positions of authority, for both old men and old women. Men, who would have been referred to as "old" even though they might have been in their fifties, earned the authority to direct this lodge through a series of sacrifices. Dorsey noted that these old men who could direct the Offerings Lodge were Spotted Bear, born in 1841, Black Horse, born in 1847, and Hawkan (Crazy), born in 1851. Hawkan directed the Offerings Lodge in 1901 and 1902. The female director in 1901 and 1902 was old lady Lump Forehead, born about 1816. She was the widow or divorced wife of Bad Man, who, according to the census of 1881, was a medicine man. Crippled had the key position of Peace-maker in the Offerings Lodge. Born in 1860, she was not chrono-logically old, but the "Seven Old Men" had selected her "long ago" for the Peacemaker position, Dorsey reported. She presided over the Tomahawk, Spear, Lime Crazy, and Dog lodges as Peacemaker as well. Crippled was a relative in-law of Chief Powderface. She was apparently divorced or widowed in 1881 but married to Ute by 1887. In the early reservation years, people made body sacrifices (fasting and, until the late 1880s, piercing the skin) to prevent or relieve a relative's suffering by taking the "hard knocks" in his or her own body, according to Jess Rowlodge. The vows addressed problems of health, lack of food, and threats from federal supervi-sion and settler aggression, from "bad people" in Warden's terms.[139]

Although very few old people became peyotists in the 1890s, the Ghost Dance movement drew in old people as well as young. Mooney wrote that Tall Bear, high in the ceremonial hierarchy, was a believer. Tall Bear apparently feared the possibility of mistakes in the lodge ceremonies, because he refused to assume his full duties as priest at the turn of the century, stating that he thought he and his family would avoid misfortunes if he retired. Jess Rowlodge stated that his mother, Owl, never lost her faith in the Ghost Dance prophecy. In fact, she kept the gifts she bought for her dead children in her trunk until the end of her life, expecting to be able to give the children the presents. Arapahos had certain regalia specifically for old men in the Ghost Dance hand game. Missionary Mary Jayne reported that in the hand game, old men had prominent roles in prayer. Old men and women also participated in the Crow Dance. Kroeber noted that old women would stand and "cry" (pray) at three poles with cloth offerings in the dance arena. Old women frequently received the property sacrifices made during the ceremony. Old people made some contribution to the success of revitalization movements by accepting them to one degree or another.[140]

On the reservation in the 1870s through the 1890s, life changed as Arapahos adjusted to their circumstances. They accepted a civilization strategy that encouraged an agricultural lifestyle, including commercial agriculture, but on their own terms, relying on communal work patterns and sharing. In this way, they maneuvered to protect their interests in relation to those of the more numerous Cheyennes and tried to make a place for themselves within the territorial economy. Although Arapaho ritual authorities redesigned the lodge system to better reflect their new circumstances, revitalization movements emerged that challenged not only the efforts of Americans to undermine Arapaho social institutions, but the Arapaho age-graded ceremonial organization as well. Arapahos provided the leadership for the Ghost Dance movement in Oklahoma. This new religion attempted to revive the prereservation world. Arapahos also developed their own version of the peyote religion, the "Arapaho way," which helped individuals cope with the world as it was.

What role did age and gender play in the way Arapahos shaped reservation life? As we have seen, the civilization strategy was developed and implemented by the cohorts of Little Raven and Walking Backward and Left Hand and Owl, people who arrived on the reservation with more horses than the younger cohorts, and people who generally had higher positions in the lodge organization. The primary leadership—the band heads and chiefs, and their wives—had senior lodge positions (Lime Crazy and Dog lodge status) and came from the most prosperous families.

Leadership for the revitalization movements came from the Medicine Grass and Bichea cohort, people whose path to prosperity and senior lodge status was blocked by reservation conditions. Married couples took on the leadership of these movements. Why did these partnerships continue to play such an important role in social change? The life careers of men and women were linked. They needed each other to support their households, mobilize political consensus and action, and pursue religious goals. Moreover, Americanization did not offer a practical solution to the difficulties of reservation life. Arapahos, including those who spent months or years in schools, realized that American ideas about age and gender would not help them meet the challenges they faced in Oklahoma, and that, in reality, they found rewards (to one degree or another) in conforming to Arapaho values. In economic, political, and religious activity, men and women continued to earn respect and prestige from kinship and marital reciprocities, respect and prestige denied them by agency-backed opportunities.

By the turn of the century, Arapahos had begun selling their allotted lands in conjunction with new federal policies ostensibly designed to assimilate Indians into mainstream America. How were the lives of the members of the Medicine Grass, Bichea, Jessie Spread Hands, and Little Raven, Jr., cohorts affected by these changes? The younger cohort of Jess Rowlodge and Myrtle Lincoln reached maturity during these years. How did they cope with the new conditions?

CHAPTER 3

LIKE A REED

Coping with a Cash Economy, 1902–1936

In November 1905, James Blindy, the son-in-law of Sitting Bull and son of Blindy, a Dog Man, was hunting on his allotment in the Canton area when he came across his settler neighbor, a frequent trespasser who took game and wood from Blindy's place. Blindy's complaints to the agency had produced no remedy. When he confronted his neighbor on that fall day, a gun battle ensued, and both men were killed. Why was James Blindy driven to violence, and why did his neighbor feel free to trespass time and again, ignoring Blindy's protests?[1]

From the turn of the century well into the 1920s, most Arapahos spent little time on their home places, preferring to pack up their belongings in wagon caravans and move to large winter or ceremonial camps nestled in timber along the streams. Some Arapaho extended families might live part of the year in wall tents or small frame houses, but they often leased their houses to settlers and lived in tents or tepees elsewhere. They tended small gardens of vegetables and corn patches when they stayed at home. The clusters of allotments were surrounded by the homes of settler families who had moved onto the reservation after 1892 to try to open farms or establish small towns, all of which depended on Arapahos and Cheyennes in one way or another. Perhaps if James Blindy had not tried to make a living on his allotment, he could have avoided confrontation. In any case, he could not count on help from the agency to protect his property.[2]

The agency for the Arapahos and Cheyennes was subdivided at Darlington, Cantonment, and Seger. Darlington was four miles northwest of El Reno, a town with a population of 7,000 in 1912. The subagency had forty buildings on twenty-six acres, as well as two government boarding schools. The Arapaho school complex had twenty-two buildings, and the water was piped in, so the sanitation had improved over past years. The Cheyenne school complex had twelve buildings. Most of the Arapaho allotments in this agency surrounded the town of Geary, opened in 1899, and two smaller towns, Bridgeport and Greenfield. Geary, served by the railroad, had a population of over 2,000 in 1902. Businesses that served the several thousand settlers and the Indians included ten groceries, four hardware stores, four lumber yards, seven saloons, three pool rooms, four feed stores, three blacksmith shops, five restaurants, three meat markets, a bottling works, two furniture stores, two cotton gins, four hotels, a flour mill, four grain elevators, two brick yards, two banks, six lawyers, seven doctors, and two newspapers. The agency at Darlington supervised 506 Arapahos in 1906, as well as the more numerous Cheyennes there. In 1920, the Darlington Arapahos numbered 496.[3]

The Cantonment agency was smaller: a few buildings, a Mennonite mission and school (which became a government boarding school), and a government trader. The town of Canton, three miles from the agency, was established in 1905 on a deceased Indian's allotment. The population in 1912 was 800. The streets had wide, covered walkways with seats in front of the stores. Older Indians sat on the benches while younger ones played billiards or ate ice cream in the stores. The Indians were great patrons of the Canton businesses: two banks, two hardware stores, two general stores, two lumber yards, two butchers, a bakery, two saloons, two grain elevators, two hotels, two restaurants, an opera house, a furniture store, a pool hall, a cotton gin, a machine shop, two stables, and one newspaper. In 1906, 242 Arapahos lived in the area administered by the Cantonment agency; in 1920, 210.[4]

Despite the 1890 agreement that promised allotments would remain in trust status for twenty-five years, Congress passed legislation in 1902 that allowed for the sale of allotments by heirs of the deceased owners. In the 1906 Burke Act, Congress permitted "competent" Indians, with the secretary of the interior's permission, to get a fee patent on their allotments. A patent in fee made the land alienable—that is, the owner could sell it and was liable for tax on it. Individuals also were allowed to apply for their pro rata share of the tribal fund from the sale of surplus land in 1892. In 1907 Congress passed legislation that allowed "noncompetent" Indians to obtain permission to sell land. In this way, Arapaho and Cheyenne resources were gradually depleted as lands were sold. By 1928 Arapahos had sold 63 percent of their land; by 1939, 68 percent.

The federal government deposited the money from the leasing and sale of allotments and the pro rata payment in what was called an Individual Indian Money (IIM) account, which was controlled by the agency superintendent. Arapaho individuals' access to this money thereby was restricted to small amounts or to purchases approved by the superintendent. Although the federal government as trustee had the responsibility for protecting the interests of their "wards," agency officials sometimes colluded with speculators and favored the interests of the settlers so that Cheyennes and Arapahos did not receive market value for their land.

With neither adequate income to buy the necessities of life nor enough land to raise livestock, Arapaho families experienced a poverty so desperate that in addition to selling wood and working for wages when they could, they mortgaged their agricultural equipment and stock to get credit to buy groceries. James Blindy needed all the wood and all the game on his land to support his wife, Lydia, and their three children. Many settlers, like his troublesome neighbor, viewed the Arapahos and Cheyennes as legitimate prey whose well-being was ignored by their federal trustee.[5]

These new conditions—individual ownership of land, the reliance on a money economy, and the intensification of federal surveillance and control—had profound effects on Arapaho society. This chapter asks how Arapaho life changed and what roles Arapahos played in those changes. I examine how federal policy affected age categories and cohorts, as well as women and men, and argue that the interplay between age and gender shaped how Arapahos created new kinds of social arrangements and rituals through which they adapted.

College Caps: Children Becoming Modern

In the Arapaho camp at the Lime Crazy ceremony in 1906, the children played around their families' tepees, or rode horses, or swam in the stream. They would have been taught to show special respect and deference to the people in the ceremony. Cleaver Warden made note of an incident there that surely was atypical. After the ceremonial activity ended and people retired to their camps at the end of the day, a group of unsupervised children went into the ceremonial tepee and disturbed the ritual objects. Subsequently, a fierce wind storm came and put the camp into some consternation because this was a sign that they were not behaving properly toward supernatural power. The priests then felt that they had to formally order all children to stay away from the lodge. These children, like others born in the twentieth century, may have had difficulty seeing their parents and grandparents as role models, given conditions in their communities.[6]

Despite this incident, adults were clearly trying to inculcate the values they had learned as children. Elderly people named children born in the late 1890s and in the early twentieth century, although it might be at home without a public feast. The name inspired the child to aspire to be worthy of it. Arnold Woolworth (in Little Raven, Jr.'s cohort) feasted elderly people to name his oldest four children born between 1898 and 1907. Children were not whipped but received lectures on proper conduct and praise for good behavior, according to Arnold's daughter Rose. Helen Spotted Wolf (born in 1888) told Inez Hilger that she was never hit but was encouraged to live up to her father's expectations and lectured by old people.[7]

Even after children entered the Arapaho boarding school at Darlington or the Cantonment boarding school, their families had influence. In late August, Arapahos camped at these schools for several days. They came to the schools on holidays to visit the children. Most students went home to their families during summer break and sometimes on weekends or holidays. There, the children's families might sponsor peyote or other ceremonies for the children's health and well-being. In 1915 Amos Two Babies's parents agreed to send him to the government school at Seger Agency. They purchased a beef and gave a feast for their eight-year-old son so that he would have supernatural assistance in the difficult school environment. Myrtle Lincoln's mother-in-law Red Feather tried to introduce Myrtle's oldest child to Arapaho ceremonies, dressing her in a dance outfit and urging her to participate. Annie Pedro's father's sister gave Annie's son a beaded cradle. Mothers still celebrated sons' first success in hunting birds or small game. Myrtle Lincoln observed that her sons, contemporaries of Arnold Woolworth's children, hunted rabbits with bows and arrows. According to Jess Rowlodge, most parents did not have their children's ears pierced ceremonially. But Arnold Woolworth paid an old warrior, who had pierced an enemy, to charge his daughter and touch her with a stick; later her ears were pierced at home. Children's graves often had toy wagons on them, so that the child could travel in the afterworld; in earlier times, the parents shot a pony on top of the grave. Children had new games, clothing, and toys, but still their lives could be shaped by the customs of their parents.[8]

By the twentieth century, these reservation boarding schools had the capacity to enroll all the school-age children healthy enough to stand the experience. Unsanitary conditions and overcrowding still threatened the children's health. For example, in 1905 two children died at the Arapaho school, and in 1908, two died at Cantonment. In 1909, out of 150 Arapaho and Cheyenne students at the newly established Cheyenne-Arapaho school (Concho boarding school) at the agency, 19 were in the hospital in September, 40 in October, and 35 in November.[9]

William Sutton, born in 1896, entered Cantonment school at the age of eight. He described his experiences there as "under military supervision." The children rose at five, drilled in formation, then ate breakfast and went to work or class by six. They attended class for half a day and worked at various jobs the remainder of the day. He recalled that they had "no privileges" and that punishments usually involved hard labor, for example, sawing wood for hours on end. Boys were instructed in farm work and girls in domestic chores (now referred to as "domestic science"). Girls learned to cook American style: cake and pudding, for example. One little girl at Concho school wrote in April 1911 that she liked to work on the kitchen detail because "we don't get hungry there because there is something to eat all the time." The older girls made the dresses for all the girls. Boys milked cows and helped on the school farm. All the children worked in the garden and planted flowers and trees. They received seven cents an hour for at least some of their effort. At Cantonment school in the 1920s, some of the Arapaho children were Harry Bates's grandson Melvin Bates and daughter Sophie Bates, Myrtle Lincoln's son Hannibal Howling Buffalo (Lincoln), James Scabby Horse's grandson Loren, and Dave Meat's daughter Pauline Meat. Eleven-year-old Melvin and Hannibal worked in the dairy. Nine-year-old Loren Scabby- horse did chores, as did eight-year-old Sophie and Pauline. At Concho, the school offered grades one through six, and at Canton- ment, one through four.[10]

Concho school was being modernized by the second decade of the twentieth century, with new courses and more entertainments for the children. The school program became more in line with public school programs. The children's classes had frequent par- ties, where they played games and had ice cream, cookies, and lemonade. The school acquired playground apparatus and built a swimming pool. The children could have music lessons, watch movies, or join the sketching club or debating society. The senior class selected a class flower and motto, and each class had a class pin. The fifth grade boys sent away for "college caps," caps that had the name of the school on them. Girls competed with other reservation schools and town schools in basketball, and boys competed in baseball. Football and track also attracted the boys.[11]

When they first entered school, Arapaho children probably felt that they were still under the watchful eye of the Arapaho community. Little children were advised and helped by their older relatives at the school. Groups of boys went on rabbit hunts, probably under the guidance of the older students. These older children translated English and might even choose an English name for a child. But the Arapaho school was closed and combined with the Cheyenne school in 1908. A few years later, both the schools at Concho and Cantonment began to admit children and youths from other tribes, including Cherokee, Ponca, and Shawnee. Arapaho children probably spoke English to a greater extent than before, and they became a minority among strangers, whereas once they were among friends and relatives.[12]

In the 1920s the Bureau (formerly the Office) of Indian Affairs (BIA) began pressing Indian parents to put their children in public schools. Until then very few Arapahos went to public schools—primarily some of the children from the Poisal and Keith families. In 1920 the Cantonment school had 97 students and 43 Cheyenne and Arapaho children were in the public schools. In 1922, 55 children enrolled at Cantonment school and 75 in public schools. In 1921 the Concho school had 142 students; 69 children were in public schools. In 1922, 176 children were enrolled at Concho, and 75 in public schools. The federal government closed the school at Cantonment in 1927. In 1923, Concho, the only reservation boarding school, had 189 students, and 307 Cheyennes and Arapahos reportedly were enrolled in public schools. Parents and tribal leaders protested the placement of children in public schools, where they were ridiculed and discriminated against and where they were a minority among non-Indians. Given the fact that the reservation boarding schools did not offer education beyond the sixth grade, genuine opportunity for youths to obtain advanced education or training rested with off-reservation schools, such as Chilocco and Haskell.[13]

The children born in the first third of the twentieth century experienced competing influences to a far greater extent than did the older cohorts. Though further discussion is beyond the scope of this book, these children's experiences shaped the post-1940s world of the Arapahos.

I Heard a Voice: Landless Arapaho Youths

Arapahos born in the 1880s had received allotments. Many had attended off-reservation boarding schools for a year or two after graduation from Concho school. They reached their thirties in the 1920s, but Arapahos still regarded the men as somewhat less than "mature" because, for the most part, they did not advance beyond the boys' lodges and could not support their families without help from their elders. Arapahos born after 1892 had even less hope of making a living from farming because they had not received allotments. Many went to Haskell or Chilocco to learn a trade, and like the other members of the Jess Rowlodge–Myrtle Lincoln cohort, struggled to mature on Arapaho terms.

Getting Along with One's Elders

During the early twentieth century, adults lectured young people about character issues, how to establish a good reputation in the community. These youths, who had been children in the late 1880s and 1890s, had already absorbed Arapaho values, and older Arapahos reinforced these values during the teen years. Jess Rowlodge (born in 1884) recalled how his father, Row Of Lodges (actually his attentive stepfather), talked to him every evening—he must support himself, do his own thinking, be patient and kind, and show respect to elderly people. Once as a teenager, Jess had let a girl ride on the back of his horse. His parents were very upset at how he risked his reputation by being with an unsupervised girl. He felt chastened by the experience. Myrtle Lincoln (born in 1888) told how her uncle Coal Of Fire lectured her—be hospitable, ignore slights, learn to work well by observing how others cooked, sewed, washed and cleaned house. This behavior would help her make a good marriage. Adults stressed the importance of respect relations between brother and sister, according to Grace Sagebark (born in 1881), and Grace added that her mother taught her to take gifts of food, clothing, and moccasins she made to her relatives. Bird White Bear (Red Woman's son, born in 1888) told Hilger that boys experienced pressure to join the Foxes and Stars. In fact, Jess Rowlodge joined the Foxes, then the Stars shortly after the turn of the century.[14]

Parents still sponsored rituals for their teenage children, occasions when young people experienced reinforcement of Arapaho values of respect and generosity between and within families. In 1924 Ben and Helen Spotted Wolf gave a feast for their niece, an orphan who lived with them, upon her successful return from three years at Chilocco. Indian custom marriage continued to be an important ritual. In 1914, when Medicine Grass's daughter Lucy (born in 1895) married Jess's brother Henry Rowlodge (born in 1879), Henry gave her relatives twenty-six horses, and her family returned the same. Henry chose her because she was a "good woman" and a "good housekeeper." When Annie Pedro (born in 1881) married John Pedro (born in 1878), their marriage was arranged by both families, as was the case with Grace Powderface's marriage to Nelson Sagebark (born in 1879). Their families exchanged gifts. Grace was still at Haskell when the marriage was arranged, and Nelson wrote to her there. Myrtle Lincoln's uncle chose her husband Howard Lincoln (born in 1881) and "put up a tent" for them, meaning there was gift exchange (but not as lavish as exchanges between more prominent families). Jess Rowlodge apparently was noticed by Carrie Lumpmouth when they were in school. She sent a friend to arrange a meeting, but apparently this did not happen. Instead, Jess explained, her brothers "picked" her as a wife for him because several of his "sisters" had married Lumpmouth boys. After he and Carrie left school, they married Indian custom with the families feasting each other and exchanging presents.[15]

Youths' work was important in the camp and at school. Myrtle Lincoln noted that fathers took their sons with them to hunt, fish, and chop wood. William Sutton, born in 1896 and cared for by his grandmother Red Face after his mother died, took care of his grandmother's horses and helped her move camp. After Myrtle's grandmother Pumpkin died, her uncle Coal Of Fire (who had been married to Pumpkin's brother Arrow's daughter) brought her to his camp, where his wife Ugly Woman (the widow of one of Pumpkin's sons) made her work sewing, beading, cooking, babysitting, and going for wood and water. Grace Powderface incorporated what she learned at school into her work at her mother's camp: she washed dishes, made bread, and sewed garments. Myrtle learned to cook American style at school—frying food and baking with flour.[16]

The schools at Concho and Cantonment could not have operated without the students' labor, and the students received some money for their efforts. Boys farmed, tended stock, and worked as teamsters hauling supplies and delivering spring water to the town of El Reno (for which the school was paid). Ralph Stanion, school superintendent in 1906, reported that girls had to take care of the Darlington school's hennery, and they tended their own garden. Myrtle Lincoln found Cantonment school a refuge from her aunt Ugly Woman. She had more time for recreation, and she earned money assisting the girls' matron. These older students might stay several years in the fourth grade at Cantonment or the sixth at Concho, working for the school. Realizing that they could not hope to support themselves by farming, many decided to attend off-reservation schools. Myrtle had wanted to go to Chilocco but could not get permission.[17]

Disillusionment

The reservation schools prepared boys and girls for farm life, but Arapahos did not have sufficient land or equipment for everyone to support themselves by farming. This is why young people hoped and expected to learn trades at Haskell, Chilocco, and Phoenix Indian School. Girls, even those such as Lucy Medicine

Grass, who went to Chilocco, could obtain work only as domestics or as school employees doing domestic work. Boys hoped for more lucrative positions, but very few obtained agency jobs. William Sutton went to Chilocco for two years, where he learned about boiler maintenance and baking bread, difficult work there and useless once he returned to Canton.[18]

Jess Rowlodge graduated from Concho, then decided to go to Haskell. This happened as the result of a vision. Older men invited him to a peyote meeting in 1904, where they prayed for him because he was grieving for his deceased father. He explained what happened during the ceremony: "I was sitting quietly, you know. . . . And I heard a voice right over my head. It talked Indian. It said, 'You stay with this [peyote] religion. You're a young man. You got a chance to go to school yet. And if you carry this out, it's going to be good for you.'" Jess attended Haskell from 1904 to 1910, where he completed the commercial course, competed in sports, played in the band, and reportedly enjoyed the experience. At Haskell Jess studied Arapaho history and treaties. When he returned, he passed the civil service exam and was hired at Seger Agency. Jess was an exception. Even Frank Shields, who had attended public school, managed to secure only a janitorial position. Some boys, unable to prosper as farmers, continued to pursue sports, where they excelled. Some of the Canton Arapahos organized a men's team (the Arapaho Indian Basketball Team, including Paul Bates and Robert Sankey) that played against town teams. But generally, members of the Jess Rowlodge–Myrtle Lincoln cohort experienced great frustration as they aged.[19]

The youths realized that school officials exploited them and that they faced discrimination in the wider society. Oftentimes, they resisted this treatment. The Arapaho school required some male students to work at the school all summer. The youths and their parents resented these work details, for which boys received little or no pay. In 1904 Bird White Bear (Red Woman's son) ran away to avoid serving his detail. Another group of youths, who were sent to Missouri to work on farms in 1924, quit and returned in disgust, claiming that their employers treated them like inferiors.[20]

Throughout this first part of the twentieth century, these young people resented that they could not get access to their funds. The interest money from the 1892 land cession went to minors' parents or guardians (sometimes school superintendents) until an allottee was eighteen. Lease money was not accessible until the age of twenty-one. William Sutton complained about Chilocco, where he felt he was not "treated like a human." He had to get the superintendent's permission to spend any of the money in his account. Eventually, he ran away. Myrtle Lincoln felt that her aunt Ugly Woman was more interested in collecting her money than in helping her. When she was at Cantonment school, her aunt tried to take her home. She arranged with the superintendent to give her aunt some of the money from the sale of her mother's allotment. After that, Ugly Woman did not "bother me again," Myrtle said.[21]

The agency superintendents felt frustration over the attitude of youths, especially those who returned from off-reservation boarding schools. Most boys followed in their father's footsteps. Girls returned to family camps, where "old time Indians" made sure they "fell back" into Indian practices. They faced ridicule and ostracism if they did not, according to Superintendent W. W. Scott. Baptist missionaries wrote that Mrs. Left Hand made it her duty to make fun of the girls who associated with the missionary women. Despite the lack of employment opportunities for men trained as mechanics and bakers, agency officials blamed the students themselves for their lack of employment. But these youths had few options, other than to attach themselves to relatives with land and income.[22]

The members of the Jess Rowlodge and Myrtle Lincoln cohort were not convinced that they could follow the example of older cohorts and have satisfying life careers. Boys questioned membership in the ceremonial organization. Bird White Bear's family tried to steer him into the Clubboard Lodge (a name for the Tomahawk Lodge commonly used in this century), which was the lodge that marked a man's maturity. He, however, decided not to enter this lodge, he told Fred Eggan. He followed the peyote religion and felt that peyote ritual—for example, walking around the altar in the tepee—might result in the violation of lodge rules, such as the prohibition against walking in front of ceremonial grandfathers.[23]

Jess Rowlodge was groomed by his family for a career in the lodge organization. In fact, he was selected as one of two boy messengers for the Clubboard Men in 1903. He, like Bird, decided against advancing beyond the Stars. Jess wanted to work on treaty matters and represent the tribe in dealings with the federal government. He felt that he could not do this if bound not to disagree with higher-ranking ceremonial men. Both Bird (the grandson of Old Sun and Mrs. Old Sun) and Jess (the grandson of Little Raven) believed that as peyote men, they could still live up to Arapaho ideals. Mennonite missionary John A. Funk noted that many young "educated" Arapahos "disregarded" their parents' religion and took up peyote ritual. Peyotism became an alternative way to seek supernatural help and a way to achieve leadership positions (in the peyote lodge) with less extensive obligations and expense. Jess, for example, was invited to be the Fire Man, despite limited experience in peyote meetings.[24]

Members of the Jess Rowlodge–Myrtle Lincoln cohort faced discrimination because of federal policies related to education and gender. After 1906, educated men were encouraged to sell part or all of their allotments to acquire money to purchase farming equipment to become better farmers. Of course, virtually all members of Jess Rowlodge's cohort had attended at least reservation schools. Women, regarded by federal officials as dependents who should be supported by their husbands, generally could keep their allotments and lease part or all of their land. The agency superintendents intended that husbands would farm (with proper equipment) their and their wife's land. For example, the superintendent encouraged Jess Rowlodge, regarded as well educated, to give up the trust status of his land. After his land fell into fee patent status, he sold eighty acres in 1916 and the remaining eighty acres in 1917. He owned inherited land, which he also sold in 1916. His wife was born too late to receive an allotment, so they lived in her family's camp. The BIA considered the relinquishment of trust status a necessary step to integration into the wider American society.[25]

In 1917 the BIA intensified the pressure on educated men to attain fee patents on their allotments, which allowed taxation of the land and resulted in its loss. By the time the members of the Jess Rowlodge–Myrtle Lincoln cohort reached their thirties, they were experiencing extreme poverty, whether or not they had been allotted in 1892. Superintendent Scott characterized their struggles as a failure of character—they "would not settle down to serious effort" when they were in their twenties and thirties. Cohort members' disillusionment with federal policy grew, and they became increasingly unconvinced that participation in the lodge organization would help them.[26]

Regardless of Arapaho views of what "maturity" meant, the BIA considered the people in the Jess Rowlodge and Myrtle Lincoln cohort to be adults. Federal agents used land policy ostensibly to make this group farm more intensively, but in actuality, that policy worked to their disadvantage economically and politically. Below, I contrast the allottees born between 1881 and 1892 with the non-allottees–that is, the individuals born between 1893 and about 1900. In the Canton area twelve men born between 1881 and 1892 lived to maturity. Two, Dave Meat and Wilbur Tabor, both married to Canton women, can be described as very successful by agency standards. Eight others had a struggle to fulfill family and community responsibilities and eke out a living by farming, working for wages, and getting lease money.

Noncompetents and Competents, Allottees and Nonallottees

Dave Meat (1885–1953), the son of Big Head 2 and Crossing Woman 1 (who died when Dave was eight), married Kate (1885–1959), Rabbit Run's daughter, in 1903. Dave went to the Mennonite Mission School and Cantonment school for about five years. Kate went for four. In 1911 he was farming his father's allotment, very success-fully according to agency reports. Declared "competent," he sold his allotment, but as the only surviving child of his parents, he managed to hold onto enough acreage through heirship to be des-cribed as a successful farmer in 1922 and 1930. Kate was declared "noncompetent" and retained her 160 acres, which provided the family with lease income as well as farm land. In a 1922 household survey, the family had a three-room house, barn, chicken house for twenty-five chickens, seven cows, five horses, and a car. They were not only prosperous by local standards, but prominent participants and donors in ceremonial life. Dave was a peyotist, and he served on committees that sponsored dances and gatherings and that built a community hall. He and Kate sponsored feasts and contributed gifts to help relatives. They participated in reciprocal exchanges; for example, Kate received a horse at a dance in Geary in 1922 and gave a cow to a woman in Geary in 1923.

Wilbur Tabor (or Washing Hands; 1883–1964) was the adopted son of Old Man and the son of Crossing Woman 2, who died when he was small. He attended the Arapaho school as a child. As a young man he married a young woman from Geary who was particularly wealthy in inherited land. The two lived in the Canton area, where they were described as devoted to each other. When she became ill, he was at her side constantly, until after a seven-week illness, she died. He sold his land but inherited her property. In 1911 he married Black Rock, or Lydia Blindy (1884–1935), the widowed daughter of Sitting Bull. Lydia had attended the Cantonment school for about six years and joined the Mennonite Church in 1904. They lived on his first wife's place, where he was described in agency records as a prosperous farmer who grew crops for sale. Lydia (like many other Arapaho women) raised chickens. In 1922 the family lived on Wilbur's father's allotment. They had a four-room house and a second house for Old Man, an orchard, eight horses, twenty-four chickens, a tractor, and a car. Lydia was declared noncompetent and retained her land. This family also participated generously in community activities, gift giving, and feasting. Wilbur was a peyotist and served on the community hall building committee. Both he and Dave Meat were excellent farmers but also lucky in that, even though they were "competents" who lost their allotments, they were the only surviving children of parents, and they inherited large parcels of land.

Most of the other eight young men with allotments struggled to support their families, farming a little, collecting small amounts of lease money, and working for wages by the day when able. Joel Smoker (1884–1943) is one such individual. The son of doctors Big Head 1 and Striking Night, he went to the mission school five years and one year at Cantonment, then married Coming On Horseback's unallotted daughter Lizzie, who died in 1913. He farmed on a relative's allotment, worked for others, and leased land. He was declared competent in 1917 and sold eighty acres of his allotment, then leased the remainder. He twice remarried, both times to women from Geary, and by 1922 his family was living in a tent on his sister's allotment, and he owned only two horses. By 1930, he was unable to work and had a very small lease income. But he was respected by the Arapaho community. When he was able, he sponsored feasts and peyote meetings and donated to community projects, such as the construction of the community hall. He was selected by the men to supervise a rabbit hunt in 1923. All eight of these men tried to live up to Arapaho ideals of generosity, although they had very limited means. Half had household IIM income in the bottom 25 percent in 1922.

Women, who were generally declared "noncompetent," usually held on to their allotted land. To relieve their family's poverty, a few requested a fee patent in 1917, often for only part of their allotment. Among the eight Canton women to reach maturity, Singing (Bessie Bighead; 1886–1935) managed to prosper by Arapaho standards, while Medicine Woman struggled. Singing was the sister of Joel Smoker and Hannibal Bighead. Both her parents were respected ceremonial people, and her mother's brothers included ceremonial men Heap Of Crows and Lime. Singing attended the Mennonite and Cantonment schools for ten years, then in 1903 married the much older Bad Man (from Medicine Grass's cohort), who died in 1914. After a brief second marriage, in 1917 she married Plenty Bears, an older Northern Arapaho who settled in Canton. He was a member of the lodge organization and became custodian of the Sacred Wheel used in the Offerings Lodge. Classified noncompetent, she had 160 acres, as well as the allotment she had inherited from her first husband. She owned a house and had a relatively large income from leases. Singing donated to community projects in addition to performing ceremonial duties. Myrtle Lincoln's husband Howard sold his land. She sold 80 acres of hers then deeded the remainder to their children, and the family collected the lease money on that land.

Medicine Woman (1886–1969) was Chief Little Raven's grand-daughter, but she was an orphan. She attended Darlington school two years and Cantonment two years, then married Lumpmouth's son Yellowhair (a member of the Little Raven, Jr., cohort from Geary). As a noncompetent she kept her allotment and leased it. When her husband died in 1918, she married his younger brother, Old Bear, who tried to farm in the Canton area. By 1930, she was a widow, Old Bear's land had been sold, and she was living off her lease money. Sometimes she and her children did not have enough to eat. Widows like Medicine Woman usually had less income than married women whose husbands might at least lease some of their land and might also have an income from farming.

Nonallottees might have a little income from their share of an inherited allotment but owned no parcel of land to farm. Usually alumni of off-reservation boarding schools, they worked for day wages in the Canton area. Alfred Whiteman, Chief White Shirt's son, was in this group but did exceptionally well, working in agency jobs or, by the 1930s, in the town of Canton. He became a fore-man of the Civilian Conservation Corps (CCC) camp in Canton in 1934. Another exception was Walter Fire. The son of Coal Of Fire and Ugly Woman, as a boy he ran away from Cantonment school, then his disappointed parents sent him to Chilocco in 1907. After he returned, they convinced him to go to Haskell, where he graduated in 1918. Walter became a relatively successful farmer using his deceased father's land and equipment. He was also a manager of a CCC camp in 1934. But most of the nonallotted men in the Jess Rowlodge cohort lived on the allotments of older relatives (often in a tent) and hired out, sometimes working for relatives. This group included Henry and Paul Bates, Robert

Sankey, and Bill Williams—all sons of men in the Little Raven, Jr., cohort.

The wives of these men usually had little or no land. Widows had the more difficult situation. Jessie Bad Looking was born in 1894, the daughter of Chief Young Bear. She married Kiser Youngman from Geary when she was fourteen and he middle aged. Kiser, one of the first Arapahos to attend the Arapaho school and an alumnus of Haskell and Chilocco, sold his allotment, and they lived with Jessie's father. In 1916 Superintendent W. H. Wisdom agreed to pay Jessie her children's IIM money because her husband could not support the family. Kiser died, leaving Jessie a widow with three small children. Superintendent E. J. Bost reported that she had no income, and he also released her children's IIM money to her.[27]

The members of the Jess Rowlodge–Myrtle Lincoln cohort probably felt pessimistic about their futures. Handicapped by federal policy, they could not become economically independent of their elders. They participated in dances and gatherings, where they could demonstrate commitment to Arapaho values of cooperation and sharing to whatever extent possible. A few of the men served in World War I, and this battle experience gave them prestige and influence at gatherings. In Canton, Henry Bates, Dan Blackhorse, Harry Williams, Bill Williams, and Alfred Whiteman were veterans. They were sons of Harry Bates, Black Horse, Bull Thunder, and White Shirt. These young people had little political influence until the 1930s, when lodge organization and chieftainship began to wane. They relied on peyote ritual for help with their problems and on their elders for economic assistance.[28]

WE ALL HAVE TO BECOME DEBTORS:
POVERTY, INEQUALITY, AND LEADERSHIP AMONG MEN

In August 1903 Bichea's thirty-three-year-old son, Dan Webster, announced to Old Crow and other Arapahos that he had made a vow to sponsor the Clubboard Lodge so that Old Crow's son George would recover from an illness. Later, he denied making the vow, and his relatives began to worry that the entire family would be the object of disapproval. They also worried about Dan's well-being. Webster's stepfather Fire felt weak and encouraged Dan to sponsor the ceremony on his behalf, volunteering to bear the expense. In this way, the family could avoid the sacrilege of ignoring the vow. The tribe then felt encouraged, Cleaver Warden reported, because all the Arapahos would have experienced misfortune from negative supernatural sanctions. At a tribal gathering, some Spear Men, headmen for Dan and other Star Men, held a council and sent for Dan, concerned that he would waver. They criticized him for his behavior and warned him that if he did not complete the vow, harm would come to his family and other Arapahos. So Dan's fellow Star Men rallied around him, and the preparations for the lodge began.[29]

This event reveals much about Arapaho life during the early twentieth century. Family members keenly felt a responsibility to help each other, and ceremonial people struggled to motivate younger Arapahos, such as Dan Webster (in the Little Raven, Jr., cohort), to follow the example they had set for a good and successful life career. In the twentieth century, men still tried to contribute to their households and to fulfill their duties to kin and community through property sacrifice. Recognition for leadership ability depended on such generosity. But federal policy about the sale and leasing of Indian land created obstacles for men trying to support their families, help kinspeople, and attain political influence. Despite their prayer sacrifices, Arapahos became increasingly poor and plagued by illness. The men of the Medicine Grass cohort and the camp Indians of the Little Raven, Jr., cohort struggled, but their difficulties paled in comparison to the problems of educated men in the latter cohort and those in Jess Rowlodge's cohort.

The Landowners

Arapaho men fished in the streams and rivers and hunted deer, wild turkey, and sage hen for food and fur-bearing animals for pelts. Men also cooperated in group hunts for coyote and wolf (regarded as pests), whose pelts they sold. But now hunting was more difficult. For example, a state ranger arrested Jess Birdshead for killing quail without a state license, so a man took some risk when he hunted for his family. The men (with help from women) continued to farm, increasingly with horse-drawn rather than walking plows. And the men in a family would cooperate, working each other's land. For example, Bichea's husband, Fire, and her son Dan Webster farmed with John Poisal, the husband of Bichea's sister Turkey and Turkey's son Tom Levi. Men also worked for day wages or a share of the crop in the fields of settlers, and helped relatives who grew cash crops like wheat.[30]

Fathers, mother's brothers, and brothers made property sacrifices on behalf of kinsmen—a horse given away when a relative participated in a ceremony or gifts to guests at a feast for a child entering school, as Two Babies did, or returning from school, as Ben Spotted Wolf did. Husbands tried to live up to their responsibilities to their wives' families. Men often married the sister of a deceased spouse, as Old Bear did. And Arapahos still observed respect relations between certain relatives. A man had to avoid his mother-in-law, and vulgar language could not be used in the presence of a sister, for example. Acknowledged kinship between relatives who were collaterally distant also supported social bonds between Arapahos. Despite these ideals, the reality was that Arapahos did not have enough pasture and feed to support large horse herds, and a family could not be self-sufficient or provide for needy relatives by farming a small plot of corn. Arapahos came to rely on cash to buy food and supplies for their households and purchase goods for property sacrifices. The greatest source of income came from leasing or selling allotments, and access to cash through inheritance of land sometimes became a source of contention and conflict between relatives.[31]

After 1902, Congress allowed the sale of inherited trust land, and federal policy treated men differently from women in matters of leasing and sale of allotted land. Federal agents would not allow men to lease all their land. They required them to reserve forty acres and farm it. The rationale for this restriction was that Indian men, characterized as naturally lazy, had to be forced to work at farming and compelled to support their dependents (their wives and children). Moreover, unless they were elderly, men were usually denied any money from their IIM for support until 1913, when the agents allowed withdrawal for the purchase of farm equipment. Again, withholding their lease and sale money was intended to make them "work" for a living.

After 1906 individuals declared "competent" obtained permission to sell their allotments and receive their share of the tribe's funds from the 1892 land cession. Officials loosely defined competency as having formal education. By 1915, as we have seen, many of the younger Arapaho men—regarded as educated by the superintendent—had already sold land and withdrawn their pro rata shares. In 1917 the commissioner of Indian Affairs ordered a Competency Commission to complete a survey of households and declare the adults "competent" or "noncompetent." The competent Arapahos—generally men from Little Raven, Jr.'s cohort who had attended off-reservation boarding school or those from Jess Rowlodge's cohort (all of whom at least attended school on the reservation)—received a fee patent on their land whether they wanted it or not. Federal officials often pressured them to sell it to raise money for farm equipment. In any case, they could not afford to pay tax on their land in fee status.

All Arapaho men faced the problem that farming in this area was extremely precarious. Few settlers could make a living, and those that did relied on leasing Indian land at less than market value. To get money to support their families, men continued to sell land and apply for IIM to support farming efforts. Equipment (purchased with funds from trust land) could be mortgaged to obtain provisions, even though this violated federal policy regarding "trust property." The agents eventually liberalized the IIM regulations so that over time, many Arapaho men lost their land or much of it and depleted their accounts. Due to graft that went unchecked by the federal government, many Arapahos sold land for less than market value. One strategy employed by Arapahos to avoid having to sell land because of their competency status was to deed some of it to a child or a noncompetent person (usually a spouse). The superintendent in Cantonment in 1911 reported that 125 Arapahos (more than half women) still had trust patents on their allotments, and 15 had obtained patents in fee (and were in the process of selling), while 103 had never been allotted. Arapahos survived by helping and sharing with one another.[32]

A few educated men from Little Raven, Jr.'s cohort worked for the agency, but these salaried positions did not necessarily help them make a long-term living. Henry North was assistant farmer. In 1906 he asked to resign, complaining that Arapahos disliked him and that Chief Bird Chief, Sr., expressed hostility to him. Carl Sweezy was also an assistant farmer in 1912. Arapahos complained about him, irate that he did not belong to the district in which he worked and that he could not interpret well. He had married an Oneida woman he had met when they worked at the government boarding school for the Kiowas. This marriage was probably a handicap in the job. He left his position.[33]

Men from the Medicine Grass cohort and camp Indians from the Little Raven, Jr., cohort had the strongest resource base because as noncompetents, they owned sizable acreage. Reports from Canton in 1911, 1917, and 1922 show this. In 1911, men born in the 1850s and 1860s took responsibility for households and needy relatives. As "uneducated" men they could not sell their own allotments but could sell those of deceased relatives (primarily children), although the BIA was slow about officially determining heirs. These men had land to farm and lease (although the settlers could not always pay what they owed) and had the benefit of their wives' contributions. Often, younger relatives helped them farm.

Bringing Good (married to Jessie Spread Hands), from the Medicine Grass cohort, owned and farmed his own allotment in 1911. He had been able to draw on his funds and Jessie on hers to build a house and buy stock and farm equipment. In Greenfield, Medicine Grass, whose two wives had died, married Mrs. White Man, who was widowed and divorced from other ceremonial men. They both had their allotments. Bichea and Fire, who lived west of Geary, had their allotments. Arnold Woolworth pointedly

told a federal official in 1914 that the older men were more prosperous than his age group.[34]

Camp Indians from the Little Raven, Jr., cohort still had land to
farm or lease. Little Raven, Jr., and his wife had their allotments,
but she died, leaving him with four children. White Shirt had
his allotment of 160 acres, as did his wife White Buffalo Woman.
The Competency Commission declared Little Raven, Jr., and White
Shirt noncompetent, so they retained their land in 1917. Striking,
born in 1878, was a younger member of this cohort. A camp Indian,
he was a noncompetent who retained his allotment, and in 1922
he owned a three-room house, barn, windmill, and car. His wife,
Myrtle, leased her allotment for $1,500 per year. They had donated
land for the Arapaho Council House and many people camped
in tents around the building.

James R. Hutchinson, a member of the Little Raven, Jr., cohort
(who had attended Haskell in the 1880s), had reestablished an
identity as a camp Indian by his devotion to a ceremonial career
and by focusing on farming rather than pursuing employment
at the agency. He still owned his allotment in 1911 and was growing
cotton and garden vegetables. He had a house and some farm
equipment. He was also declared noncompetent. He had eighty
acres and had deeded the other eighty to his wife Ugly Woman
(the sister of his first wife, Minnie Yellow Bear, who had died).
Although he had attended Haskell for three years, James convinced
the commission that he could not read and write. In 1922, James
was fifty-five. He and Ugly Woman had a three-room house and
a barn. He cultivated his eighty acres with the help of younger
men, and his wife had lease income. The educated members of this
cohort did not fare as well. At least half lived in tents on other
people's allotments. Their land was gone, and they had no tools.[35]

Contrast the situation of Hutchinson with that of Frank Harrington, another member of this cohort, who identified himself
as "educated." Frank requested and obtained a fee patent on his
allotment and sold it. In 1911 he was camped in a tent on the
allotment of Red Man, a camp Indian related to him. He helped

Red Man farm, and his wife Amy (b. 1887; from Myrtle Lincoln's cohort) still had her allotment. In 1917 he was living in a tent, and his wife (who had been to school on the reservation reportedly for fourteen years) previously had been allowed to sell eighty acres but was declared noncompetent in 1917. They still had eighty acres of her allotment. In 1922 he lived in a tent in Striking's camp. In his tent was his collection of books.

Another educated man of this cohort was Francis Lee, a Carlisle alumnus. In 1911 he was among the most prosperous. His and his wife's allotments were in trust, and he farmed extensively. In 1917 he had 120 acres in trust and had given his wife 40 acres. He was farming and working in a store in Canton, and he leased land for $140 per year. He had a house, barn, well, horses, and farm equipment. He told the commission that he did not want a patent, but they declared him competent. He died the next year in the Spanish flu epidemic, but his land was sold shortly before or after his death. The men of Jess Rowlodge's cohort were declared competent, and they sold their land.[36]

And what of the men in the Poisal family? How did they fare in the early twentieth century? John Poisal (the son of Snake Woman and the trapper-trader John Poisal) had the respect of Indian agents and local businessmen for his successful ranching operation in the late nineteenth century. Like his father, he chose to associate and affiliate with Arapahos. Over time, he had four Arapaho wives and one Cheyenne wife. After the Jerome agreement, he had no choice but to take an allotment west of Geary, for his profitable ranch had been appropriated by settlers. In the Geary area he farmed in cooperation with other Arapahos. His children, all with family names (Robert, John, Matilda, and Margaret) went to the Arapaho school. All but one died small. He was vulnerable to American racial ideology. As an Indian, he was a ward of the government, and the superintendent controlled his IIM and interfered in his life. His entrepreneurial skills could not be put to good use. On the other hand, as a biracial man, he was thought to have inherited competency from his "white" father, so he had to sell his land. He had little choice but to help his brother-in-law Fire. He died in 1907.

John's son Robert (1892–1915) also farmed in Geary and did road work with Arapahos. John's nephew Joe Poisal (the orphaned son of his brother Robert and an Arapaho woman) was born in 1878. He farmed with other Arapahos, attended community meetings, signed community petitions to the commissioner of Indian Affairs, and visited his and his wife's relatives. His wife, Eva, was the daughter of Chief Big Mouth, so this was a prestigious match. Eva had attended Carlisle fourteen years. She still had her allotment in 1917, but declared "competent," he had sold his. These two men were full-fledged members of the Arapaho community.

In contrast, the sons of the women in the Poisal family tended to model themselves after their American fathers. Henry Meagher (born in 1878), the child of a white man and Margaret Poisal's daughter Jenny, was not a participating member in Arapaho society, although he went to Haskell and was celebrated there for his military service in the Spanish American War. He identified himself as white in 1937.

Except for the eldest, the sons of Mary Keith grew up in the Kingfisher area on their white father's ranch. Benny, her eldest son (born in 1868), was a scout at Fort Reno. He married a Cheyenne woman and ranched in the South Canadian River area. The others married American women and sent their children to public school as soon as they could. They resented the BIA's restrictions on their freedom to handle their own property and obtained fee patents as soon as possible. Two of Mary's grandsons, the eldest sons of her daughter Josephine and Peter Shields, a white man, were Haskell alumni who worked for the BIA. One, J. E., or Eddie, Shields (born in 1879), married a Sioux woman and worked at Chilocco and Riverside Indian schools. He was the government farmer in Geary from 1912 to 1914 and then became principal of Concho school. Arapahos got along with him, probably because he understood Arapaho values. In fact, Julia Prentiss wrote Mary Jayne that the BIA wanted to replace Eddie Shields as school principal with a white man: "We are fighting to keep him." Inspector O. McPherson ridiculed him for his humble demeanor: given the fact that he looked more like a white man than an Indian, he "should deport himself with greater dignity." He felt that Shields set a bad example because he had the "appearance and bearing of a common farm laborer." McPherson thought he should have the "bearing of a gentleman."[37]

Redefining Chieftainship

Because of the widespread poverty and the emerging economic inequalities, district (formerly band) leaders could not really provide for the needy in a substantial way. Gradually, the expectations surrounding leadership changed, and the civilization strategy gave way to a more militant one as the intermediary chiefs complained vigorously and sought legal redress for their people.

Early in the century the lodge organization had enough support to generate considerable consensus and motivate people to fulfill community and ceremonial responsibilities. This is what Frank Harrington tried to explain to Reverend John A. Funk, but Funk regarded the Arapahos' support for their value system as stubborn recalcitrance: he found Arapahos to be deceptive, like "a reed which is prostrated by the force of the wind but which, after the wind ceaseth, rises up again and stands boldly erect." [38]

The elder brothers (headmen) of lodge men still had authority over their juniors. This authority was supernaturally sanctioned, so that senior lodge men could ask junior ones to do work around the camps. Rather than shooting a horse belonging to someone reluctant to attend a tribal ceremony or contribute to it, they "fined" a person a blanket or trimmed his horse's tail (a form of ridicule). Ceremonial grandfathers worked to keep the peace, and the grandfather-grandson relationship supported consensus-based politics. Warden explained that both grandfather and grandson should agree on any subject. For example, if the grandfather should say, "I think the (IIM) payments are rather slow and therefore advise you chiefs and headmen to call another feast for consultation with the agent," the grandson should say, "Yes, my grandfather is right." The grandfathers took responsibility for the behavior of their grandsons, working to smooth over social conflicts in

which they were involved. Lodge activity was considered "work," and Arapahos rejected the missionaries' and agents' idea that it was not. The letters of Frank Harrington at Canton reveal that lodge men and women had great control over members of the community and that, in special circumstances—such as Mennonite converts disrupting a tribal ceremony—they would use oratory to criticize individuals quite harshly. The Mennonite missionary arguably failed in Canton largely because of the opposition of lodge people—not to Christianity per se, but to Reverend Funk's attack on Arapaho values.

In Canton, the men who reached the Lime Crazy Lodge by 1906 included Henry Sage, Black Horse, Sitting Bull, Rabbit Run, Bringing Good, Heap Of Crows, Broken Rib, Deaf, and Coal Of Fire—all members of Medicine Grass's cohort—and Mixed Hair and Lime, from the Little Raven, Jr., cohort. In Greenfield, the Lime Crazy Men included Hail, Gun, Bald Head, Tony Pedro, Black Lodge, Medicine Grass, and Young Bear—from Medicine Grass's cohort—and Cut Nose and Circle Left Hand, from the Little Raven, Jr., cohort. Probably most men in the Medicine Grass cohort belonged to the lodge organization, although all of them may not have gone as far as the Lime Crazy Lodge.[39]

The positions of district leaders, referred to as chiefs, had supernatural sanction. Old Crow, head priest until his death in 1904, then Hawkan, presided over a chief's induction: by accepting a pipe from the priest, the chief swore an oath to help his people, especially the needy families and individuals, and the chief's wife had to agree to support him. These chiefs were role models. When Congress passed legislation in 1903 to enable the sale of deceased Indians' allotments (in violation of the 1890 Jerome agreement, Arapahos insisted), Left Hand instructed chiefs not to sell land. Young Bear of Greenfield did, and he was suspended from the chieftainship for about three years—he had "no voice" in council, according to Jess Rowlodge. Left Hand's son Grant had ambitions to become a chief, but he developed a drinking problem in the mid-1890s. Left Hand refused to support him, admonishing him to demonstrate that he could be depended on to help the needy. Eventually, years after Left Hand's death, Grant repaired his reputation. Chiefs spoke at gatherings, including camp meetings sponsored by churches, extolling Arapaho values. They also tried to set an example for industry, submitting agricultural exhibits at Indian fairs and supporting school attendance at the agency schools.[40]

The intermediary chiefs (those who acted as spokesmen in Washington) represented Arapahos in dealings with the federal government by persuading constituents and articulating group consensus. In Canton, Rabbit Run and Bringing Good (from the Medicine Grass cohort), and Little Raven, Jr., White Shirt, and Lime (from the Little Raven, Jr., cohort) were intermediary chiefs. Chiefs went on delegations to Washington, signed petitions to federal officials, and met with local superintendents and politicians to try to shape federal policy and its implementation.

The older men Rabbit Run and Bringing Good belonged to the Lime Crazy Lodge. Bringing Good went on the 1911 delegation and both went on the 1915 delegation. Rabbit Run went to Washington in 1917, and Bringing Good in 1920. They were both delegates to the Black Hills council, a meeting of several Plains tribes that hoped to file a claim against the federal government for a treaty violation that resulted in their being forced from the Black Hills area. Rabbit Run and his wife Bitchea divorced in 1920, but Jessie Spread Hands remained a chief wife until Bringing Good died.

Little Raven, Jr., and White Shirt attained chieftainship by 1909; they both went as chiefs on the delegation to Washington that year. Little Raven, Jr., was a lodge man and also an Offerings Lodge grandfather and Lodge Maker. After Jenny Bringing Good died in childbirth in 1915, he married Bitchea, a ceremonial authority who had divorced from Rabbit Run. They lived on their lease money. He went on delegations in 1917 and 1926, and some Arapahos viewed him as head chief (probably because of his family's prominence). White Shirt's father was a "Spanish" boy from Texas captured by Arapahos, who became a respected warrior. White Shirt was married to Anna, Little Raven, Jr.'s sister, then, after she died, to White Buffalo Woman (sister to Lime's wives) after she divorced from Lime. He was a lodge man, and he and his wife relied on lease money. Lime was a Lime Crazy Man by 1906 and an elder brother to Jess Rowlodge's Fox (and presumably Star) society. He went on the 1915, 1920, and 1926 delegations. He had been on the police force as a young man and possibly in conflicts, because he directed the sham battle at the Indian Fair in 1911. Lime had two wives, Spotted Woman (the chief wife) and Long Hair.

In Greenfield, the chiefs were Hail, Young Bear, and Medicine Grass (from the Medicine Grass cohort) and Circle, Cut Nose, and Arnold Woolworth (from Little Raven, Jr.'s cohort). Hail (married to Cross Killer), Young Bear (married to Woman Going Ahead), and Medicine Grass (married to Singing Woman, the widow of Black Coyote, after his prior wife died) were Lime Crazy Men. Hail was on the 1917 delegation, and Young Bear and Medicine Grass, on the delegations of 1920 and 1926, and both attended the Black Hills council. Left Hand's son Circle became a district chief in 1902. Married to Lulu Blind (Carlisle and Haskell alumna), he went on the 1908 and 1909 delegations and died in 1910. Cut Nose (married to Big Heart), one of the highest ranking Offerings Lodge authorities, went on the 1917 delegation. They both joined the Lime Crazy Lodge in 1906. Arnold Woolworth, a Carlisle alumnus who returned to camp life, became a district chief in 1906 and a Lime Crazy Man in 1913, and he went on the 1909 (as interpreter), 1911, and 1926 delegations. He was married to Black.

While the camp Indians and the educated Indians who reidentified as camp Indians participated in politics and had opportunities to influence others, the very small group of men who retained an "educated" identity could not achieve the recognition they needed to attain chieftainship or influence the community generally. Their loyalties appeared to be suspect, dating from the time of the Jerome Commission, when some served as interpreters and, in the minds of many Arapahos, misinterpreted to the disadvantage of Arapahos. In fact, according to Jess Rowlodge, at a council in the early twentieth century, two of these interpreters spoke to the people assembled there, admitting that they had been bribed and apologizing to the tribe. Some of these educated men were also at times criticized by family members for dishonesty—for example, misinterpreting in heirship hearings or forging signatures on documents. Of one, Myrtle Lincoln said that he was a "white man," not a good man. Of course, since landownership was an important basis for authority, influence, and personal autonomy, these landless men had less clout than those who had been able to retain their land as noncompetents.[41]

Arapahos relied on delegations of Arapaho and Cheyenne chiefs who traveled to Washington to protest injustice and advocate for treaty rights. Thus, chiefs had to be well versed in Arapaho history, especially treaty rights. The 1909 delegation aggressively opposed the fee patents and payment of pro rata shares of the tribal fund, insisted that graft undermined the responsible management of their lands, and urged that the trust status of their land be extended beyond the twenty-five years agreed to in 1890. They protested the restrictions on IIM payments—ten dollars a month from an individual's land sale funds and minimal distributions of lease money. Little Raven urged the government to permit payments of twenty-five dollars a month, because when they could not pay their grocery bill, they mortgaged property, which they subsequently lost. Referring to the Jerome agreement, White Shirt advocated for the extension of "treaty obligations." He pointed out that if the trust fund were to be paid out, the unallotted children of the tribe would receive no financial benefit—it was a tribal fund and should be perpetuated. Two educated men, Cleaver Warden and Frank Harrington, went with Little Raven and White Shirt, primarily to interpret. Neither Cleaver nor Frank opposed fee patents. The 1909 delegates' complaints largely went ignored.

In 1911, the delegation continued to press their demands. They wanted a promise that the trust status of their lands would be extended, and they complained bitterly about the hardship that the supervision of their IIM accounts entailed. Concerned about the plight of "landless" Arapahos, they proposed that the lands of deceased children be assigned to unallotted Arapahos. Arnold

Woolworth pointed out that the maximum monthly payment of twenty-five dollars would not support a family, and therefore Arapahos went into debt to the storekeepers: "We all have to become debtors to the class of traders who accommodate us." The delegation did receive a promise that the government would not close the boarding schools, which they viewed as a treaty right. Arnold told the commissioner he could speak English but that he felt unqualified to manage his own affairs.

The 1915 delegation tried to prevent the classification of Arapahos into "competent" and "noncompetent" categories, urged the extension of the trust period, and complained again about the hardship brought by the IIM regulations. The 1917 delegation was gratified to hear that the trust period would be extended ten years. Cut Nose complained about the IIM restrictions, to no avail: "The old people, old men, old women, blind people, sick people, crippled people, they are allowed only the small sum of ten or fifteen or twenty dollars monthly. That is not enough." In 1920 the delegates again argued for support for boarding schools, and federal officials reassured them. They wanted the commissioner's support for their claim against the government for treaty violations, and he promised to help. They complained that the IIM restrictions were still a hardship, although the monthly cap was raised to one hundred dollars. The superintendent at Cantonment agreed, arguing that a dollar was worth half what it was when the regulation was made. In 1926 the delegates persisted, urging that the trust status of their land be extended beyond 1927 and pleading for help for the "patent in fee element," in Young Bear's words. Arnold Woolworth used Jess Rowlodge as his interpreter when he spoke for the addition of grades to the Concho school.

Arapaho chiefs tried to protect the Arapaho community's interests, challenging and confronting the BIA on policies that made it impossible for families to become self-supporting. The government officials held up the settlers as an example of the successful agricultural way of life to which Arapahos should aspire. This justified leasing and selling land to settlers—they were to serve as role models. The old ways represented by "unprogressive" old people had to be discarded. Men had to be forced to work to provide for dependents.

But Arapahos realized that Americans in general had no interest in Indians succeeding at farming and that there was little reason to model themselves after them. Settlers often did not pay for their leases, and they often failed at farming. Tradesmen cheated Arapahos, and even missionaries participated in the land grab. To generate income for their towns, settlers also promoted the Indian dances and camps that the BIA tried to discourage. Missionaries, with whom Arapahos interacted, pointed out these failings. Mary Jayne wrote that settlers were not interested in the welfare of Indians or the work of missionaries. Reverend Funk wrote that the settlers needed the Gospel as much as the Indians did and that the white people were "a Godless" bunch, poor role models for Indians. Arapahos rejected the notion that they were "childlike" and needful of supervision; they realized they were being exploited. Men were not "lazy"—it was impossible for them to support their families. And the ideologies of age and gender relations promoted by the BIA made no sense to Arapahos. Families could not survive without the contribution of women's and old people's income, and old people had major economic and political responsibilities.[42]

The members of the Medicine Grass cohort and the camp Indians of the Little Raven, Jr., cohort challenged the BIA's rationale for the policies concerning trust property, instead attributing their poverty to the government's failure to keep its promises, the use of Indian resources to help struggling settlers, and the graft of officials and settlers who cheated them at every turn. They steadfastly maintained their right to sue the government for treaty violations, their right to a land base that would support tribal members well into the future, and the value of their ideals about sharing and respect that helped them cope with their circumstances. This was council talk as well as the speech of delegates.

During the early twentieth century, Arapahos redefined chieftainship: district chiefs organized and inspired people, drawing on their memories and experiences in the nineteenth century, but they could not provide work or support for people in their districts. Chiefs took responsibility for securing permission to hold tribal ceremonies and for convincing the federal government to end its repressive policies toward native religion. They successfully petitioned the superintendents most years. Moreover, the highest levels of political and ceremonial leadership fused; that is, when the men chosen by Left Hand and his peers reached old age, they did not retire, as Left Hand did, but remained as district and intermediary chiefs while directing ceremonial activities. The age span of the chiefs who went as delegates in 1911 was 49–54; in 1917, 56–63; and in 1926, 64–74. Poverty worked as a leveler so that districts rather than individual families had to take responsibility for gatherings. Still, senior lodge men and their wives provided leadership in the initial struggles with the BIA; however, by about 1930, their influence was on the wane.

Committees formed in the districts to do ceremonial and celebration work and, over time, political work, for the Arapaho community. In 1910 each district selected representatives to serve on the committee that managed the Indian Fair, where Cheyennes and Arapahos camped. The fair had Indian dances and games, horse races, and exhibits, and was supervised by chiefs, but some managerial positions were held by other men, including those in Jess Rowlodge's cohort. The horse races provided great entertainment, and some Arapaho men raised horses especially trained to race. Jess Rowlodge explained that the people in each district would "vote" on where to have the Christmas, Easter, and Thanksgiving camps. For these celebrations, the districts had committees and an associated "club of women" that supervised the preparation of the food (or feast) for the event. The committees raised money to buy food (increasingly purchased food, including canned goods and crackers), and women in the community would be asked to prepare it. The committee would also direct the work of the holiday camp, seeing, for example, that boys hauled in wood. The committee collected donations of property and money and gave away horses, according to Myrtle Lincoln, to demonstrate their worthiness for the job. These committees probably gradually replaced the lodge organization's role in camp organization and control, but lodge men and women served on them.[43]

The first mention in the record of a Christmas committee is in the Canton area in 1921 (although according to Arapahos, they existed before that), and the members included chiefs Little Raven, Jr., Young Bear, and White Shirt, as well as Chase Harrington (Frank's brother), an educated man from Little Raven, Jr.'s cohort, and two from Jess's cohort, Dave Meat and Hannibal Bighead. The chiefs must have been convinced that district chiefs should be prominent participants in these community gatherings because by the 1930s, they chose men from Jess Rowlodge's cohort as district chiefs (although not as intermediary chiefs). In Canton, these new chiefs were Dave Meat and Wilbur Tabor, both with farms and income, and presumably willing to shoulder the burden. In the 1920s the Canton and Geary-Greenfield communities had committees that raised money and organized the labor to build council halls ("round halls," where people met and danced). Chiefs including Rabbit Run, Bringing Good, and Lime served as committee officers, and other men from the Little Raven, Jr., and Jess Rowlodge cohorts worked on the hall committee.[44]

The Rise of Peyotism

Aside from their political duties, the lodge men of the Medicine Grass cohort and later the camp Indians in the Little Raven, Jr., cohort served as religious leaders—as doctors, ceremonial grandfathers, and peyote chiefs. A man often had all these roles, but by the 1930s, most Arapahos primarily relied on peyotism for help.

Men still fasted to obtain power to cure. Arapahos used their services even though they sometimes accepted treatment from the agency physicians. Deaf was relied on for cures, and he was the head of the medicine men until he died in 1910. Thereafter, Ute (another member of the Medicine Grass cohort) led the medicine men. Once a year they met and under the leader's direction replenished their powers. Men whose power was from the same spirit being were organized into a society (for example, the Lizard,

Beaver, and Thunderbird societies). People could join several of these groups if they qualified. Blackman fasted for power and trained several men, including Arnold Woolworth, who took twenty-five or thirty lessons, each one requiring the learning of certain songs, before he used the powers. Gun, Sharp, Medicine Grass, Young Bear (of Canton), and Lumpmouth were medicine men, and among Deaf's apprentices were Hoof (from Little Raven, Jr.'s cohort). Broken Rib doctored and was noted for being able to control storms. Grace's husband, Nelson Sagebark (born in 1879), fasted for curing power. Arapahos had great respect for doctors. Jess Rowlodge recalled with awe a curing ceremony in which Ute "sucked out" (drew out of the body) a man's illness using Thunderbird medicine.[45]

Arapahos also pledged lodge ceremonies to recover from illness and other trouble throughout the early twentieth century, even though they struggled to adapt to the deaths of the elderly priests. The symbolism of the lodges focused on health and character development. According to Jess Rowlodge (who had been a messenger boy in all the lodges as far as the Lime Crazy Lodge), the grandfathers of these lodge men gave their grandsons paint to live by and food to live on. The paint referred both to the religious duties and the blessing that derived from joining the lodges—its spiritual component—and the food referred to the social support represented by the exchange of food in the ceremony. Arapahos camped in a circle at these ceremonies, with each of the three main districts occupying a particular place in the circle. A successful ceremony brought benefits to all Arapahos, and all were expected to contribute in some way.[46]

Cleaver Warden took detailed notes at the 1903 Clubboard Lodge ceremony (formerly known as the Tomahawk Lodge). The camp formed on 18 October and the next day the Star Men selected their headmen, who chose grandfathers for the Stars. These Star Men were to be inducted and elevated to the Clubboard Lodge. The headmen also chose men who would receive the honor of carrying special regalia (degrees) and divided the new Clubboard Men into Stout and Short groups. The inductees rehearsed their dance, while headmen encouraged them with accounts of their war exploits, and families in the camp invited each other to feasts. On 20 October, the grandfathers, instructed by elderly priests, made the regalia (with the help of women) and applied symbolic paint designs to the bodies of the Clubboard Men. They had another dance rehearsal in the evening. On 21 October, the grandfathers applied paint again, and their grandsons danced in the evening. On 22 October the grandsons again received paint and also the regalia. They danced in public, and the dancing was followed by a race between the Stouts and Shorts.

The new Clubboard Men all were members of the Little Raven, Jr., cohort—fifteen camp Indians and twenty-two educated men. This group represented half the members of the cohort. The camp Indians from Canton were Singing Man, Little Raven, Jr., Hoof, and White Shirt, and the educated Indians, Francis Lee and James R. Hutchinson. From Greenfield, the camp Indians were Lone Man, Straight Crazy, and Otter Robe (actually, a few years older than the others), and the educated men were Grant Left Hand and Arnold Woolworth. The headmen, who were members of the Thunderbird Lodge (formerly called the Spear Lodge), belonged to the Medicine Grass cohort (except for Cut Nose, who had risen to a ceremonial position beyond his actual years). The grandfathers came from the Left Hand, Medicine Grass, and Little Raven, Jr., cohorts, for they qualified by having gone through the Clubboard Lodge. Two of the Stars did not participate and instead sent substitutes. Henry North (an alumnus of Carlisle and Haskell) sent Dan Dyer (Annie Pedro's brother), a younger man from the Kit Foxes, and Casper Edson (a Carlisle alumnus) sent his younger brother Richard. According to Warden, North and Edson forfeited the right to be "prominent in dances," or to advise in councils. They had, in essence, stalled in their life course toward "manhood." One young man, Black Bear, was actually a Kit Fox, whose well-off and prominent "father" Red Wolf persuaded the directors to allow him to skip the Stars and become a Clubboard Man.[47]

The symbolism of the lodge reinforced Arapaho ideas about the creation and regeneration of life. The spatial organization of the lodge and the painting of dancers reminded spectators of the male and female components of the life force, as well as the origin story in general. The activities of the Short and Stout divisions represented the concept of reciprocity in gender relations and in social relations in general. For the Clubboard Men, the lodge experience helped them "in the pursuit of manhood privileges," and the wearing of the Clubboard paints was a prayer sacrifice (along with the gifts of food and other items to headmen and grandfathers) for fertility and prosperity.

At various times during the ceremony, the headmen struck the drum (around which sat the singers for the ceremony) and told about their exploits in battle. The war stories about success "stimulated people's minds to ward off illness and depression" and bestowed "manhood" and "future blessings," wrote Warden. In other words, the headmen symbolically transferred the power associated with their success to the Clubboard Men. When the grandfathers made the regalia, they or old men (substituting for them) told stories about the taking of scalps. For example, Chief Left Hand transferred one of the high-degree clubboards to Arnold Woolworth, telling how he once used it in battle. Arnold received it and gave four war whoops. The Arapahos in the camp circle contributed materials (for example, canvas) to build the lodge structure, as well as exchanged food and supported the participants by singing, dancing, and cheering. Clowns, the spectacle of the dancing, and the fun of the race between the Shorts and Stouts—where the loser was pelted with dirt—all held the interest of the crowd. Warden mentioned that at various times there was disagreement or confusion about the proper way to conduct the ritual and the participants had to improvise, for example, by substituting a horse tail for a buffalo tail in the regalia.[48]

The families and the community as a whole expected men of the Little Raven, Jr., cohort to join the lodge organization. Arapahos believed, as Jess Rowlodge explained, that "if they think enough of Indian life and want to be somebody in their old life, they join." In reality, though, confidence in the lodges' efficacy appears to have waned, or reliance on peyote may have seemed more promising. As mentioned, two of the Star Men did not participate in the 1903 Clubboard Lodge. The Arapahos held another Clubboard Lodge in 1911, ostensibly for the men in Jess Rowlodge's cohort. Like Jess, Bird White Bear would have been eligible, and he felt pressure from his wife and his relatives to join the Clubboard Lodge, but he believed that membership would be an obstacle in his life, especially because it would be "dangerous" for a peyote man because of the "grandfather business." He told Eggan he knew of cases where men who tried to be both peyote and lodge men had had accidents.

The lodge ceremonies reinforced the stature, influence, and authority of the men of the Medicine Grass cohort. Warden's description of the Lime Crazy ceremony held in 1906 shows why it impressed Arapahos as a "spectacular" dance and why the participants were viewed with awe. Young Bull's wife Bushy Head vowed the ceremony, and her husband was Lodge Maker. Her vow was a prayer for recovery from illness, but Arapahos felt that the prayer sacrifice would benefit them all. The ceremony took place during the second week in September. On 6 September, the priests began preparations, the new Lime Crazies gathered material from the camps to build the lodge, and the headmen selected Long Hair (from Colony) and Swapping Back (from the Geary area) to carry the special regalia. In the evening, rehearsals for the dance took place and the initiates offered their wives to the priest (a body sacrifice). On 7 September, the grandfathers worked on the regalia and painted the dancers, who continued to rehearse. The following day, they continued these activities and the offering of wives ("visiting," in Warden's words) again occurred.

On the last day, the warriors' accounts accompanied the bestowal of regalia, then the Lime Crazy Men walked through the camp, behaving and talking in inappropriate ways. Four headmen—Black Coyote, Little Left Hand, Spotted Corn, and Big Belly—and their wives made a fire under the direction of Dog Lodge members. When the coals were red hot, the priests, headmen, and then the dancers walked on them. The Lime Crazy Men stomped on the coals until the fire died. Then people retreated to their tepees or tents, and the Lime Crazy Men began to shoot arrows (their regalia included small bows and arrows), killing several dogs. They insulted people, using vulgar language. Attached to their regalia was the "crazy root," which protected them from retaliation. They were so contrary that when their grandfathers invited them to eat, they had to do so by asking them not to eat. The Lime Crazy Men doctored six or seven invalids while their relatives begged them not to cure them. At the Lime Crazy Lodge that took place in 1913, Jess Rowlodge told Hilger with amazement that the dancers walked in the fire.[49]

The Lime Crazy Lodge again took place in Canton in 1913, according to Jess Rowlodge. The Thunderbird Men had all camped, waiting to be inducted, but before the ceremony began, four or five left Canton and avoided participating. They were all peyote men; one was Cleaver Warden (a 1903 Clubboard Man). James R. Hutchinson vowed a Thunderbird Lodge in 1919 so that his wife would recover from an illness. It was possible for lodge men to repeat a ceremony if a member so vowed. It is also possible that Hutchinson used a substitute when this lodge presumably was held prior to 1913. Another Clubboard Lodge was held sometime after this. Apparently, only a few men from Jess Rowlodge's cohort joined, including Dan Blackhorse and Henry Bates, but Howard Lincoln refused. According to his wife, Myrtle, "We want[ed] to live the way we wanted to live . . . . It's pretty hard for anybody to be in them groups. They have to help, take care of somebody else's family."[50]

The men of the Offerings Lodge also had the respect of Arapahos because their prayers helped everyone in the tribe. As in the Lime Crazy Lodge, miraculous occurrences during the ceremonies impressed the people. Although some years, only a few men fasted and danced, and some superintendents used sanctions against participants, Arapahos held the Offerings Lodge almost every year. Many men and women sang during the ritual, which was essential to the success of it. Most family members of participants also contributed in some way. According to Myrtle Lincoln, Charles Campbell (as the keeper of the Sacred Wheel) and Ute (the priest)

directed the ceremony about 1909. After 1917, according to Jess
Rowlodge, Charles Campbell was a Lodge Maker. Lodge Makers
also included Young Bull (from Medicine Grass's cohort) and two
Carlisle alumni from Little Raven, Jr.'s cohort, Philip Pratt and
Neatha Seger. Jim Warden identified directors of the Offerings
Lodge during the first two decades of the century: Sage, Blackman,
Two Babies, and Ute—all members of the Medicine Grass cohort.
No description of the Offerings Lodge exists after Dorsey's in
1902, but the 1923 ceremony, attended by other tribes as well as
Arapahos, received considerable attention.

The Arapaho chiefs asked Superintendent L. S. Bonnin for permission to hold the seven-day ritual in Geary, and he told them
to finish in three days. The religious leaders decided to conduct
the ritual properly and risk punishment from Bonnin rather than
from the Creator. Bonnin, furious, sent the Cheyenne police to take
the names of the heads of households camped there beyond the
allotted time. Bonnin was also outraged when he was informed
that the wives of the Lodge Makers had had "visits" (symbolic
intercourse only, according to the Arapaho chiefs) with the priests.
In this rite, power was transferred from the Creator to the woman,
then to the Lodge Maker. The trouble over the ceremony led the
Arapahos close to "open rebellion," according to Bonnin, and he
decided to cease his interference. The camp circle at the ceremony included the Seger, Cantonment, and Darlington districts,
and the Lodge Maker Young Bull had visited these communities
and collected donations of horses, cattle, money, blankets, and
other goods for the priests and the keeper of the Sacred Wheel.
He took his ceremonial pipe to the leaders, which, after smoking,
obligated the community to support Young Bull. In return, they
would share in the blessing.

Five men fasted and danced. The government farmer reported
that three of the dancers lived in the Cantonment subagency.
Young Bull and his wife Bushy Head had the Lodge Maker role,
and Lewis Miller (Old Crow's son) reportedly took an "active part"
(probably in wearing a particular paint or possibly as a second
Lodge Maker). One woman and three men priests directed the

ritual, and these were the last who knew the procedures: Ute, Man Going Up Hill, Big Belly, and the woman priest, Singing After. From the list furnished by the police (which apparently focused on the Geary Arapahos), fifteen "participants" were members of Medicine Grass's cohort, including Hail, Young Bear, Medicine Grass, Cut Finger, Blackman, Ute, and Spotted Corn. Over thirty-four of the names belonged to members of the Little Raven, Jr., cohort: for example, Dan Webster, Arnold Woolworth, and Grant Left Hand. Camp Indians and educated Arapahos were there. About sixteen other men were from Jess Rowlodge's cohort. Many of these men were sons of older Offerings Lodge men, such as Lone Man, Fire, Straight Crazy, and Hail. After 1923, Carlisle alumnus Noble Prentiss served as Lodge Maker several times, and in 1937 he and Little Raven, Jr., vowed the ceremony together.[51]

Besides the opposition from the superintendent at Darlington, Arapahos faced another threat to the Offerings Lodge. The Sacred Wheel used in the ceremony was cared for by Charles Campbell and his wife Singing After until they divorced in 1921. Her father Heap Of Hair had been the keeper, and after he died, they dug up the wheel, which was buried with him. Campbell went blind, Arapahos thought because of improper treatment of the tribal bundle. Singing After began to demand expensive presents for the use of the wheel. In 1923, Young Bull was embarrassed and the ritual delayed because he had difficulty meeting her demands. In 1928, the Arapahos held a council at which "all the men and women lodges" agreed to send for a duplicate wheel from the Northern Arapahos because of the exorbitant demands of Singing After. Plenty Bears, a Northern Arapaho priest, brought a wheel, married a Southern Arapaho, and they took the wheel to subsequent ceremonies. The chiefs told the superintendent that Singing After's demands were unprecedented: the wheel was tribal, not personal, property.[52]

Despite devotion to lodge ceremonies and use of medicine men, the Arapahos' troubles continued. They turned to other faiths, usually in conjunction with the Offerings Lodge—a revival of the Ghost Dance, Christianity, peyotism, and reliance on a combination of these rituals. Around the second decade of the century, Heap Of Crows revived the Ghost Dance and organized a group of followers for a brief time. Most people who still had faith in the Ghost Dance prayed and had visions privately. Myrtle Lincoln recalled that some men at Canton had hand game bundles used as "a way of prayer." Mixed Hair, Young Bear, and Striking led these rituals. Mixed Hair died in the flu epidemic in 1918, and Young Bear, in 1929. The bundles were buried with the owners.[53]

At first, Arapahos showed little interest in Christianity. In Canton, some Arapahos argued against it by insisting that because Christ could not save himself from his enemies, his power was weak. The Mennonites began by trying to convert children at their two schools. When the schools closed, the work with Arapahos continued from the Arapaho Mennonite Church in Canton, led by Reverend Funk. Funk's assistant was the educated youth from Little Raven, Jr.'s cohort, Frank Harrington, who worked with him to translate the Bible into Arapaho. Funk insisted that converts must give up gambling, dancing, gift giving, smoking, Indian custom marriage, and peyote. He set church members against other Arapahos, whom he referred to as "heathens," and encouraged his flock to disrupt Arapaho gatherings and ceremonies. As a result, the lodge men actively opposed Funk's work. Before a chapel was constructed, Funk paid a lodge man one dollar to meet in his unused home. When this man learned that they planned to report the names of Arapahos violating the BIA moral code, he raised the rent to five dollars, which Funk could not afford. Eventually, Frank Harrington quit—he became disillusioned when Funk refused his advice to try to persuade rather than threaten lodge men. Funk's congregation reached fourteen in 1902, seventy in 1906, and sixty in 1908 and 1914. But attendance was poor at services.

For a few years in the early part of the century, several men educated by the Mennonites worked to undermine all religious activity except Christianity. Jess Rowlodge referred to them somewhat derisively as "the Christian Six": Frank Harrington, Henry Lincoln, Wilbur Tabor, Mathew Spotted Wolf, Ben Spotted Wolf, and Striking. Striking joined the church late in life. Jess Rowlodge recalled that the first four eventually became disillusioned with Christianity. Myrtle Lincoln commented that one of these men and another educated man from the Little Raven, Jr., cohort took a medicine bag from the home of an elderly doctor after that person died, and they sold the bag. Because they "bothered" the bag, one died suddenly, and the other had a stroke.[54]

The Baptists, led by Reverend F. L. King and his wife, Mabel, established the Arapaho Baptist Mission in the Greenfield-Geary area. He and his wife welcomed Arapahos into their home, where they fed and entertained them, and they camped with Arapahos during their native ceremonies. The Kings welcomed peyotists and followers of traditional ceremonies (presumably hoping to gradually persuade them to abandon non-Christian faiths). Frank Harrington noted that Baptists were less strict than the Mennonites and concentrated on doing "good works." Arapahos camped around the mission where Baptists distributed clothing, pulled teeth, and lent books and tools. Chiefs were invited to address the people and to eat with the Kings.

Reverend King wrote that he was a guest in Black Coyote's tepee during the 1903 Clubboard Dance, where he ate bread, crackers, coffee, beef, dog, rice, tomatoes, and apples. In 1905 the church had twenty-two members, but nonmembers were welcomed to eat and attend the Christian celebrations, where Arapahos received gifts. Mrs. King explained in 1907, "When the Indians go away from home they bring their valuables here to be stored, to keep bad white men from stealing them, so at times the mission looks like a regular second-hand store." In 1908 Reverend King noted that he worked seven years before he got a convert; finally, four influential lodge men joined (without renouncing other faiths), and his converts numbered thirty. Chiefs Left Hand and Hail converted. At the Christmas camp in 1915, Arapahos played hand games and danced and received gifts and dinner from the Baptists. An Arapaho chief prayed at the event as well. James R. Hutchinson had a vision that convinced him to join the Baptist Church in Geary. Camp meetings continued to attract Arapahos into the 1920s.[55]

Mrs. King commented that the faith of converts depended on the health of their children. The high infant mortality among Christians and non-Christians alike encouraged Arapahos to appeal for help every way they could. Good results strengthened religious commitment, and if prayers in one kind of ritual did not bring help, others could be tried. Elements of peyote ritual and Christianity were often combined in peyote ceremonies, and elements of native religion were incorporated into the Arapaho Baptist Church, especially in the form of Arapaho hymns. The experiences of Mennonite converts Frank Harrington and William Meeks also illustrate that belief in Arapaho concepts about the supernatural coexisted with belief in Christianity.

Frank Harrington's mother was Big Nose, and his father was Bull Going Down, who died about 1876, when Frank was ten, leaving him an "orphan." Later, she married the warrior Spread Hands as a co-wife. From childhood Frank was taught to respect men who claimed to cure from supernatural power. He thought the first Mennonite missionary S. S. Haury was a "civilized medicine man" because he doctored the sick. Frank went into the "prairies and woods" praying for a "spirit" to reveal itself (fasted for a helper). His mother wanted him to herd the family's stock. But against his mother's wishes, he ran away to the Mennonite school at Cantonment when he was twelve. In other words, he thought his vision experience validated his apprenticeship to the Mennonite missionary. Later, Harrington worked with the chiefs to get permission from the government for the 1918 Offerings Lodge.

Harrington's replacement as Funk's assistant was William Meeks. After Meeks's conversion, he dreamed that he should fast on a bluff. That night something "hummed around him." A lizard spirit came to him and offered the power to heal sick people. The spirit told him such doctoring would not interfere with Christianity. So Meeks eventually became a member of the Lizard doctors' society. One of the deacons of the Arapaho Baptist Church was James R. Hutchinson of Canton. He also was a lodge man and a peyote chief.[56]

The Arapahos accepted individuals' participation in more than one faith largely because of the expectations of reciprocal respect that characterized lodge as well as kinship relationships. Senior and junior people felt an obligation to help each other. Left Hand eventually accepted the Baptist faith, while his sons became peyotists as well as Baptists. Hail and his wife, Cross Killer, also accepted the Baptist faith at the same time they were Offerings Lodge leaders. Their son Mathew was a ceremonial man and a peyotist. Medicine Grass was a senior lodge man, and his son-in-law Henry Rowlodge was a peyotist. Little Raven, Jr., and his wives Jenny, then Bitchea, were ceremonial people all their lives but acted as Offerings Lodge grandfather and grandmothers to men and women who were peyotists and Christians. The Arapaho position contrasts with the Cheyenne view that peyote people acted as a kind of faction. Records from this era show considerable conflict between Cheyenne Christians and peyotists, and ceremonial people and others, perhaps in part because the Cheyennes lacked the age-grade tradition.

The expansion of and increased reliance on the peyote religion helped transform Arapaho society because it effectively drew together men (and their wives) from the Jess Rowlodge cohort, buttressing social ties and supporting political activity even without lodge membership. Many Arapahos became members as the result of a cure during the ritual. When Sitting Bull was old, he had a stroke, brought on, Arapahos said, by the violation of rules associated with Ghost Dance theology. In any case, peyote men cured him in a peyote ceremony, and subsequently he announced that the peyote religion was a true one and became a peyotist. The peyote chiefs in Canton, including Osage, Broken Rib, and Heap Of Crows (from the Medicine Grass cohort) and James R. Hutchinson, Mixed Hair, and White Shirt (from Little Raven, Jr.'s cohort) drew many Arapahos into their ceremonies by offering to pray for or cure them. Canton men from Jess Rowlodge's cohort who practiced peyotism included Dan Blackhorse, Ben Spotted Wolf, John Hoof, and Dave Meat. Bichea's sons John (from Jess's cohort) and Daniel Webster (from Little Raven, Jr.'s cohort) also embraced the peyote religion.

Individuals who had problems could vow to sponsor a peyote ritual in return for supernatural aid (as was the practice in the lodge organization and Ghost Dance hand game). In fact, Arapaho ideas about religious practice affected the development of the peyote religion. There was a hierarchy in the peyote organization— a man had to be "ordained," that is, trained by a peyote chief before he could lead a meeting. Feathers used in the regalia correlated with ritual experience: men new to the ritual used roadrunner feathers, and senior people used the feathers of flickers. When a man became a member of the peyote organization, he and his entire family had to follow rules. For example, a peyote family should not "talk mean," according to Myrtle Lincoln, whose husband Howard practiced the peyote religion.[57]

Once established, the peyote organization successfully recruited many or most of Jess Rowlodge's cohort. Although a young man had to apprentice, he did not have the expense and extensive social duties associated with the lodge organization. And he could introduce ritual innovations. Jess Rowlodge noted that his brother Henry made changes in the ritual once he became a peyote chief. Arapahos also accepted peyote because they believed it helped curb alcoholism. The peyote religion precluded the use of alcohol, which had become a problem for Arapahos after the establishment of towns (where there were saloons). In 1912, Superintendent Byron White at Canton reported that the peyotists had founded societies (district "chapters") and tried to enforce rules against drinking alcohol. These chapters also created or reinforced social bonds among peyotists. Superintendent Scott at Darlington in 1914 noted that the use of peyote increased from year to year. The believers collected money and sent delegates to Mexico to bring back the plant. At first they had their ceremonies at remote locations to avoid detection from the superintendents.

By 1917, the peyote ritual was "widespread," and Superintendent Robert Daniel at Canton wrote that its use was "unrestricted." Peyote meetings often had participants from several tribes, so the cultural exchange that took place in the 1890s continued into the twentieth century. The Arapahos and Cheyennes successfully worked with other tribes in Oklahoma to obtain a state charter for the Native American Church in 1919, which undercut the ability of the superintendents to repress the ceremonies and elicited pride and confidence in this movement. In 1924 the peyote organization was still actively recruiting. By the 1930s peyotism, led by people in the Jess Rowlodge and Myrtle Lincoln cohort, had become the religion with the most Arapaho participants.[58]

Political Reorganization

In the 1920s the federal government began to dismiss the idea of chieftainship. Officials viewed these elderly men as relics of the past and put pressure on the Cheyennes and Arapahos to select younger, bilingual, boarding school–educated men as representatives. Arapahos still respected and recognized these chiefs but began to give more responsibility to younger men, who felt great frustration over their lack of political influence, as well as their economic circumstances. The superintendents organized "farm chapters" in the districts, and although Arapahos showed more interest in the fair committee and in preparing for the fair than attending chapter meetings, this district organization became the basis for district committees, where Arapahos discussed community affairs and chose representatives for a tribal council. People in the Jess Rowlodge–Myrtle Lincoln cohort participated extensively.

In 1928, with strong pressure from the superintendent, the tribes organized a general (Arapaho and Cheyenne) tribal council, the members of which were elected from their districts. The Arapaho districts—Calumet (a subdistrict of the Cheyenne-Arapaho, or Darlington, agency), Geary, Greenfield, Canton, Carlton (a subdistrict of Cantonment agency), and Seger—at first sent two representatives, then four to allow for broader participation. Deliberations in this council continued a tradition of speakers not directly contradicting or criticizing each other, translation of Arapaho and Cheyenne into English and vice versa, and the unwillingness to allow spokespersons to do anything other than articulate consensus. From the Arapaho point of view, the council's job was to pursue a legal claim against the government for violation of the 1851 treaty among other things. They also felt very uneasy about their prospects because the federal government had consolidated the agencies and schools at Concho in 1927. Their fears contributed to a willingness to incorporate younger, more recently educated people into the council.

Until a new business council was organized in 1937 under the Oklahoma Indian Welfare Act, chiefs—including Little Raven, Jr., White Shirt, Medicine Grass, Arnold Woolworth, and Ute—were elected to the general tribal council from their districts. So were younger men, including men from the Little Raven, Jr., cohort and Jess Rowlodge's cohort (including Dan Blackhorse, Walter Fire, and Hannibal Bighead from Canton, and Tom Levi and Wakefield Young Bear from Greenfield). Eddie Shields also participated occasionally. Gradually, the younger men became the majority on the council. In 1932 Chief Arnold Woolworth, Chief White Shirt, and Jess Rowlodge, now a full-fledged spokesman, went to Washington as the Arapaho delegates. The Cheyennes and Arapahos accepted the Oklahoma Indian Welfare Act, organizing an elected constitutional government in 1937. The main support initially came from the landless families who saw the promise of land assignments and economic development.[59]

Federal land policy provoked a shift from the civilization strategy to one in which the Arapaho chiefs directly challenged these policies and determined to seek legal redress in U.S. courts. At the same time, peyotists defied American sanctions against peyote ritual, eventually prevailing. Not unrelated to this success, the peyote organization grew in popularity, especially among the Jess Rowlodge cohort. Chiefs from the Little Raven, Jr., cohort and their wives retained their positions well into old age, although Arapahos redefined chieftainship to stress lodge-related kinds of qualifications and knowledge, rather than the ability to help others economically. In time, the members of the younger cohorts challenged the leadership of these older men. This challenge, abetted by a federal policy that privileged young over old men, resulted in the Arapahos accepting an elected constitutional government in conjunction with the Cheyennes. Some Arapahos faithfully continued the lodge ceremonies, which reaffirmed ideas about gender balance and the age-hierarchy principle, including the mutual obligations between old and young Arapahos. On the other hand, both the old and young cohorts rejected for different reasons some of the political roles formerly associated with the age hierarchy.

HE COMPLIED WITH HER DEMANDS: NEW OPPORTUNITIES FOR WOMEN

When Baptist missionary Robert Hamilton visited an Arapaho and Cheyenne camp in 1903, he saw hundreds of white tents along a stream, and beside most of the tents were wagons and small indiscernible patches of white. Everywhere groups of dogs ran helter-skelter. Upon closer inspection, he saw that the white patches were actually flocks of relatively motionless chickens tethered with rawhide like horses had been in prereservation days. Once in camp, he saw women doing their work. Some washed clothes with soap-weed in the stream, and some sewed on machines in their tents. The women owned the tents, chickens, sewing machines, dogs, many of the wagons, and much of the stock. In the twentieth century, Bichea, Jessie Spread Hands, Myrtle Lincoln, and the other women in their cohorts faced new challenges because of federal policies that impoverished Arapaho families. They adapted in ways that both reconfigured and reinforced Arapaho notions of gender in the economic, religious, and political realms of Arapaho life.[60]

Economic Contributions

Women persisted in viewing themselves as economic partners with men in their households. They gathered plants, gardened, farmed, worked for wages, and sold the products of their labor. They also used their Individual Indian Money (IIM) payments to bolster their ability to contribute to the household, despite resistance from the superintendents who felt that men should support their wives, whom the superintendents viewed as dependents. Women realized that the superintendents' ideas would not work for their families.

Women gathered wild grapes, plums, onions and other plants, then dried them. They also tended vegetable gardens and dried the corn that they and their husbands grew. As in prior years, they sliced, pounded, and dried beef in the same manner that they had prepared buffalo. Arapahos no longer wore hide clothing, except on ceremonial occasions, but women made clothing out of cloth for the family, increasingly using sewing machines they purchased with their IIM accounts. Not only school-educated women used sewing machines—from the Bichea cohort, Yellow Woman (widowed in 1902 and now Mrs. Spotted Corn), and from the Jessie Spread Hands cohort, Big Heart (Mrs. Cut Nose), bought sewing machines in February 1912. Missionaries, especially the Baptists, and the field matron in Geary invited women to use their machines, gave out fabric, and organized sewing groups so that sewing became a group activity much enjoyed by women. Mary Jayne, a single woman who worked as a missionary, showed many women how to make a star quilt and how to make semi-tailored garments.[61]

Generally, women refused to wear the clothes of white women (tailored dresses, aprons, jackets, hats, and shoes). They made "old time" or "Indian style" "neat and modest" (loose fitting) calico dresses, and wore moccasins and "Indian shawls." Thus, Jayne felt gratification when Mrs. Old Camp put a pocket in her camp dress. Women made shirts for Arapaho men, who also wore some purchased "citizens'" clothing. At the local Indian fair, women won prizes for work based on the new technologies. They received prizes for garments by camp Indians and for those by returned students, as well as for bread (both made in camp and in the house—that is, over camp fire and in ovens). In 1934, the Emergency Conservation Corps allocated one-third of its local budget for Indian women to make garments for issue to poor Indians—Arapaho women worked in groups on this project.[62]

Arapaho households needed cash to buy food and supplies. Many women raised chickens on their home places, where they had chicken coops. When they traveled to tribal gatherings like the one Hamilton visited, they probably took the chickens with them so that they would not be stolen. In 1907, Fieldy Sweezy (from the Little Raven, Jr., cohort) told the superintendent that his wife, Jeanette (from Jessie Spread Hands's cohort), told him she was going to raise chickens. White Buffalo Woman (Mrs. White Shirt) moved a building to her place to use as a hen house in 1922. Superintendent Freer reported in 1912 that one-third of the Indian women had chickens, so this kind of project took initiative and some money to buy a few birds. The women sold their chickens' eggs in the towns. The *Carrier Pigeon* reported in 1913 that Yellow Woman (Mrs. Spotted Corn) brought her eggs to market. The income belonged to the woman who owned the chickens.

Arapahos still valued beaded ceremonial clothing and regalia, so women continued to develop these skills, and they entered their work at the Indian fairs. They also sold beadwork made for non-Indians, such as belts, moccasins, and purses, to missionaries who marketed some of it. The Dutch Reformed Church's Mohonk Lodge at Colony bought beadwork from Bitchea (Mrs. Tony Pedro) and Ute Woman, as well as other Arapaho women, who also sold beadwork to James Mooney, who needed it for the 1904 World's Fair. Mary Jayne noted that Straight Crazy's wife, Curley Hair, made miniature tepees for sale. In the 1920s Mrs. Young Bull regularly took her work to Anadarko to sell to visitors at the Indian fair there, and women sold beadwork in the local towns.[63]

Women's labor helped support their families in other ways. Wives helped their husbands farm and farmed by themselves. Myrtle and Howard Lincoln worked together, using a walking plow. She and her mother-in-law Red Feather planted wheat and sold the crop. Women worked beside their husbands in the settlers' wheat and cotton fields, usually for a daily wage. Several—for example, the wives of Tom Levi, Henry North, and Frank Sweezy— worked for hire transporting goods in their wagons. Myrtle Lincoln also helped her husband chop wood to sell.[64]

Arapaho women rejected the superintendents' expectations that they should be dependent on their husbands, fathers, or brothers and that they needed government supervision to manage their property. Instead, they viewed themselves as partners with their husbands or, if unmarried, as heads of household supporting their families. In 1913 Superintendent F. E. Farrell made a point of crediting Bichea with her husband Fire's good garden, but gardens generally needed the labor of both husband and wife. Husbands and wives partnered each other in much of their work, and husbands respected their wives' views. For example, when Henry North worked as an agency farmer, he had difficulty getting along with other Arapahos. His wife, Nancy, convinced him to resign because she was dissatisfied with the situation. Similarly, Ben Miles resigned his job as farmer because his wife disliked living in the district where he was stationed. As Jim Warden put it, the woman was "boss of the home," "head of the house." Actually, she managed the household economy and "owned" the food. Myrtle Lincoln's husband brought her his pay from the wage work he did and told her to decide how to spend it.[65]

Ideally, men respected women's property rights, but occasionally women asked the superintendents to intervene. For example, at Singing First's request, Superintendent George Stouch canceled her husband Smith Curley's sale of her mules. If a couple divorced, the woman took her property. In 1913 when John Fire's wife left him, she took with her a wagon and team and so many farming implements that he could no longer farm.[66]

In their independence, women exasperated the superintendents. They sought and often obtained permission to lease their own land, rather than allowing the government farmer to make the lease for them. And they aggressively tried to negotiate for the highest price once they had control. Ethel Black Wolf, who had attended Haskell, Carlisle, and Chilocco, and then returned to work at reservation schools until she married the widower William Meeks in 1905, inherited her brother's land. She refused to accept what a settler offered, insisting on what she thought a fair price in 1908. In 1916 Singing Woman set about making improvements on land she inherited from Black Coyote so that she could lease it for more money. Good Warrior (Mrs. Earl White Shirt) asked her leaser for a steer "on time"; after his refusal, she threatened not to lease to him in 1910. Myrtle Striking and her mother Bitchea (Mrs. Rabbit Run) refused to agree to lease their land for the price Superintendent Byron White recommended: Bitchea seemed "to think that every time a new lease is made it should be higher than the one before." Myrtle always followed her mother's lead, he wrote. Superintendents also complained that women gambled among themselves, playing bone dice and the cup and pin game while betting moccasins, belts, and purses.[67]

Women provided crucial support for their families by leasing their land. Even those with the same or more education than their husbands generally received noncompetent status and, with their lands in trust, collected lease income twice a month. In Geary, Molly Candy (married to Black Bear since 1898) went to school seven years on the reservation but kept the trust patent on her land. In Jessie Spread Hands's cohort, thirty-eight women in Canton, who had not been to school, received noncompetent status. There were seven women who had been to school for several years, but they were also declared noncompetent. For example, Ethel Black Wolf (Mrs. William Meeks), despite her off-reservation education, was declared noncompetent and held on to her 160 acres in 1917. The one exception in Canton was Jessie Spread Hands, who was allowed to sell her allotment before 1917, probably because Bringing Good was considered a very good farmer, and they had enough land for their farm. In Myrtle Lincoln's cohort, almost all the women, despite their years in reservation schools and their ability to read and write, received a noncompetent designation, for example, Myrtle Lincoln, Ellen Bates (with five years at Carlisle), Lydia Tabor (married to Wilbur Tabor), Amy Harrington (married to Frank Harrington), and Ruth Tucker (married to Dan Tucker). If a woman in this cohort requested a fee patent, she was given it, presumably because these women were in their twenties and thirties and "educated." Agency records show that among all the Arapahos, five women requested competent status, including Annie Pedro.

If women were allowed to sell inherited land, these larger sums could be drawn on with the superintendents' permission, although he often refused it. When Good Killer wanted to use some of her IIM to build a house on her husband Tom Levi's land, Superintendent Charles Shell denied her request. He insisted that she was "entitled to support by her husband." In other words, it was her husband's responsibility to build her a house. Shell also refused to allow wives to sell the hay on their allotments if their husbands were able to work. Women collectively had somewhat more cash in their IIM accounts than men, but probably more important, superintendents allowed women to draw more money from their accounts than men could. Women tried to demonstrate that they would use their money to support their family farm. In fact, Buffalo Fat was allowed to buy a team for $300 for her husband Cut Finger and an $80 wagon for her son-in-law. Ada Feathers received money to buy farm equipment for her husband Henry Lincoln. Bitchea bought farm equipment for Rabbit Run.[68]

But Lime's wives Spotted Woman and Long Hair could not persuade officials that Lime would farm with the team they wanted to buy. In 1905 Lime's wives' request was denied because officials believed the women would use the team to visit other households. Of course, this attitude hindered women's efforts to fulfill cere-monial and kinship duties and to work as midwives. Superin-tendents tried to ensure that the women's money would be spent only for equipment or farm animals, or for subsistence in hardship cases. In 1905 Superintendent Stouch announced that he would approve no purchases of silk cloth (used for dance outfits), jewelry, beads, trunks (associated with traveling), or buggies (associated with visiting rather than farming). In 1908 Lydia Blindy (at the time, James's widow) received five dollars to buy food and clothing for her children. Superintendent White told her to buy no candy, fruit, or beads.[69]

These IIM accounts provided a new source of security for unmarried women, although they still could be at a disadvantage. Divorces were generally Indian custom, and where the State of Oklahoma did not recognize a divorce, a woman had no claim on her children's money. The father collected. But widows and divorcees could lease their land and collect their interest payments from the tribe's cession fund (about sixteen dollars annually). Even so, life could be difficult. Take the case of Bear Woman. Unmarried at forty-two and lacking close relatives to provide for her, she had to sell her allotment to get income on which to live. She realized she was heir to no land and that her income would soon be depleted. She begged the superintendent for some of her land sale money to buy chickens and turkeys to raise commercially. That could be her means of support, she thought.[70]

Arapahos felt that matters of income were largely out of their control. Not only did the superintendents' decisions seem discriminatory and arbitrary, but people whose parents, siblings, or children had long lives inherited less land than those whose allotted family members died. The fact that women could more reliably count on getting money from leases allowed them to maintain, even increase, their importance to household economies and to community projects.

The experiences of most of the Poisal women were colored by the fact that superintendents considered their biracial status when determining whether they received a fee patent or not. Their marriages to white men also made their families less susceptible to the superintendents' control because the federal officials had no authority over their husbands' income or business decisions. Jenny Meagher's third husband was Dr. A. Jackson, a doctor in El Reno. Her daughter Maggie Munder married a white man and lived in Arkansas. Jenny applied for and received fee patents on all their allotments in 1905.

Mary Poisal Keith's daughters also married white men. One, Josephine Shields (born in 1861), lived in Calumet all her life, and her husband and a son farmed her 160-acre allotment and raised cattle. She entered her garden produce in the Indian Fair of 1912. Prosperous, she did not want a fee patent in 1917, but one was given anyway, because she was one-fourth Arapaho and "reads and writes." Later, she apparently bought land in town. Her daughters all married white men from the Calumet area and had little involvement in the Arapaho community, although their children briefly attended the Arapaho school before entering public school. Their husbands prospered by farming their wives' allotments; against their wishes, these women received fee patents as a result of the Competency Commission's work in 1917. Presumably, their husbands paid property tax on the land thereafter, because they remained in the Calumet area. These families seem to have been considered part of the settler, rather than the Arapaho, community in Calumet.

On the other hand, the children of Robert and John Poisal had Arapaho mothers. John's daughters were participating members of the Arapaho community. Ella (born in 1880) married a Cheyenne, as did all her children. Nellie married a Northern Arapaho. They remained "wards" of the government. Robert's children, orphans looked after by his relatives, included Anna (born in 1874) and Mary (born in 1879). They were integral members of the Arapaho community at Seger. Anna married an Arapaho, Theodore Haury, and Mary wed a white man, Joe Wisel, but the family associated closely with Arapahos.[71]

Women used their money not only for subsistence purposes. They tried to fulfill their duties toward family and community by making prayer sacrifices on behalf of relatives, and they did their best to live up to behavioral ideals regarding family members. Women had a major responsibility to their children. While a woman was pregnant, family members had to be careful not to frighten her lest the child be damaged—and such cases had happened, Hilger learned. Fathers and mothers both practiced food taboos. Pregnant women had to avoid the meat of certain animals in order to prevent birth defects. Long Hair admitted to Hilger that she ate rabbit (taboo to pregnant women), and her child had a harelip. Women used midwives, who made teas and incense to ensure a safe delivery. They gave birth on their knees, holding on to a stake. Myrtle Lincoln, for example, gave birth to all her children with the assistance of a midwife. The midwife placed the afterbirth in a tree so that the child would grow up well. The navel cord was placed in a beaded bag, the designs symbolizing prayers for the child's good health. In many cases, cradle boards were passed down rather than being made especially for each child, but these gifts represented familial duty.[72]

The nursing mother had to avoid certain foods. As added insurance, a mother could make body sacrifices for her children. Long Hair sacrificed the small finger of her left hand and the ring finger of her right hand at the joint. Mothers helped sponsor feasts and gift giving as property sacrifices for children. Grandmothers and father's sisters did the same. Women sacrificed cloth by tying it to the rafters of the Offerings Lodge. Arapahos also sponsored peyote ceremonies for children's birthdays as a prayer for the children's health. And when a child died, objects he or she needed for the afterlife were still placed on or in the grave.[73]

Women had obligations to their siblings and in-laws. Frank Harrington's sister and her daughter showed support for him when, after he became a Mennonite convert, they agreed to be baptized. Women continued to take gifts to their brother's wife and children, especially moccasins and clothing. Relations with in-laws called for respect, sometimes in the form of avoidance. Bird White Bear explained to Fred Eggan that respect relations continued to the extent possible in the Arapahos' new circumstances. For example, when in-laws lived in the same house, avoidance was complicated. Hilger noted that Arnold Woolworth's daughters-in-law did not want to enter a room where he was. One commented, "If I talk to him he would think that I have no respect for him." Myrtle Lincoln helped her mother-in-law Red Feather with household work, and Red Feather gave gifts to her and her children. Myrtle exchanged gifts with her sister-in-law and avoided her father-in-law.

Long, stable marriages (reinforced by proper relations with in-laws) continued to be the ideal. In fact, at the 1902 Offerings Lodge, the priest Old Crow recognized several "old married couples" on the last day of the ceremony, praising them and lecturing young people on the merits of a stable marriage. Indian custom marriages continued to be the norm for young and old from the turn of the century to at least the late 1920s, although they often occurred in conjunction with a legal ceremony, primarily so that heirship rights would not be challenged. In these weddings, families exchanged property, "a horse for a horse," as Myrtle Lincoln put it. There were still elopements. Walking Woman eloped but separated from the man after three days because her family refused to acknowledge the marriage.

The perceived need for polygamy had decreased in the early twentieth century. And the superintendents did what they could to break up polygamous families. In some cases the parties continued their relationship surreptitiously. Long Hair, married to Lime as a co-wife with her sister Spotted Woman, told Hilger that "white people" insisted they separate, but she continued to "live with him" until he died. Her sister was "too crippled to take care of him so I stayed and took care of them both." Actually, she separated and married another man, then when her husband died, returned to Lime, but she probably did continue to help her sister and Lime when she was married. By 1920 superintendents Bonnin and Charles Coggeshell reported from their respective agencies that Arapaho males numbered 371 and females 335. Young women married monogamously. Only a few elderly women were co-wives.[74]

Women also gave support to the men in their family—husbands, brothers, and sons especially—through their contributions to ceremonial events, especially by their work as singers. For example, women composed and sang war party songs for the Arapaho soldiers in World War I, songs that were prayers for their safe return. All but one of the Arapaho soldiers returned. Their mothers and sisters played a central role in the victory dances held in Geary and Canton. Frances Densmore learned from veteran Bret Rising Bear (the son of Pipe Woman and Lester Rising Bear, a lodge man and Carlisle alumnus) that at his victory dance, two women carried German helmets on lances like scalps in "the old days." The soldiers related their experiences. Bret was a rifleman in France, and he was wounded. The women interpolated the names of the soldiers in the old war songs that once praised warriors returning with scalps, and they composed new words that reflected the times: "The German got scared and ran and dragged his blanket along." Bret took the name of his mother's father, Yellow Horse, a renowned Arapaho warrior, to reflect his accomplishment and future prospects.[75]

Ritual Partnerships: Peyote, Christianity, and the Grass Dance

Bird White Bear told Eggan that husbands and wives were a ceremonial team. In the lodge organization, the participation of women still was an essential part of the ritual. In the 1903 Clubboard ceremony, Warden described the lodge symbolism as a dramatization of creation and the role of the male and female principles in that process. He also documented the key role women played in helping to establish and strengthen bonds between the junior and senior men and between and within families. Wives of Clubboard initiates, wives of the headmen (or elder brothers), and grandfathers' wives prepared, delivered, and redistributed sacred food (primarily meat and rice soup). Preparation of food for a ceremony was a kind of ritual act, a form of prayer thought. To initiate the ceremony, the headmen's wives took food to the grandfathers' camps, and later the grandfathers' wives took food to the wives of the Clubboard Men, who ate the sacred food. The next day the Clubboard Men's wives took food to the grandfathers' wives. These women ate inside the lodge; women who had no husbands participating sat and ate outside the lodge. Wives redistributed some of the food to friends and relatives.

The wives of the grandfathers made the regalia worn by the Clubboard Men. They brought sinew to the priests, who made thread from it, which the women used to ornament buckskin with quills or corn shucks (a substitute). The women sat in the lodge in the same position as women did when doing quillwork on a tepee or robe. The grandmother-granddaughter relationship was one of respect.

The wives of the Clubboard Men also stood behind or beside their husbands when they danced, and the women cheered when the men received the regalia. The women in the grandfathers'

families danced behind or beside them. The wives of the Clubboard Men helped reinforce the bond between the men by forming
two groups, each of which went to the rehearsals of the Short or
Stout men and joked with the men. The wives of the Short Men
went with the Stout men and vice versa. As "brothers'" wives,
this kind of joking was permissible.[76]

In the 1906 Lime Crazy Lodge, Warden's notes show that Bushy
Head (born in 1858), the wife of Young Bull, made the vow, then
had to convince her husband to serve as the Lodge Maker. The
people in the community congratulated her for taking a step toward
higher sacred knowledge. As in the Clubboard ceremony, granddaughters and grandmothers exchanged food. In addition, the
wives of the Lime Crazy Men had two "visits" with the grandfathers—in these encounters, sacred knowledge passed from the
grandfather to the wife, who transferred it to her husband. The
wives of the grandfathers made the regalia: first, they received
paint from the priests, then they made the regalia. The wives of
the Lime Crazy Men also received paint. The headmen's wives
played a central role in the preparation of the sacred fire, in
which the Lime Crazy Men danced. The headmen's wives cut
the wood for the fire, and both they and their husbands received
instructions from the priest on the way to lay the fire. The women
relatives of the wives helped them with food, labor, and property
(for gifts). These lodge ceremonies reinforced ideas expressed in
the origin stories, for example, concepts about gender balance
and reciprocity.[77]

The "highest degree in womanhood" was that of woman priest
in the Offerings Lodge. Crippled may have succeeded Lump
Forehead in this position. Crippled was also the Peacemaker, or
the woman priest, in the 1903 and 1906 lodge ceremonies. Warden
described her role in the Clubboard Lodge as crucial to the ceremony. She essentially "made" or ordained the new priest Mountain, and the ceremony could begin only on her "order." She
activated the sacred and life-giving ceremony, as the personifica-
tion of the female principle in the life force. She had to be "paid"
with a gift for her acts. Crippled also participated as Peacemaker

in the Lime Crazy Lodge. She was the wife of Ute, who succeeded Hawkan as Offerings Lodge priest. After Arapahos ceased to hold the age-graded lodge ceremonies, the Peacemaker role continued to be central to the Offerings Lodge. Crippled died in 1917 and apparently was succeeded by Singing After, married to Lodge Maker Charles Campbell.

Singing After was the woman director in the 1923 Offerings Lodge. Bushy Head, who was the Lodge Maker's wife in that ceremony (and in several other Offerings Lodges), was the daughter of Lump Forehead and probably was undertaking a series of sacrifices to achieve her mother's position. Another woman who made a major sacrifice in the 1923 ceremony was Virginia Lone Lodge (Mrs. Hannibal Bighead), who was a member of Myrtle Lincoln's cohort. She was singled out by the superintendent, so she may have been the second woman to have made a "visit" (Bushy Head was the other). Virginia was the granddaughter of Mrs. Old Sun, and her parents had high lodge positions. Little Raven, Jr., served as Lodge Maker several times. His wife Bitchea (divorced from Rabbit Run in 1920) would have had high status when she married him and would have been a great help to him as he earned more authority. These ceremonial people maintained their ceremonial careers by marrying other ceremonial people after the death or divorce of a spouse. The Offerings Lodge could not have continued to be held without the leadership of the women who helped direct it.[78]

Doctoring power also remained important in Arapaho life into the 1930s, due in no small part to the commitment of women. One of the members of Deaf's society of doctors was Red Feather. She succeeded her brother and treated patients with his bundle. Red Feather attended the spring ritual opening of the bundles led by Deaf, and people vowed to make property sacrifices to her bundle to obtain a cure. Other women doctors included Big Woman (Mrs. Lumpmouth) and Bad Teeth (Mrs. Strong Bull). Ugly Woman (Mrs. Coal Of Fire), Myrtle Lincoln's aunt, was a specialist in bloodletting; she taught Myrtle this technique. Red Feather was also a midwife, as was Striking Night (Mrs. Big Head), who helped Myrtle Lincoln with the births of her children from 1909 into the 1920s. The women Hilger talked to had used midwives for their children's births: Long Hair from Jessie Spread Hands's cohort and women from Myrtle Lincoln's cohort, including Helen Spotted Wolf, Grace Sagebark, and Lucy Medicine Grass. Women doctors still used sterility medicine; in fact, Lucy's mother Pretty Woman had this ability and used it to sterilize one of her daughters.[79]

The search for new religious options continued in the twentieth century, though enthusiasm waned for all but peyotism. The Spanish flu epidemic in 1918 killed a shockingly high number of Arapahos, and poverty contributed to the high incidence of tuberculosis. In this context, women in the Bichea and Jessie Spread Hands's cohorts sought help from several religions. Bethhebah and her husband Heap Of Crows revitalized the Ghost Dance. Rather than dancing, the believers had prayer meetings. They often had visions on these occasions. Several people had hand game bundles and presided over ceremonies that people vowed as a prayer sacrifice. Pipe Woman had a hand game bundle, and she composed songs in her effort to obtain help for others. Mixed Hair, with his wife Good Looking, had a bundle. Myrtle Lincoln also identified Young Bear and his wife, Bad Looking, and Striking and his wife, Myrtle (who was Mrs. Rabbit Run's daughter) as bundle owners. Women also achieved renown for the hand game songs they composed.[80]

Sometime between 1914 and 1916, Killing First in Canton asked one of her relatives among the Gros Ventres at Fort Belknap, Montana, to transfer a Grass Dance ceremony to her. This Grass Dance leader came to Canton, and the Arapahos there helped Killing First (from Jessie Spread Hands's cohort) gather a great deal of property for this man, who instructed her and her husband, Red Man. In this ceremony, which people could vow as a prayer sacrifice, women wore or carried the regalia: four war bonnets, four staffs, a whip, and two pipes. The old warriors Sitting Bull and Plenty Bears chose women to carry the regalia, women whose husbands and other family members could contribute property to be given away when they received the regalia.[81]

Myrtle Lincoln named Lydia Tabor (Sitting Bull's daughter, married to Wilbur Tabor) as the leader of the women. Lydia was in Myrtle's cohort, and she had tried to convince Myrtle's husband, Howard, to join the lodges (she was Myrtle's "mother," that is, Myrtle's grandfather's daughter). Myrtle also indicated that Red Feather tried to mentor Myrtle's little daughter Rose to encourage her to participate. With one exception, the other Grass Dance women belonged to Myrtle's cohort as well: Virginia Lone Lodge (Mrs. Hannibal Bighead), Susie Scabby Bull (Mrs. Saul Birdshead), Myrtle Striking, Hazel Sponner (Mrs. Harry Williams), Zada Lime (Long Hair's daughter), Lena Beard and Sarah Wolf Chief (Mrs. Bull Tongue's daughters and Walking Backward's granddaughters), and Medicine Woman, or Martha (a granddaughter of Chief Little Raven, married to Lumpmouth's son Old Bear). "Old Mrs. Bringing Good," or Jessie Spread Hands carried a staff. These young women probably intended that even though they could not attain senior lodge women positions, they could have special influence in their community as Grass Dance women. Jessie may have joined because by the time she married Bringing Good, he already had an established lodge career with his first wife.[82]

Some women attended Christian services, usually in addition to "Indian" rituals, and women dreamed songs about Christianity and could exert leadership in church activities, especially in the Baptist Church. Big Heart and her husband, Cut Nose, and Little Bird and her husband, the medicine man Blackman, attended Baptist camp meetings in 1911, to the great satisfaction of the missionaries. Women spoke (probably to give testimony) at church meetings. When Chief Hail and his wife, Cross Killer, went to the Kiowa-Comanche-Apache agency in 1908 to attend a camp meeting, they stopped for the night on the way home, camping by the side of the road. They went to sleep in their wagon "with the spell of the Indian singing on them," missionary King wrote. Mrs. Hail dreamed of a spirit being who came to her and taught her a hymn. When she awoke, she taught it to Hail, and it eventually became a standard for the Arapahos. The Baptists reported that the Arapaho deacons worked *with their wives* to support the church.

A group of Arapaho women formed a women's society to support church functions: Prairie Woman, Black Coyote's mother-in-law, was "chief" of the society in 1908.

Myrtle Lincoln also commented that the Christian men (the "Christian Six" mentioned by Jess Rowlodge) who, for a while, opposed Indian ceremonies in the early years of the century, had the help of their wives; however, Myrtle Striking and Lydia Tabor obviously did not remain opposed to Indian religion and may have influenced their husbands to be less rigid.[83]

Arapaho women provided essential support to the spread of peyotism and its acceptance as the major faith in the mid-twentieth century. In 1910 Baptist missionary G. Lee Phelps went into a peyote ceremony and observed twenty-six men and women in white sheets (a garment associated with a religious activity) participating in the ritual. Clearly, women had become regular participants since Kroeber's time. Usually the wife of the peyote chief served as the water woman, and Arapahos viewed these wives as ceremonial partners. Annie Pedro always participated, she said, because her husband John was a peyote chief. When a person vowed to sponsor a peyote meeting as a prayer sacrifice, women prepared the food for the ceremony, as they did for hand games and lodge ceremonies. Jess Rowlodge also pointed out that many women participated in peyote meetings, and that they sang with the men. Some had the fire tender position. He viewed the women's roles as singers and composers of songs to have been crucial in the growth of the peyote movement. They "preserved the songs" better than the men, he said.

Rowlodge described the main peyote leaders in Canton as Heap Of Crows, Mixed Hair, White Shirt, and Jim R. Hutchinson "and their wives," Bethhebah, Good Looking, White Buffalo Woman, and Ugly Woman, respectively. Recall that these ceremonial teams also led in the other religious faiths of the time. Once, Rowlodge recalled, Sitting Bull was talking during a rest period in the ritual, and he started to recount his war experiences to other men there. His wife Dropping Lip interrupted and reminded him that he should not mix words about violence with words about good or peaceful thoughts. According to Rowlodge, he immediately "complied with her demands." They acted as a ceremonial team, each able to intervene and exercise authority in matters of ritual. In Greenfield, Rowlodge named Cut Nose and his wife, Big Heart, and Gun and his wife, Woman, as peyote leaders.

Rowlodge also identified Crooked Foot (from the Jessie Spread Hands cohort) as a peyote chief and an important leader in the movement. She was married to Long Hair, and they were senior people in the lodges as well. She made her own songs and developed unique ritual components. Her husband "ran" the meeting, but the water woman brought Crooked Foot the sacred objects used in the ceremony. Long Hair's sister Long Nose always sat beside Crooked Foot. After Long Hair died, Crooked Foot married Grant Left Hand, a lodge man and peyotist.[84]

New Political Partnerships

Women had political influence and probably authority, although the record on this is not extensive. According to Bird White Bear, wives of Lodge Makers (and probably other senior lodge women) had particular political influence: their "words were honored." In Canton, the senior women (those with Lime Crazy rank) were Bitchea (Mrs. Rabbit Run), Ugly Woman (Mrs. Coal Of Fire), Spotted Woman (Mrs. Lime), Bad Looking (Mrs. Young Bear), Good Looking (Mrs. Mixed Hair), Red Mouth (Mrs. Henry Sage), Bethhebah (Mrs. Heap Of Crows), Singing Woman (Mrs. Black Horse), and Dropping Lip (Mrs.. Sitting Bull). Bitchea (as Mrs. Rabbit Run, then Mrs. Little Raven, Jr.), Spotted Woman, Dropping Lip, and Jessie Spread Hands (Mrs. Bringing Good) also had chief's wife status. Half belonged to Bichea's cohort and half to the Jessie Spread Hands cohort. In Greenfield, the senior women were Cross Killer (Mrs. Hail), Big Heart (Mrs. Cut Nose), Woman (Mrs. Gun), Blackfeet Woman (Mrs. White Owl), Woman Going Ahead (Mrs. Young Bear), Hide In The Night (Mrs. Bald Head), Bitchea (Mrs. Tony Pedro), and Julia (Black) Woolworth (Arnold's wife, who was Cut Finger's sister and a member of Myrtle Lincoln's cohort).

Cross Killer, Woman Going Ahead, and Julia Woolworth were chief's wives.

As in the past century, wives contributed to and shared in their husbands' status, in large measure by their generosity and reciprocal gift giving. The chiefs' wives used their money and ceremonial authority to help their husbands generate support for their political agenda of opposing federal land policy and pursuing legal claims. For example, they and other women donated money for the expenses of the delegations. The chiefs' wives helped their husbands retain their influence and authority into old age.

Women made their wishes known in community councils. The government farmer in 1902 wrote that men considered women's views and generally deferred to them (presumably on matters that fell within their sphere). As women's role as landowners assumed great importance, federal land policy became their concern. In 1934 in a district meeting in Geary, when Arapahos discussed whether to accept the Oklahoma Indian Welfare Act, two old women spoke to the council from their perspective as landowners. Sage Woman (Mrs. Two Lances) and Hecha spoke against the proposed legislation. Sage Woman, from Jessie Spread Hands's cohort, and her husband were Lime Crazies and prominent people in Calumet. Hecha was the widow of Red Wolf, a Lime Crazy Man. She belonged to Bichea's cohort, and in her first marriage was a co-wife. With her second husband, Red Wolf (an elder brother of the 1903 Clubboard Men), she mentored the Clubboard Men and their wives. Jess Rowlodge also identified Hecha as one of the women respected for her ability to pray for "life." [85]

Apparently, women felt they could take their concerns to their district chiefs and that these men would pursue these matters with federal officials. The 1917 delegation had instructions from women to protest the superintendents' control of their IIM accounts. Cut Nose, chief and delegate, told officials, "We have a good many widow women, some with children, and they have good incomes but they have no teams, wagons, horses, harness." He argued that these women had to visit their relatives in different districts and needed the transportation. Ellen Theok (Mrs. Harry Bates) wrote the superintendent in 1925, referring to the chiefs: "I will see that they make a complaint to the commissioner of Indian Affairs about the two Indian women cooks at Cantonment school. My children complain." Ellen, from the cohort of Myrtle Lincoln, was a granddaughter of Little Raven and a Carlisle alumna, who married Harry after his first wife died.[86]

When men's district committees were organized, women's committees served concomitantly, in charge of gender-specific duties but also most likely participating in discussions and decisions about the date and place of gatherings. In the 1920s in Canton, women as well as men donated money to the council hall building project, so perhaps the income they had from leasing and selling land gave them the means to participate in new ways. The council hall took the place of the chief's tepee. Women as well as men signed petitions to federal officials. In 1923, twenty-two women at Seger (including some from the Poisal family) joined men in signing a petition requesting to elect district representatives. In 1933, fifteen Arapaho women (generally from Myrtle Lincoln's cohort) as well as several men in Canton signed a petition to the commissioner protesting their people's circumstances.[87]

At the time the federal government was attempting to remove the old chiefs from leadership positions, their wives and other women of the Bichea and Jessie Spread Hands cohorts supported the chiefs. The result was a general tribal council that included both chiefs and the young men of Jess Rowlodge's cohort. Superintendent Charles Berry reported in 1934 that women participated in district council meetings and voted for their district representatives to the general council, although no women ran for office. The young women of Myrtle Lincoln's cohort helped their husbands press for economic aid and more political authority for landless Arapahos. Their support was an important factor in the Arapahos' acceptance of the Oklahoma Indian Welfare Act and elective, representational, constitutional government.[88]

As we have seen, women took advantage of their access to money as well as other opportunities in the religious sphere to partner their husbands in various ways, including in the pursuit of a political agenda that involved a turn away from the civilization strategy toward a more defiant one. Women in Myrtle Lincoln's cohort gave essential support to their husbands' efforts on behalf of the landless Arapahos. Women in Bichea's and Jessie Spread Hands's cohorts assisted their husbands to pursue political goals and retain authority well into old age and, in the process, supported their own life careers.

Two Elements That Control These Lands: Redefining Old Age

In 1911 Red Woman, a seventy-two-year-old widow, Buffalo Lodge Woman, and member of Owl's cohort, had a prophetic dream. She saw the death of Lena Black Horse (Mrs. Mathew Spotted Wolf), her daughter-in-law. She wept profusely, and later that day, Lena died. Old people like Red Woman (Mrs. Spotted Wolf) generally inspired great respect and even awe because of their perceived access to supernatural forces. By the 1930s, the cohort of Medicine Grass and Bichea had reached old age. Many in the Little Raven, Jr., and Jessie Spread Hands cohort had also. Arapahos relied on old people to conduct funerals and called on them to name children and otherwise bless them. For example, Arnold Woolworth, whose children were born in the first decade of the century, asked his grandmother Old Lady Hawk to name his oldest child. The doctor Old Lady Digging (one of Trunk's daughters) named his daughter Rose. The doctor Old Man Calf Head and Old Lady Gun, the wife of the doctor Gun, named his third and fourth children. Old people presided over all the ceremonies— both household and tribal—held during these years. Not only did their advanced age signal that they had obtained supernatural assistance, but an old person's children surviving to adulthood also indicated a blessing from the Creator.

Old people set the example of good conduct, regularly displaying generosity to others, which they could afford to do, given their generally sizable IIM accounts. The Indian correspondent for the Canton newspaper recorded many feasts given by individuals and attended by all the people in the district and sometimes other districts. For example, in 1921, Arapahos gave seven feasts, including three of seventy-five-year-old Coming On Horseback (from Medicine Grass's cohort) and one of sixty-year-old Little Raven, Jr. In 1922, Coming On Horseback (a renowned warrior, who was called upon to tell his war stories at tribal ceremonies) gave two feasts, sixty-five-year-old Young Bear gave one, Little Raven, Jr., gave one, and two old women, Ugly Woman (Mrs. Coal Of Fire) and Dropping Lip (Mrs. Sitting Bull) gave feasts. In 1923 Coming On Horseback gave three feasts, and Medicine Dance and Bringing Good (from Medicine Grass's cohort) gave feasts.[89]

During these years, the term "old" came to mean more than chronological age. To have this title, a person had to qualify as a ceremonial person. For example, Dan Tucker, Sore Thumb, Red Man, and Hoof were all born between 1860 and 1862—they were members of the Little Raven, Jr., cohort—but the Indian correspondent referred to the latter three (camp Indians) as "chiefs" (which Arnold Woolworth noted was a contemporary term used for an "old" man and not literally an indication of intermediary chieftainship), but Dan Tucker, the Carlisle alumnus who had been on the margins of Arapaho ceremonial life, was referred to as "Dan Tucker." Myrtle Lincoln referred to Jessie Spread Hands as "old Mrs. Bringing Good," although she was born in 1867 and still in her late forties during the Grass Dance rituals in which she participated.[90]

Economic Contributions

In the new money economy of the twentieth century, the old people played a key role in household economy for the first time. When the federal government discontinued rations, elderly Arapahos received the food for a time, and they shared it with family members. The IIM of the aged was supervised by the agency superintendents, who put them on a monthly allowance—at first ten dollars, later twenty dollars or a little more. For example, when sixty-one-year-old Fire became physically unable to farm, Cantonment Superintendent White authorized fifteen dollars a month to him and ten dollars a month for his wife, Bucket. A year later, White also approved thirty dollars for a new tent and furnishings. Since the superintendents were wont to give younger people money only for "subsistence," the old people in an extended family bought groceries for all. They often took on the care of grandchildren, especially "orphans." And the old men allowed younger ones to use their farming equipment either for a share of the crop or to fulfill kinship responsibilities. Old people generally still had their allotments. This land base came to be relied on by younger generations in several ways. The old person's allotment was the site of the home place, where the extended family lived, and younger men and women farmed it. Old women were sometimes allowed their IIM to buy stock and farm equipment for younger male relatives. As Chief Sage from west Geary put it in 1934, "There is only two elements that controls these lands; they are the old men and women."

Even though the income of elderly people usually helped their younger relatives, sometimes parents depended on an adult child, for care more than income. In 1912 Reverend Funk noted that when John De Brae died, White Rabbit, his aged and nearly blind father, who had been cared for by John, fell into a deep depression. Other Arapahos, fearing suicide or an accident, "watched him" and comforted him. A few old people (educated members of the Little Raven, Jr., cohort) had little or no land and depended on a wide range of kin for help.[91]

One of the issues that the chiefs raised on delegations to Washington was the amount of the monthly IIM payment. They argued that, given the responsibility of old people, the amount should be increased because they could not get credit. The superintendents' attitude was that agedness meant that an individual was not competent to manage his or her money and could not be trusted with larger amounts. Of course, older people, as "noncompetents," usually held on to their allotments, and they often inherited quite a bit of land from their allotted children who did not survive childhood. Because elderly people inherited a great deal of land from deceased children and sometimes spouses or other relatives, generally they had large IIM accounts, which could be drawn on for developing farms if not for other purposes. In 1912, of the twelve elderly Arapahos in Canton, six were in relatively well-off households. They had household income that was higher than 63 percent of the other Arapahos. In 1917, two-thirds of the elderly people's households were well off; in 1927, 70 percent. Most old people over the 1912–27 period had large incomes at least some of these years. Compared with other age groups, elderly people were the largest percentage of the well-off category.[92]

Differentials

Although old people in general lived more secure lives than in past eras and were influential, not every old person achieved prominence and a relatively good standard of living. Education was a factor, but so was marital history and the state of a person's health. If we look at the lives of the elderly (from the Medicine Grass and Bichea cohort) in the Cantonment area, several couples, who had long stable marriages, were particularly well off: Heap Of Crows and Bethhebah, and Sitting Bull and Dropping Lip. Sitting Bull and his wife had adult children. Heap Of Crows did not, although his wife was very close to her sister's children. Sitting Bull's economic fortunes fell drastically in his last years because the North Canadian River overflowed and destroyed his allotment. Rabbit Run and Bitchea were also a prominent couple until they divorced in 1920, when he was sixty-six. These were all ceremonial people, and the latter two couples held chieftainship positions. Rabbit Run and Bitchea had higher than average income, as did Sitting Bull and Dropping Lip (until the flood). Bringing Good and Jessie Spread Hands (who died in 1946, outliving her husband by eleven years) and Broken Rib and Turkey (married since 1912) had years of both high and low income from leases and sales. All these couples often permitted camps on their land or invited people to feasts.

What about widowers or men without stable marriages? Medicine Dance, a doctor, became a widower in 1921. Drawing a small monthly allowance, he lived on his wife's daughter Traveler's place in a tent, and Traveler took care of him. Old Man Tabor's wife died in 1916, and he then lived with his son Wilbur. After Rabbit Run and Bitchea divorced, he was briefly remarried, then divorced again. Afterwards, he lived with his daughter Kate (Mrs. Dave Meat). The superintendent visited this household in 1922: Rabbit Run and his two sons-in-law and their families "were eating dinner, all sitting around in a circle on the floor in one room. They all had stewed meat, bread, potatoes, coffee and canned pears . . . . The white looking place in the roof of the house was caused by a room being tore off by Bitchea, former wife of Rabbit Run. The room was built onto the house with her funds, so when she got a divorce from him she took her part of the house with her." Rabbit Run collected $368 annual rental on his allotment. Coming On Horseback's wife died, and he remarried; he had no children but considerable income. These old men received care and contributed income to the household in which they lived. Without a wife, though, a man's political influence greatly declined.

Widows outnumbered widowers. Having adult children was important to women's well-being, especially if they needed care. Striking Night, the midwife and widow of Big Head, was taken care of by her children. Short Woman, widow of ceremonial man Old Bear, remarried Bird Chief, Jr., another ceremonial man, and after he died, she lived with her daughter. Red Woman (widow of Spotted Wolf, who died in 1898, and mother of Bringing Good, Ben Spotted Wolf, and Harry Bates) was a ceremonial authority and midwife, and she lived with her son Harry until she died at the age of eighty.

Single women in good health who had children could be heads of household. Ugly Woman (Coal Of Fire's widow) had a farm on her husband's allotment, and her sons and other relatives worked it. She married Rabbit Run in 1925, which allowed them to work as a ceremonial team. But they soon divorced. She was an assertive woman, who had a leadership role in the extended family household, in which income was pooled. Traveler had been Scabby Bull's widow until she married his brother Sitting Bull briefly, then Cleaver Warden in 1907. They divorced and Cleaver married Singing After (the custodian of the Sacred Wheel). Traveler had several children, and her daughter and son-in-law lived with her. She had two old men living on her place (Medicine Dance and Singing Man), who also contributed to the household. She drew on her IIM, and her son-in-law farmed. Traveler died still "head" of the family farm in 1942 at the age of eighty. Red Feather (Myrtle Lincoln's mother-in-law and Beaver's widow) remarried a younger man, Chase Harrington (an educated member of the Little Raven, Jr., cohort). He and some of his relatives lived on Beaver's allotment, as did the Lincolns, and they farmed her land. Assertive and active, like Ugly Woman and Traveler, she drew a monthly allowance and worked as a doctor.

Women without children did not fare so well, especially if in poor health. Good Looking (Mixed Hair's widow) had no living children. She was nursed through the flu by Walter Fire's family, but died. Walter was her brother's son. Bucket (Fire's widow) was respected for her knowledge of Arapaho history, so much so that the chiefs obtained her testimony about the Black Hills treaty. Bucket lived eleven years after Fire's death, and the superintendent paid money from her account to others to care for her since she had no reliable relative who would take responsibility. Singing Woman (widow of Black Horse) was childless. After Black Horse died, she remarried, but her husband died in 1926. By this time, she was feeble and paralyzed, according to the superintendent. She moved to the allotment of some relatives, who drew on her funds. She died in 1930 at the age of seventy-four. The formidable Mrs. Left Hand, also childless, left Greenfield after the death of Left Hand in 1911. She eventually moved to Canton, where she married Left Hand's widowed brother Red Man, fourteen years her junior, and lived ten more years after his death in 1924. They lived much of their married life in a tent on James R. Hutchinson's allotment (he was her "son-in-law"), drawing on their lease income. Probably with great satisfaction, Bear Woman (Left Hand's divorced wife) moved with her son Grant into Chief Left Hand's house.

Several members of the cohort of Little Raven, Jr., and Jessie Spread Hands also reached old age by the 1920s. Camp Indians Little Raven, Jr., White Shirt, and Lime had attained prominence as chiefs and ceremonial men, a position they shared with their wives. Little Raven, Jr. (who died in 1938 at the age of seventy-seven) had married Bitchea (who died in 1941), the divorced wife of Rabbit Run. All these couples had adult children. Little Raven, Jr.'s wife Bitchea had a sizable income. His and White Shirt's families had income in the top 25 percent. In 1930 Lime was living with both Spotted Woman (his ceremonial partner) and Long Hair and several adult children. The family's income was relatively high in relation to the Arapaho community in general.

But what about the educated members of this cohort? Five had reached old age by 1930. James R. Hutchinson was a ceremonial man, who had identified himself with the camp Indians, and he and his wife Ugly Woman had an average income. Ira Sankey (another of Owl's sons) was a ceremonial man, an Offerings Lodge participant, married to a camp Indian whose income put the family in the average range. Ira's son contributed to the household and helped him farm, which made the extended family fairly prosperous by Arapaho standards. Harry Bates was married to Ellen Theok, and they had several adult children who helped him farm. Both Harry and Ellen had held onto their land when agency officials reported in 1917 that neither could read nor write (obviously an incorrect assumption). Harry lived humbly, not identifying himself as "educated." He seems to have participated primarily in Mennonite rituals, and is credited with composing the only Arapaho hymn used in that church. Dan Tucker and John Williams, who had counted on prospering as educated Arapahos, had little or no income. After his divorce from his American wife, Tucker married a young school girl who died within a year. A few years later, he married White Shirt's daughter Ruth (from Myrtle Lincoln's cohort). Their children died when they were small, and Ruth died at the age of thirty-seven. Dan lived alone the last fourteen years of his life, doing a little farming and collecting some lease money. John Williams married Birdshead's daughter Red

Woman and managed to get the superintendent's permission to sell half of her allotment as well as his own in 1908. They had no adult children and struggled to support themselves. Tucker and Williams probably felt great frustration.[93]

In the Geary area, Medicine Grass died in 1931, gratified that he had been able to deed land to his daughter Lucy. Bichea died in 1934, proud of her long life, the rank she had achieved in the lodge organization, her surviving children and grandchildren, and the fact that she had been able to give land to her grandchildren. When she died, she was living with her son John. Owl died in 1921. She spent the last years of her life living with her sons Ira Sankey and Jess Rowlodge, using her money to help their families.[94]

The Incorporation of New Religions

In the late 1920s, the ceremonial and political authority of elderly people faced some challenges. Ceremonial authorities still made an essential contribution to Arapaho religious life by directing rituals and validating innovations that enabled ceremonial life to thrive. The old warriors, including Sitting Bull, Coming On Horseback, and Plenty Bears, told their war stories at appropriate times in the lodge ceremonies, animating regalia and transferring blessings. Ute became the head of the doctors' society and was renowned for his ability to make rain, according to Bird White Bear. Another old doctor cured Bird of paralysis when the agency doctor failed. Hail had his son Mathew (a member of Jess Rowlodge's cohort) treated by an Arapaho doctor. Arapahos could rely on doctoring even as they occasionally accepted care from the agency or other physicians. And the priesthood survived. White Eyed Antelope, Mountain, Old Crow, and Tall Bear were all dead by 1908, and Mrs. Little Raven died in 1911. But Bull Thunder and his wife, Striking In Night, and Hawkan and his wife, Grass Singing, succeeded them. Bull Thunder and his wife died in 1917 and Hawkan, in 1918. Ute (from Medicine Grass's cohort) and his wife, Crippled, succeeded them, and he lived until 1950, remarrying ceremonial women twice after Crippled died: Blackfeet Woman (White Owl's widow) and Singing Woman (the widow of Black Coyote, then of Medicine Grass). Several other elderly men assisted Ute.

Singing After, who held the highest women's position in the Offerings Lodge, lived until 1964. Mountain's widow Join In The Party (from Jessie Spread Hands's cohort), a doctor in her own right and qualified to cut the center pole in the lodge, remarried Elmer Sweezy (an alumnus of Halstead and Carlisle) and lived until 1931. Bitchea, Tall Bear's widow, married Carlisle alumnus Neatha Seger, who subsequently became a Lodge Maker on several occasions and thus qualified to be the grandfather of the Lodge Maker. He and Young Bull had reached old age by the 1920s, when they were Lodge Makers. Noble Prentiss (another Carlisle alumnus and a member of Little Raven, Jr.'s cohort) became a Lodge Maker in his late forties and continued his leadership role into the late 1930s. By this time Little Raven, Jr., had become a priest, assisting Ute. So some of the members of Little Raven, Jr.'s and Jessie Spread Hands's cohort, as well as older people, remained committed to the perpetuation of the lodge ceremonies.[95]

Nonetheless, the spread of peyote cut into the number of participants in the Offerings Lodge. In 1925, only five men sacrificed themselves. But elderly people did not oppose peyotism. In fact, many of the Indian doctors, including Ute, used peyote in curing patients, whether or not they were peyotists. And there were other opportunities for ritual expression. Old men went with younger ones visiting tribes throughout Oklahoma (as they had done in the 1890s) to attend dances and participate in gift giving. The World War I veterans showed particular interest in these events.[96]

Other factors worked to discourage participation in the lodge organization. Not only did people in Jess Rowlodge's and Myrtle Lincoln's cohort feel that the lodge organization created obstacles to their economic and political aspirations, but Arapahos also had a considerable amount of fear that mistakes might be made and supernatural punishment follow. Bird White Bear noted that the women's sacred bags from the Buffalo Lodge had been buried with their owners because young people were "afraid of" the ceremony. Jess Rowlodge concluded that many "educated ones" did not care to keep up their "training," so ultimately the sacred ritual objects used in the lodges were sent to the Northern Arapahos in Wyoming.

A few old people accepted Christianity. Left Hand had lost his faith in the Ghost Dance by the beginning of the century. Blind then, he attended Baptist services, at first to encourage Arapahos to give up using liquor, as the missionaries were urging. Then he had a dream vision in which he saw the missionary proclaim that if Arapahos converted, sickness would disappear. He recognized that Jesus made a body sacrifice, so he was able to relate his life to the missionary's teachings. He took the "Jesus Road" by 1907 but also declared that he would continue to believe in Indian medicine and the Sacred Flat Pipe. In fact, Jess Rowlodge reported that he gave a feast for the Beaver doctors during their rituals. Other old people participated in the lodges and in Christianity.[97]

Political Participation

The Bureau of Indian Affairs also opposed the perpetuation of Arapaho ceremonial organization, as well as chieftainship. By the 1930s superintendents had begun to ignore and belittle the chiefs. For example, when a delegation of chiefs took their concerns to the superintendent, he referred to them as "former chiefs" who had "honorary positions" only. This undermined them politically, and may have discouraged Arapaho participation in the ceremonies that the chiefs essentially led. Ute, for example, was a chief as well as a priest. Once praised as progressives who farmed successfully and supported the schools, now they were obsolete nonprogressives who, because of their age and association with the ceremonial life, could not provide leadership for the modern community. Officials described them as impediments to progress, even though these same individuals had smoothed the Arapahos' transition to farming and formal education. In Washington, the commissioner of Indian Affairs refused to receive the chiefs as delegations, insisting on English-speaking representatives.

At the same time, the men and women of Jess Rowlodge's and Myrtle Lincoln's cohort felt great frustration with their circumstances.

Relatively landless, in the 1930s they were dependent on the old landowners, and they had no political apparatus to express their concerns other than the council meetings, where they tried to influence the chiefs and older men and women. When Commissioner John Collier proposed a reorganization plan with provisions for economic development—land assignments and loans—and elective representative government, the younger generation enthusiastically supported the change.[98]

The agency superintendent had begun the process of political change in 1928, when he encouraged the men of Jess Rowlodge's cohort to organize a joint general council based on the model of the farm chapter organization in each district. The members of the farm chapters were largely members of Jess Rowlodge's cohort. The districts chose representatives, who occasionally came together with Cheyenne representatives. The joint general council elected three officers. The chiefs agreed to participate because the work of the general council was to be the pursuit of the court claims against the United States, and the council got approval to send a chief and a young bilingual, educated man from each tribe to Washington. Arapahos viewed the chiefs as knowledgeable about the treaties upon which their claims were based. In 1928 Jess and Henry Rowlodge were two of the officers of the council. In Canton, the president of the district council was Dave Meat. Wilbur Tabor also served on the council. Chief White Shirt and Jess Rowlodge went as delegates to Washington in 1930 and 1931.

After that, the commissioner approved only one delegate per tribe, and the council selected Jess Rowlodge. In the Greenfield and Geary area, elderly chiefs Medicine Grass, Ute, and Arnold Woolworth served on the council alongside Jess and Henry Rowlodge. In the Cantonment district, elderly Little Raven, Jr., and White Shirt served with Hannibal Bighead and Dan Blackhorse. This was the pattern in 1932 and 1933—old chiefs and young men from Jess's cohort making up most of the council membership. In 1933 Arapahos sent a petition to the commissioner of Indian Affairs. Men from the Medicine Grass, Little Raven, Jr., and Jess

Rowlodge cohorts signed, as well as several women. The women signatories generally were from Myrtle Lincoln's cohort or were younger women born in the first decade of the century and married to men of Jess's cohort. Virginia Lone Lodge (Mrs. Hannibal Big-head) was one. In 1929 the general council had adopted a constitution that called for four representatives from each of the six Arapaho districts (so that most families would have representation), and the representatives had to include chiefs and headmen as well as young educated people (although only men actually ran for election). This was the compromise for which the old people had worked. The constitution also provided for no compensation for council members.[99]

The chiefs and the older landowners opposed the Indian Reorganization Act, legislation proposed by Collier. The chiefs were sympathetic to the plight of the young, "landless" people, though. Little Raven, Jr., commented that "the pleadings of the younger element of the tribe seems to haunt me." The opposition was in response to Collier's plan to buy allotments and put them in trust for the tribe. This plan was eventually dropped largely because of the protests from allottees all over the country. Another bill, which pertained to Indians in Oklahoma (the Oklahoma Indian Welfare Act), passed Congress, and the younger Arapahos pressed for reorganization under its provisions. In 1937 the Cheyennes and Arapahos voted to reorganize their joint council.[100]

The younger generation of Arapahos—Jess Rowlodge's and Myrtle Lincoln's cohort—accepted the idea of elective government (one person, one vote) and decision making by majority vote, but the people elected (again, people primarily from Jess Rowlodge's cohort) did not have a record of accomplishment or generosity that older Arapahos believed validated authority. Most of those elected were poor, and in the new constitution, the elected representatives were to receive per diem. So rather than expressing generosity by providing for others, the representatives received tribal funds for attending meetings. And most important, despite new leadership, Arapahos obtained no relief from poverty or the

paternalistic controls of the federal government. In the new constitution, the Arapaho and Cheyenne governments were combined,
the number of Arapaho representatives was cut from twenty-four
to fourteen, and none of the elected representatives had to be
chiefs. As a result of the tension between the understandings and
interests of old and young, a new form of government did emerge.
It would result in the undermining of Arapaho political process
in the post-1936 years.[101]

In the twentieth century, poverty and the Arapahos' realization
that BIA policy marginalized them economically and politically
led to more defiant and aggressive political strategies in dealings
with the United States. Arapahos recognized that federal land
and IIM policy discriminated on the basis of age and gender. Some
Arapahos could take advantage of these policies to make new
kinds of contributions to household and community and perhaps
parlay that into political influence. The disadvantaged began to
develop forms of resistance to these inequalities, both in relation to
the United States and to the landowning Arapahos. The potential
tension between women and men, fostered by discriminatory
federal policies, developed instead into new partnerships in
households and communities as Arapahos realized that such
policies would not work for them. They drew on ideas about
reciprocities that under the direction of old people continued to
be expressed in age-graded and Offerings Lodge ceremonies.

Leadership practices, though, came under challenge as tension
developed between older and younger cohorts. Initially, leadership for the new militancy came from senior lodge people and the
chiefs and their wives. Later, the Jess Rowlodge–Myrtle Lincoln
cohort worked to challenge that leadership. Goals and understandings diverged between men and women in the older cohorts
and those in the Jess Rowlodge–Myrtle Lincoln cohort. Age group
reciprocities promoted in lodge ceremonies mitigated these tensions,
but the inequalities between the landowning older Arapahos
and the landless younger ones eventually resulted in the end

of intermediary chieftainship and the democratization of leadership institutions. In conjunction with the new political direction,
peyotism, with its more individualistic organization, became the
most widespread religious ritual and drew young people away
from the lodge organization.

Chief Hail in Ghost Dance clothing, 1901. Hail (1856–1925) was an Offerings Lodge grandfather, a headman for the 1903 Clubboard Men, and a Lime Crazy Man. He was also a Ghost Dance leader and a leader in the Baptist Church at Geary, and a district and an intermediary chief during the twentieth century. He and his wife probably received the Ghost Dance shirt and dress from Sitting Bull. The painted designs on his shirt symbolize his visions during the Ghost Dance ritual. Note the drum in the background with a group of men and a group of women singers. Photo by Mrs. Ollie Gilham, Hickox Collection. Courtesy of the Research Division of the Oklahoma Historical Society (9563).

Mrs. Hail in Ghost Dance clothing, 1901. Mrs. Hail (Cross Killer) lived from 1865 to 1952. She was the chief wife in a polygamous household. Cross Killer was an Offerings Lodge grandmother, wife of a headman of the Clubboard Lodge, a Lime Crazy Woman, as well as a leader in the Ghost Dance and Baptist Church. She probably was one of the seven women who received a Ghost Dance dress from Sitting Bull. The designs on the dress represent her visions during the ritual. She and Hail had a farm in the Greenfield area, where she raised chickens. Note the stove inside the tent, an adaptation of the time. After Hail died, she married another ceremonial man. Cross Killer had one son who lived to maturity. Photo by Mrs. Ollie Gilham, Hickox Collection. Courtesy of Research Division of the Oklahoma Historical Society (9573).

Arapaho wall tent with quilled ornaments, Cheyenne-Arapaho Reservation, 1913. After buffalo robes could not be obtained, women made quilled ornaments for canvas tepees. The ornaments on this wall tent could have been transferred from a woman's tepee by the owner or inherited by another woman who used them, probably after a ceremony of which no record exists. The circular ornament represents the course of Whirlwind Woman as she circled the earth, making it increase in size. She is credited with making the first of these ornaments to represent her act of creation. Campbell Collection. Courtesy of Western History Collections, University of Oklahoma (342).

2nd night's rehearsal with Clubs + etc.

Second night's rehearsal, Clubboard Lodge, 1903. This drawing is from Cleaver Warden's sketch-book. It shows how Arapahos viewed the ritual and highlights the important roles Arapaho women as well as men played in the ceremony. This scene represents a moment when the women relatives of the Clubboard Men and the grandfathers supported the men publicly. In the center on the right is the pledger of the ceremony, Dan Webster (1870–1946), with his mother, Bichea, wife Pueblo Woman, and probably his sister Molly and his mother's sister Turkey dancing with him facing his grandfather, Striking Back (1856–1910). Striking Back is dancing with his women relatives, including his wife Road Maker and probably his sister Buffalo Fat, and daughters of his other two sisters. Striking Back holds the club that he will give Dan during the ceremony. To the southeast is a woman clown, holding an "awkward looking" wand in imitation of the Clubboards. To her right are the headmen for Dan and the other new members of the Clubboard Lodge. A drum, to be used during the dance, sits on the ground, and two messenger boys rest beside it. South of them are several old men who are encouraging the dancers. In the northeast corner of the drawing are the women relatives of the grandfathers. They have brought food and water in pails to "provision the grandchildren," which initiates an exchange between grandfathers and grandsons to help establish the bond between the families of the men. To the far left on the ground is a bisected circle, painted red and black. Cleaver Warden refers to this as a symbol of the "foundation" of the lodges, including the theme of gender complementarity. On the far west sit the four priests of the ceremony: from top to bottom, Crippled (1860–1920), the woman priest for the ceremony and the holder of the Peacemaker position in the tribe; Old Crow (1828–1904), one of the men priests for the ceremony and holder of a Seven Old Men position for many years; White Eyed Antelope (1832–1908), another of the men priests and a newly selected Old Man; and Mountain (1843–1905), the third of the men priests and the most recently selected Old Man. Cleaver Warden and George A. Dorsey Collection. Courtesy of The Field Museum (CN91205d).

Bull Thunder and his wife, ca. 1910. This long-married, respected couple sat for a formal portrait. The photograph was used as a postcard during a time when Oklahoma settlers invited and advertised Native participants to their celebrations to attract visitors and paying customers. Bull Thunder (1838–1917) was a band headman at Cantonment in the 1880s and, along with his wife Striking In Night, became a priest of the lodges, probably achieving the Old Men's Lodge. He holds his pipe and wears the white sheet that indicates his ritual status and the peace medal he received from the government as an intermediary chief. Striking In Night (1851–1917), a co-wife early in her marriage, likely had achieved the Buffalo Women's Lodge, and she and Bull Thunder were a chief couple (chief and chief's wife) at Cantonment in the 1890s. Striking In Night had two sons who lived to maturity. Photo by Hudson. Courtesy of Mennonite Library and Archives, Bethel College.

Lizard and his wife Shoshone Woman, Seger Colony, 1904. Lizard (1847–1926) was a Lime Crazy Man and an Offerings Lodge participant who assisted one of the grandfathers in 1902. Shoshone Woman (1855–1928) was a high-ranking women's authority in the Rabbit Lodge and an apprentice to the woman priest in the 1901 Offerings Lodge. She was the sister of Spotted Bear, a high-ranking Lodge Maker. As the wife of Old Horse, she had been a Lodge Maker's wife and qualified to be a grandmother of the wives of Lodge Makers. After Old Horse died, in about 1890 she married Lizard, whose rank in the Offerings Lodge was lower than hers. Lizard had had six brief marriages before, but his union with Shoshone Woman lasted all their lives. They are in "traditional" clothing appropriate for a tribal gathering and may be in the process of giving gifts. E. Palmer Collection. Courtesy of Research Division of the Oklahoma Historical Society (21082.12).

Coal Of Fire, his wife, and their children, ca. 1906, El Reno. Coal Fire (1858–1920) was Trunk's son. During the 1890s he was a freighter, and in the early 1900s, a relatively prosperous farmer. With his wife Ugly Woman (shown here), he rose to the Lime Crazy Lodge in 1906. Coal Fire married Ugly Woman (1856–1928) in 1894. She was a co-wife, but three years later the other wife, Snake Woman (apparently the boss wife), died and Ugly Woman became his ceremonial partner. Ugly Woman had been married twice before, divorced once, and widowed once. After Coal Of Fire died, she married a high-ranking ceremonial man, Rabbit Run. She and Coal Of Fire are well dressed in Indian style for this formal portrait, along with their three children, who are wearing American-style clothes—Walter (born in 1896), James (born in 1903), and Matilda (born in 1904) Fire. Several other children died when they were small. Photo by H. J. Stevenson. Courtesy of the Research Division of the Oklahoma Historical Society (3860).

James R. Hutchinson, his wife, and his daughter, 1901. James Hutchinson (1867–1944) was the son of the high-ranking warrior and band leader Cut Finger, who died when James was fourteen. He went to the Arapaho School, then to Haskell for about three years during the mid-1880s before returning to the reservation, where he freighted and worked for wages. His first wife was Chief Yellow Bear's daughter Minnie, who died in 1894. His daughter May (1892–1907) was the child of Minnie. James married Ethel Black Wolf, then Minnie's younger, widowed sister Ugly Woman (1876–1930), who had been married to one of Trunk's sons. He and Ethel soon divorced. With Ugly Woman (shown here), he rose to the Thunderbird Lodge and was an Offerings Lodge participant, peyote chief, and deacon in the Baptist Church. He became a relatively prosperous farmer who raised wheat and cotton for sale, and Ugly Woman raised chickens. Although he had been educated at Haskell, he reidentified as a camp Indian. Ugly Woman had one son who lived to maturity and six others who died when they were very young. Photo by Mrs. Ollie Gilham, Hickox Collection. Courtesy of Research Division of the Oklahoma Historical Society (9479.4).

Joel Bighead and his wife, 1908. Joel Bighead (Smoker; 1884–1943) was the son of Big Head 1 and Striking Night, both doctors. His wife Lizzie (Woman in Sight; 1886–1913) was his first wife, whose father was the accomplished warrior Coming On Horseback. They were legally married and had several children, all of whom died when they were small. After she died, Joel married two more times. He went to school on the reservation for about six years. In 1911 he was helping older men farm, and in 1917 he was declared "competent" and given a fee patent on his land. They are photographed in camp, probably at a gathering, in front of a brush windbreak. He wears an Omaha Dance outfit. Photo by Dedrick Talonga, H. H. Henston Collection. Courtesy of Research Division of the Oklahoma Historical Society (8128).

CONCLUSION

Making Gender, Making History

Little Raven, Jr.'s life experiences reflect the opportunities and constraints many in his cohort encountered. He was a child in a prosperous family in prereservation days; in his youth, a camp Indian who did not attend school; a young man who worked as a scout and helped older men freight; a mature man who became a chief and a high-ranking ceremonial authority; and an old man who had land and income as well as respect for his ceremonial knowledge, yet whose leadership was challenged by younger Arapahos. His first wife, Jenny, younger than he, married him when she was very young, thereby avoiding school, rose with him in the ceremonial organization, and became a chief wife. His second wife, Bitchea, older than he, was first the wife of a warrior, chief, and senior lodge man, and she already had ceremonial authority equal to or greater than Little Raven, Jr.'s when she married him in her later years. These three helped Arapahos transition to an agricultural economy, played roles in the Arapahos' embrace of the Ghost Dance, and supported the chieftainship all their lives as they struggled to persuade the United States to abide by its agreements with Arapahos. Their lives, as well as the lives of their contemporaries, reveal how cohort histories and partnering between women and men operated to produce major transformations in Arapaho life.

COHORTS IN HISTORY

In the prereservation era, the Arapahos lost their position of preeminence in their homeland, where they were rich in horses and able to trade buffalo robes for the goods they wanted, and they suffered large losses in population from war and disease. Their reversal of fortune came relatively quickly because of the Colorado gold rush, as well as the migration of the Cheyennes, Sioux, and other groups into their area. Rejecting American ideas that they could not be trusted to adjust to American expansion, leaders focused on trying to be conciliatory in dealings with Americans to prevent army attacks and to secure the federal government's guarantee of a territory reserved to them where they could live safely, according to their own values. They had allies among traders, some military officers, and some federal officials. Others in the army and federal bureaucracy, as well as most settlers, opposed Arapaho efforts. By the mid-1860s, Arapahos had lost their homeland and needed to find a new one. To accomplish this, and to avoid the constant attacks borne by their Cheyenne allies, intermediary chiefs had to be able to persuade other Arapahos to cooperate and to adhere to the agreements they made at treaty councils.

The members of the Little Raven and Walking Backward cohort experienced both the good times and the decline. They understood what was at stake, and they held the senior positions in the political and ceremonial organization at the time of the treaty councils. In a sense, they were in the right place at the right time. Allying with Americans interested in peace rather than war, they developed the strategy of conciliation to ensure the survival of the Arapahos, who were in a more precarious position than the other nomadic tribes on the southern plains after the loss of their winter range in Colorado. These women and men supported the chiefs and chiefs' wives, who belonged to their cohorts.

The chief couples (chiefs and their wives) had authority in the lodge system and wealth that they used to implement the conciliatory strategy. Chiefs' wives played an important part in mobilizing public support, just as they had in supporting military expeditions and facilitating trade. The duties of the Little Raven and Walking Backward cohort included the encouragement of military accomplishments by the members of the junior lodges. So their promotion of the conciliatory strategy meant that they had to contain the ambitions of the younger warriors and their wives. This involved a change in the social roles associated with the lodge organization. It is likely that as the Little Raven–Walking Backward cohort aged, its members gained increased influence because they had survived the dangers of their time. In any case, although the members of the younger Owl and Left Hand cohort had fully engaged in the military struggle, because of their junior ceremonial status, they deferred to the decisions of the older Little Raven and Walking Backward cohort and accepted the conciliatory strategy.

When the Arapahos arrived on the reservation in 1870, the Little Raven and Walking Backward cohort was still influential. Arapahos began a struggle to retain as much political independence as possible and to defend their interests in relation to the more numerous Cheyennes. They adopted a "civilization strategy" with regard to the federal government's programs, accepting innovation but on their own terms. Their success in obtaining the reservation within Arapaho hunting territory and preventing army attacks validated for the Owl and Left Hand cohort the wisdom of the conciliatory strategy and gave credence to the civilization strategy. The members of the Little Raven–Walking Backward cohort became old, then died during the early years on the reservation. In the 1870s and 1880s, prominent couples from the Owl and Left Hand cohort gradually assumed leadership positions in the lodge organization and succeeded to chieftainship. They took responsibility for promoting and implementing the civilization strategy, and the Arapahos made a transition to an agricultural economy.

By this time, the Owl–Left Hand cohort had entered the senior lodges, and they had large horse herds that they had brought with them to the reservation. The chiefs and chiefs' wives used their ceremonial status and wealth to mobilize the members of their cohort and the cohort of Medicine Grass and Bichea to accept new economic institutions, such as freighting and ranching, which they shaped to fit Arapaho ones. They took advantage of competing visions of the civilization program and schisms among Americans— different administrations, personality differences among agents, different school options, and animosity between the military and civilian branches of the federal government—to mitigate policies to which they objected. Senior Arapaho leaders instructed the agency police (largely from the Medicine Grass cohort) to conceal some aspects of Arapaho life from agents. While sending enough children to school to satisfy the agents, they insisted on their children's return to camp life. Freighting, stockraising, and farming involved communal labor and the sharing of the products of that labor. Because of a perceived continued threat from the Cheyennes and other tribes in the region, the federal government placated the chiefs to a considerable degree and tolerated the lodge organization and polygamy, which gave leaders the opportunity to perpetuate their authority while protecting the agency personnel. In this way, Arapahos convinced federal officials that they accepted the civilization program while living according to Arapaho religious and social values.

The men and women in the Medicine Grass–Bichea cohort had accepted an apprenticeship of sorts to the older cohort, working under their leadership on freight trains and in ranching operations, in this way embracing the civilization strategy. They realized that warfare could no longer be a route to advancement. But economic circumstances on the reservation had deteriorated by the 1890s. By the time they reached maturity, they had lost confidence both in the American officials' promises and in the Arapaho ceremonial hierarchy's ability to secure supernatural help for them. They began to assume the leadership for a series of revitalization movements that transformed Arapaho life. The members of the Medicine Grass–Bichea cohort were, in a sense, in the right place at the right time to lead the spread of the Ghost Dance complex and the peyote religion, challenging both the federal government's civilization agenda and the comprehensive authority of senior lodge people.

The members of the Jessie Spread Hands–Little Raven, Jr., cohort came to the reservation as children. They accepted the authority of the senior Arapahos, who accommodated them by reorienting the lodge ceremonies to modern conditions. But the boarding school policy of the federal government threatened to create a schism between "educated" and "uneducated" youths. Some, like Jessie, went to off-reservation schools, where teachers groomed them to reject the Arapaho way of life. Camp Indians, however, stayed on the reservation and, like Little Raven, Jr., who had his wives' help and was mentored by his prosperous family, began careers in the lodge organization.

Soon after the educated Arapahos returned to the reservation, they became disillusioned. Realizing that they faced discrimination and lack of opportunity, many reidentified as camp Indians. As young men, they joined the lodge organization and worked with their families freighting and farming. Girls contributed to the economic, political, and ceremonial activities of their households in what amounted to a refusal to accept the dependent role advocated in the boarding schools. Some of the educated youths showed stirrings of rebellion against the senior Arapaho cohorts by objecting to guardianships, preying on school girls (in the case of boys), or refusing marriages proposed by their families. Most of the boarding school students, however, eventually found a niche respected by Arapahos: the boys instructed older Arapahos in farming, and the girls made clothes and showed others how to sew on machines. In the end, the majority of people in the Jessie Spread Hands–Little Raven, Jr., cohort helped the Arapahos make the transition to an agricultural economy.

The beginning of the twentieth century brought new problems for Arapahos, who lived in allotment clusters surrounded by a much larger population of American settlers. Agency superintendents sought to implement new assimilation programs designed to transfer land from Indian to non-Indian ownership and to control the income from allotted lands. Due to the loss of most of their land, families could not support themselves by farming, and wage work opportunities could not compensate. Arapahos leased their allotments and gradually sold off most of their land. Bureau of Indian Affairs personnel could not control income from wages, but lease and land sale money from trust land (Individual Indian Money, or IIM) had to be supervised by the trustee (the United

States). As "unearned" income, it became the focus of the assimilation program, as superintendents withheld money in order to force Indians to work and spend their money in ways compatible with American values. In distributing these trust funds, superintendents discriminated against men and young people in general.

Arapahos recognized the discriminatory and exploitive nature of the federal land policies and turned away from the civilization strategy they had used to appease and reassure Americans and toward more defiant and assertive politics. Leaders directly challenged federal officials' views on age and gender issues and began a decades-long effort to sue the federal government for its violation of agreements made by treaty and otherwise. The members of the Medicine Grass–Bichea cohort and camp Indians in the Jessie Spread Hands–Little Raven, Jr., cohort did what they could to resist the assimilation program, using their own funds to travel to Washington, delegation after delegation, succeeding, Arapahos thought, in getting the trust status of their allotments extended and having some measure of success at liberalizing the IIM regulations.

Elderly people played an especially important economic role in households. They had retained allotments and had more access to their funds than did other Arapahos. The Arapahos who could provide for others were the landowners, that is, those few elderly men and women from the Owl–Left Hand cohort still living, the members of the cohort of Medicine Grass and Bichea, the camp Indians from the Jessie Spread Hands–Little Raven, Jr., cohort, and most of the educated women from the cohort of Jessie Spread Hands. Wives and husbands continued to "partner" by pooling income to support the extended family household. Families and communities shared their resources with others, both reinforcing social bonds and providing help for people in need. Although disputes over inheritance could strain family relations, and the discriminatory policies of the BIA created economic inequalities, the deeply felt obligation to share prevented the concentration of wealth in particular families or individuals. Groups of men and women community leaders (lodge and committee people) led reciprocal exchanges between families and communities at dance gatherings that gradually took the place of chiefs' families' generosity.

During most of this era, the cohort of Jessie Spread Hands and Little Raven, Jr., provided political leadership. Most of these people owned land and often had senior lodge positions. Several couples held the chieftainship. The educated male members of the Little Raven, Jr., cohort had lost their lands and largely been discredited as leaders, unless they reidentified as camp Indians and attained noncompetent status. Jessie's and Little Raven's cohort reached old age by the 1920s, when they had more access to income than younger Arapahos. Their ceremonial authority also helped them convince Arapahos to support the more assertive political strategy and to participate in communal sharing and lodge ceremonies that increasingly centered on the Offerings Lodge while the age-graded lodges decreased in importance. The intermediary chiefs in the Little Raven, Jr., cohort, and their wives, challenged the age-graded model of leadership by retaining chieftainship positions while moving into the priesthood—fusing the two kinds of leadership previously associated with different age groups. By this time, chieftainship itself had become redefined as based on ceremonial authority rather than the ability to support followers economically. The lodge people tolerated the peyote organization as well as Christianity, often because they had obligations to support ceremonial grandchildren. Some even embraced the Christian or peyote religion, which facilitated the Arapahos' acceptance of participation in many faiths.

Increasingly dissatisfied with the leadership provided by the Little Raven, Jr., and Jessie Spread Hands cohort, the younger people—the cohort of Jess Rowlodge and Myrtle Lincoln—began to challenge the Arapaho age hierarchy while resisting the policies of the BIA. This "landless" group of men (and a few women) had been educated for a number of years in reservation schools and sometimes at Haskell or Chilocco as well. They had been forced, encouraged, or allowed to sell allotments or had been born too late to have received an allotment and had few opportunities for gainful employment. So they had to depend on older Arapahos for economic assistance. Opting not to commit to the lodge organization, however, they embraced peyotism and gradually assumed leadership in the district chapters of the Native American Church, and their efforts culminated in the peyote religion becoming the most prominent one among Arapahos.

This cohort also took advantage of the BIA's policy to replace chieftainship with an elective, representative government. Men and women thought they could get economic reform and political input by co-opting the reorganization program that was authorized by the Oklahoma Indian Welfare Act of 1936. They both challenged paternalistic BIA policies and insisted that the chiefs accept their input. They were, in a sense, in the right place at the right time to move into political positions by becoming the mainstay of the elected district councils, then the 1938 business committee. Jess Rowlodge became a leader in this elected council and Myrtle Lincoln's husband, Howard, served as a representative for Canton Arapahos. In no small part because the Jess Rowlodge–Myrtle Lincoln cohort supported reorganization so enthusiastically, the Arapahos became one of the Oklahoma tribes to accept a new Western form of government after 1936.[1]

Comparison of cohort histories explains how and why particular cohorts challenged American domination at certain points in time, taking responsibility for the formation and implementation of successive strategies of conciliation, civilization, and assertiveness. These comparisons also show how and why particular cohorts altered the ideas and social arrangements integral to the age hierarchy. After reservation settlement, the meaning of maturity had to change when warfare and buffalo hunting ended. A man's reaching his twenties or thirties was no longer necessarily associated with participation in councils. The senior cohorts reoriented the lodges to community service to provide new avenues to maturity, albeit deferred. The meaning of old age changed in the early twentieth century as members of the Little Raven, Jr.–Jessie Spread Hands cohort retained politicoeconomic authority instead of "retiring." These leaders assumed high ceremonial authority as well, effectively fusing two kinds of leadership. By the 1930s, tensions between this cohort and the one junior to it led to the beginnings of a challenge to the authority and political influence of elderly Arapahos. The age-graded lodge system did survive, somewhat attenuated, to the 1920s, and the role of gender in sociocultural change is only clear when gender is considered in interplay with age. Some women in senior cohorts with membership in senior lodges had more influence than men in junior cohorts, just as women or men in senior lodges had authority and influence in relation to other women or other men in their own cohort. But over time, the Arapaho age hierarchy underwent major transformations that produced some leveling of inequalities.

Comparison of subsets within cohorts shows why particular individuals provided leadership during major transformations. Differences between men and women in the aggregate were far less important than differences between women or differences between men. As discussed in more detail below, leadership was associated with marriage. Married women had more political influence in council decisions than unmarried ones, and in the polygamous households in the nineteenth century, the boss wife had the most influence. Men could not succeed in leadership roles without a wife's help. In the twentieth century, access to IIM accounts and landownership provided unmarried women with more economic security and more influence, particularly in the 1930s. Men's and their wives' political roles largely depended on their rank within the ceremonial lodge organization. Once on the reservation, attendance at the off-reservation boarding schools affected Arapahos' lodge membership. A very small minority of these educated men in the Little Raven, Jr., cohort opted not to continue to advance in the lodge system, and they and their wives (educated or not) became politically marginalized. Individuals with political ambitions maintained marriages with people who would partner them ceremonially.

Gender in History

In identifying the actual men and women who had sufficient influence and authority to effect social transformations, we see the crucial role marriage played in these transformations. Ceremonial authority from the lodge system served as the keystone of leadership, and married couples had to proceed through these lodges together as they aged. Over time, married couples consistently had the important leadership roles. Leadership came from couples married a long time who had high ceremonial rank, such as Bull Thunder and Striking In Night, and women and men who, though married to each other after the death or divorce of their spouses, both had high ceremonial rank (for example, Left Hand and his wife Woman Going In or Little Raven, Jr., and his wife Bitchea). Before they came to the reservation and for many years after, leading couples could use their relative wealth, as well as their status in the lodge organization, to attract followers. By the twentieth century, economic differentials had leveled out, but the chiefs and their wives could still use their lodge status to exert authority and influence. Ritual authority emanated from the interaction of male and female principles of power, both of which were necessary to the regeneration of "life," to health and prosperity. Arapahos relied on this ritual source of power before and after reservation settlement to cope with the constant dangers and stresses in their lives.

Both men and women tried to improve their position in the household and community through marital relationships, as well as through individual achievements and sacrifices. In their marriages, women might try to displace the boss wife or divorce so that they could marry a man monogamously or a higher-ranking man. This is what Owl did. Achieving a long, stable marriage to an ambitious man or woman also helped one's life career. Ceremonial people who lost their spouses remarried other ceremonial people, thus maintaining their positions. Men also could try to arrange marriage to a woman in a more prominent family to get assistance from her father and brothers. For example, Row Of Lodges repeatedly married daughters of Little Raven, maintaining an alliance between the Bad Faces (the most prominent band) and his own, the less prominent Blackfeet band.

"Partnering," necessary to leadership as well as to a successful life career in general, involved wives and husbands and men and women who were kin (brothers and sisters, especially). Economic, political, and religious partnerships operated as reciprocities that required respect as well as various kinds of exchanges. When kinspeople or in-laws felt they did not receive the respect to which they were entitled, they might leave their families, as Night Killer did when her brother insulted her. Occasionally, young Arapahos chose suicide as a response to poor treatment by a relative. Wives and husbands might use divorce as a sanction for good behavior, for example, to prevent stinginess. Spouses who divorced in the twentieth century took their personal property with them, including valuable machinery or the roof of a house (as Bitchea, Rabbit Run's wife, did). The threat of negative socioeconomic as well as supernatural sanctions encouraged the expected reciprocities.

Partnerships reflected the ideals of a gender system based on complementarity. Gender balance survived the American encounter, but not as a result of conservatism or resistance per se. Over time, this "balance" was manifested in different ways, and the gender system was actually reworked repeatedly by people who made innovative choices and by others who accepted the choices as reasonable.

In prereservation times, women and men did different kinds of work, which was viewed as an equal exchange. Both kinds of work were necessary for the group to survive. In terms of property ownership, women owned food, tepees, their tools, and some horses. Men owned their tools and sometimes more horses than the women in their households. Women and men both responded to new trade opportunities, partnering in producing hides for the market and dividing the manufactured goods they received. Leaders came from prosperous families.

On the reservation, men and women both used contacts with federal officials to defend their property rights and to assert new kinds of property rights. Men owned wagons and most of the horses; women owned food and tepees or tents. A man and his wife (or the boss wife in polygamous families) divided the goods they got when they sold crops and delivered freight. Men and women still did different kinds of work, as well as the new kinds of work. Men involved themselves in cattle raising (for subsistence), and women gardened. But men and women worked together freighting and farming (growing corn and some cotton), and sometimes cutting wood. By the late nineteenth and early twentieth centuries, both men and women were working with plants (farming and cutting wood), and women sold rawhide ropes, which altered the prior division of labor. The chiefs and their wives came from the most prosperous households with large herds of horses and cattle and several freight wagons.

In the twentieth century, Arapahos primarily relied on cash, and the old gender-based division of labor was of much less importance. Both women and men worked in agriculture, either growing their own crops or hiring out to settlers as family labor. Wives and husbands pooled their IIM income, a practice that was a new manifestation of complementarity. Food, clothing, and housing (canvas tepees, wall tents, and frame houses) all were purchased. Houses and farm machinery could be owned by both men and women. Economic differentials still existed (in IIM accounts), but poverty was so widespread that women's and men's committees rather than individual families took responsibility (through collection of donations) for raising money for camp celebrations and construction of council halls.

Leadership in prereservation times required partnered wives and husbands to use household resources and ceremonial authority to motivate others to cooperate in subsistence activity or in political work. The wives of band headmen and chiefs used food and property, and the men lent horses or mentored other men to influence behavior. Couples with membership in the Dog and probably the Buffalo lodges had the most influence in council decisions. Both women and men had a stake in the success of the conciliatory strategy, and one or the other might be the more ambitious. Women and children feared capture or attack, and men experienced high casualties in battle. Both women and men attended treaty councils to establish peace and obtain supplies. The senior lodge women advised junior women, just as senior lodge men shaped the views and influenced the behavior of their juniors. During these years, Arapahos accepted a new form of marriage between Arapaho women and American men, who did not have families who could enter into reciprocities to the extent Arapahos or people from other tribes could. But these women's husbands could cooperate with the men in their wives' families to promote the conciliatory strategy the way John Poisal and Thomas Fitzpatrick did with Left Hand, brother and mother's brother to their wives.

Once on the reservation, political decisions centered no longer on communal hunts and warfare but on the organization of new kinds of communal labor and the ability to obtain help from the federal government to support agricultural efforts and prevent settlers and outlaws from stealing Arapaho property. Both women and men had a stake in the success of freighting, stockraising, and haying. Both women and men sold property to settlers to support political gatherings and delegations, and both influenced council decisions, including the Arapahos' consent to allotment. The chiefs' wives helped formulate the goals of the delegations, and the wife of the principal chief went to Washington with the chiefs. With the end of warfare and buffalo hunting, Arapaho men had lost opportunities for individual achievement, as had women who generally lost the means for quillwork on buffalo hides. But senior lodge people, including chiefs and their wives, reoriented the lodge organization to support success on the reservation, and they influenced their juniors to support the civilization strategy. The men and women in the senior lodges also partnered in promulgating the Ghost Dance, and the seven men and seven women leaders apparently came from these lodges.

In the twentieth century, the chiefs and their wives still came from the membership of the senior lodges, but their resources were more limited. These couples did have home places (combined allotments still in trust) where landless Arapahos could camp. Rather than providing for their followers economically, these couples had ceremonial authority and knowledge of treaty relations that they used to formulate a more assertive stance toward the federal government and motivate junior Arapahos to support their political work. Role models for the value of reciprocity, they provided leadership on the committees that took over "provisional" work on behalf of Arapaho communities. Young women who formed part of the group of landless Arapahos helped their husbands' efforts to propel Arapahos toward elective, constitutional government in the 1930s.

The political work of leaders in the prereservation era drew support from the ceremonial organization, especially the age-graded and Buffalo lodges, that offered supernatural sanction for political roles and that had the support of all Arapahos. In prereservation times, wives and husbands used their property to make prayer sacrifices on behalf of each other and their children, in lodge ceremonies and in other kinds of religious acts. Both male and female sources of power had to work together in the lodge ceremonies in order for Arapahos to receive supernatural help.

On the reservation, chiefs and chiefs' wives drew on authority earned in the Buffalo, age-graded, and Offerings lodges to maintain their positions. Women's quillwork was on the decline, which undermined the opportunity for women to establish positions of influence based on their degrees in quillwork. But the women of the senior lodges and the chiefs' wives partnered their husbands in the Ghost Dance religion and, through their vision experiences, expanded their opportunities for leadership.

By the twentieth century, many of the men of the junior lodges made the transition with their wives to the senior lodges, but these couples also had leadership roles in the Ghost Dance hand game and in the peyote religion. Over time, Arapaho participation in the age-graded lodges and ultimately in the Offerings Lodge declined as Arapahos tried to find comfort and remedy for their difficult circumstances, by turning to peyotism and Christianity (usually in combination). Chiefs and chiefs' wives retained their lodge-based authority, and this authority helped them hold on to the chieftainship even though the age-grade system called for the succession of younger people. These couples were also leaders in the peyote religion, Christianity, or both, and the women asserted their authority in relation to the men's—usually by preparing sacred food and regalia, preparing the ground for the peyote ceremony, and making prayer songs and prayers for both peyote and Christian rituals. The women and men in the younger cohort (that of Jess Rowlodge and Myrtle Lincoln) committed themselves to the peyote organization rather than to the age-graded lodge system, and this association helped them organize effectively for political reorganization.

Some Comparisons

The Arapaho experience suggests new lines of research in several areas. First, the question of women's status in Plains societies during the hide trade era should be reexamined. I have taken issue with the idea that women's status declined with the introduction of the horse and participation in the buffalo robe trade. This argument, developed by Alan Klein and others, is that before the advent of equestrian hunting and full participation in the hide trade, nomadic groups such as the Arapahos hunted collectively, that is, women and men participated in the impound method of hunting buffalo. They collectively owned the meat and consumed most of it. The products of the hunt, including hides, were equally distributed among all families. Thus, there were minimal inequalities of wealth among individuals and households. Under these circumstances, men and women had relatively equal status. Once the horse was employed in hunting, the chase method replaced impounding, and the individual hunter owned the meat, Klein argued. Hunting became the "domain of men." Women owned the horses they received from men, but theirs were "the least valued mounts."

Women's status further declined, according to Klein, when Euro-American traders began to buy large numbers of buffalo hides.

Women had to spend more time processing (or tanning) hides for the market, and men had control over women's work. Men owned these hides, though they gave some to women for domestic use. To purchase more trade goods, men obtained greater numbers of hides. They began to take more than one wife in order to increase production. Female captives were also added to this labor pool. In short, the argument is that the workload of women increased, yet they did not share in the profits, because men controlled and distributed trade goods. The elaboration of the duties of men's societies further raised the prestige of men in relation to women because societies took over responsibilities once fulfilled by kinship groups. Although scholars have shown that certain kinds of craft work, religious roles, and war-oriented activity brought some women honor, Klein's argument that women had "near-slave" status is generally accepted. Women's leadership roles would have been negligible. Others have added that male ascendancy led to women's loss of personal autonomy in sexual behavior and marriage.[2]

Klein's conclusions, based on sources on Northern Plains societies, are problematic. And the Southern Arapaho case contrasts with his characterization of Plains gender relations. The ethnographic, biographical, and documentary sources on the Arapahos show that respect relations between men and women prevailed, women's "status" had more to do with their relations with other women than with men, and both women and men owned valuable property and traded hides. Arapaho religion operated to support respect relations among Arapahos and to strongly sanction against abuse of relatives, wives, and in-laws. Both the male and female "principles" were necessary to life, and male and female economic and ritual roles were reciprocal and had a charter in origin narratives.

In practice, gender relations took place in the context of family relations, where women and men depended on each other economically, politically, and ritually. Individuals could withdraw support if they felt they had not been given proper respect. Women were grandmothers, mothers, fathers' sisters, sisters, sisters-in-law, and mothers-in-law, as well as wives. Institutionalized respect relations between a man and his mothers, sisters, and fathers' sisters helped ensure a man's success in life. These women as well as a man's wives made many kinds of body and property sacrifices on his behalf—for hunting, warfare, health, and the quest for supernatural aid generally. They also helped ensure the health and success of his children. A man had an obligation to give horses and other property to women who helped him in this way. Women owned packhorses and saddle horses, which made their work easier and contributed to the prosperity of the entire household. Women also might receive horses trained for other tasks as gifts and could inherit horses from fathers and brothers. They could give horses to or for others as sacrifices. Women had the right to distribute the food they prepared, and Arapahos regarded this preparation as well as other work women did as an equal exchange for men's work. Food was an essential part of ritual sacrifice, that is, its preparation was sacred and symbolic of the female principle of "life."

The accounts of traders and travelers reveal that Arapaho women traded for and owned manufactured goods, including tools, cloth, and beads. Nineteenth-century observers saw Arapaho women going on hunts, helping butcher buffalo, and taking at least some, if not all, the meat back to camp on packhorses. Sacred ritual permeated buffalo hunting, and the women's Buffalo Lodge played a major role in ensuring the success of the hunt. Women as well as men sold buffalo meat to traders and travelers, and there was no indication that men exclusively owned meat from a buffalo hunt. At Bent's trading post, Arapaho women as well as men brought in hides to sell. In short, wives and other female relatives who helped butcher, preserve, and cook food, and dress hides had a *right* to buffalo meat and hides. The gifts and property sacrifices of women often included trade goods (for example, cloth on men's robes and beaded moccasins). Note that when alcohol abuse on the part of some men led to a disruption in this pattern, women leaders resisted. A delegation of Arapaho chiefs' wives asked the agent to defend their rights. Men routinely traded for the goods women wanted, including jewelry, beads, awls, and cloth. Trading for these kinds of goods can be seen as an acknowledgment of women's right to a share. Wives of important men went to councils with them and received trade goods in person, taking charge of goods received at treaty councils and other meetings with Americans.

Close scrutiny of Klein's sources on Northern Plains groups actually provides support for my findings and offers no firm evidence that women were marginal to the hunt and the hide trade. For example, he points to the work of Regina Flannery and John Ewers to argue that women were absent from the buffalo hunt, did not go on horse raids, and owned only horses of less value than men. Ewers actually found that women went on war parties and horse raids. Neither Flannery nor Ewers, whom he cites, actually support his assertion that women's horses were *less valued* than men's. And, according to Rudolph Kurz, writing in 1851, when Assiniboines hunted, the women butchered the meat and hauled it to camp, for it belonged to them.[3]

Klein's argument that men owned the buffalo hides and that women did not trade hides, or that if women traded they merely acted as agents for their husbands, is not supported by his sources, namely, Flannery, Kurz, Edwin Denig, and Henry Boller. On the contrary, Flannery's consultants, who prepared hides for trade, told her that the man of the household consulted with the women of the household about what trade goods they wanted and that he was supposed to follow through, especially if they wanted something for ceremonial reasons (beads, cloth, awls, for example). One of her consultants, born in 1854, traded her robe to get something for her child. Denig, writing about the Crows in 1854, noted that husbands and wives negotiated with each other about what to get from the trader in return for hides and that, if there was affection between them, the wife prevailed. Sometimes the husband and wife would divide the hides and each would trade for what he or she wanted. Kurz, whom Klein also cites as support for his position, actually wrote that among the Upper Missouri tribes, women had "a share" in the dressed hides, which they exchanged for trade goods. Boller, in the upper Missouri region in 1858, saw that women traded the hides they dressed.[4]

At Fort McKenzie in August 1833, Prince Maximilian noted that when Blackfeet men were selling robes for whisky without consulting the women, women knew they would not profit from their labor, so they would "tan the skins only half-way and badly," which would adversely affect the price. This indicates the strong possibility that Blackfeet women were also entitled to a share (half?) of the profit and, by their actions, protested the men's inappropriate behavior.[5]

One of the problems with Klein's argument is that he treats women in the aggregate and outside the family context. Women in households had different roles and statuses. Klein assumes that wives and captives tanned hides for the market. In fact, women in a household included many divorced, widowed, and unmarried women, all of whom were relatives of the husband or wife. All these women worked as a group on various projects, particularly hide preparation, under the direction of an older or senior women, or the "boss wife" in a polygamous household. The senior woman had the major role in deciding how to distribute household resources and to assign work. Increased production of hides was likely possible because of the efforts of a man's or his wife's temporarily unmarried women relatives, as well as captives. Captive women (not including women adopted into Arapaho families when young) had low status and probably did not marry. Without relatives in camp, they could be subject to abuses that Arapaho women could more easily avoid. Klein ignores sources that describe the claims women had on men generally. For example, on the Upper Missouri, both Maximilian and Kurz commented that sisters could claim a brother's property. Kurz noted that unmarried women lived in extended families and worked as members of the household, "glad to be part of" a family. Whether they were glad or not, they could help a man's wives tan hides and probably have the status of kinswomen, entitled to a share of household resources. Flannery reported that brothers and sisters among the Gros Ventres expected to grant each other's requests. It does not appear even on the Upper Missouri, where tribes were more extensively committed to the hide trade than on the southern plains, that all women in a household were without rights or access to valued property.⁶

There seems to be the assumption on the part of some scholars that women lost personal autonomy in marital relations and sexuality because they tanned hides for the market. Klein argues that increased polygamy came from men's desire to have more hides processed, and that polygamy undermined the status of women. But polygamy was certainly a reaction to the high death rate of men in warfare, and women could benefit from this kind of marriage. It was a man's duty to marry the widow of his brother and support his brother's children. A marriage by a man to sisters usually brought women social support and welcome assistance with the household work. And marriage initiated and maintained social alliances between families that were strengthened by a man marrying sisters and that helped both women and men in these families.⁷

The argument that women had no choice in marriage is also suspect. Senior family members could pressure young women to agree to the husband selected for them through the family's negotiations. But for Arapaho women (and women of other tribes), the first marriage could also be the result of a courtship. After a young man won a girl's favor, he approached his family to propose the marriage. Getting the consent for a marriage involved women, such as mothers and fathers' sisters, on both the groom's and the bride's side. In cases where the girl had not been courted, she had the option of trying to persuade her brother to abandon the proposed marriage, even though ideally she would show respect for him by agreeing. Elopement was another option to avoid an arranged marriage and a way for young women to subvert the wishes of older relatives or a recalcitrant brother.

Arapahos were among the groups in which, after the first marriage, women more readily refused men they did not want, and women could initiate divorce, sometimes because they opposed their husband's taking a co-wife or because they preferred some-one else. The ideal resolution of an adultery case was for the husband to accept a payment and to show no anger. Being abusive disgraced a man. Women controlled contraception with the help of women doctors and could insist on child spacing through abstinence.

What about the view that the important role men's "military societies" played in the nineteenth century diminished the importance of women's roles? The standard work on the Arapaho lodge organization is Alfred Kroeber's. His studies would seem to show that women played little part in the six "men's" ceremonies. But Kroeber, while he identified the themes of gender reciprocity in his research on symbolism in Arapaho designs, apparently did not understand the key role played by women in the Tomahawk, Spear, Lime Crazy, and Dog lodges. He treated the Spear Lodge (which he did not observe) most extensively, referring to the ceremony as "made by men" and describing the regalia as made by the grandfathers. He mentions only that women relatives of the dancers prepared food for the grandfathers, and wives of grandfathers brought food to the dancers. He mentioned that "old women" or the "old men's wives" " may be present" and that old women sing. In his description of the Tomahawk Lodge, there was no mention of women whatsoever. He noted that in the Lime Crazy Lodge, the grandfathers and their wives taught the elder brothers and their wives how to build the fire, and that the dancers' wives went away from camp with the "old men," who transferred a sacred root to them so that they could transfer it to their husbands. He explained that this was a sort of simulation of sexual coitus but did not link it to the origin story. He mentioned that the grandfathers' wives painted the wives of the Dog Men and that a sacred root was transferred from grandfather to wife to Dog Man.[8]

Kroeber does not put the activities of women in the broader context of the origin stories and does not mention the Peacemaker's role, the wives' manufacture of the regalia, the interaction of wives and dancers in the ritual of the Short and Stout Men, the political influence grandmothers had over their ceremonial granddaughters, the symbolism of food exchange, or the fact that wives attained the same rank as their husbands when they progressed through the lodge series.

Much of the research on nineteenth-century gender relations on the plains should be reevaluated in the context of the available sources. And comparative work on, for example, Northern and Southern Plains socioeconomic organization and the relative importance of and customs surrounding captivity could lead to more nuanced understandings of gender relations in this era.

The transition made by big game hunters to agriculture and the spread of revitalization movements during late nineteenth-century reservation life are important issues in the study of Native peoples in the Dakotas, Montana, Wyoming, Oklahoma, and beyond. One argument is that the transition to reservation life was more difficult for men than for women because they lost the valued roles of hunter and warrior. On the other hand, the Arapaho case, and work elsewhere—for example, on the importance of Native ranching—shows that both men and women made major economic adaptations. They had new valued economic roles and perpetuated old political and religious roles, often in new form. More study of these transitions in local contexts is needed. How can local differences be explained? Were there inconsistencies in the application of federal policy? As Katherine Osburn showed, the roles of Ute women apparently offered more of a threat to assimilation goals than men's roles did, and agents applied harsher negative sanctions to women than to men. How did variation in the way civilization policy was applied affect gender relations and the potential for both women and men to initiate adaptations and transformations?[9]

Regarding revitalization movements, we can build on James Mooney's work about the initial acceptance and diffusion of the Ghost Dance by making comparisons of how the movement developed in local contexts over time. Clearly, the Arapahos devoted themselves to the Ghost Dance more enthusiastically and for a longer time than other tribes on the southern plains. Unsanitary conditions at the Arapaho school, as well as the high death rate at off-reservation boarding schools, traumatized mothers and fathers. Women's Ghost Dance visions reunited them with their children. Mothers from Bichea's and Jessie Spread Hands's cohorts played as important a role in the Ghost Dance movement as Sitting Bull and the other men leaders. Without the women's commitment, the religion would not have taken such a hold on the Arapahos, and the fame of Arapaho Ghost Dance leaders would not have spread so widely. The Arapaho case suggests that the role of women in the movement has probably been ignored and points to the importance of local factors in the degree to which the new religion took hold, the patterns of its proselytism, and the development of an associated complex of rituals (such as the Ghost Dance hand game). What kinds of patterns can we find and account for on other reservations during the 1890s and the early years of the twentieth century?

Boarding school attendance in the late nineteenth and early twentieth centuries is also a subject that has drawn considerable interest. Some work explores how the environment of these schools subjected children to close supervision, corporal punishment, and a general pattern of domination, as well as to different educational programs for boys and girls that introduced foreign ideas about gender. Recent scholarship documents how children in the school environment resisted these forms of dominance and, in so doing, created and reinforced both tribal and Indian identities. But there is no systematic study of students after they returned to their home communities. Was the school civilization program successful with them? Were boys and girls affected differently? How did the adult lives of boarding school children compare with those of young people who never attended school or who attended on-reservation schools? I addressed these questions by comparing the lives of off-reservation and reservation school alumni and the life careers of those Arapahos who never attended school. For the most part, educated women and men reidentified as camp Indians at the same time they introduced new skills to their community because identity as an "educated" Arapaho was decidedly not advantageous. Marital choices were important in the reidentification process. How typical are the experiences of Arapaho returned students? This is another subject that calls out for comparative research.[10]

How does the Arapaho experience in the pre–World War II twentieth century compare with what we know about other Native peoples? Federal policy with regard to landownership was inconsistent. Among the Utes, married women did not receive allotments, but single women did, which especially disadvantaged divorced women, who lost access to land and income from it. In the Arapaho case, all women had allotments, which actually improved the circumstances of single, including divorced, women. Recent research contradicts earlier expectations that capitalistic agricultural and industrial expansion would marginalize women economically. As in the Arapaho case, both men and women generally participated in wage work and household provisioning. But little attention has been given to issues relating to the effects of the post-allotment leasing and sale of land, which regularly provided cash income and produced economic inequalities. How were gender systems affected when income from landownership largely replaced the traditional division of labor between men and women? Patricia Albers found that the lease money of married women was credited to their husbands' accounts, although women could use this income as "leverage" within the household. Clearly, decision making could be influenced by individual ownership of land and income differentials. In the Arapaho case, beginning in the early twentieth century, these economic changes contributed to political and religious transformations, including greater influence for the elderly. What happened in other Native communities?[11]

Peyotism (originating in the late nineteenth century, but proliferating in the twentieth) spread throughout Native communities. The standard work on the peyote religion is Omer Stewart's. Stewart's exhaustive study does not mention women's participation or leadership in Plains communities. It would seem to be a general conclusion that in the peyote religion, women occupied a subordinate position in the Plains region. For Arapahos, however, the pattern of partnering between husband and wife became central to peyotism, and women performed leadership roles. Arapahos avoided the bitter conflict between adherents of peyotism and Christianity that characterized the Cheyenne community.

Senior lodge men and women tolerated and supported junior ones regardless of religious choices by their participation in Christian, peyote, and lodge ceremonies in one way or another. This helped promote community-wide tolerance. How does Arapaho peyotism compare with peyote organization in other communities in terms of gender roles, twentieth-century historical development, and links to political transformation?[12]

By following the life careers of the women and men in particular cohorts through time, we see multiple strategies at work. The men and women of different cohorts, married and unmarried individuals, and educated and not formally educated Arapahos maneuvered within and against both the sociocultural framework they accepted as children and the American projects they were subjected to all their lives. The life careers of Little Raven, Walking Backward, Owl, Left Hand, Medicine Grass, Bichea, Jessie Spread Hands, Little Raven, Jr., Jess Rowlodge, Myrtle Lincoln, and their contemporaries are not merely relevant to individuals. These Southern Arapaho stories offer a window onto the way history makes gender and gender makes history.

Abbreviations

AMLS	Arapaho Manual Labor School, 1881–1903, Cheyenne-Arapaho Records
CAR	Cheyenne-Arapaho Records
CC	*Calumet Chieftain*, Calumet, Oklahoma
Census of 1881	Tenth Census of the United States, Indian Division, Population, Arapaho, April 1881, Census Records
CF	Concho Agency Central Files
CFC	Cantonment Agency Central Files
CFCA	Cheyenne-Arapaho Agency Central Files
CIA	Commissioner of Indian Affairs
CP	*Carrier Pigeon*, Cheyenne-Arapaho Records
CR	*Canton Record*, Canton, Oklahoma
CT	*Cheyenne Transformer*, Darlington, Oklahoma, Oklahoma Historical Society
CVR	*Canadian Valley Record*, Canton, Oklahoma
DD	Doris Duke Collection
Dorsey MS	George A. Dorsey manuscript, Cleaver Warden and George A. Dorsey Collection
Eggan FN	Fred Eggan Field Notes
GB	*Geary Bulletin*, Geary, Oklahoma
Hilger FN	M. Inez Hilger Field Notes

HME	*Home Mission Echoes*, Union Theological Seminary, New York
IIF	Individual Indian Files, Cheyenne-Arapaho Records
IIM	Abstracts of Individual Indian Bank Accounts, Cantonment, 1918–1927
IR	Reports of Inspection, 1873–1900
Kroeber FN	Alfred Kroeber Field Notes, 1900, Manuscript 2560a
LB, Canton	Letterbooks, Cantonment Agency, Cheyenne-Arapaho Records
LB, Darl	Letterbooks, Darlington Agency, Cheyenne-Arapaho Records
LB-ER	Cheyenne-Arapaho Letterpress Books, Carnegie Library
LR	Letters Received by the Office of Indian Affairs, 1881–1907
LRCA	Letters Received by the Office of Indian Affairs, 1824–81, Cheyenne and Arapaho Agency
LR-Cen. Supt.	Letters Received by the Office of Indian Affairs, 1824–1881, Central Superintendency, Census Records
LRUA	Letters Received by the Office of Indian Affairs, 1824–81, Upper Arkansas Agency
LSBIA, Canton	Letters Sent to the Bureau of Indian Affairs, Cantonment Agency, Cheyenne-Arapaho Records
LSCIA, Darl	Letters Sent to the Commissioner of Indian Affairs, Darlington Agency, Cheyenne-Arapaho Records
LT files	Land Transaction Case Files, 1904–87
Menn	*The Mennonite*, Mennonite Library and Archives
Michelson MS	Truman Michelson Manuscripts

MJ	Mary Jayne Collection
MLS-C	Miscellaneous Letters Sent, Cantonment Agency, Cheyenne-Arapaho Records
MLS-D	Miscellaneous Letters Sent, Darlington Agency, Cheyenne-Arapaho Records
Mooney MS	James Mooney Collection
NA	National Archives, Washington, D.C.
NNI	Notes Not Incorporated (by Warden, in Dorsey MS)
PR	Post Records
RCAO	Record of Indian Children Attending Off-Reservation Schools, Concho Agency
RCIA	*Annual Reports of the Commissioner of Indian Affairs*, U.S. Office of Indian Affairs
RED	Records of the Education Division
SC	Special Cases, 1821–1907
SRC	Superintendents Annual Narrative and Statistical Reports, 1907-38, Cantonment Agency
SRCA	Superintendents Annual Narrative and Statistical Reports, 1907-38, Cheyenne-Arapaho Agency
SW	Sallie J. Williams Manuscript
Warden FN	Warden Field Notes and Sketches, Papers of Cleaver Warden, Cleaver Warden–George A. Dorsey Collection
W-D	Cleaver Warden–George A. Dorsey Collection, The Field Museum, Chicago

NOTES

INTRODUCTION

1. Leacock pioneered studies of women's loss of status due to colonization and capitalism—see Etienne and Leacock, *Women and Colonization*. Other scholars subsequently took up the issue of women's status. Osburn, *Southern Ute Women*, and Ackerman, *A Necessary Balance*, documented the persistence of gender balance under conditions of neocolonialism. Albers argued that in some groups, women's status declined, and in others, it rose—see "From Illusion to Illumination," 139–45. The essays in Shoemaker's edited volume took this approach, showing that women often resisted marginality and Euro-American gender ideology and that in a particular society, women could simultaneously lose and gain status or lose it in one realm and gain it in another—see 9, 13–14, 20, 95. See also Harkin and Kan, "Native American Women's Responses to Christianity." Pesantubbe, *Choctaw Women*, and Johnston, *Cherokee Women in Crisis*, examined women's status in different realms.

2. In *Cherokee Women*, Perdue found that in the face of elite Cherokee men's domination of politics, nonelite women insisted on common ownership of land and women's property rights. On Native women in the fur trade, see Brown, *Strangers in Blood*; Van Kirk, *Many Tender Ties*; and, more recently, Thorne, *Many Hands of My Relations*. Murphy showed that in the Great Lakes area, women and men, Indian and Creole, played a major role in producing food and lead for the market, helping to develop the regional frontier economy (*Gathering of Rivers*). Kan examined how Tlingit women (and men) created a Tlingit version of Orthodox Christianity ("Clan Mothers and Godmothers"). Sleeper-Smith found that, as the center of matrifocal households involved in trade, Native women married to French men in nineteenth-century Wisconsin played a major role in frontier Catholicism (*Indian Women and French Men*). In Barr's interesting study of the Texas borderlands, she considered how women as captives, slaves, wives, and emissaries were used in Indian-Spanish negotiations over trade

and peace, and how Native gendered standards and practices framed these negotiations (*Peace Came in the Form of a Woman*).

3. In an egalitarian gender system, men and women both were expected and entitled to participate in production, marital arrangements, exchange, leadership, and ritual, and both genders had sources of prestige admired by the group as a whole. Relative prestige is allocated on nongender grounds. Sherry B. Ortner argued that within this framework of egalitarianism, "balance" is always challenged in some areas or instances (that is, hegemonies are always partial), and these challenges may or may not become transformative over time. Once American and Arapaho gender systems engaged, both systems were challenged. As Ortner argues, gender strategies were crosscut by other strategies. In the Arapaho case, gender, age, and "national" strategies were either in conflict or served each other, providing a possible sense of alternatives (see *Making Gender*, 151–52, 156). Studies of Native and American engagement have addressed issues of gender and (national) identity (or cultural persistence, generally), but the issue of age has been slighted. Foner has made this point cross-culturally. She argued that age (as well as gender, class, and race) should be considered a system of inequality; age and gender hierarchies articulate, and age hierarchies play an important role in, historical process (*Ages in Conflict*).

4. I have drawn on Ortner's "subaltern practice theory." She argues for a dialectical relationship between structural (sociocultural) constraints and the interested practices of social actors "on the ground." A "structure," or "sociocultural framework," is a hegemonic system—a relatively pervasive but not totally consistent framework of meanings and practices embedded in social relations of power and influence. These sociocultural frameworks have a determining effect on human action and on the shape of events. But, Ortner argues, actors may reproduce the social and cultural world as given or produce something new. If social practices are enabled and constrained by hegemonies, how can hegemonies be transformed by practices? Hegemonies are always "partial," that is, there are always "slippages in reproduction, erosions of long-standing patterns, and moments of disorder and outright 'resistance.'" Hegemonies are intrinsically unstable because social actors recognize tensions between the world as hegemonically constructed and the world as lived experience. This framework is useful for explaining both reproductions and transformations. Encounters between colonial regimes and Native peoples become sites of "alternative practices and perceptions" and of multiple forms and degrees of agency "that may become the bases of resistance and transformation." History is shaped by social practices "within and against existing 'structures.'" As Ortner puts it, "history makes people, but people make history" (*Making Gender*, 1–20, 139–72, and 181–212; quotes on 17, 18; *Anthropology*, quoted on pp. 2, 9). Ortner primarily draws on Raymond Williams's Gramsci-based approach and Marshall Sahlins's historical application of practice theory, as well as feminist theory.

5. Mannheim, "The Problem of Generations," 304; Ryder, "Cohort as a Concept"; Spitzer, "Historical Problem of Generations"; Elder, "Perspectives on the Life Course." For a pioneering sociological study using this approach, see Elder, *Children of the Great Depression*, and the more recent Elder and Conger, *Children of the Land*. Elder's focus is on how historical events influenced cohorts, not on how cohorts influenced events.

Chapter 1. Rules of Life

1. Talbot, *Journals*, 25–26.

2. Dodge, *Report of the Expedition*, 25. Arapahos told Henry Dodge in 1835 that they had migrated into Wyoming and Colorado from the upper Marias River in Montana. Arapahos were equestrian by the 1740s. In the eighteenth century, the Arapahos were on the northern plains in five divisions. The Gros Ventres were on the Saskatchewan River, and the other four were south and southeast of them. By the nineteenth century, probably due to epidemics that cut into the band populations, these four had combined into one, subsequently known as Arapahos (L. Fowler, "Arapaho," 840). See Toll on the Arapahos' occupation of the Colorado area (*Arapaho Names and Trails*).

3. Trudeau, "Trudeau's Description," 168, and "Journal," 31, 38; Tabeau, *Tabeau's Narrative*, 153–54. Tabeau, who was on the upper Missouri River in 1803–05, wrote that Arapahos depended on Cheyennes in trade negotiations. See Berthrong's *Southern Cheyennes*; Moore's *Cheyenne Nation* and *Cheyenne*; and Powell, *People of the Sacred Mountain*, on Cheyenne history.

4. John, "An Earlier Chapter," 383, 385, 389–92. Mexico became independent in 1821, and the United States expanded into what is now Texas, Arizona, and New Mexico after defeating Mexico in 1848.

5. Williams, "Ezekiel Williams' Adventures," 203; Stuart, "Robert Stuart's Journal," 192. For background on the fur trade in the region, see Dale, *Ashley-Smith Route*.

6. James, *Account of Long's Expedition*, 16:55, 197–98, 208; 17:156–57; Bell, *Journal*, 192. In the early nineteenth century, Crow was the trade language used by the tribes and the Americans on the plains. "Arapaho" is probably the Crow name for the tribe (that is, *alappaho*). See James, *Account of Long's Expedition*, 15:220; L. Fowler, "Arapaho," 860.

7. J. Fowler, *Journal*, 57–58, 60–61, 63–65, 68, 70.

8. Dodge, *Report of the Expedition*, 24–27, 35; Lavender, *Bent's Fort*, 114, 179. Dodge wrote that Gros Ventres visited the Arapahos on the Arkansas River in 1824. On the Gros Ventres, see L. Fowler, *Shared Symbols*. Arapahos used metal from kettles and barrel hoops to make arrow heads rather than stone after they had regular access to trade goods (see Michelson MS 2267, "Story of Medicine

Grass," 1929). On the relationship between American expansion and the intensification of warfare, see L. Fowler, *Columbia Guide*.

9. Sage, *Rufus B. Sage*, 5:266; Pancoast, *Quaker Forty-Niner*, 193–94; Parkman, *Journals*, 2:398–400; Parkman, *Oregon Trail*, 291; Bell, *Journal*, 204; Frémont, *Expeditions*, 1:219, 712–13; Talbot, *Journals*, 26–27; Thomas Fitzpatrick to Thomas Harvey, 18 September 1847 in *RCIA* 1847, 238–49. Talbot reported that the Arapahos had 325 lodges, and their Gros Ventre allies, 60 or 70 lodges, in 1843 (p. 25), and Thomas Fitzpatrick reported that there were 350 lodges of Arapahos, 280 lodges of Cheyennes, and 800 lodges of Sioux.

10. Smith, "E. Willard Smith Journal," 166; Frémont, *Expeditions*, 1:199–200, 437–38, 714; Talbot, *Journals*, 19–22; Sage, *Rufus B. Sage*, 5:66–68, 233, 256; Abert, *Report*, 113; Parkman, *Oregon Trail*, 226–27, 304–308; Garrard, *Wah-to-yah*, 136; Harvey to CIA, 5 September 1846 in *RCIA* 1846, 282–88.

11. Kearny, *Report*, 212 (and see also Hughes, "Doniphan's Expedition," 181); Abert, *Report*, 6, 113; C. Bent, "Charles Bent Papers," 155, 159; Fitzpatrick to Harvey, 18 September 1847, in *RCIA* 1847, 238–49; Fitzpatrick to D. D. Mitchell, 24 September 1850, in *RCIA* 1850, 50–56; Garrard, *Wah-to-yah*, 165–66, 346–47; Heslep, "Santa Fé Trail," 371–73 (and see Cooke, *Scenes and Adventures*, 391, and Pancoast, *Quaker Forty-Niner*, 190–92). For more discussion of friendly chiefs, see L. Fowler, *Arapahoe Politics*.

12. L. Fowler, *Arapahoe Politics*, 28–29, 32; Kappler, *Indian Treaties*, 2:594–96; Mitchell to L. Lea, 17 October 1852, in *RCIA* 1852, 65–68; Fitzpatrick to A. Cumming, 19 November 1853, in *RCIA* 1853, 366, 368; J. W. Whitfield to Cumming, 27 September 1854, in *RCIA* 1854, 94–96; W. W. Bent to Charles Mix, 20 October 1858, LRUA; W. W. Bent to Superintendent of Indian Affairs, 5 October 1859, in *RCIA* 1859, 137–39; Richardson, *Beyond the Mississippi*, 173; Michelson MS 2267, "Story of Medicine Grass," 1929. Congress subsequently amended the treaty of 1851; the tribes agreed to annuity payments for fifteen instead of fifty years.

13. Jackson, "Diary," 213; W. W. Bent to Superintendent of Indian Affairs, 5 October 1859 in *RCIA* 1859, 137–39; S. G. Colley to William Dole, 30 September 1863 in *RCIA* 1863, 134–35; Richardson, *Beyond the Mississippi*, 189.

14. Robert C. Miller to J. Haverty, 14 October 1857 in *RCIA* 1857, 141–48; A. B. Greenwood to J. Thompson, 25 October 1860 in *RCIA* 1860, 228–30 (and see Richardson, *Beyond the Mississippi*, 303); Albert G. Boone to Dole, 26 October 1861 in *RCIA* 1861, 105–106; John Saville to [?] Hollaway, 15 April 1863, LRUA; Hafen and Ghent, *Broken Hand*, 274. On the Treaty of 1861, see Kappler, *Indian Treaties*, 2:807–11. Shavehead's band joined with the Arapahos after his death; his successor could have taken his name (Miller to A. Robinson, 17 August 1858 in *RCIA* 1858, 96–100). Agent Colley took Chief Spotted Wolf and Neva as delegates to Washington, where Spotted Wolf told President Abraham Lincoln that the things he saw on the trip seemed "like some kind of magic" (Viola, *Diplomats in Buckskins*, 100).

15. Saville to Hollaway, 15 April 1863, and J. Leavenworth to W. Dole, 4 March 1864, both in LRUA; Colley to Dole, 2 September and 20 October 1864 in *RCIA* 1864, 242–44; U.S. Senate, *Report of the Secretary of War on the Sand Creek Massacre*, 29–30, 73, 93, 116, 135–37. On the Sand Creek Massacre, see G. Bent, *Life of George Bent*, 137–63 (especially 149, 159, 162, 256–57), and L. Fowler, *Arapahoe Politics*, 314 n28. See also Greene and Scott, *Finding Sand Creek*. When he was in Little Raven's tepee, Henry M. Stanley met the recently returned Arapaho boy who had been in a circus ("A British Journalist Reports," 274).

16. "Treaties with Arapahoes et al.," in *RCIA* 1865, 515–27; Kappler, *Indian Treaties*, 2:887–92 (see also G. Bent, *Life of George Bent*, 165, 177, 247–48); Kingman, "Diary," 449; Record of Council with Arapaho and Cheyenne at Fort Zarah, 10 November 1866, in Documents Relating to the Negotiations of Ratified and Unratified Treaties. Kingman, who met Margaret at the treaty council in 1865, described her as "the creature of many loves, the subject of many sorrows." The 1865 treaty set aside 640 acres in fee for each of the Poisals: Margaret Wilmot and her children, Andrew and Virginia; Mary Keith and her children, William, M. J., and Frances; Matilda Pepperdin and her daughter, Margaret; and Robert and John Poisal.

17. H. Douglas to Whom It May Concern, 30 April 1867, Letters Received, Camp Supply, PR; Leavenworth to Commissioner of Indian Affairs, 2 September 1867 in *RCIA* 1867, 314–15; *Chicago Tribune*, 11 April 1867; Jones, *Treaty of Medicine Lodge*, 26, 74–76, 107–108, 111, 128, 141–2, 151, 174–82, 210; Stanley, *My Early Travels*, 1:49, 60–61, 229–31, 261; Transcript of the Minutes and Proceedings of the Indian Peace Commission, v. 1, 8/6–11/26/1867, Records of the Indian Division, Entry 665, Records of the Office of the Secretary of the Interior, RG 48, NA, pp. 113, 115–20; Kappler, *Indian Treaties*, 2:984–89.

18. J. Butterfield to Murphy, 5 February 1868, LRUA; E. Wynkoop to Thomas Murphy, 19 August 1868 in *RCIA* 1868, 71–73; G. Bent, *Life of George Bent*, 313–27; B. Darlington to E. Hoag, 6 September 1869 in *RCIA* 1869, 382–83; Henry Asbury to C. McKeever, 3 May 1869, Letters Sent, Camp Supply, PR; Darlington to Hoag, 1 September 1870 in *RCIA* 1870, 265–67.

19. The origin stories were recorded only in fragmentary form, but George Dorsey's unpublished manuscript and Cleaver Warden's notes often cite the appropriate origin story for the everyday and ceremonial activities Dorsey describes (see W-D). George Dorsey began studying Arapaho life in 1899. Working for The Field Museum in Chicago, he made many visits to the Southern Arapahos and one to the Northern Arapahos. He hired Cleaver Warden, a bilingual Southern Arapaho, to help him interview Arapahos. Warden (1869–1932) completed some interviews working alone, and he attended ceremonies and took notes for Dorsey. Dorsey also brought Hawkan, an elderly Arapaho man, to Chicago, where he interviewed him. Most of Dorsey's and Alfred L. Kroeber's information came from men in the Medicine Grass cohort: Black Horse, Coming

on Horseback, and Osage; and Tall Bear from Little Raven's cohort. These men described life in the mid-nineteenth century. Dorsey also directly observed the Offerings Lodge of 1901 and 1902, and his description of the lodge provides mythological referents for the ceremonial acts in this ritual (*Arapaho Sun Dance*). Kroeber also provided links to particular origin stories in his publications on decorative symbolism and ceremonial lodges (1903–07; in *Arapaho*) and in his field notes (Kroeber FN). Kroeber was on staff at the American Museum of Natural History in New York and used Warden and other interpreters when he interviewed Arapahos. The origin stories alluded to by Dorsey, Kroeber, and Warden are published in Dorsey and Kroeber, *Traditions*. Some of the stories have more than one version that differ in fairly minor respects. Variant versions are probably due to the Southern Arapahos coming from four different tribal divisions. For more discussion of origin stories, see Anderson, *Four Hills*. Anderson focuses on homologous relationships between social "functions" (for example, rituals), space, time, and color, and his book provides a good explanation of culturally constituted forms of "personhood," and how, in mythological time, animal, human, and spirit or other-than-human beings metamorphosed into each other. My approach to the stories is to use the ethnohistorical method to focus on how Arapahos linked certain stories to particular activities and relationships over real time.

20. On the story of the Pipe Being and the tribal bundle, see Dorsey and Kroeber, *Traditions*, pp. 1–2 and 13–19, and W-D, Dorsey MS, 153. On Whirlwind Woman, see Dorsey and Kroeber, *Traditions*, 97–98; Kroeber, *Arapaho*, 60–61, 109–110, 121–22, 361, and 373; and W-D, Dorsey MS, 34–35, 92–94, 156–57. The symbolism on the regalia of the Buffalo Lodge and the bags of the Seven Old Women is the same (W-D, Dorsey MS, 153, and Warden NNI, "Miscellaneous Notes," "Women's Sacred Bags"). Actually, there was a third gender described by Kroeber as men who lived as women. Arapahos told Kroeber that they had no women who dressed and lived as men (*Arapaho*, 19–20). This is the only reference to this third gender that I found, and I was not able to identify any particular individuals who could be described thus, although Jess Rowlodge told Hilger that Arapahos knew about one such person "in old times" (17 May 1941, Hilger FN). Why did these individuals disappear from the record? Perhaps it was because of negative sanctions from federal agents. Alfred W. Bowers reported that "berdaches" customarily helped dig the hole for the center pole in the Hidatsa Sun Dance, but in 1879 the agent forcibly stripped the Hidatsas' only berdache of his "feminine attire, dressed him in men's clothing, and cut off his braids." The berdache fled to the Crow Agency (*Hidatsa*, 315). For an overview of the berdache in Native America, see W. Williams, *Spirit and the Flesh*.

21. On the lodge symbolism, see Dorsey and Kroeber, *Traditions*, 31–41 and 42–48; W-D, Dorsey MS, 146, 153, 204–205, Warden FN, Notebook on Symbolism and Notebook on Arapaho Lodge Ceremonies and Regalia, and Warden NNI,

"Arapaho Ceremonials," and "Buffalo Women's Lodge." On the story of Blue Feather, see Dorsey and Kroeber, *Traditions*, 404–18. Some examples of stories from *Traditions* that serve as charters: paying damages for adultery (29–31), scalping (341–50), women's quillwork (239–46, 404–18), women's victory dance (49–50).

22. On the four hills of life concept, see Kroeber, "Arapaho Dialects," 71–138. On the Four Old Women, Cleaver Warden mentions these beings in "Buffalo Women's Lodge" (W-D, Warden NNI), and see Cooper, *Gros Ventres*, 18. The Four Old Women do not appear in the origin stories recorded by Dorsey and Kroeber. This concept might have been most familiar to the Gros Ventre and Big Lodge divisions of the Arapahos because they probably had the most contact with the village peoples on the Upper Missouri. The Four Holy Women appear prominently in Hidatsa origin stories. The First Creator created earth from mud underneath the waters, then created males of various species. Village Old Woman then created the females of each species as well as the Four Holy Women "in the groves of the four directions." These were supernatural beings represented by the Holy Woman Society of the Hidatsas. When any ceremony was performed, these "aged females" represented the "Holy Women" and Village Old Woman. They prepared ceremonial grounds and dug the hole for the center pole in the Sun Dance and had a "benevolent" role (Bowers, *Hidatsa*, 297, 315, 323–24). One could speculate that the Arapaho woman who serves as Peacemaker in the lodge ceremonies is a more modern representative of these Four Old Women. The Hidatsas and neighboring Mandans had age-graded societies and a Buffalo Lodge, and as Ewers noted, the Mandan Goose Society Pipe bore a striking similarity in overall shape and design (a bird head in relatively the same position) as that of the tribal Flat Pipe of the Arapahos ("owned" by the Big Lodge division) and the Gros Ventre division (*Plains Indian Sculpture*, 186). Arapahos were participants in trade rituals, alliances, intermarriages, and apprenticeships that involved several tribes in the eighteenth century, so it is likely that ideas and ceremonies were exchanged.

23. Hilger, *Arapaho Child Life*, 10, 40–42, 72–73, 102, 171–72; Kroeber, *Arapaho*, 18–19; Eggan FN, 1:69; 2:85.

24. Hilger, 52–53, 82. Hilger learned that Arapaho women used contraceptive techniques but did not abort (pp. 9–11). She interviewed elderly Southern Arapahos using interpreters during the years 1935 and 1941. Fred Eggan interviewed Jess Rowlodge (Owl's son) and Bird White Bear (Red Woman's son), two bilingual Southern Arapahos in 1933. For an extensive description of his findings on Arapaho kinship, see Eggan, "Cheyenne and Arapaho Kinship," 35–95.

25. Hilger, *Arapaho Child Life*, 75–6, 78–9.

26. Ibid., 78, 106–107; W-D, Dorsey MS, 194.

27. Truman Michelson, "Narrative," 596–99; Michelson MS 2182, "Life of Mrs. White Bear," 1929; LT files, 1445 and 1541 (genealogies are based on many files because an individual's file may lack details that appear in others' files).

Michelson hired Jess Rowlodge to interview for him. Rowlodge's interviews with Bichea, Red Woman, and Medicine Grass were written in Arapaho, then translated into English by Rowlodge.

28. Hilger, *Arapaho Child Life*, 78, 106–107, 113; Talbot, *Journals*, 25–26; Richardson, *Beyond the Mississippi*, 172; Michelson MS 2267, "Story of Medicine Grass," 1929; W-D, Dorsey MS, 161–97.

29. Michelson MS 2267, "Story of Medicine Grass," 1929; LT files, passim; Hilger, *Arapaho Child Life*, 79, 109, 119. On the lodges, see Kroeber, *Arapaho*, 159, 178–79, 211, 222–23, and W-D, Warden NNI, "Buffalo Women's Lodge." On decorative symbolism of children's clothing, see Kroeber, *Arapaho*, 44, 49.

30. Hilger, *Arapaho Child Life*, 140–41; Michelson MS 2182, "Life of Mrs. White Bear," 1929.

31. Hafen and Ghent, *Broken Hand*, 197, 274–76, 278, 284–89, 298, 319–20, 343–51; Powell, *People of the Sacred Mountain*, 1:220; McMechen, "The Model of Auraria-Denver," 125; LT files, passim; Lecompte, "John Poisal," 353–54, 356; U.S. Census 1860, Denver, Arapahoe, Kansas Territory, M653_348, p. 111, image 114, households 4239 and 4240 (John Poisel [Poisal] and L. J. Wilmot) and U.S. Census 1860, Kickapoo, Leavenworth, Kansas Territory, M653_350, image 366 (L. J. Wilmott), U.S. Bureau of the Census House Diary, 1854–1862, 1851: 103–104 and House Diary, 19–20 September 1856; Record of First Communions and Confirmations, 1851–1877; "White Pupils and Others, Non-Potawatomi," all in Jesuit Mission and College Records. Wand, *Jesuits in Territorial Kansas*, 19, 24; Daughters of the American Revolution, *Vital Historical Records of Jackson County*.

32. Simmons, *Kit Carson*, 26–27, 43–44, 46–49.

33. Hilger, *Arapaho Child Life*, 76, 77; Eggan FN, Bird White Bear, 1:47; Eggan, "Cheyenne and Arapaho Kinship," 42, 50–51, 53, 64. Eggan points out that when relatives do not live in the same band, Arapahos "emphasize the extension of attitudes rather than of behavior" toward these "distant relatives" (42).

34. Kroeber, *Arapaho*, 11, 18; Hilger, *Arapaho Child Life*, 68–70; Eggan, "Cheyenne and Arapaho Kinship," 51. On Row Of Lodges's name, see DD, Jess Rowlodge, T-454:2–4.

35. Hilger, *Arapaho Child Life*, 172; Eggan FN, Bird White Bear, 1:28; Michelson MS 2267, "Story of Medicine Grass," 1929.

36. Hilger, *Arapaho Child Life*, 59, 71, 77, 110, 128; Kroeber, *Arapaho*, 15, 18, 228–29, 298, 418, 450; Kroeber FN, 26:20.

37. *CT*, 24 December 1880; Left Hand, "Chief Left Hand," 3–4; on Sitting Bull, DD, Myrtle Lincoln, T-588:23; Michelson MS 2267, "Story of Medicine Grass," 1929.

38. Kroeber, *Arapaho*, 181–82; Hilger, *Arapaho Child Life*, 102, 110, 118. On the effect of youths' dances on the people in the camp, see W-D, Warden NNI, "Arapaho Social Organization—Tribal Organization."

39. Dorsey, *Sun Dance*, 5; Kroeber, *Arapaho*, 294; Eggan, "Cheyenne and Arapaho Kinship," 54.

40. Kroeber, *Arapaho*, 14; Hilger, *Arapaho Child Life*, 70–71, 198–99; Michelson, "Narrative," 599–600.

41. Hilger, *Arapaho Child Life*, 68–72, 76; Eggan FN, Bird White Bear 1:47; Kroeber, *Arapaho*, 11, 15, 18; Eggan, "Cheyenne and Arapaho Kinship," 50–53, 64. Customs at puberty may have varied with the families' means. Warden noted that when a woman's menstrual period began, she told her husband, "I am a medicine woman" (W-D, Warden FN, "Notes on the Clubboard Lodge"). And Gros Ventres told Regina Flannery that a man's penis was given its shape by a woman's vagina during intercourse (personal communication, 1979).

42. Kroeber, *Arapaho*, 11; Hilger, *Arapaho Child Life*, 111, 183; Eggan FN, Bird White Bear, 1:36.

43. W-D, Warden FN, "Symbolism on Buffalo Robes."

44. Michelson, "Narrative," 599–600; Michelson MS 2182, "Life of Mrs. White Bear," 1929.

45. DD, Jess Rowlodge, T-690:9–12. Dorsey recorded a longer version of this story (*Sun Dance*, 5–7).

46. Kroeber, *Arapaho*, 15; Hilger, *Arapaho Child Life*, 73–75, 199–200; Michelson, "Narrative," 599, 601.

47. Michelson MS 2182, "Life of Mrs. White Bear," 1929; Henderson and Petersen, *American Pictographic Images*, 47; W-D, Warden NNI, "Notes on Arapaho Clothing." In one story, referred to in connection with the Tomahawk Lodge, Nih'óóOoo, the trickster, attempted to deceive and seduce women, who assaulted and ridiculed him (Dorsey and Kroeber, *Traditions*, 109–10). The drawings collected by or made by Southern Arapahos and Carlisle alumnus Frank Henderson in 1882 include twelve in which women appear. In one, a scene in camp, a woman addresses a man getting ready to pursue buffalo: "Wait. I want to smoke in pipe first." Ten other drawings are courting scenes, usually of women in the process of chopping wood, meeting and talking with men (in *American Pictographic Images*).

48. Hafen and Ghent, *Broken Hand*, 274–77, 289; Lecompte, "John Poisal," 357; J. Morrison to Wynkoop, 14 December 1868, LRUA; Henry Meagher, 18 June 1937, Indian Pioneer Papers; Old Man [Robert Poisal] 359 and John Poisal 20, Census of 1881.

49. Simmons, *Kit Carson*, 77, 79, 86, 88. Adaline's marriage was short lived, and she subsequently married a man of her own choice.

50. Kroeber, *Arapaho*, 12–13; Eggan, "Cheyenne and Arapaho Kinship," 58–60; Eggan FN, Bird White Bear, 1:72–73; Jess Rowlodge, 3:23–24; Hilger, *Arapaho Child Life*, 201–203; W-D, Warden NNI, "Notes on Arapaho Social Organization—Indian Marriage."

51. Michelson, "Narrative," 602; Michelson MS 2182, "Life of Mrs. White Bear," 1929.

52. Eggan FN, Bird White Bear, 1:23; Eggan, "Cheyenne and Arapaho Kinship," 60.

53. Kroeber, *Arapaho*, 7; Boone to Dole, 16 November 1861, LRUP. A band of Plains Apaches camped with Arapahos from 1861 to 1867.

54. Hilger, *Arapaho Child Life*, 49, 200, 207–208; Kroeber, *Arapaho*, 13; Eggan FN, Bird White Bear, 1:7–12; 3:27; Eggan, "Cheyenne and Arapaho Kinship," 61.

55. Hilger, *Arapaho Child Life*, 194, 196, 204–205, 208; Kroeber, *Arapaho*, 14; Hilger FN, Salt Friday, 12 August 1940. On Owl, LT files, 1357.

56. DD, Myrtle Lincoln, T-588:27–28; Stuart, "Robert Stuart's Journal," 192; Bell, *Journal*, 199; James, *Account of Long's Expedition*, 16:208–209; J. D. Miles to E. A. Hayt, 20 January 1880, LRCA.

57. Simmons, *Kit Carson*, 15, 23, 26, 35–36, 39, 41; Ratified Treaty 341, October 14, 1865, p. 30, Documents Relating to the Negotiation of Ratified and Unratified Treaties.

58. Hafen and Ghent, *Broken Hand*, 220; Lecompte, "John Poisal," 353–58; U.S. Census, 1860, Denver, Arapahoe, Kansas Territory, p. 111, NA; Albert Keith, 13 July 1937, 4946, pp. 93, 96–97, Indian Pioneer Papers; Powell, *People of the Sacred Mountain*, 1:220.

59. Hafen and Ghent, *Broken Hand*, 251, 261; Lecompte, "John Poisal," 357; U.S. Census, 1860, Kickapoo, Leavenworth, Kansas Territory, Image 366, U.S. Bureau of the Census; *Chicago Tribune*, 24 October 1867; *Cincinnati Commercial*, 27 October 1867.

60. Kroeber, *Arapaho*, 109–110; Eggan FN, Bird White Bear, 1:58; Frémont, *Expeditions*, 1:199, 713; Chittenden and Richardson, *Life, Letters and Travels*, 2:682; W-D, Warden NNI, "Miscellaneous Notes—Fire."

61. Michelson MS 2182, "Life of Mrs. White Bear," 1929; Kroeber FN, 21:15 and 24:4; Kroeber, *Arapaho*, 26, 29, 91, 140–42; W-D, Dorsey MS, 111. Women also owned dogs that were important to the household. They carried and, in winter, pulled loads; alerted the family to the approach of others; and ate the refuse of the camp. Women put up small tents for their dogs in the winter (see Toll, *Arapaho Names and Trails*, 23).

62. James, *Account of Long's Expedition*, 16:198; Bell, *Journal*, 197–98, 201; Lavender, *Bent's Fort*, 148; Richardson, *Beyond the Mississippi*, 173; Jones, *Treaty of Medicine Lodge*, 179; Grinnell, *Cheyenne Indians*, 1:273 (Grinnell noted that the Cheyennes sold hides dressed by captive women).

63. Kroeber, *Arapaho*, 16; Hilger, *Arapaho Child Life*, 109; W-D, Warden NNI, "Notes on Arapaho Social Organization—Indian Marriage"; Eggan FN, Bird White Bear, 1:21–22, 24; Eggan, "Cheyenne and Arapaho Kinship," 52–57.

64. Dorsey, *Sun Dance*, 5–7; Hilger, *Arapaho Child Life*, 104; DD, Jess Rowlodge, T-221:7–14 and 237:28–31.

65. Kroeber, *Arapaho*, 56–58; Hilger, *Arapaho Child Life*, 9, 10, 12, 45, 54–55, 141–42; Michelson MS 2182, "Life of Mrs. White Bear," 1929; Dorsey, *Sun Dance*, 181; W-D, Warden NNI, "Notes on Arapaho Social Organization—Birth"; LT files, 2338. Ewers suggested that epidemics and population reduction by warfare caused changes in warfare, political and social organization, and

religious beliefs and practices on the southern plains. Smallpox struck once each generation, and high losses among children and teenagers could have stimulated attention to religious ceremonies to protect health ("Influence of Epidemics," 104–115).

66. Hilger, *Arapaho Child Life*, 8, 9, 12, 196, 208; Kroeber, *Arapaho*, 14; Ford, *March of the First Dragoons*, 71; Whitfield to CIA, 5 January 1855, and Boone to Dole, 16 November 1861, LRUA. Polygyny is the anthropological term for a marriage in which a man has more than one wife. I use the term polygamy because most readers are more familiar with it.

67. Lewis, "Manly-Hearted Women," 173–87.

68. Hilger FN, Salt Friday, 12 August 1940; W-D, Dorsey MS, 59–72, and Warden NNI, "Notes on Arapaho Clothing."

69. Kroeber, *Arapaho*, 13–14; Eggan FN, Bird White Bear, 1:61, and Jess Rowlodge, 2:115; Hilger, *Arapaho Child Life*, 211–14; W-D, Warden NNI, "Notes on Arapaho Social Organization: Ho-Nar-Tha-tis, Pay Damages" and "Notes on Arapaho Clothing"; and Dorsey MS, 59–72; Eggan, "Cheyenne and Arapaho Kinship," 62; DD, Myrtle Lincoln, T-617:37–38; Michelson MS 2182, "Life of Mrs. White Bear," 1929.

70. Dorsey, *Sun Dance*, 186–87; Hilger, *Arapaho Child Life*, 174; Kroeber FN, 26:16; Parkman, *Oregon Trail*, 315–16; James, *Account of Long's Expedition*, 16:214–18; Bell, *Journal*, 207.

71. DD, Myrtle Lincoln, T-588:23–24, and Jess Rowlodge, T-203:27–29, 204:11–12, and 237:30–31; Hilger, *Arapaho Child Life*, 181–82.

72. Michelson MS 2182, "Life of Mrs. White Bear," 1929, and 2267, "Story of Medicine Grass," 1929.

73. LT files, 2338; DD, Myrtle Lincoln, T-610:14.

74. Smith, "E. Willard Smith Journal," 166; Boone to Robinson, 14 March 1861, LRUP (the request was not granted but two of the Kiowa delegates took their wives); Stanley, "A British Journalist Reports," 277, 283 (Stanley quotes Little Raven saying, "God damn them mean squaws," but this may be an English gloss); *Cincinnati Commercial*, 4 November 1867, 2.

75. W-D, Warden NNI, "Notes on Dog Lodge"; Dorsey, *Sun Dance*, 7, 103, 127, 130; Kroeber, *Arapaho*, 284–85, 292; Eggan FN, Jess Rowlodge, 2:51–55, and Bird White Bear, 67, 77.

76. W-D, Warden FN, Notebook 2, Clubboard Lodge, and "Body Paint for Lime Lodge," and Warden NNI, "Notes on Buffalo Women Lodge" and "Dog Lodge"; Kroeber FN, 26:27; Kroeber, *Arapaho*, 160–61, 165, 168, 190, 198–200. Dorsey noted that Arapahos believed that some paints had more heat than others and thus were harder to bear.

77. Kroeber, *Arapaho*, 210, 213–14; W-D, Warden FN, "Notes on Buffalo Women Lodge"; *Rocky Mountain News*, 19 July 1862.

78. Dorsey and Kroeber, *Traditions*, 42–48 and 31–41 (in this version, the rescued woman, held captive by Buffalo Steer, teaches Arapahos the Buffalo

Lodge ceremony and establishes the Seven Old Men and Seven Old Women);
W-D, Warden NNI, "Notes on Buffalo Women Lodge"; Kroeber, *Arapaho*, 212–25.

79. W-D, Warden NNI, "Notes on Arapaho Social Organization—Supersti-
tions," and Dorsey MS, 59; Kroeber, *Arapaho*, 59–64, 70–77; Hilger, *Arapaho
Child Life*, 181; Dorsey and Kroeber, *Traditions*, 97–98.

80. Kroeber, *Arapaho*, 65–66; W-D, Dorsey MS, 17–18, 22, and Warden NNI,
"Notes on Arapaho Tipi," and Warden FN, "Notes on Symbolism."

81. W-D, Dorsey MS, 27–28, and Warden NNI, "Miscellaneous Notes—Robes";
Kroeber, *Arapaho*, 29–35.

82. Kroeber, *Arapaho*, 66–68; W-D, Dorsey MS, 92. Beaded cradles were decorated differently, according to Kroeber (69). Women's quilled robes often had
the Whirlwind Woman design.

83. Kroeber, *Arapaho*, 451; Hilger, *Arapaho Child Life*, 16–17, 124, 135–37; W-D,
Warden NNI, "Notes on Arapaho Social Organization: Birth."

84. Dorsey, *Sun Dance*, 7; Eggan FN, Bird White Bear, 2:65–66; W-D, Warden
NNI, "Notes on Dog Lodge."

85. Hilger, *Arapaho Child Life*, 141–42; Kroeber, *Arapaho*, 16, 38–40, 46, 58,
109–10, 121–22; Dorsey, *Sun Dance*, 181, 186–87; Kroeber FN 26:4; W-D, Dorsey
MS, 39–59 and Warden FN, "Notes on Arapaho Clothing."

86. Hilger, *Arapaho Child Life*, 170–71; Eggan FN, Bird White Bear, 1:58;
Michelson MS 2994, "Ethnological Notes," 1926.

87. Hilger, *Arapaho Child Life*, 180; Talbot, *Journals*, 20, 25; Abert, *Report*, 113;
Garrard, *Wah-to-yah*, 136; Boone to Dole, 14 December 1861, LRUA.

88. Hilger, *Arapaho Child Life*, 197; Kroeber, *Arapaho*, 18, 294, 298; Dorsey,
Sun Dance, 7; DD, Jess Rowlodge, T-221:12–13; Eggan, "Cheyenne and Arapaho Kinship," 50, 51, 53.

89. W-D, Warden NNI, "Pipes."

90. Hilger, *Arapaho Child Life*, 12, 24–28, 40, 42, 55, 188; Kroeber, *Arapaho*,
18–19; Eggan, "Cheyenne and Arapaho Kinship," 56–57; W-D, Warden NNI,
"Spirits of the Water"; Eggan FN, Bird White Bear, 1:13–22; Michelson MS
3087, "Interview with Cleaver Warden," 1928.

91. W-D, Warden NNI, "Notes on Arapaho Social Organization: Ho-nar-tha-ti,
Property Damages"; Eggan FN, Jess Rowlodge, 2:115; Eggan, "Cheyenne and
Arapaho Kinship," 62. Hilger also recorded cases among the Northern Arapahos
where a husband physically abused an unfaithful wife. Divorce is referenced
in an origin story in which the culture hero Nih'óóOoo (the trickster) divorces
from Whirlwind Woman because he can not keep up with her (Michelson MS
2994, "Ethnological Notes," 1926).

92. Eggan FN, Jess Rowlodge, 2:115; Eggan, "Cheyenne and Arapaho Kinship," 62; Hilger, *Arapaho Child Life*, 211–16.

93. DD, Jess Rowlodge, T-206:19–20; Michelson MS 2267, "Story of Medicine
Grass," 1929. Shortly after the death of Big Mouth, his son Little Big Mouth

(who subsequently became known as Big Mouth) was the leader of a small band that lived near the Comanches and, according to Little Raven, kept "separate from the rest of the tribe." Big Mouth may have been ostracized at this time (8 December 1866, Report of a Council, Documents Relating to the Negotiations of Ratified and Unratified Treaties).

94. Dorsey, *Sun Dance*, 184–87; James, *Account of Long's Expedition*, 16:14–18; Bell, *Journal*, 204, 207; Ruxton, *Ruxton of the Rockies*, 231–32; Michelson MS 2267, "Story of Medicine Grass," 1929, and 3345, "Narrative of the Old Moccasin Society by Little Left Hand," 1932; Hilger, *Arapaho Child Life*, 198.

95. Hilger, *Arapaho Child Life*, 58, 60, 63; Eggan FN, Bird White Bear, 1:70; Dorsey, *Sun Dance*, 184–87.

96. W-D, Warden FN, "Notes on Symbolism" and Dorsey MS, 17–18, 39–59; Hilger, *Arapaho Child Life*, 116.

97. W-D, Warden NNI, "Miscellaneous Notes—Shields," and Dorsey MS, 39–59, 203–208.

98. See LT files on wives; DD, Jess Rowlodge, T-206:30–32 and 239:18–19 on the 1867 treaty and 206:6–8 on Trunk; on Powderface, see *CT*, 24 December 1880; on Left Hand, see Left Hand, "Chief Left Hand"; on Big Mouth, see Hoag to H. R. Clum, 1 November 1871, LRUA; and on Little Raven's son, see Wynkoop to Murphy, 19 August 1868, *RCIA* 1868, 70–73.

99. Michelson MS 2994, "Ethnological Notes," 1926, and 3087, "Interview with Cleaver Warden," 1928; Eggan FN, Bird White Bear, 1:65; W-D, Warden NNI, "Notes on Arapaho Social Organization—Tribal Organization"; "Mode of Electing Headmen"; "Election of Chiefs"; and "Miscellaneous Notes—Taking the Office of Chief"; and Dorsey MS, 40–41.

100. J. Fowler, *Journal*, 57, 61, 64–65, 68; James, *Account of Long's Expedition*, 16:208–209; Bell, *Journal*, 192–94, 198; Frémont, *Expeditions*, 1:200–201; Talbot, *Journals*, 21–22; Parkman, *Oregon Trail*, 304–308, and *Journals*, 2:475–76; Garrard, *Wah-to-yah*, 136–37.

101. Fitzpatrick to Harvey, 18 September 1847, *RCIA* 1847, 238–49; Lowe, *Five Years a Dragoon*, 87–88; Chittenden and Richardson, *Life, Letters and Travels*, 2:673–84; Wildman, "Letters," 38–39, 67; I. Hayden to Assistant Adjutant General J. Kellin, 2 September 1861, Letters Sent, Fort Larned, PR; Stanley, *My Early Travels*, 1:249.

102. Mooney, *Ghost Dance*, 986–87; Kroeber FN, 21:36; Michelson MS 3087, "Interview with Cleaver Warden," 1928; W-D, Warden NNI, "Tomahawk or Clubboard Lodge," and Dorsey MS, 98. The ceremonial organization worked to promote unity through the reciprocal ties within and between the lodge memberships and to encourage centralization of authority through the Seven Old Men. The Southern Arapahos inducted only one age set (that is, a group of men inducted into a lodge at the same time) into a lodge, which strengthened the bond between people from all the camps. This system developed in a particular

historical context. Compare the Gros Ventres, who lacked the Seven Old Men tradition and who had several age sets in each lodge, which lacked the unity and centralization characteristic of the Arapahos. See L. Fowler, "'Look at My Hair,'" 82–90.

103. Michelson MS 3345, "Narrative of the Old Moccasin Society by Little Left Hand," 1932.

104. Kroeber, *Arapaho*, 8–9; W-D, Warden FN, "Arapaho Ceremonials." On clowns, see Warden FN, "Notebook on the Lime Crazy Lodge," 50.

105. Michelson MS 2267, "Story of Medicine Grass," 1929; W-D, Warden NNI, "Notes on Arapaho Social Organization—Mode of Electing Headmen"; Kroeber, *Arapaho*, 155.

106. Kroeber, *Arapaho*, 182–88; Dorsey, *Sun Dance*, 67; W-D, Warden FN, Notebooks 1 and 2 on the Clubboard Lodge and Warden NNI, "Notes on Clubboard Lodge."

107. Kroeber, *Arapaho*, 188; Kroeber FN, 25:29; W-D, Warden NNI, "Notes on Clubboard Lodge," and Warden FN, Notebooks 1 and 2 on the Clubboard Lodge.

108. Kroeber, *Arapaho*, 158–62, 165. The Thunderbird Lodge is also known as the Spear Lodge.

109. Kroeber, *Arapaho*, 173–176; W-D, Warden NNI, "Notes on the Thunderbird Lodge."

110. Kroeber, *Arapaho*, 168–170, 173, 176, 178; Eggan FN, Bird White Bear, 2:71; W-D, Warden NNI, "Notes on the Thunderbird Lodge."

111. Kroeber, *Arapaho*, 189–93; W-D, Warden FN, "Notebook on Lime Crazy Lodge."

112. Kroeber, *Arapaho*, 188–90, 192–93, 195–96; W-D, Warden FN, "Notebook on Lime Crazy Lodge."

113. Kroeber, *Arapaho*, 196–200; W-D, Warden NNI, "Notes on Dog Lodge" and Warden FN, "Arapaho Ceremonies."

114. Kroeber, *Arapaho*, 197, 201–207; W-D, Warden NNI, "Notes on Dog Lodge" and Warden FN, "Arapaho Ceremonies."

115. Kroeber, *Arapaho*, 152; Dorsey, *Sun Dance*, 162, 167, 182–84, and passim.

116. Hilger, *Arapaho Child Life*, 124–25, 127–29, 135–37; Kroeber, *Arapaho*, 436; W-D, Warden NNI, "Miscellaneous Notes—Medicine." Occasionally a youth dreamed that he became a woman, according to Kroeber. This was regarded as a gift from a spirit helper, and it brought medicine power. This third gender role involved men living as women and married to men.

117. See LT files, passim, on Little Raven's relatives and wives.

118. Mooney MS, 1910a; Kroeber, *Arapaho*, 30, on Little Raven's mother. On Trunk, see DD, Jess Rowlodge, T-206:6–8, and Kappler, *Indian Treaties*, 892, where Trunk appears as Haversack; LT files, passim.

119. Hilger, *Arapaho Child Life*, 5–6, 41–42, 57, 59, 61, 75–76, 204; Kroeber, *Arapaho*, 17, 28, 418.

120. Hilger, *Arapaho Child Life*, 104; Sage, *Rufus B. Sage*, 5:266, 301; Michelson MS 2267, "Story of Medicine Grass," 1929.

121. W-D, Dorsey MS, 59–72, 74 and Warden NNI, "Notes on Arapaho Clothing"; Kroeber, *Arapaho*, 22, 24–25, 27–28; Eggan FN, Jess Rowlodge, 2:101; Dorsey, *Sun Dance*, 192–212.

122. Kroeber, *Arapaho*, 206–207; W-D, Warden NNI, "Sweat Lodge" and Warden FN, "Arapaho Ceremonies."

123. Kroeber, *Arapaho*, 207–209; W-D, Warden FN, "Arapaho Ceremonies."

124. W-D, Warden NNI, "Notes on Arapaho Social Organization—Birth" and "Spirit of the Waters" and "Notes on Arapaho Clothing," and Dorsey MS, 59–72, 74.

125. Kroeber, *Arapaho*, 30–35, 70–77, 209–10.

126. Sage, *Rufus B. Sage*, 4:274–75.

127. Dorsey, *Sun Dance*, passim.

128. Ibid. The Rabbit spirit being was important to the Algonkian-speaking peoples in the woodlands area, where Arapahos presumably once lived before moving onto the plains.

CHAPTER 2. SEEING SIGNS AND WONDERS

1. *CT*, 10 May 1884. This chapter is based on information from documentary sources (see Berthrong, *Cheyenne and Arapaho Ordeal*, for more background on agency history); the ethnographic work of Inez Hilger, Alfred Kroeber, George Dorsey, and Cleaver Warden; and the personal accounts of Arapahos interviewed by Inez Hilger, Fred Eggan, and Julia Jordan (see DD).

2. D. B. Dyer to C. W. Darling, 30 April 1884, LB, Darl, 7. Fort Reno was established in July 1875. A subagency, Seger Colony, opened in 1886, when John Seger took a group of Arapahos and Cheyennes to settle on the Washita River.

3. Seger, *Early Days*, 73–77. The name Neatha means "white man"; Neatha took John Seger's last name.

4. Hilger, *Arapaho Child Life*, 75; W-D, Warden FN, "Arapaho Ceremonials," 5; S. S. Haury to J. D. Miles, 15 August 1883, p. 69, *RCIA* 1883. On discipline, see also Hilger FN, especially interviews of Jess Rowlodge, 18 May 1941, and Helen Spotted Wolf (b. 1888), 26 May 1941. Hilger interviewed several Arapahos, who told her about their childhoods on the reservation in the 1880s and 1890s.

5. Bass, *Arapaho Way*, 8; Hilger, *Arapaho Child Life*, 24, 41, 61–62; Dorsey, *Sun Dance*, 179–80; DD, Jess Rowlodge, T-236:4, 240:24, 475:12; Hilger FN, Jess Rowlodge, 22 May 1941. Julia Jordan's interviews with Jess Rowlodge in the Duke Collection took place during 1967–69. Genealogical information throughout the chapter is from LT files.

6. Hilger FN, Jess Rowlodge, 18 and 28 May 1941; Arnold Woolworth, 18 and 27 May 1941; Grace Powderface Sagebark, 14 May 1941; and Helen Spotted Wolf, 26 May 1941. Bass, *Arapaho Way*, 35; DD, Jess Rowlodge, T-41:14, 198-2:13, 204:30–31, 220:29; Myrtle Lincoln, T-617:32–33; Annie Pedro, T-242:2–3; LT files, 2221, 2232, 2234, 2259. Julia Jordan's interviews with Myrtle Lincoln took place during 1969–72, and with Annie Pedro, in 1968.

7. Bass, *Arapaho Way*, 46, 51; Hilger FN, Jess Rowlodge, 17 and 22 May 1941.

8. B. Darlington to E. Hoag, 26 August 1871, p. 472, and A. Standing and Julia Cattell to E. Hoag, 25 August 1871, p. 474, both in *RCIA* 1871; Miles to Hoag, 28 August 1872, p. 251, *RCIA* 1872; Miles to E. P. Smith, Report for December 1875, in LB, Darl, 1; Miles to William Nicholson, 31 August 1876, p. 46, *RCIA* 1876. For additional background on the reservation schools, see Mann, *Cheyenne-Arapaho Education*.

9. Miles to CIA, 1 September 1880, p. 69, *RCIA* 1880; J. Seger to Miles, 15 August 1881, p. 71, and Miles to CIA, 1 September 1881, p. 67, both in *RCIA* 1881; G. D. Williams to CIA, 22 August 1887, p. 77, *RCIA* 1887; Arapaho Manual Labor Boarding School, Statistics Relating to Indian Schools, 1882–1909:4 (1898), 7–9, RED.

10. J. Seger Reports, 31 January, 30 April, 31 May 1881, AMLS; DD, Jess Rowlodge, T-41:4, Annie Pedro, T-241:12; Bass, *Arapaho Way*, 65; letter from Josie Poisal, 28 June 1888, in *Menn*, August 1888:165.

11. DD, Jess Rowlodge, T-239:21; Misc. School Records, 1875–83, CAR; J. M. Lee to CIA, 13, 15, and 25 February 1886, LB, Darl, 11; C. E. Campbell to R. Pratt, 8 October 1879, LB-ER, 1; *CT*, 13 September 1883.

12. On hair cutting and whipping, Hilger FN, Jess Rowlodge, 17 May 1941; Kroeber, *Arapaho*, 18–19, 365–66; DD, Jess Rowlodge, T-240:24–26.

13. Census of 1881, passim; Bass, *Arapaho Way*, 64; on orphans, see Miles to H. Price, 5 July 1881, LB-ER, 1.

14. Census of 1881, passim; Report of John Seger, 1 July 1881, AMLS; Seger to CIA, 23 August 1900, p. 501, *RCIA* 1900; DD, Jess Rowlodge, T-235:18, Myrtle Lincoln, T-617:34.

15. Bass, *Arapaho Way*, 51; Miles to E. A. Hayt, 1 February 1879, LB-ER, 1; Seger to Miles, 15 August 1881, p. 72, *RCIA* 1881, and Seger to CIA, 3 August 1893, p. 445, *RCIA* 1893; DD, Jess Rowlodge, T-237:2. Despite disclaimers of corporal punishment, John Seger bragged about whipping Arapaho boys.

16. John Seger, 31 March 1881, and W. Thomas, 29 April 1882, AMLS; Miles to Nicholson, 14 July 1876, LB, Darl, 1; *CT*, 18 December 1883, 10 October 1884, and 15 February 1885; J. Woodard to Price, 2 February 1883, LB, Darl, 6; Robert Gardner, 28 June 1887, p. 4, IR; D. B. Hirschler, 30 November 1882, LR 1882-22320; *Menn*, September 1885 and February 1888; on language, see H. Voth to Lee, 1 September 1886, p. 124, *RCIA* 1886, and E. White to CIA, 4 December 1888, LR 1888-30019.

17. I. Dwire to C. Ashley, 5 August 1891, p. 348, *RCIA* 1891; W. Montgomery to A. E. Woodson, 1 July 1895, p. 248, *RCIA* 1895; Charles Nesler, 30 October 1897 (7969), p. 4, IR; J. Duncan to CIA, 4 September 1900, p. 328, *RCIA* 1900; Council with Cheyenne and Arapaho, 21 March 1895, SC 147-13100-1891.

18. Miles to CIA, 1 September 1882, p. 55, *RCIA* 1882; Ashley to CIA, 27 August 1889, p. 186, *RCIA* 1889; Dwire to Ashley, 20 July 1892, pp. 380–81, *RCIA* 1892; Dwire to Ashley, 30 June 1893, p. 251, and George Westfall to Woodson, 20 September 1893, p. 255, both in *RCIA* 1893; W. Dew to George Stouch, 24 August 1901, p. 318, *RCIA* 1901; James M. Haworth, 14 February 1883, p. 1, and Frank Armstrong, 25 November 1886, p. 2, and Gardner, 28 June 1887, p. 2, all IR; Arapaho School, 1:27, Statistics from Monthly School Reports, 1895–96, RED; Stouch to CIA, 12 January 1901, LSCIA, Darl, C; J. S. Krehbiel, 3 April 1894, in *Menn*, July 1894.

19. Ashley to CIA, 7 September and 8 July, 1889, LB, Darl, 27; Ashley to CIA, 10 March 1892, LB, Darl, 33; Dyer to J. D. Atkins, 4 April 1885, LB-ER, 5; Williams to L. H. Jackson, 30 August 1888, LB, Darl, 25; Quarterly Report, 30 September 1889, AMLS.

20. Hilger FN, Grace Sagebark, 14 May 1941; Woodson to CIA, 28 August 1896, p. 246, *RCIA* 1896. On work assignments, see Census of 1881, passim; DD, Jess Rowlodge, T-157:17–18, 205:19–21, 352:8, 30–31.

21. DD, Jess Rowlodge, T-238:20, and Myrtle Lincoln, T-624:2–3, 14, 18, 20; Hilger FN, Grace Powderface Sagebark, 14 May 1941, Jane Hungry Wolf, 12 August 1940, and Jess Rowlodge, 17 May 1942; Census of 1881, passim.

22. W-D, Dorsey Correspondence: Cleaver Warden to George Dorsey, 5 December 1903; Hilger, *Arapaho Child Life*, 122; Dorsey, *Sun Dance*, 8–9, 24–32; DD, Jess Rowlodge, T-204:8. Participants were Walter Finley, Black Bear, George Black Hat, Don Brooks, Charles Campbell, Dan Dyer, Ben Franklin, Good Warrior, Jay Gould, Cecil Geary, George Hocheny, Francis Lee, James Monroe, Charley Old Horse, Noble Prentiss, Hartley Ridge Bear, Short Man, Singing Man, Dan Webster, Dan Wheeler, Arnold Woolworth.

23. DD, Jess Rowlodge, T-172:26, 203:1–2, 5–7, 10–12, 204:9, and Myrtle Lincoln, T-666-1:3.

24. Bass, *Arapaho Way*, 52; Census of 1881, 117. Orphans could activate kinship networks when they matured, establishing reciprocal duties with siblings and others.

25. Miles to Hayt, 20 March 1878 [M528], LRCA; Miles to Nicholson, 31 August 1876, p. 48, *RCIA* 1876; Miles to Nicholson, 31 August 1877, p. 84, *RCIA* 1877; Miles to CIA, 1 September 1880, pp. 69–70, *RCIA* 1880; John McNeil, 9 September 1878, p. 3, IR; Census of 1881, passim; Miles to Hayt, 1 February 1879, LB-ER, 1; C. Krehbiel, 17 January 1890, in *Menn*, March 1890; DD, Jess Rowlodge, T-352:8.

26. Woodson to CIA, 5 February 1896, LR-1896-6523; DD, Annie Pedro, T-242:20, 25; S. S. Haury to Miles, 15 August 1883, p. 69, *RCIA* 1883; Hirschler report, 30 June 1882, AMLS.

27. DD, Jess Rowlodge, T-237:12–14, 17–21, 238:22–23, and Annie Pedro, T-242:8, 10–11.

28. Miles to Hayt, 20 March 1878 [M529], LRCA; Haworth, 14 February 1883, p. 16, IR; report of J. Schmidt, *Menn*, March 1891, 91.

29. Report of Anna Schmidt, *Menn*, April 1891, 109; H. L. Weiss to Board of Missions, Report for July 1894, Board of Missions/General Correspondence; Woodson to CIA, 28 August 1896, p. 246, *RCIA* 1896; 10 April 1898 and 10 October 1899, MJ, Diaries.

30. DD, Myrtle Lincoln, T-617:23; John Williams to H. Voth, 30 July and 2 August 1887, Henry R. Voth Collection, box 8, folder 47; Edmund Mallet, 18 September 1889, p. 3 (5798), IR; Montgomery to Superintendent of Indian Schools, 1 July 1895, p. 248, *RCIA* 1895; Ashley to H. W. Sheeler, 27 September 1890, LB, Darl, 31; Woodson to CO, 23 April 1894, LB, Darl, 44; Woodson to Col. E. P. Pearson, 6 November 1895, LB, Darl, 57; Woodson to CIA, 10 August 1898, LB, Darl, 76.

31. On Bichea's daughter Molly, see LT files, 1690; Haury to Miles, 18 August 1881, p. 75, *RCIA* 1881.

32. RCAO, passim; Lee to CIA, 1 September 1885, LB, Darl, 9; *CT*, 10 December 1880 and 25 March 1881; Miles to Price, 9 February 1882, LB, Darl, 4; *School News*, September 1880, March 1881, and *Eadlekeatahtoh*, February 1882. For background on American ideas about women's role in nineteenth-century America, see Welter, "The Cult of True Womanhood." Women were expected to be pious, pure, domestic, and submissive.

33. On Henry North, see *School News*, December 1882, and Miles to J. K. Mizner, 22 August 1877, LRCA. For background on Carlisle, see Bell, "Telling Stories." The Arapahos at Carlisle kept a low profile compared with many from other tribes. In 1884, eleven Arapahos went to Chilocco in Oklahoma; eight in 1887. In 1883, eight Arapahos went to White Manual Labor Institute in Iowa.

34. *Indian Helper*, 4:3 (31 August 1888); 5:43 (24 June 1890); 5:33 (18 April 1890); 10:7 (September/October 1890).

35. *Menn*, February 1888. Halstead was a contract school, supported partly by the United States government.

36. William P. Ames, "Highlights of Haskell Institute," 1936, manuscript at Haskell Cultural Center and Museum; Paul Hogan to C. Robinson, 27 August 1887, LR-1887-23084; Ashley to C. Meserve, 17 February 1891, LB, Darl, 32.

37. DD, Jess Rowlodge, T-352:28; *CT*, 25 June 1881; Henry North for Black Coyote to T. J. Morgan, 26 January 1893, LR 1893-3800; Dyer to Pratt, 18 October 1884, LB-ER, 4; Pratt, *Battlefield and Classroom*, 53.

38. On the Poisal family, see RCAO and Dyer to Atkins, 4 April 1885, LB-ER, 5.

39. *CT*, 25 January 1881; Ashley to Pratt, 9 August 1892, LB, Darl, 36.

40. Williams to Atkins, 31 March 1887, LB, Darl, 20; Dyer to CIA, 9 August 1884, p. 76, Lee to CIA, 31 August 1886, p. 116, and Williams to CIA, 22 August 1887, p. 77, all in *RCIA* 1884, 1886, and 1887; Lee to CIA, 10 December 1885, LB, Darl, 9.

41. On Dan Tucker, see *CT*, 30 April 1885; Hirschler to Voth, 29 August 1888, Henry R. Voth Collection, box 4; and Woodson to D. Tucker, 1 July 1895, LB, Darl, 50. On Peter Arrow, see Voth's report for September 1888 in *Menn*, February 1889.

42. *School News*, 2:12 (May 1882); *CT*, 25 June and 26 September 1882. On the importance of correspondence between students and their families, see Child, *Boarding School Seasons*.

43. Woodson to CIA, 9 February 1894, LR 1894-5995; Voth to CIA, 8 September 1890, p. 185, and Dwire to Ashley, 5 August 1891, p. 348, both in *RCIA* 1890 and 1891; Dorsey, *Sun Dance*, 25; W-D, Warden FN, "Clubboard Lodge." On Paul Boynton, see F. Glasbrenner to G. Coleman, 9 March 1895, LB, Darl, 54 and Woodson to S. Janus, 3 June 1896, LB, Darl, 62.

44. *Indian Helper* 5:19 (10 January 1890), *Red Man* 9:4 (March 1889) and 10:5 (June 1890). On Francis Lee, see *Menn*, November 1889, 26, and on Harry Bates, see *Menn*, March 1890, 92, and July 1893, 78.

45. On Bessie Red Pipe, see Lee to Haury, 1 August 1886, and Lee to L. Miles, 10 August 1886, both in LB, Darl, 16; on Jessie Bringing Good, see Woodson to Col. Pearson, 6 November 1895, LB, Darl, 57 and Janus to Woodson, 4 and 17 January 1896, LB, Canton, 3; on Lulu Blind, see Pratt to W. Hailman, 11 June 1895, LR-1895-24433, Westfall to Woodson, 19 January 1894, LB, Darl, 39, and Paul Faison, 5 December 1895, IR.

46. DD, Jess Rowlodge, T-267:2; Montgomery to Woodson, 9 May 1895, LB, Darl, 55; Glasbrenner to CIA, 7 March 1895, LB, Darl, 54; Woodson to Seger, 20 April 1894, LB, Darl, 44. On Minnie Yellow Bear, see *Indian Helper* 3:14 (11 November 1887) and 3:22 (13 January 1888).

47. Ashley to H. W. Wheeler, 2 June 1890, LB, Darl, 31; Report of the Jerome Commission, Irregularly Shaped Papers.

48. Information on the histories of these individuals is taken from multiple sources, primarily agency correspondence, LT files, and ethnographic data from James Mooney, Warden, and Dorsey. Cleaver Warden was among this early group going to Carlisle, but when he returned, he settled at Colony. Fox and Star members included camp youths Little Raven, Jr., and Circle and educated youths Francis Lee, Grant Left Hand, Dan Webster, and Jesse Bent.

49. Michelson MS 3345, "Narrative of the Old Moccasin Society by Little Left Hand," 1932.

50. Michelson MS 2267, "Story of Medicine Grass," 1929.

51. Bass, *Arapaho Way*, 41; Michelson MS 2267; Miles to Hoag, 1 September 1873, p. 221, *RCIA* 1873; Miles to CIA, 31 August 1878, pp. 54–55, *RCIA* 1878; Miles to Hoag, 4 February 1876, LB, Darl, 1; Miles to Hayt, 19 September 1879,

LRCA; Miles to Hoag, Report for January-February 1873, LRUA; Ben Clark to Mizner, 16 May 1877, Ben Clark Collection.

52. Bass, *Arapaho Way*, 41; DD, Jess Rowlodge, T-144:21–23, 157:11, 14, 238: 18–19.

53. Bass, *Arapaho Way*, 54; DD, Jess Rowlodge, T-237:23, 25–26; J. A. Covington to Miles, 5 January 1878, LRCA; *CT*, 10 February 1883; Enrollment Lists and Census Records (hereafter Enrollment), CAR.

54. Miles to Nicholson, 31 August 1877, p. 83, *RCIA* 1877; Miles to Nicholson, 31 August 1876, p. 47, *RCIA* 1876; Miles to Hayt, 20 September 1878, LRCA; Miles to CIA, 1 September 1880, p. 68, *RCIA* 1880; Miles to Price, 22 November 1881, LB, Darl, 3; *CT*, 25 May 1882 and 24 December 1880.

55. Miles to CIA, 18 August 1883, pp. 60–62, *RCIA* 1883; DD, Jess Rowlodge, T-157:8–9.

56. Bass, *Arapaho Way*, 11; *CT*, 20 February 1886; Miles to Nicholson, 31 August 1876, pp. 48–49, *RCIA* 1876; Miles to Nicholson, 31 August 1877, p. 82, *RCIA* 1877; Miles to CIA, 1 September 1882, p. 56, *RCIA* 1882; Miles to CIA, 18 August 1883, p. 64, *RCIA* 1883; Lee to CIA, 25 January 1886, LB, Darl, 11; Enrollment, 14 February 1878; Census of 1881, 117; Freight and Transportation File, ca. 1877, all CAR. The census shows that most Arapaho men had one or two horses; thirty-six had none. Thirty-one (16 percent) had four or more. Prominent middle-aged chiefs individually owned ten or more, for example, Bird Chief. Most Arapaho families had six or more horses.

57. *CT*, 25 May 1881; Bass, *Arapaho Way*, 44–47; Williams to CIA, 22 August 1887, p. 78, *RCIA* 1887.

58. J. Covington to Miles, 19 August 1881, p. 77, *RCIA* 1881; Bass, *Arapaho Way*, 47; Miles to CIA, 31 August 1879, pp. 59 and 61, *RCIA* 1879; Miles to CIA, 31 August 1878, p. 55, *RCIA* 1878; Report of W. Murray, 30 November 1876, Farmers File, CAR; A. Dalles to Assistant Adjutant General, 21 July 1879, Letters Sent, Camp Supply, 6, PR; Williams to CIA, 22 August 1887, p. 78, *RCIA* 1887.

59. Bass, *Arapaho Way*, 26, 39; DD, Jess Rowlodge, T-125:18, 144:19, 157:16–18, 20–21, 235:18, 20, 237:16, 352:5–7, and Annie Pedro, T-242:12–13; Gardner, 24 November 1883 (4871), IR; Armstrong to L. Lamar, 24 July 1885, File 1885-29393, SC 9; *Morning Star* 7:2 (1886). Row Of Lodges and the Poisals were in the Blackfeet band. Mooney noted that Arapahos arrived on the reservation in five bands: Bad Faces, Pleasant Men, Blackfeet, and two others that I could find no record of. Warden noted that the two main bands were Ugly Faces and Funny People (which referred to their small tepees, that is, their lack of prosperity)—Mooney, *Ghost Dance*, 957; W-D, Warden NNI, "Notes on Arapaho Social Organization—Tribal Organization."

60. DD, Jess Rowlodge, T-144:15; Miles to Hoag, January-February report 1873, LRUA; Enrollment 1874, 1877, 14 February 1878, 1884, CAR; Miles to Smith, 4 February 1875, LRCA; Miles to Nicholson, 25 February and 18 September

1876, both in LB, Darl, 1; "Arapaho Wagon List," and Freight and Transportation File (n.d.); Census of 1881, 20, 359, 365, all in CAR; *CT*, 25 June and 26 September 1882 and 15 May 1885; Miles to Price, 2 July 1883, LB, Darl, 2; Gardner, 24 November 1883 (4871), IR; Lee to CIA, 24 August 1885, LB, Darl, 9; Williams to Atkins, 13 August 1887, LB, Darl, 20; Woodson to H. North, 9 November 1894, LB, Darl, 47; Henry Meagher, 18 June 1937, 4652, p. 53, Indian Pioneer Papers (Henry was an eyewitness to the murder). The Creek bandit was initially captured by the Seminole Lighthorsemen and brought to jail, but he escaped.

61. H. Smith to CIA, 14 June 1894, File 1894-22833, SC 147; DD, Jess Rowlodge, T- 157:8–9, 16–17, 23, 32 and 352:5–7, 26. On Bringing Good, see Ashley to CIA, 6 July 1892, LR 1892-24452, and Ashley to William Grimes, 18 July 1892, LB, Darl, 36. The Cheyennes also had allotment clusters, largely to the west of the Arapahos.

62. Woodson to CIA, 1 September 1897, p. 228, *RCIA* 1897; John Faber to G. Stouch, 24 November 1902, Farmers File, CAR.

63. Bass, *Arapaho Way*, 23–24; DD, Jess Rowlodge, T-157:29–30, 235:13–15, 352:12–13, 20.

64. W-D, Warden NNI, "Notes on Arapaho Social Organization—Election of Chiefs."

65. DD, Jess Rowlodge, T-205:23, 25–26, 33–34; 239:19, 21–22; 352:13, 29–30.

66. Hilger FN, Lucy Rowlodge, 27 May 1941, and Arnold Woolworth, 27 May 1941; LT files, 1465 and 1466; Mooney, *Ghost Dance*, 898; Dorsey, *Sun Dance*, 16–20, 142.

67. W-D, Warden FN, "Arapaho Ceremonials," and Warden NNI, "Thunderbird Lodge," "Lime Lodge," and "Dog Lodge"; DD, Jess Rowlodge, T-205:15–16.

68. W-D, Warden FN, "Arapaho Ceremonials" and Warden NNI, "Notes on Arapaho Social Organization—Mode of Electing Headmen."

69. On war parties, see Darlington to Hoag, 9 February 1871; L. E. Compton to Assistant Adjutant General, 21 November 1873; Covington to Miles, 30 June 1873; Miles to Hoag, 11 July 1873; Meeting between Northern and Southern Cheyenne and Arapaho and Commissioner of Indian Affairs, 13 November 1873; Miles to Smith, 16 and 20 June 1874, all in LRUA; and Covington to Smith, 16 August 1875, LRCA. On ranking, see Census of 1881, passim; Clark, *Indian Sign Language*, 43; DD, Jess Rowlodge, T-206:19–20. On Adobe Walls, see Berthrong, *Southern Cheyennes*, 384–86. The 1881 census ranks Arapaho "warriors" and "chiefs" (war chiefs).

70. Michelson MS 3345, "Narrative of the Old Moccasin Society by Little Left Hand," 1932. On guarding the agency, see Miles to Smith, 23 May 1874, LRUA. On enforcing conformity, see Dyer to CIA, 9 August 1884, p. 75, *RCIA* 1884; Woodson to CIA, 28 August 1896, p. 246, *RCIA* 1896.

71. Bass, *Arapaho Way*, 14; Indian Police, 1 December 1881, CAR; Miles to CIA, 31 August 1878, p. 55, *RCIA* 1878; Dyer to CIA, 9 August 1884, LB-ER, 1;

Williams to CIA, 22 August 1887, p. 78, *RCIA* 1887; Woodson to CIA, 20 September 1893, p. 247, *RCIA* 1893; Miles to J. Brown, 5 May 1881, LB-ER, 1; Woodson to Black Coyote, 10 October 1893, LB, Darl, 40; Woodson to Little Left Hand, 30 April 1895, LB, Darl, 55.

72. W-D, Warden FN, "Arapaho Ceremonials," and Warden NNI, "Notes on Arapaho Social Organization—Tribal Organization and Mode of Electing Headmen."

73. Dorsey, *Sun Dance*, 15–20, 70, 72, 85–86, 126–27, 160.

74. Kroeber, *Arapaho*, 418–19, 427–29, 431, 434–39; W-D, Warden NNI, "Miscellaneous Notes—Black Man's Story about the Medicine (Stone)"; DD, Jess Rowlodge, T-163:26–27, 39–40, 164:2–3, 7–10, 13–17, 690:4–6, and Myrtle Lincoln, T-585:13, 608:10–11, 14, 23–25, 691:3–6.

75. In 1884 bands of seven or eight families were headed by members of the Left Hand cohort, including Powderface, Road Traveler, Fire, Bull Thunder, Birdshead, and Big Mouth, and two members of the Medicine Grass cohort, Black Wolf and Scabby Bull (Enrollment, CAR). In 1887 beef bands were headed by Deaf, Fire, Bull Thunder, Birdshead, Black Wolf, Scabby Bull, Road Traveler (Enrollment, Cantonment, CAR). In 1892 Arapaho beef bands at Cantonment were led by Fire, Bull Thunder, Birdshead, Arrow from Left Hand's cohort, and Scabby Bull, Black Wolf, Deaf, Henry Sage, Theok Raven, Bad Man, and Black Horse from the Medicine Grass cohort (S. H. Jones to William Pulling, 13 June 1892, LB, Darl, 35). By 1894 the heads of all the beef bands in Cantonment were members of the Medicine Grass cohort (Woodson to C. Briscoe, 16 August 1894, LB, Darl, 46). The names of the intermediary chiefs appear in the transcripts of councils—see note 81.

76. On Little Raven's political career: Darlington to Hoag, 26 August 1871, p. 470, *RCIA* 1871; Miles to Hoag, 12 March 1873, LRUA; *CT*, 25 September 1880; Miles to Price, 7 January 1882, LR 1882-1024; Miles to CIA, 20 March 1884, LR 1884-5886; J. H. Potter to R. Williams, 23 June 1885, LR 1885-16697 and War Department to CIA, 24 February 1885, LR 1885-4459. On genealogy, see LT files, passim, and Census of 1881, 117.

77. LT files, passim.

78. On Left Hand: Miles to Hoag, January-February 1873 report, LRUA; Enrollment 1874, CAR; Journal of the Sixth Annual Session of the General Council of the Indian Territory, Okmulgee, 3–15 May 1875 (H975-1442), LR-Cen. Supt.; Miles to Hayt, 18 September 1878, LRCA; Miles to CIA, 7 March 1881, LR 1881-4532; Miles to Price, 7 January 1882, LR 1882-1024; Council with CIA, 3 December 1884, Letters Sent, 39, Indian Division, Records of the Office of the Secretary of the Interior, RG 48; Proceedings, Report of Jerome Commission, 1890–93, Irregularly Shaped Papers 78; Ashley to CIA, 24 October 1891, LR 1891-38601; Ashley to CIA, 31 March 1891, LR 1891-12394; Mitchell to Browning, 5 May 1893, LR 1893-17373; Council with Cheyenne and Arapaho, 19 March

1895, File 13100-1891, SC 147; Woodson to Pearson, 21 May 1897, LB, Darl, 69; Talk with Arapahos, 30 March–6 April 1898, LR 1898-146691/2. See LT files, passim, for genealogy.

79. On Scabby Bull: E. Beaumont to Assistant Adjutant General, 24 February 1880, LRCA; Enrollment 1874, 1880, and 1881, CAR; Miles to Price, 7 January 1882, LR 1882-1024; Report of the Jerome Commission, Irregularly Shaped Papers; Ashley to CIA, 31 March 1891, LR 1891-12394, 21 November 1891, LR 1891-42064, and 24 October 1891, LR 1891-38601; Woodson to CIA, 9 February 1894, LR 1894-5995; Woodson to Pearson, 21 May 1897, LB, Darl, 69; LT files, passim.

80. On Black Coyote, see LT files; Dorsey, *Sun Dance*, 182; Mooney, *Ghost Dance*, 776, 897.

81. For transcripts of councils, see Miles to Price, 3 July 1882, LR 1882-12454 and Miles to Price, 7 January 1882, LR 1882-1024; E. Mitchell to D. M. Browning, 5 May 1893, LR 1893-17373; Ashley to CIA, 18 May 1893, LR 1893-18546; Talk with Arapahos, 30 March-6 April 1898, LR 1898-14669½. On the different perspectives of Americans, see *CT*, 10 April and 10 July 1882, 27 June 1883, and 26 June 1886; W. Pollock, 12 June 1879, IR; MJ, Diaries, 9 April 1898, 6 April 1899, 15 June 1900; O. Woodard to Miles, 1 October 1881, LR 1881-17913.

82. On the Jerome agreement, see the transcript in Report of the Jerome Commission, Irregularly Shaped Papers, and Hagan, *Taking Indian Lands*, 61–84, esp. 70, 74. See L. Fowler, *Tribal Sovereignty*, for a discussion of American ideology during the administration of the reservation.

83. Lee to Little Raven, 25 February 1886, LB, Darl, 12.

84. Mooney, *Ghost Dance*, 894–97, 900–903; Ashley to CIA, 30 January 1890, LR 1890-3278 and 22 September 1891, LR 1891-34757.

85. Kroeber, *Arapaho*, 352, 354, 411, 427; Mooney, *Ghost Dance*, 895.

86. On Sitting Bull, see DD, Jess Rowlodge, T-159:10, 235:5–6; LT files, 2189, 2259, 2382; Mooney, *Ghost Dance*, 896–97. On Arapaho scouting, see L. Fowler, *Arapahoe Politics*. On Black Coyote, see LT files, 1342, and Mooney, *Ghost Dance*, 897–98.

87. Kroeber, *Arapaho*, 319, 326, 427, 431; Mooney, *Ghost Dance*, 326, 431, 897, 899, 909, 919–21, 1012; DD, Jess Rowlodge, T-159:7, 15, 19, 24; Myrtle Lincoln, T-613:16. On visits to the Otos, Poncas, Pawnees, Apaches, and Caddos, see, for example, Woodson to M. Nichols, 21 August 1894, LB, Darl, 46; Woodson to M. Nichols, 14 July 1894 and Woodson to S. Skinner, 25 June 1894, both in LB, Darl, 45; P. Sisney to Woodson, 11 July 1899, LB, Canton, 5; Woodson to Sisney, 27 October 1899 and Woodson to Indian Agent, Ponca, 20 November 1899, both in LB, Darl, 84; Woodson to J. Randlett, 28 September 1899, LB, Darl, 83; Fred Winterfair to Stouch, 13 October 1900, LB, Canton, 7.

88. Kroeber, *Arapaho*, 368–82; DD, Myrtle Lincoln, T-586:1–2, 13–14, 668:2; WD, Warden NNI, "Notes on Arapaho Games," and Dorsey MS, 168–79.

89. Kroeber, *Arapaho*, 319–20, 340, 342, 348–49, 351–52, 354–55, 357, 363–68; Mooney, *Ghost Dance*, 901, 921–22; Dorsey, *Sun Dance*, 136. The Crow Dance eventually became a more secular dance, known as the Omaha Dance or war dance.

90. DD, Jess Rowlodge, T-159:7–9, 170-1:5 and 2:18–21, 172:9, 18–19, 247:34. See also Stewart, *Peyote Religion*, 106–108, 189. Plains Apaches are sometimes referred to as Kiowa-Apaches; perhaps this is why Kroeber credited the Kiowas with transferring peyote to Arapahos.

91. Kroeber, *Arapaho*, 320–21, 398–410; Bass, *Arapaho Way*, 76; DD, Jess Rowlodge, T-247:12; W-D, Warden FN, "Peyote Ceremony" and "Miscellaneous Notes: Mescal Fan." Peyote was administered as a tea for cures in Arapaho households.

92. Michelson, "Narrative."

93. Bass, *Arapaho Way*, 27–30; DD, Myrtle Lincoln, T-658:1–5, 12, 16–17, 19, 25, 27, 30.

94. DD, Jess Rowlodge, T-157:16, 19–20, 352:33–34.

95. *CT*, 30 September 1884; Dyer to CIA, 22 July 1885, p. 79, *RCIA* 1885; Kroeber, *Arapaho*, 91–92; Bass, *Arapaho Way*, 11–14, 27–30, 35, 53–54; MJ, Diary, 3 May 1898, 5 March and 6 April 1899.

96. Bass, *Arapaho Way*, 11–14, 45–46; DD, Myrtle Lincoln, T-616:25–26.

97. Miles to Hoag, 28 January, and January/February Report, 1873, LRUA; Bass, *Arapaho Way*, 60; Miles to William Nicholson, 31 August 1877, p. 82, *RCIA* 1877.

98. Miles to Price, 7 July 1882, LB, Darl, 5; DD, Jess Rowlodge, T-41:11, 125: 5–7, 237:22, 475:13; Myrtle Lincoln, T-588:11–12, 658:20; Richard Dodge to Assistant Adjutant General, 4 March 1880, Letters Sent, Cantonment, 1, PR.

99. *GB*, 17 October 1901; Winterfair to Woodson, 2 January 1899, LB, Canton, 5; Winterfair to Stouch, 30 January 1900, LB, Canton, 6; Property Clerk to Agent, 17 August 1894, LB, Darl, 42.

100. Hilger, *Arapaho Child Life*, 209; Kroeber, *Arapaho*, 10–11; DD, Myrtle Lincoln, T-624:17–18, and Jess Rowlodge, T-41:10–11; Pratt, *Battlefield and Classroom*, 52; Michelson, "Narrative," 609–10.

101. Hilger FN, Lucy Rowlodge, 27 May, Long Hair 20 May, Jess Rowlodge 17 May, Helen Spotted Wolf 26 May, all 1941; *CT*, 26 September 1882.

102. Michelson, "Narrative," 602–608 and MS 2182, "Life of Mrs. White Bear," 1929; LT files, 1357, 1445, 1540, 1541; Covington to Smith, 27 March 1875, LRCA; DD, Jess Rowlodge, T-236:25; Miles to R. Pratt, 28 September 1881, p. 19, *RCIA* 1881; Miles to CIA, 10 July 1883, LR-1883-12759. On White Bear's imprisonment, see Petersen, *Plains Indian Art*, and Lookingbill, *War Dance*. A. Standing reported that on White Bear's return home after five years in the east, his brother, "a large great fellow, came to the wagon, lifted him in his arms and kissed him and among parents and friends he was borne away" (*Morning Star* 1:3, May 1880).

103. Voth to Ashley, 4 September 1889, p. 312, *RCIA* 1889; Ashley to CIA, 28 August 1890, pp. 179, 181, *RCIA* 1890; Ashley to CIA, 19 March 1891, LB, Darl,

30; Woodson to CIA, 28 August 1896, p. 246, *RCIA* 1896; S. Janus to Woodson, 17 January 1896, LB, Canton, 3; Woodson to CIA, 26 January 1897, LB, Darl, 66; Woodson to Probate, 22 August 1897, LB, Darl, 71. The chiefs complained to Inspector C. C. Duncan about Woodson's interference in marital customs (Report of 13 July 1896, 5018, IR).

104. Woodson to CIA, 1 September 1897, pp. 225–26, *RCIA* 1897; Woodson to CIA, 28 August 1896, p. 246, *RCIA* 1896.

105. Miles to Mizner, 1 May 1876, LB, Darl, 1; Census of 1881, passim; Williams to CIA, 25 August 1888, p. 89, *RCIA* 1888.

106. Ashley to CIA, 19 March 1891, LB, Darl, 30; Janus to Woodson, 17 January 1896, LB, Canton, 3; Woodson to CIA, 28 August 1896, p. 248, *RCIA* 1896; Woodson to CIA, 1 September 1897, p. 225, *RCIA* 1897; Hilger FN, Long Hair, 16 May 1941; Letter from James Scabby Horse, 15 March 1890, *Menn*, July 1890, 150.

107. Census of 1881, passim; Michelson, "Narrative," 599.

108. Census of 1881, 117.

109. LT files, 2343.

110. W. DeLesdernier to Pulling, 19 February 1890, LB, Darl, 31; F. Winterbottom to Woodson, 25 August 1897, LB, Canton, 4; Woodson to Winterbottom, 13 August 1897, LB, Darl, 70; Dodge to Assistant Adjutant General, 4 March 1880, Letters Sent, Cantonment, 1, PR.

111. Woodson to CIA, 28 April 1897, LB, Darl, 68; Ashley to Seger, 10 April 1893, LB, Darl, 36; Woodson to Coleman, 5 February 1895, and Woodson to R. Davis, 18 February 1895, LB, Darl, 53.

112. Woodson to CIA, 20 September 1893, p. 247, *RCIA* 1893; Pulling to Ashley, 11 June 1892, LB, Canton, 1; Woodson to CIA, 26 January 1897, LB, Darl, 66.

113. J. Witcher to Agent, 31 July 1902, Indian Customs file, CAR.

114. W-D, Warden NNI, "Buffalo Women's Lodge"; Kroeber, *Arapaho*, 220; DD, Myrtle Lincoln, T-452:28, Jess Rowlodge, T-204:11–12, 205:15–16; Pratt, *Battlefield and Classroom*, 52.

115. E. A. Carr to Assistant Adjutant General, 24 November 1875, LRCA; Reports of 31 February 1881, 30 June 1887, 30 September 1888, and 31 March 1889, AMLS; J. Meagher to C. Schurz, 12 February 1880, and Miles to CIA, 24 February 1880, both in LRCA; Pollock, 10 March 1880, IR; Woodson to CIA, 4 September 1893, LR 1893-33816; Woodson to M. Munder, 18 March 1896, LB, Darl, 60; Albert Keith, 15 July 1937, 4946, p. 97, Indian Pioneer Papers; J. Williams to Sallie Williams, 25 and 30 October and 2, 3, 15, 26 November 1873, SW.

116. Journal of the Sixth Annual Session of the General Council of the Indian Territory, Okmulgee, Indian Territory, 3–15 May 1875, p. 31, LR-Cen. Supt.; DD, Jess Rowlodge, T-203:3, 236:30–31; Dorsey, *Sun Dance*, 37.

117. Michelson, "Narrative," 608–10.

118. J. Williams to Sallie Williams, 15 November 1873, SW; Pratt to CIA, 4 November 1884, LR 1884-21179; Counsel with Cheyenne and Arapaho, 3 December 1884, Letters Sent 39:250; *Indian Helper* 7:13, 14 (4 and 11 December 1891).

119. LT files, 1008; W-D, Warden NNI, "Dog Lodge."

120. DD, Jess Rowlodge, T-163:2, 164:12, 14–15, 17; Myrtle Lincoln, T-453:1, 608:10, 14, 666-1:3.

121. Dorsey, *Sun Dance*, 25–32, 118; DD, Jess Rowlodge, T-204:7. Grass Singing probably was being trained to take over the duties of her elderly co-wife and sister.

122. Dorsey, *Sun Dance*, 16, 19–20, 72–73; LT files, 1146; Eggan FN, Bird White Bear, 2:66.

123. Information on the senior women is based on Warden's field notes and Dorsey, *Sun Dance*, passim.

124. Mooney, *Ghost Dance*, 775, 779, 899, 901, 909, 918–19, 923–24, 962, 974–75, 1007, 1032, 1036, 1038–39; Katie Left Hand and Woman Going In, Lincoln Township, Blaine County, Oklahoma, Twelfth Census, 1900, 7A penned, U.S. Bureau of the Census; LT files, 1357 and 2190; DD, Jess Rowlodge, T-159:15; Kroeber, *Arapaho*, 326, 346–48; H. Voth's report, p. 154, *Menn*, July 1891; W-D, Warden NNI, "Miscellaneous Notes—Buckskin Dress."

125. MJ, Diary, 9 April 1898; DD, Myrtle Lincoln, T-586:2; W-D, Dorsey MS, 168–79; Kroeber, *Arapaho*, 370, 373.

126. Mooney, *Ghost Dance*, 901; Kroeber, *Arapaho*, 363–67.

127. Kroeber, *Arapaho*, 398–405; W-D, Warden NNI, "Miscellaneous Notes—Mescal Fan"; DD, Jess Rowlodge, T-170:9, 13, 172:7.

128. Bass, *Arapaho Way*, 20; Mooney, *Ghost Dance*, 986, 989.

129. Kroeber, *Arapaho*, 12, 17–18, 22, 24–25, 28; W-D, Warden NNI, "Notes on Arapaho Clothing."

130. Census of 1881, 117, 158; Indian Census Rolls, 1892, 1901; Hilger FN, Jess Rowlodge, 24 May 1941. There was also a painted record of the history of the ceremonial lodges kept by one of the Seven Old Men, but in 1858 he buried it with his wife, even though he did not have the authority to do so (see Dorsey and Kroeber, *Traditions*, 19).

131. Census of 1881, passim; Indian Census Rolls, 1887, 1892, 1901; Kroeber, *Arapaho*, 30.

132. DD, Jess Rowlodge, T-125:19–20, 206:16, 20; Kroeber, *Arapaho*, 206–208.

133. Dorsey, *Sun Dance*, 26, 30–33, and passim; Kroeber, *Arapaho*, 207–209; W-D, Warden FN, "Arapaho Ceremonials," and Warden NNI, "Lime Crazy Lodge"; DD, Myrtle Lincoln, T-658:33, Jess Rowlodge, T-172:15, 247:35–36.

134. Kroeber, *Arapaho*, 161, 165; W-D, Warden FN, "Arapaho Ceremonials" and notebook, "Lime Crazy Lodge," p. 7; Dorsey, *Sun Dance*, 24–26, 30.

135. Kroeber, *Arapaho*, 30–35, 209–210; W-D, Warden FN, "Symbolism on Various Kinds of Buffalo Robes" and "Arapaho Ceremonials." I cannot establish the identity of Cedar Woman. She was probably born in 1841, the daughter of Moon and Deer Woman. There was a Deer Woman who was one of the Seven Old Woman, so Cedar Woman might have had the background and inclination. A widow, she lived west of Geary, where Bird In Tree lived. This woman

died in 1916. The other possibility is a woman living in the South Canadian district, who lived from 1853–1917. She seems rather young to have received the bundle, but her father was Tall Bear, and her first husband was Broken Cup (the son of Little Raven), so she would be Backward's grandson's wife.

136. Kroeber, *Arapaho*, 70–77.

137. DD, Jess Rowlodge, T-204:11–12; Annie Pedro, 241:10–11.

138. Hilger, *Arapaho Child Life*, 35; Kroeber, *Arapaho*, 16; W-D, Warden NNI, "Cradles," and FN, "Cradles."

139. Dorsey, *Sun Dance*, 24, 26; LT files, 1066, 1071; W-D, Warden FN, "Arapaho Ceremonials"; DD, Jess Rowlodge, T-204:5.

140. Mooney, *Ghost Dance*, 975; DD, Jess Rowlodge, T-159:27–28, 247:13–14, 18; MJ, Diaries, 9, 10, 30 April 1898; Kroeber, *Arapaho*, 321, 363, 365–66, 379–80; W-D, Warden FN, notebook, "Clubboard Lodge," 1:16–17.

CHAPTER 3. LIKE A REED

1. *CVR*, 23 November 1905.

2. William B. Freer, Narrative Report, 1910, SRCA; Report from Canton, 30 June 1911, Agents Reports File, CAR; W. Breuninger report, 30 June 1915, Farmers File, CAR; R. Newberne report, 29 April 1915, CFCA 150-49351-1915; C. T. Coggeshell, Statistical Report, 1921, SRC; L. S. Bonnin, Statistical Report, 1921, SRCA; E. J. Bost, Statistical Report, 1927, SRC; Bost to F. McKenzie, 13 May 1927, CF 024.

3. George Stouch to CIA, 14 August 1905, pp. 293–94, in *RCIA* 1905; *GB*, 23 January and 24 April 1902; Stouch to O. Franz, 31 July 1906, LB, Darl, 69; W. W. Scott, Narrative Report, 1920, SRCA.

4. Byron White, Narrative Report, 1910, SRC; *CVR*, 30 May 1907 and 18 July 1912; White, 7 August 1906, Cantonment, Agents Reports File, CAR; Coggeshell, Statistical Report, 1920, SRC.

5. L. Fowler, *Tribal Sovereignty*, 48, 93. The Indian Appropriations Act of 1902 (or Dead Indian Land Act) allowed adult heirs of deceased allottees to sell inherited trust land. Minors could sell inherited lands through court-appointed guardians (32 U.S. Stat. 245, 275). The Burke Act provided that, with the secretary of interior's permission, competent Indians could get a fee patent on their allotment, which allowed for it to be taxed and sold; the commissioner of Indian Affairs supervised the expenditure of land sale funds (34 U.S. Stat. 182–83, 1015, 1018). The Indian Appropriations Act of 1907 allowed noncompetent Indians to sell their land. For more background on agency history, see Berthrong, *Cheyenne and Arapaho Ordeal*.

6. W-D, Warden FN, "Lime Crazy Lodge, 1906," 7 September 1906, p. 40.

7. Hilger FN, Lucy Rowlodge, 27 May 1941; Rose Arpan, 17 May 1941; Carl Sweezy, 14 May 1941; Helen Spotted Wolf, 26 May 1941; Arnold Woolworth, 18 May 1941; Jess Rowlodge, 18 May, 1941; Eggan FN, Jess Rowlodge, 2:94 and 3:48.

8. Hilger FN, Arnold Woolworth, 18 May, and Jess Rowlodge, 17 May 1941; Eggan FN, Jess Rowlodge, 3:56, 57; Hail to Charles Shell, 20 May 1907, Indian Dances file, CAR; *Cheyenne and Arapaho Sword*, 1 February 1901; *CR*, 18 August 1921; DD, Myrtle Lincoln, T-664:7, 695:15; Annie Pedro, T-242:20; *CP*, 15 September 1910, and 15 February and 1 December 1911; *Geary News*, "Tepee Talk, 35 Years Ago," 28 September 1950. Children received commercial toys on the missionaries' Christmas trees: for example, dolls, jumping jacks, and jack-in-the-boxes (MJ, Diaries, 21 January 1901).

9. Statistics from Monthly School Reports, Cheyenne-Arapaho Agency, 1:12, 2:10, 6; 3:7, 9, RED.

10. DD, William Sutton, T-67:6–7 (interviewer Susan Brandt); *CP*, 1 November 1910, 1 February and 15 April 1911; Semi-Annual School Reports, box 4, Cantonment 1926, RED.

11. *CP*, 15 January, 1 February, 1 April, 1 and 15 May 1911; 15 July 1912; 28 February 1913. See Riney, *The Rapid City Indian School*.

12. *CP*, 1 January and 15 November 1911; Scott, Narrative Report, 1918, SRCA; Bost, Narrative Report, 1922, SRC; R. L. Spalsbury report, 24 October 1921, CFCA 150-88173-1921.

13. Coggeshell, Statistical Report, 1920 and Bost, Statistical Report, 1922, in SRC; Bonnin, Statistical Reports, 1921, 1922, 1923, all in SRCA.

14. Hilger FN, Jess Rowlodge, 18 and 22 May, and Grace Sagebark, 14 May 1941; DD, Jess Rowlodge, T-352:31; Myrtle Lincoln, T-588:6–7, 624:14; Eggan FN, Bird White Bear 2:63.

15. *CR*, "Indian News," 19 June 1924; Hilger FN, Grace Sagebark, 14 May, and Lucy Rowlodge, 27 May 1941; DD, Annie Pedro, T-242:15–16, Myrtle Lincoln, T-452:21, 588:8, and Jess Rowlodge, T-203:16 and 266:13–15.

16. DD, Myrtle Lincoln T-608:2, 4–8, 624:20, 658:14, and Arthur Sutton, T-634:23; Hilger FN, Grace Sagebark, 14 May 1941.

17. *CP*, 1 December 1910 and 1 January 1911; Ralph Stanion to CIA, 26 July 1906, p. 304, *RCIA*, 1906; Cantonment Boarding School, 1926, box 4, Semi-Annual School Report, RED.

18. DD, William Sutton, T-67:5, 9–10; *CP*, 15 July 1912.

19. DD, Jess Rowlodge, T-248:4, 265:24–27, 266:3, 5, 7; CP, 15 April 1912 and 15 August 1910; *CR*, "Indian Items," 8 March 1923. Jess requested books on Arapaho ethnology and Charles Kappler's book on Indian treaties (C. F. Hauke to H. Peairs, 4 May 1909, CFCA 034-33810-1909).

20. Stouch to C. Ruckman, 13 July 1903, MLS-D, 59; W. Leonard to J. Seger, 9 July 1904, MLS-D, 63; Stouch to Farmers, 20 June 1906, MLS-D, 69; Stouch to

CIA, 2 February 1904, LSCIA, Darl, H; G. Myers to CIA, 1 August 1905, p. 295, *RCIA* 1905; Bonnin, Narrative Report, 1924, SRCA.

21. DD, William Sutton, T-67:8, 15–16, Myrtle Lincoln, T-608:8.

22. Scott, Narrative Report, 1917, SRCA; Shell to CIA, 16 October 1906, LR 1906- 92330; *HME* 8 (10) 1905:6.

23. Eggan FN, Bird White Bear, 2:62–63.

24. *Menn*, 1 June 1905; DD, Jess Rowlodge, T-240:2, 248:4, 34.

25. DD, Jess Rowlodge, T-352: preface.

26. Scott, Narrative Report, 1917, SRCA.

27. S. Lincoln report, 21 April and 7 June 1911, and Farmer to Bonnin, 30 September 1930, Farmers File, CAR; W. McConihe to CIA, 7 February 1911, CFC 150-15553-1911 and "Walter Fire," CFC 127-36178-1918; "Charles Tabor," F. E. Brandon to CIA, 4 August 1921; "Lester Meat," Bost to CIA, 4 March 1922, "Roy Youngman," Bost to CIA, 27 September 1922, and "Charles Youngman," W. H. Wisdom to CIA, 6 December 1916, all in IIF; Journal of Cheyenne and Arapaho Competency Board, 1917, 4:495, 502, 5:581, 662, 670, 710; CFC: Industrial Survey, 1922–23, 20, 125, 177, 183, 197, and CFCA, Industrial Survey, "Jesse Rowlodge"; *CR*, 1 February 1934; *Menn*, 20 August 1908.

28. Scott, Narrative Report, 1918 and 1919, both in SRCA; *CVR*, 22 November 1917, 21 and 28 February, 11 April 1918, 29 August, and 26 September 1918, and 26 June and 25 September 1919; *CC*, 14 June 1917 and 8 August, 3 October, 19 December 1918.

29. W-D, Warden FN, "Clubboard Lodge," 1903, 1:1–4.

30. DD, Myrtle Lincoln, T-585:18, 32; *CVR*, 16 January 1919; *CR*, 8 December 1921, 9 November and 9 March 1922, 22 February and 22 November 1923; Logan to Freer, 17 April 1911, Farmers File, CAR.

31. Eggan FN, Jess Rowlodge, 2:114 and Bird White Bear, 1:19; Interview with Jess Rowlodge, July 1929, p. 23, Michelson MS 1791.

32. Agents Reports, 1911, CAR; F. E. Farrell, Narrative Report, 1913, Scott, Narrative Report, 1915, and Bonnin, Narrative Report, 1920, all in SRCA; Walter West, Narrative Report, 1913, and Coggeshell, Narrative Report, 1920, both in SRC; J. McLaughlin to secretary of interior, 17 January 1903, LR 1903-5966; H. Traylor report, 31 October 1917, CFCA 150-1917.

33. North to Shell, 15 January 1907, and J. Logan to Freer, 12 October 1912, both in Farmers Files, CAR.

34. Lincoln report, 10 May 1911, Farmers File, CAR; J. Brown report, 28 April 1914, CFCA 150-48369-1914; Journal of Cheyenne and Arapaho Competency Board, 1917, 5:735.

35. Lincoln report, 5 and 7 June 1911, Farmers File, CAR; Journal of Cheyenne and Arapaho Competency Board, 1917, 5:642, 666, 727; CFC, Industrial Survey, 1922–23, 1:94, 2:190.

36. Lincoln report, 28 April 1911, Farmers File, CAR; Journal of Cheyenne and Arapaho Competency Board, 1917, 5:584, 672; CFC, Industrial Survey, 1922–23, 1:77.

37. Stouch to Logan, 19 July 1905, MLS-D, 65; T. Otterby to Agent, 31 May 1909, Freer to Otterby, 10 March 1910, and Logan to Freer, 17 April 1911, all in Farmers Files, CAR; Council Meeting, 28 June 1910, CFCA 053-23044-1910; Petition from Colony, 13 February 1911, CFCA 056-11558-1911; O. M. McPherson, 18 September 1915, CFCA 150-1915; *CR*, 1 December 1921; Henry Meagher, 18 June 1937, 4652, p. 51, Indian Pioneer Papers; J. Prentiss to M. Jayne, 6 February 1914, MJ, Correspondence.

38. *Menn*, 16 February 1905.

39. *Menn*, 14 May 1908, 4 March 1909, and 10 November 1910; Superintendent to CIA, 15 August 1918, Indian Dances File, CAR; W-D, Warden FN, notebook, "Clubboard Lodge," 1903, 2:174–76, and "Lime Crazy Lodge," 1906.

40. DD, Jess Rowlodge, T-159:23–24, 239:16, 25–26, 240:1, 373:3; Eggan FN, Jess Rowlodge, 2:88–89. In the Industrial Survey of the Cheyenne-Arapaho Agency, 1922, Grant Left Hand is referred to as a chief.

41. On Lime, see Farrell to CIA, 29 April 1913, CFCA 047-54838-1913. On the apology, see DD, Jess Rowlodge, T-144:16; Myrtle Lincoln, T-453:8.

42. Shell to CIA, 18 January 1908, CFCA 056-4520-1908; Proceedings, 28 May 1909, CFC 056-15976-1909; Proceedings, 11 February 1911, CFCA 056-14461-1911 (quote, p. 12); F. Hubbolt to Red Bird et al, 16 February 1911, CFC 154-15327-1-1911; Hearings, 26 October 1915, CFC 056-112404-1915; Hearings, 17 January 1917, CFCA 056-5805-1917 (quotation, p. 6); *CVR*, 1 February 1917; Hearings, 12 February 1920, CFCA 056-14620-1920; Coggeshell to CIA, 7 April 1920, CFC 056-16919-1920; Hearings, 15 February 1926, CFCA 1828-1926 (quotation, p. 2); Charles Burke to A. Woolworth, 17 February 1926, CFCA 056-8405-1926; Hearing, 1 June 1926, CFC 056-29615-1926. On conflicted viewpoints among Americans, see *Menn*, 25 June 1903 and 4 March 1909; MJ, Diaries, 20 March 1902; L. Fowler, *Tribal Sovereignty*, 48–91. On the claims era, see Cobb and Fowler, *Beyond Red Power*, pp. xv, 178–79.

43. DD, Jess Rowlodge, T-240:23, and Myrtle Lincoln, T-615:2; *CR*, 20 July 1922; *CP*, 15 September 1910; Freer to Additional Farmer, 11 July 1910, Farmers File, CAR; Freer, 1 January 1910, Narrative Report, SRCA 1910.

44. *CR*, 1 December 1921; Building Committee to Bost, 4 March 1922, in Indian Councils File, CAR. Another chief selected from Jess Rowlodge's cohort was Tom Levi (Dan Blackhorse to C. Berry, CF 064, 1937).

45. Hilger FN, Arnold Woolworth, 18 May 1941, Rose Arpan, 18 May 1941, Grace and Nelson Sagebark, 14 May 1941, Lucy Medicine Grass, 27 May 1941; DD, Jess Rowlodge, T-163:26–32, 664:13, and Myrtle Lincoln, T-585: 12–14, 695:16.

46. Eggan FN, Jess Rowlodge, 2:53, 91.

47. On the daily events, see W-D, Warden FN, "Clubboard Lodge," Notebook 1:61–64, 77, 90–95, 97–98, 124–38; 2:166–67, 187–94, 202. And for the names of the participants, see the same manuscript, 1:10–13, 20, 55–56. The names of the other dancers are Black Bear, James Monroe, Lester Rising Bear, Jesse Bent, George Black Hat, Clarence Powderface, Lewis Miller, Kiser Youngbear, James Paints Yellow, Short Man, Noble Prentiss, Night, Cleaver Warden, Tom White Shirt, James A. Hutchinson, Man Going Up Hill, Ben Miles, Ohnano, Coyote Robe, Alex Yellowman, Fieldy Sweezy, Jock Bull Bear, and Smith Curley. The grandfathers were Striking Back, Spotted Corn, Black Crow, Washee, Bird Chief, Jr., Black Coyote, Bears Lariat, Pawnee, Young Bear, and Two Lances. The headmen were Blackman, Heap Of Crows, Middle Man, Little Chief, Bird Chief, Sr., Red Wolf, Hail, Big Nose, Lizard, Black Horse, Sitting Bull, Cut Nose, Tony Pedro, Deaf, Rabbit Run, Thunder, Broken Rib, Sage, and Bald Head.

48. Ibid., 1:9, 18, 20, 57, 59, 60, 89, 95, 98, 122, 126–27; 2:188, 198, 200–203. There is a literature on clowning, too extensive to mention here. Often, clowns call attention to values expressed in ritual.

49. W-D, Warden FN, "Lime Crazy Lodge, 1906," 66–101, 110; Hilger FN, Jess Rowlodge, 22 May 1941. The other Lime Crazy dancers were Fire, John Washee, Long Hair, Lone Lodge, Two Lances, Curley, Little Bird, Bird Chief, Jr., Ute, Big Nose, Sagebark, and Big Belly. The grandfathers in the Lime Crazy Lodge were Rabbit Run, Hail, Tall, Black Bear, Sage, Cut Nose, Gun, and White Owl.

50. Hilger FN, Arnold Woolworth, 27 May 1941, and Jess Rowlodge, 22 May 1941; DD, Jess Rowlodge, T-205:17, 240:4, Arthur Sutton, T-634:3, 6, Jim Warden, T-679:8, Myrtle Lincoln, T-588:4–5, 607:14 (quoted); *CP*, 1 September 1911; *CVR*, 7 August 1919; J. Goss to Ruckman, 13 August 1919, Indian Dances File, CAR. White Shirt sponsored a Clubboard Dance in 1931. This may have been the one Blackhorse and Bates joined (Bonnin to White Shirt, 26 June 1931, Indian Dances File, CAR). Lowie, *Plains Indian Age Societies*, 933.

51. DD, Myrtle Lincoln, T-607:7, 12, 19–20, 452:25, Jess Rowlodge, T-458:8, and Jim Warden, T-679:4–7; Kish Hawkins to Bonnin, 11 October 1923, CFCA 062-64212-1921; *CC*, 20 August 1925.

52. Eggan FN, Bird White Bear, 2:66; Hilger FN, Jess Rowlodge, 22 May 1941; Bonnin to C. Warden, 21 September 1928, Indian Dances File, CAR.

53. DD, Jess Rowlodge, T-159:12, 15–16, and Myrtle Lincoln, T-586:1–2, 13–14.

54. *Menn*, 6 November 1902, 12 February 1903, 22 September 1904, 13 September 1906, 21 February and 30 May 1907, 13 February 1908, 15 April and 5 August 1909, 11 August 1910, and 3 December 1914; DD, Jess Rowlodge, T-159: 12–13, and Myrtle Lincoln, T-607:3.

55. Frank Harrington to Mennonite Mission Board, 15 April 1909, Board of Mission Correspondence; MJ, Diaries, 28 March 1902 and 5 July 1905; *HME* 7, 12 (1903): 6; 10, 3 (1907): 4; 10, 10 (1907): 11, 8 (1908): 8; *CC*, 22 January 1915; Hamilton, *Gospel*, 194. A Baptist missionary also worked briefly among the

Powderface band on the South Canadian (see Phelps, *Tepee Trails*). On the Baptist missionaries, see also Wasson, *One Who Was Strong*, and Women's American Baptist Home Mission Society, *Thirty-Six Years Among Indians*.

56. *HME* 10, 1 (1907): 6–7; *Menn*, 20 November 1902; Hilger FN, Jess Rowlodge, 17 May 1941; DD, Jess Rowlodge, T-164:8–9, 373:13–14.

57. "Peyote," in United States, House of Representatives, Hearings on HR 2614, 67th Cong., 2d sess. (1918), p. 191; West to CIA, 10 December 1912 and 4 September 1913, "Sitting Bull," IIF; DD, Jess Rowlodge, T-159:8–10, 247:17, John Sleeper, T-681:11–12, 19–20, 22, and Myrtle Lincoln, T-695:7. Cheyenne conflict over peyotism is mentioned in L. Fowler, *Tribal Sovereignty*, 64, 108. On the indigenization of peyote, see Lassiter, Ellis, and Kotay, *Jesus Road*.

58. DD, Jess Rowlodge, T-172:37; White, Narrative Report, 1912, and R. Daniel, Narrative Report, 1917, SRC; Scott, Narrative Report, 1919, and Bonnin, Narrative Report, 1924, SRCA; Scott to CIA, 23 December 1914, CFCA 126-137105-1914; Freer to CIA, 19 February 1912, Liquor Traffic and Peyote File, CAR.

59. On farm district councils, see CFCA 100-6949-1923, passim, and Bonnin, Narrative Reports, 1926 and 1929, SRCA, and Bost, Narrative Report, 1926, SRC; Bonnin to CIA, 10 May 1928, and tribal council minutes, 29 January 1932, in CF 064, 1928 and 1932.

60. R. Hamilton to H. Morehouse, in MJ, Diaries, 1903:79–80.

61. DD, Myrtle Lincoln, T-658; Hilger FN, Grace Sagebark, 14 May 1941; Phelps, *Tepee Trails*, 60; William Mitchell report, 22 July 1922, Farmers File, CAR; MJ, Diaries, 18 January and 30 April 1902; *HME* 10, 1:6–7, January 1907.

62. Phelps, *Tepee Trails*, 30; MJ, Diaries, 22 March and 28 March 1902; Indian Fair Program, 1912, in CFCA 047-83974-1912; Stouch to T. Ferguson, 24 July 1905, MLS-D, 66; *CC*, 6 and 20 September 1912; W. N. Sickels to CIA, 20 January 1934, CFCA 150-7293-1934.

63. Frank Sweezy to Shell, 1 April 1907, and Mitchell report, 28 October 1922, both in Farmers Files, CAR; MJ, Diaries, 5 and 7 1903; *GB*, 7 May 1903; F. Staley to CIA, 6 May 1905, LSBIA, Canton, 2; Freer, Narrative Report, 1913, and Bonnin, Narrative Report, 1925, SRCA; D. Young Bull to Bonnin, 29 September 1922, Family Relations file, CAR; *CP*, 15 May 1911, 1 May 1912, 31 March and 2 June 1913; Page, *In Camp and Tepee*, 76.

64. DD, Myrtle Lincoln, T-452:2–3, 7–9, 691:12; *CP*, 15 November 1910; Stouch to Logan, 4 April 1905, MLS-D, 65; Stouch to F. Sweezy and Stouch to H. North, 27 July 1905, both in MLS-D, 66.

65. *CP*, 2 June 1913; North to Freer, 20 April 1911 and Freer to CIA, 16 October 1912, and Logan to Freer, 17 October 1912, all in Farmers File, CAR; DD, Jim Warden, T-677:6, and Myrtle Lincoln, T-588:7.

66. Stouch to H. Todd, 2 June 1905, MLS-D, 66; *CP*, 2 June 1913.

67. White to H. Schiffner, 11 November 1908, LB, Canton, 19; *CC*, 21 July 1916; White to G. Hoyo, 6 August 1910, MLS-C, 22; White to Ruckman, 29 January

1907, MLS-C, 15; 25 March 1907, MLS-C, 16; DD, Myrtle Lincoln, T-624:4–7; Bonnin, Narrative Report, 1924, SRCA.

68. Shell to Logan, 30 January 1907, MLS-D, 3; Shell to North, 19 July 1907, MLS-D, 8; White to Shell, 11 November 1908, MLS-C, 9; White to Stouch, 3 March 1906, MLS-C, 5; Stouch to White, 7 June 1905, MLS-D, 66. On women and land-ownership, see Journal of Cheyenne and Arapaho Competency Board, 1917.

69. Stouch to W. Lindsey, 29 May 1905, MLS-D, 66; W. Randolph to W. Kelley, 15 August 1905, MLS-C, 4; White to B. Groves, 6 April 1908, MLS-C, 9.

70. West to CIA, 7 February 1913 and 4 October 1912, IIF.

71. Stouch to CIA, 2 May 1905, LR 34658-1905; CC, 20 September 1912, 13 September 1917, 19 December 1918; LT files, passim.

72. Hilger FN, Long Hair, 20 May 1941, and Helen Spotted Wolf, 26 May 1941, Grace Sagebark, 14 May 1941, Lucy Medicine Grass, 27 May 1941, Jess Rowlodge, 17 and 22 May 1941, and Anna Mixed Hair, 15 May 1941; DD, Myrtle Lincoln, T-453:9 and 608:10, 14–15, and Annie Pedro, T-242:20.

73. Hilger FN, Long Hair, 16 May 1941; CR, 18 August 1921.

74. Menn, 11 February 1904; Eggan FN, Bird White Bear, 1:19–22; DD, Myrtle Lincoln, T-624:9, 14–17; Hilger FN, 18 May 1941, and Long Hair, 16 May 1941; Dorsey, Sun Dance, 142; Bonnin and Coggeshell, Statistical Reports, 1920, SRCA and SRC; White to Shell, 21 April 1908, LB, Canton, 17. It is difficult to state conclusively why the ratio of men to women changed so much in this century. The death rate for men went down after the end of warfare, and apparently the death rate for girls in the schools was higher than that of boys (probably because girls worked indoors in unsanitary conditions).

75. Densmore, Cheyenne and Arapaho Music, 22, 49–50, 64, 71, 74; CVR, 26 June and 25 September 1919. The Arapaho who was killed in France was Straight Crazy's son Henry Shawnee.

76. Eggan FN, Bird White Bear, 1:63; W-D, Warden FN, notebook, "Clubboard Lodge, 1903," 1:18–19, 62, 68, 72–73, 89, 97–100, 106, 2:166–74, 191, 195, 200–201, 204, 207–208. Aside from respect relationships, Arapahos practiced "joking" behavior between brothers-in-law and between brothers-in-law and sisters-in-law.

77. W-D, Warden FN, "Lime Crazy Lodge," 2–4, 41–43, 54–56, 58–59, 65, 82–83, 86.

78. Eggan FN, Bird White Bear, 2:67; DD, John Sleeper, T-681:15; W-D, Warden FN, notebook, "Clubboard Lodge, 1903," 1:28–30, 80–81; Bonnin to CIA, 8 October 1923 and K. Hawkins to Bonnin, 11 October 1923, in CFCA 062-64212-1921.

79. DD, Myrtle Lincoln, T-607:2–3, 608:10, 14, and Jess Rowlodge, T-164:12, 14–15, 17–19; Hilger FN, Long Hair, 20 May 1941, Helen Spotted Wolf, 26 May 1941, Grace Sagebark, 14 May 1941, Jess Rowlodge, 28 May 1941, Arnold Woolworth, 27 May 1941, and Lucy Medicine Grass, 14 and 27 May 1941.

80. Densmore, Cheyenne and Arapaho Music, 50, 51, 64, 71, 74; DD, Jess Rowlodge, T-159:12, 15–17, and Myrtle Lincoln, T-586:1–2, 13–14, 668:2–3.

81. DD, Myrtle Lincoln, T-613:3–15, 664:5–10, 12–14, 668:4–5, 10–12.

82. Ibid., T-613:3–15, 664:4–5, 10–12. See Flannery, "Changing Form and Functions," on the Gros Ventre Grass Dance.

83. DD, Myrtle Lincoln, T-626:2; Hamilton, *Gospel*, 190–91; *HME* 8, 10 (1905): 6 and 11, 8 (1908): 8; *CP*, 15 February and 1 November 1911.

84. Phelps, *Tepee Trails*, 51, 52, 54; DD, Jess Rowlodge, T-159:6–8, 170:5–7, 9, 13, 15, 18–19, 172:7–9, 19, and Annie Pedro, T-242:18–19. On the Peyote religion in the twentieth century, see Swan, *Peyote Religious Art*. Jess Rowlodge recalled that Apache women had their own peyote meetings in the early days (DD, T-170:7, 16).

85. Eggan FN, Bird White Bear 2:67; J. Witcher to Indian Agent, 31 July 1902, Indian Dances File, CAR; Minutes of Geary District Meeting, 8 February 1934, CF 20; DD, Jess Rowlodge, T-203:15.

86. Proceedings, 17 January 1917, p. 6, in CFCA-056-5805-1917; E. Bates to Bost, 28 September 1925, in LT files, 2306.

87. DD, Jess Rowlodge, T-240:23; Building Committee to Bost, 4 March 1922, Petition from Dance Hall Committee, Cantonment to CIA, 5 July 1922, and Petition from Seger District to CIA, 29 January 1923, all in Indian Councils File, CAR; Petition from Cantonment to CIA, 22 December 1933, CFCA 059-1934.

88. Superintendent to John Collier, Questionnaire, July 1934, CF 064.

89. *Menn*, 16 November 1911; Hilger FN, Arnold Woolworth, 14 May 1941, and Jess Rowlodge, 17 May 1941; *CR*, 29 September, 20 October, 8 and 29 December 1921, and 5 January, 11 and 18 May, 22 June, 17 August, and 12 November 1922, and 18 January, 22 February, 5 April, and 10 and 24 May 1923.

90. *CR*, 26 April 1923 and 25 June 1925; Hilger FN, Arnold Woolworth, 27 May 1941; DD, Myrtle Lincoln, T-664:8.

91. Stouch to CIA, 25 August 1903, LSCIA, Darl, H; White to CIA, 15 June 1911 and 15 August 1912, both in IIF; minutes of Geary district council meeting, 8 February 1934, CF 020; *Menn*, 9 May 1912.

92. Proceedings, 28 May 1909, CFC 056-15976-1909; Proceedings, 17 January 1917, CFCA 056-5805-1917; Bonnin, Narrative reports, 1921 and 1927, SRCA; Bost, Narrative Report, 1927, SRC; IIM, passim.

93. Report of R. L. Spalsbury, 14 November 1930, Educational Survey Forms, RED; IIM, passim; LT files, passim; on Bucket, see *CR*, 27 March 1924. The description of Rabbit Run's household is from the Industrial Survey, Central Files, Cantonment, p. 149.

94. Michelson, "Narrative," 610; LT files, 1357. Red Woman lived with her son Bird when she was very old.

95. Hilger FN, Jess Rowlodge, 17 May 1941, Henry and Lucy Rowlodge, 27 May 1941, Grace Sagebark, 14 May 1941, and Rose Arpan, 18 May 1941; Eggan FN, Bird White Bear, 2:65, 71; Goss report, 18 November 1922, Farmers File, CAR; DD, Jim Warden, T-679:4–7. Arapahos avoided the agency hospital, which opened in 1916. It came to be used as a place to confine tuberculosis patients (Scott, Narrative Report, 1917, and Bonnin, Narrative Report, 1922, SRCA,

and Daniel, Narrative Report, 1917, and Bost, Narrative Report, 1927, SRC). In 1906, the Southern Arapaho priests Bull Thunder and Mrs. Bull Thunder, White Eyed Antelope and Mrs. White Eyed Antelope, and Crippled sent for Northern Arapaho priests Buffalo Fat and wife and Big Bellied Bear to help direct the ceremony. Southern Arapaho priests directed the 1903 Clubboard Lodge (Old Crow, White Eyed Antelope and wife, Mountain, and Crippled).

96. *CC*, 20 August 1925; *CR*, 21 September and 23 November 1922.

97. Eggan FN, Bird White Bear, 1:81; DD, Jess Rowlodge, T-163:7, 164:2–3, 7–9, 13–14, 203:7; Left Hand, "Chief Left Hand."

98. Conference with Superintendent, 14 March 1933, p. 6, CF 064.

99. Petition to CIA, 22 December 1933, CFCA 059-1934. For the history of the general council and its members, see the council minutes, 1928–36, CF 064. (See also L. Fowler, *Tribal Sovereignty*, 99–111.)

100. Little Raven to C. Berry, 4 December 1934, CF 064. For the politics surrounding the introduction of the Oklahoma Indian Welfare Act, see CF 020, especially for 1934. For background on the New Deal era, see L. Fowler, *Columbia Guide*, and Cobb and Fowler, *Beyond Red Power*.

101. For the problems in Arapaho tribal government after the Oklahoma Indian Welfare Act, see L. Fowler, *Tribal Sovereignty*.

CONCLUSION

1. Jess Rowlodge worked on the claim as a member of the Cheyenne and Arapaho business committee for many years and eventually saw the tribes win their claim against the United States. In his later years, though, he told Hilger that he did not think Arapahos gave him proper recognition for his contribution on the claim work. His wife, Carrie Lumpmouth, died in 1940. They had two daughters. He married a Northern Arapaho, Sarah Coolidge (the daughter of Sherman Coolidge, a Northern Arapaho who worked as an Episcopal missionary among the Northern and Southern Arapahos), in 1953. In his old age, he was poor like most elderly Arapahos. Rowlodge died in 1974. Myrtle Lincoln died that same year. Her husband, Howard, had died in 1947, and she survived all but two of her seven children. One son was killed in World War II. Myrtle was respected for her abilities as a singer and because she was a Gold Star Mother. She worked for several years cleaning houses in Canton. Both she and Rowlodge were respected for their fluency in Arapaho.

2. Klein, "Political-Economy of Gender"; Weist, "Plains Indian Women," 257–59, 264; Liberty, "Plains Indian Women Through Time," 141–44. Also see Albers, "From Illusion to Illumination," 142–43; Knack, "Women and Men," 60.

3. Klein (1983) cites Flannery, *Gros Ventres*, 66, and Ewers, *Horse in Blackfoot Indian Culture*, 28–29, to support his assertion that women owned horses of less value than men. Flannery noted only that Gros Ventre men did not own

horses trained to pull a travois. Ewers wrote that Blackfoot men owned herds of unbroken horses and horses trained for war, hunting, and racing; women owned horses trained for riding and transport, but they could inherit other horses or trade for them or receive them as gifts. Ewers also reported that wives who were childless not uncommonly went to war or on horse raids as participants with their husbands (190). Kurz, *Journal*, 146.

4. Flannery, *Gros Ventres*, 81–82; Denig, *Five Indian Tribes*, 156–57; Kurz, *Journal*, 176; Boller, *Among the Indians*, 301.

5. Wied, *People of the First Man*, 107.

6. Kurz, *Journal*, 155, 176; Wied, *People of the First Man*, 242; Flannery, *Gros Ventres*, 112.

7. Klein relies on Lewis's work, in which Lewis concludes that polygyny increased with Blackfoot involvement in the hide trade (*Effects of White Contact*, 45).

8. Kroeber, *Arapaho*, 151, 160–61, 165, 190, 193, 198–200.

9. Powers is often cited as support for the idea that men but not women lost meaningful roles after settling on reservations. In *Oglala Women*, 3, 128, she cites Clark Wissler as her source. Neither Wissler's nor Powers's work was based on historical documents. Recent histories document, as I have for the Southern Arapahos, that in the early reservation years, men continued to have important political duties and accomplished many of their goals. Men commonly made a transition from hunting to ranching and freighting or other occupations. See L. Fowler, *Columbia Guide*, 91–95. See also Poole, "Reservation Policy"; Albers, "Sioux Women"; Mellis, *Riding Buffaloes*; Osburn, *Southern Ute Women*.

10. Several excellent studies explore student life in off-reservation boarding schools—including curriculum, discipline, health, and resistance. On resistance, see McBeth, *Ethnic Identity*; Lomawaima, *They Called It Prairie Light*; Ellis, *To Change Them Forever*; Child, *Boarding School Seasons*. Riney examined the ways in which parents influenced school policy and the treatment of students in *Rapid City Indian School*. See also the following studies, which focus more on the assimilative process: Trennert, *Phoenix Indian School*; Adams, *Education for Extinction*; Lindsey, *Indians at Hampton Institute*. On the problems boarding school alumni had obtaining employment in government positions, see Emmerich, "'Right in the Midst'"; Ahern, "Experiment Aborted."

11. Osburn, *Southern Ute Women*. The wage work of men and women is documented in Ackerman, *A Necessary Balance*. Osburn and Albers, "Sioux Women," 195, note that money from leasing and selling allotments was important to household economy. See also Knack and Littlefield, *Native Americans and Wage Labor*, and the essays by M'Closkey on Navajo, Shepherd on Hualapai, and Cattelino on Seminole in Hosmer and O'Neill, *Native Pathways*, 73–74, 115–16, 216.

12. Stewart, *Peyote Religion*. See Albers, "From Illusion to Illumination," 146.

Bibliography

Archival Sources

Abstracts of Individual Indian Bank Accounts. Cantonment, 1918–1927. Concho Agency. Records of the Bureau of Indian Affairs, Record Group 75. National Archives, Southwest Region, Fort Worth, Texas.

Ames, William P. "Highlights of Haskell Institute," 1936. Haskell Cultural Center and Museum, Haskell Indian Nation University, Lawrence, Kansas.

Board of Missions. General Correspondence. Mennonite Library and Archives, Bethel College, North Newton, Kansas.

Cantonment Agency. Central Files, 1907–39. Records of the Bureau of Indian Affairs, Record Group 75. National Archives, Washington, D.C.

Census Records. Archives and Manuscript Division. Oklahoma Historical Society, Oklahoma City.

The Cheyenne and Arapaho Sword. Mennonite Library and Archives, Bethel College, North Newton, Kansas.

Cheyenne-Arapaho Records. Archives and Manuscript Division. Oklahoma Historical Society, Oklahoma City.

Cheyenne-Arapaho Agency. Central Files, 1907–39. Records of the Bureau of Indian Affairs, Record Group 75. National Archives, Washington, D.C.

Cheyenne-Arapaho Letterpress Books, 1878–81. Carnegie Library, El Reno, Oklahoma.

Clark, Ben. Collection. Western History Collections. University of Oklahoma, Norman.

Concho Agency. Central Files. Records of the Bureau of Indian Affairs, Record Group 75. National Archives, Southwest Region, Fort Worth, Texas.

Documents Relating to the Negotiations of Ratified and Unratified Treaties with Various Indian Tribes, 1801–69 (T494). Records of the Bureau of Indian Affairs, Record Group 75. National Archives, Washington, D.C.

Duke, Doris. Collection, American Indian Oral History, 1972. Western History Collections. University of Oklahoma, Norman.

Eggan, Fred. Field Notes. Personal possession.

Hilger, M. Inez. Field Notes. Hilger Papers. National Anthropological Archives, Smithsonian Institution, Washington, D.C.

Indian Census Rolls, 1888–1940 (M595). Records of the Bureau of Indian Affairs, Record Group 75. National Archives, Washington, D.C.

Indian Pioneer Papers. Western History Collections. University of Oklahoma, Norman.

Industrial Survey, 1922–23. Central Files—Cantonment Agency and Cheyenne-Arapaho Agency. Records of the Bureau of Indian Affairs, Record Group 75. National Archives, Washington, D.C.

Irregularly Shaped Papers. Report of the Jerome Commission, 1891–93. Records of the Bureau of Indian Affairs, Record Group 75. National Archives, Washington, D.C.

Jayne, Mary. Diaries, Correspondence. Mary Jayne Collection. Western History Collections. University of Oklahoma, Norman.

Jesuit Mission and College Records, 1832–1967. Kansas State Historical Society, Topeka.

Journal of Cheyenne and Arapaho Competency Board, 1917. Records of the Bureau of Indian Affairs, Record Group 75. National Archives, Washington, D.C.

Kroeber, Alfred. Field Notes, 1900 (MS 2560a). National Anthropological Archives. Smithsonian Institution, Washington, D.C.

Land Transaction Case Files, 1904–87, Entry 12. Concho Agency. Records of the Bureau of Indian Affairs, Record Group 75. National Archives, Southwest Region, Fort Worth, Texas.

Left Hand. "Chief Left Hand: His Life Story" (as told to F. L. King), 1907. Archives and Manuscript Division. Oklahoma Historical Society.

Letters Received by the Office of Indian Affairs, 1881–1907. Records of the Bureau of Indian Affairs, Record Group 75. National Archives, Washington, D.C.

Letters Received by the Office of Indian Affairs, 1824–1881. Central Superintendency, 1851–80 (M234). Records of the Bureau of Indian Affairs, Record Group 75. National Archives, Washington, D.C.

Letters Received by the Office of Indian Affairs, 1824–1881. Cheyenne and Arapaho Agency, 1875–80 (M234). Records of the Bureau of Indian Affairs, Record Group 75. National Archives, Washington, D.C.

Letters Received by the Office of Indian Affairs, 1824–1881. Upper Arkansas Agency, 1855–74 (M234). Records of the Bureau of Indian Affairs, Record Group 75. National Archives, Washington, D.C.

Letters Sent, 1849–1903. Indian Division. Records of the Office of the Secretary of the Interior, Record Group 48 (Entry A1-656). National Archives, Washington, D.C.

The Mennonite. Mennonite Library and Archives, Bethel College, North Newton, Kansas.

Michelson, Truman. Manuscripts. National Anthropological Archives. Smithsonian Institution, Washington, D.C.

Mooney, James. Manuscript 1910a. James Mooney Collection. National Anthropological Archives, Smithsonian Institution, Washington, D.C.

Post Records. Records of U.S. Army Continental Commands, 1821–1920, Record Group 393. National Archives, Washington, D.C.

Record of Indian Children Attending Off-Reservation Schools, 1882–1896. Concho Agency. Records of the Bureau of Indian Affairs, Record Group 75. National Archives, Southwest Region, Fort Worth, Texas.

Records of the Education Division. Records of the Bureau of Indian Affairs, Record Group 75. National Archives, Washington, D.C.

Records of the Indian Division. Records of the Secretary of the Interior, Record Group 48 (Entry 665). National Archives, Washington, D.C.

Reports of Inspection, 1873–1900. Records of the Field Jurisdiction of the Office of Indian Affairs, 1873–1900. Record Groups 48 and 75 (M1070). National Archives, Washington, D.C.

Special Cases, 1821–1907. Records of the Bureau of Indian Affairs, Record Group 75. National Archives, Washington, D.C.

Superintendents Annual Narrative and Statistical Reports, 1907–38. Cantonment Agency. Records of the Bureau of Indian Affairs, Record Group 75 (M1011). National Archives, Washington, D.C.

Superintendents Annual Narrative and Statistical Reports, 1907–38. Cheyenne-Arapaho Agency. Records of the Bureau of Indian Affairs, Record Group 75 (M1011). National Archives, Washington, D.C.

Voth, Henry R. Collection. Mennonite Library and Archives, Bethel College, North Newton, Kansas.

Warden, Cleaver, and George A. Dorsey Collection, 1901–06. The Field Museum, Chicago.

Williams, Sallie J. Manuscript. Kenneth Spencer Research Library, University of Kansas, Lawrence.

NEWSPAPERS

Calumet Chieftain
Canadian Valley Record
Canton Record
Cheyenne Transformer
Chicago Tribune
Cincinnati Commercial
Geary Bulletin

Geary News
Home Mission Echoes
Indian Helper, Carlisle Indian School
Morning Star (Eadle Keatah Toh), Carlisle Indian School
Red Man, Carlisle Indian School
Rocky Mountain News
School News, Carlisle Indian School

BOOKS, ARTICLES, AND REPORTS

Abert, J. W. *Report of Lieut. J. W. Abert of his Examination of New Mexico In the Years 1846–47*. 30th Cong., 1st sess., 1848. S. Doc. 23.

Ackerman, Lillian A. *A Necessary Balance: Gender and Power among Indians of the Columbia Plateau*. Norman: University of Oklahoma Press, 2003.

Adams, David Wallace. *Education for Extinction: American Indians and the Boarding School Experience, 1875–1928*. Lawrence: University Press of Kansas, 1995.

Ahern, Wilbert H. "An Experiment Aborted: Returned Indian Students in the Indian School Service, 1881–1908." *Ethnohistory* 44, no. 2 (1997): 263–304.

Albers, Patricia C. "From Illusion to Illumination: Anthropological Studies of American Indian Women." In *Gender and Anthropology: Critical Reviews for Research and Teaching*, ed. Sandra Morgen, 132–70. Washington, D.C.: American Anthropological Association, 1989.

———. "Sioux Women in Transition: A Study of Their Changing Status in Domestic and Capitalist Sectors of Production." In *The Hidden Half: Studies of Plains Indian Women*, ed. Patricia Albers and Beatrice Medicine, 175–234. Lanham, Mass.: University Press of America, 1983.

Anderson, Jeffrey D. *The Four Hills of Life: Northern Arapaho Knowledge and Life Movement*. Lincoln: University of Nebraska Press, 2001.

Barr, Juliana. *Peace Came in the Form of a Woman: Indians and Spaniards in the Texas Borderlands*. Chapel Hill: University of North Carolina Press, 2007.

Bass, Althea. *The Arapaho Way: A Memoir of an Indian Boyhood*. New York: Clarkson N. Potter, 1966.

Bell, Genevieve. "Telling Stories Out of School: Remembering the Carlisle Indian Industrial School, 1879–1918." Ph. D. dissertation, Stanford University, 1998.

Bell, John R. *The Journal of Captain John R. Bell*. Volume 6 in The Far West and the Rockies Historical Series, 1820–1875, ed. Harlin M. Fuller and LeRoy R. Hafen. Glendale, Calif.: Arthur H. Clark, 1957.

Bent, Charles. "The Charles Bent Papers." *New Mexico Historical Review* 30 (1955): 154–67, 252–54, 340–52.

Bent, George. *Life of George Bent*. Written from his letters, by George E. Hyde. Ed. Savoie Lottinville. Norman: University of Oklahoma Press, 1968.

Berthrong, Donald J. *The Cheyenne and Arapaho Ordeal: Reservation and Agency Life in the Indian Territory, 1875–1907*. Norman: University of Oklahoma, 1976.

————. *The Southern Cheyennes*. Norman: University of Oklahoma Press, 1963.

Boller, Henry A. *Among the Indians: Eight Years in the Far West, 1858–1866*. Ed. Milo Milton Quaife. Chicago: Lakeside Press, 1959.

Bowers, Alfred W. *Hidatsa Social and Ceremonial Organization*. Lincoln: University of Nebraska Press, 1992.

Brown, Jennifer S. H. *Strangers in Blood: Fur Trade Company Families in Indian Country*. Vancouver: University of British Columbia Press, 1980.

Child, Brenda J. *Boarding School Seasons: American Indian Families, 1900–1940*. Lincoln: University of Nebraska Press, 2000.

Chittenden, Hiram Martin, and Alfred Talbot Richardson, eds. *Life, Letters and Travels of Father Pierre-Jean de Smet*. 4 vols. New York: Francis P. Harper, 1905.

Clark, William Philo. *The Indian Sign Language*. Philadelphia: L. R. Hammersly, 1885.

Cobb, Daniel M., and Loretta Fowler, eds. *Beyond Red Power: American Indian Politics and Activism since 1900*. Santa Fe, N.Mex.: School for Advanced Research Press, 2007.

Cooke, Philip St. G. *Scenes and Adventures in the Army*. Philadelphia: Lindsay and Blakiston, 1859.

Cooper, John M. *The Gros Ventres of Montana: Part II, Religion and Ritual*. Ed. Regina Flannery. Washington, D.C.: Catholic University of America Press, 1957.

Dale, Harrison Clifford. *The Ashley-Smith Explorations and the Discovery of a Central Route to the Pacific, 1822–1829*. Glendale, Calif.: Arthur H. Clark, 1941.

Daughters of the American Revolution. *Vital Historical Records of Jackson County, Missouri, 1826–1876*. Kansas City: Kansas City Chapter of the Daughters of the Revolution, 1933–34.

Denig, Edwin Thompson. *Five Indian Tribes of the Upper Missouri*. Ed. John C. Ewers. Norman: University of Oklahoma Press, 1961.

Densmore, Frances. *Cheyenne and Arapaho Music*. Southwest Museum Papers 10. Los Angeles, 1936.

Dodge, Henry. *Report of the Expedition of the Dragoons, Under the Command of Col. Henry Dodge, to the Rocky Mountains, during the Summer of 1835*. 24th Cong., 1st sess., 1835, H. Doc. 181.

Dorsey, George A. *The Arapaho Sun Dance: The Ceremony of the Offerings Lodge*. Field Columbian Museum Publications 75. Anthropological Series 4. Chicago, 1903.

Dorsey, George A., and Alfred L. Kroeber. *Traditions of the Arapaho*. Field Columbian Museum Publications 75. Anthropological Series 5. Chicago, 1903.

Eggan, Fred. "The Cheyenne and Arapaho Kinship System." In *Social Anthropology of North American Tribes*, 2nd ed., ed. Fred Eggan, 35–95. Chicago: University of Chicago Press, 1955.

Elder, Glen H., Jr., *Children of the Great Depression: Social Change in Life Experience*. Chicago: University of Chicago Press, 1974.

——. "Perspectives on the Life Course." In *Life Course Dynamics: Trajectories and Transitions, 1968–1980*, ed. Glen H. Elder, Jr., 23–49. Ithaca: Cornell University Press, 1985.

Elder, Glen H., Jr., and Rand D. Conger. *Children of the Land: Adversity and Success in Rural America*. Chicago: University of Chicago Press, 2000.

Ellis, Clyde. *To Change Them Forever: Indian Education at the Rainy Mountain Boarding School, 1893–1920*. Norman: University of Oklahoma Press, 1996.

Emmerich, Lisa E. "'Right in the Midst of My Own People': Native American Women and the Field Matron Program." *American Indian Quarterly* 15 (1991): 201–16.

Etienne, Mona, and Eleanor Leacock, eds. *Women and Colonization: Anthropological Perspectives*. New York: Praeger, 1980.

Ewers, John C. *The Horse in Blackfoot Indian Culture*. Bureau of American Ethnology Bulletin 159. Washington, D.C.: Smithsonian Institution, 1955.

——. "The Influence of Epidemics on the Indian Populations and Cultures of Texas." *Plains Anthropologist* 18, no. 60 (1973): 104–15.

——. *Plains Indian Sculpture: A Traditional Art from America's Heartland*. Washington, D.C.: Smithsonian Institution Press, 1986.

Flannery, Regina. "The Changing Form and Functions of the Gros Ventre Grass Dance." *Primitive Man* 20 (1947): 39–70.

——. *The Gros Ventres of Montana: Part I, Social Life*. Washington, D.C.: Catholic University of America Press, 1953.

Foner, Nancy. *Ages in Conflict: A Cross-Cultural Perspective on Inequality Between Old and Young*. New York: Columbia University Press, 1984.

Ford, Lemuel. *March of the First Dragoons to the Rocky Mountains in 1835:The Diaries and Maps of Lemuel Ford*. Ed. Nolie Mumey. Denver: Eames Brothers Press, 1957.

Fowler, Jacob. *The Journal of Jacob Fowler*. Ed. Elliott Coues. Lincoln: University of Nebraska Press, 1970.

Fowler, Loretta. "Arapaho." In *Handbook of North American Indians: Plains*, vol. 13, pt. 2, ed. Raymond J. DeMallie, 840–62. Washington, D.C.: Smithsonian Institution Press, 2001.

——. *Arapahoe Politics, 1851–1978: Symbols in Crises of Authority*. Lincoln: University of Nebraska Press, 1982.

——. *The Columbia Guide to American Indians of the Great Plains*. New York: Columbia University Press, 2003.

——. "'Look at My Hair, It is Gray': Age Grading, Ritual Authority, and Political Change among the Northern Arapahos and Gros Ventres." In *Plains Indian Studies: A Collection of Essays in Honor of John C. Ewers and Waldo R. Wedel*, ed. Douglas H. Ubelaker and Herman J. Viola, 73–93. Washington, D.C.: Smithsonian Institution Press, 1982.

——. *Shared Symbols, Contested Meanings: Gros Ventre Culture and History, 1778–1984*. Ithaca, N.Y.: Cornell University Press, 1987.

————. *Tribal Sovereignty and the Historical Imagination: Cheyenne-Arapaho Politics.* Lincoln: University of Nebraska Press, 2002.

Frémont, John Charles. *The Expeditions of John Charles Frémont.* 3 vols. Ed. Donald Jackson and Mary Lee Spence. Urbana: University of Illinois Press, 1970–84.

Garrard, Lewis H. *Wah-to-yah and the Taos Trail.* Ed. Ralph P. Bieber. Glendale, Calif.: Arthur H. Clark, 1938.

Greene, Jerome A., and Douglas D. Scott. *Finding Sand Creek: History, Archeology, and the 1864 Massacre Site.* Norman: University of Oklahoma Press, 2004.

Grinnell, George. *The Cheyenne Indians: Their History and Ways of Life.* 2 vols. New Haven, Conn.: Yale University Press, 1923.

Hafen, LeRoy R., and W. J. Ghent. *Broken Hand: The Life Story of Thomas Fitzpatrick, Chief of the Mountain Men.* Denver: Old West, 1931.

Hagan, William T. *Taking Indian Lands: The Cherokee (Jerome) Commission, 1889–1893.* Norman: University of Oklahoma Press, 2003.

Hamilton, Robert. *The Gospel among the Red Men: The History of Southern Baptist Indian Missions.* Nashville, Tenn.: Sunday School Board of the Southern Baptist Convention, 1930.

Harkin, Michael, and Sergei Kan, eds. "Native American Women's Responses to Christianity." Special issue, *Ethnohistory* 43, no. 4 (1996).

Henderson, Frank, and Karen Daniels Petersen. *American Pictographic Images: Historical Works on Paper by the Plains Indians.* New York: n.p., 1988.

Heslep, Augustus M. "The Santa Fé Trail." In *Southern Trails to California in 1849,* Southwest Historical Series, vol. 5, ed. Ralph P. Bieber, 351–860. Glendale, Calif.: Arthur H. Clark, 1937.

Hilger, M. Inez. *Arapaho Child Life and Its Cultural Background.* Bureau of American Ethnology Bulletin 148. Washington, D.C.: Smithsonian Institution, 1952.

Hosmer, Brian, and Colleen O'Neill. *Native Pathways: American Indian Culture and Economic Development in the Twentieth Century.* Boulder: University Press of Colorado, 2004.

Hughes, John T. "Doniphan's Expedition." In *Doniphan's Expedition and the Conquest of New Mexico and California.* Ed. William Elsey Connelley, 113–524. Topeka: privately published, 1907.

Jackson, George A. "George A. Jackson's Diary, 1858–1859." Ed. LeRoy R. Hafen. *Colorado Magazine* 12, no. 6 (1935): 201–14.

James, Edwin. *James's Account of S. H. Long's Expedition, 1819–20.* 4 vols. Volumes 14–17 in Early Western Travels, 1748–1846, ed. Reuben Gold Thwaites. Cleveland, Ohio: Arthur H. Clark, 1905.

John, Elizabeth A. H. "An Earlier Chapter of Kiowa History." *New Mexico Historical Review* 60, no. 4 (1985): 379–97.

Johnston, Carolyn Ross. *Cherokee Women in Crisis: Trail of Tears, Civil War, and Allotment, 1838–1907.* Tuscaloosa: University of Alabama Press, 2003.

Jones, Douglas C. *The Treaty of Medicine Lodge: The Story of the Great Treaty Council as Told by Eyewitnesses.* Norman: University of Oklahoma Press, 1966.

Kan, Sergei. "Clan Mothers and Godmothers: Tlingit Women and Russian Orthodox Christianity, 1840–1940." *Ethnohistory* 43, no. 4 (1996): 613–41.

Kappler, Charles J. *Indian Treaties, 1778–1883*. Mattituck, N.Y.: Amereon House, 1972.

Kearny, S. W. *Report of a Summer Campaign to the Rocky Mountains in 1845*. 29th Cong., 1st sess., 1845, H. Doc. 2.

Kingman, Samuel A. "Diary of Samuel A. Kingman at Indian Treaty in 1865." *Kansas Historical Quarterly* 1, no. 5 (1932): 442–50.

Klein, Alan M. "The Political-Economy of Gender: A 19th Century Plains Indian Case Study." In *The Hidden Half: Studies of Plains Indian Women*, ed. Patricia Albers and Beatrice Medicine, 143–73. Lanham, Mass.: University Press of America, 1983.

Knack, Martha C. "Women and Men." In *A Companion to the Anthropology of American Indians*, ed. Thomas Biolsi, 51–68. Malden, Mass.: Blackwell, 2004.

Knack, Martha C., and Alice Littlefield. *Native Americans and Wage Labor: Ethnohistorical Perspectives*. Norman: University of Oklahoma Press, 1996.

Kroeber, Alfred L. *The Arapaho*. Lincoln: University of Nebraska Press, 1983.

———. "Arapaho Dialects." *University of California Publications* 12 (1916): 71–138.

Kurz, Rudolf. *Journal of Rudolph Friederich Kurz*. Ed. J. N. B. Hewitt. Trans. Myrtis Jarrell. Lincoln: University of Nebraska Press, 1970.

Lassiter, Luke Eric, Clyde Ellis, and Ralph Kotay. *The Jesus Road: Kiowas, Christianity, and Indian Hymns*. Lincoln: University of Nebraska Press, 2002.

Lavender, David. *Bent's Fort*. Garden City, N.Y.: Doubleday, 1954.

Lecompte, Janet. "John Poisal." In *The Mountain Men and the Fur Trade of the Far West*, vol. 6 of 10 vols., ed. LeRoy R. Hafen, 353–58. Glendale, Calif.: Arthur H. Clark, 1968.

Lewis, Oscar. *The Effects of White Contact Upon Blackfoot Culture, with Special Reference to the Role of the Fur Trade*. American Ethnological Society Monograph 6. New York: American Ethnological Society, 1942.

———. "Manly-Hearted Women among the North Piegan." *American Anthropologist* 43, no. 2 (1941): 173–87.

Liberty, Margot. "Plains Indian Women Through Time: A Preliminary Overview." In *Lifeways of Intermontane and Plains Montana Indians*, 137–50. Occasional Papers of the Museum of the Rockies 1. Bozeman: Montana State University, 1979.

Lindsey, Donal F. *Indians at Hampton Institute, 1877–1923*. Urbana: University of Illinois Press, 1995.

Lomawaima, K. Tsianina. *They Called It Prairie Light: The Story of Chilocco Indian School*. Lincoln: University of Nebraska Press, 1994.

Lookingbill, Brad D. *War Dance at Fort Marion: Plains Indian War Prisoners*. Norman: University of Oklahoma Press, 2006.

Lowe, Percival G. *Five Years a Dragoon*. Kansas City, Mo.: Franklin Hudson, 1906.

Lowie, Robert H. *Plains Indian Age Societies: Historical and Comparative Summary.* Anthropological Papers of the American Museum of Natural History 11, pt. 13. New York: The Trustees, 1916.

Mann, Henrietta. *Cheyenne-Arapaho Education, 1871–1982.* Niwot: University Press of Colorado, 1997.

Mannheim, Karl. "The Problem of Generations." In *Essays on the Sociology of Knowledge,* ed. and trans. Paul Kecskemeti, 276–322. London: Routledge and Kegan Paul, 1952.

McBeth, Sally J. *Ethnic Identity and the Boarding School Experience of West-Central Oklahoma American Indians.* Washington, D.C.: University Press of America, 1983.

McMechen, Edgar C. "The Model of Auraria-Denver of 1860." *Colorado Magazine* 12, no. 4 (1935): 121–26.

Mellis, Allison Fuss. *Riding Buffaloes and Broncos: Rodeo and Native Traditions in the Northern Great Plains.* Norman: University of Oklahoma Press, 2003.

Michelson, Truman. "Narrative of an Arapaho Woman." *American Anthropologist* 35, 4 (1933): 595–610.

Mooney, James. *The Ghost-Dance Religion and the Sioux Outbreak of 1890.* Fourteenth Annual Report of the Bureau of American Ethnology. Washington, D.C.: Bureau of American Ethnology, 1896.

Moore, John H. *The Cheyenne.* Cambridge, Mass.: Blackwell, 1996.

———. *The Cheyenne Nation: A Social and Demographic History.* Lincoln: University of Nebraska Press, 1987.

Murphy, Lucy Eldersveld. *A Gathering of Rivers: Indians, Metis, and Mining in the Western Great Lakes, 1737–1832.* Lincoln: University of Nebraska Press, 2000.

Ortner, Sherry B. *Anthropology and Social Theory: Culture, Power, and the Acting Subject.* Durham, N.C.: Duke University Press, 2006.

———. *Making Gender: The Politics and Erotics of Culture.* Boston: Beacon, 1996.

Osburn, Katherine M. B. *Southern Ute Women: Autonomy and Assimilation on the Reservation, 1887–1934.* Albuquerque: University of New Mexico Press, 1998.

Page, Elizabeth M. *In Camp and Tepee: An Indian Mission Story.* New York: Board of Public and Bible-School Work of the Reformed Church in America, 1915.

Pancoast, Charles Edward. *A Quaker Forty-Niner.* Ed. Anna Paschall Hannum. Philadelphia: University of Pennsylvania Press, 1930.

Parkman, Francis. *The Journals of Francis Parkman.* Ed. Mason Wade. New York: Harper and Sons, 1947.

———. *The Oregon Trail: Sketches of Prairie and Rocky-Mountain Life.* Boston: Little, Brown, 1925.

Perdue, Theda. *Cherokee Women: Gender and Culture Change, 1700–1835.* Lincoln: University of Nebraska Press, 1998.

Pesantubbe, Michelene E. *Choctaw Women in a Chaotic World: The Clash of Cultures in the Colonial Southeast*. Albuquerque: University of New Mexico Press, 2005.

Petersen, Karen Daniels. *Plains Indian Art from Fort Marion*. Norman: University of Oklahoma Press, 1971.

Phelps, General Lee. *Tepee Trails, Putting the Indian's Feet in the Jesus Road*. Atlanta, Ga.: Home Mission Board, Southern Baptist Convention, 1937.

Poole, Carolyn Garrett. "Reservation Policy and the Economic Position of Wichita Women." *Great Plains Quarterly* 8, no. 3 (1988): 158–71.

Powell, Peter John. *People of the Sacred Mountain: A History of the Northern Cheyenne Chiefs and War Societies, 1830–1879*. New York: Harper and Row, 1981.

Powers, Marla N. *Oglala Women: Myth, Ritual, and Reality*. Chicago: University of Chicago Press, 1986.

Pratt, Richard Henry. *Battlefield and Classroom: Four Decades with the American Indian, 1867–1904*. New Haven, Conn.: Yale University Press, 1964.

Richardson, Albert D. *Beyond the Mississippi: From the Great River to the Great Ocean*. Hartford, Conn.: American, 1867.

Riney, Scott. *The Rapid City Indian School, 1898–1933*. Norman: University of Oklahoma Press, 1999.

Ruxton, George. *Ruxton of the Rockies*. Ed. LeRoy R. Hafen. Norman: University of Oklahoma Press, 1950.

Ryder, Norman B. "The Cohort as a Concept in the Study of Social Change." *American Sociological Review* 30 (1965): 843–61.

Sage, Rufus. *Rufus B. Sage: His Letters and Papers, 1836–1847*. Vol. 4–5 in The Far West and the Rockies Historical Series, 1820–1875, ed. LeRoy R. Hafen and Ann W. Hafen. Glendale, Calif.: Arthur H. Clark, 1956.

Seger, John H. *Early Days Among the Cheyenne and Arapahoe Indians*. Ed. Stanley Vestal. Norman: University of Oklahoma Press, 1979 [1924].

Shoemaker, Nancy, ed. *Negotiators of Change: Historical Perspectives on Native American Women*. New York: Routledge, 1995.

Simmons, Marc. *Kit Carson and His Three Wives: A Family History*. Albuquerque: University of New Mexico Press, 2003.

Sleeper-Smith, Susan. *Indian Women and French Men: Rethinking Cultural Encounter in the Western Great Lakes*. Amherst: University of Massachusetts Press, 2001.

Smith, E. Willard. "The E. Willard Smith Journal, 1839–40." In *To the Rockies and Oregon, 1839–1842*. Vol. 3 in The Far West and the Rockies Historical Series, 1820–1875, eds. LeRoy R. Hafen and Ann W. Hafen, 151–95. Glendale, Calif.: Arthur H. Clark, 1955.

Spitzer, Alan B. "The Historical Problem of Generations." *American Historical Review* 78 (1973): 1353–85.

Stanley, Henry M. "A British Journalist Reports the Medicine Lodge Peace Councils of 1867." *Kansas Historical Quarterly* 33, no. 3 (1967): 249–320.

————. *My Early Travels and Adventures in America and Asia.* 2 vols. London: Marston, 1895.

Stewart, Omer C. *Peyote Religion: A History.* Norman: University of Oklahoma Press, 1987.

Stuart, Robert. "Robert Stuart's Journal." In *The Discovery of the Oregon Trail*, ed. Philip Ashton Rollins, 3–263. New York: Charles Scribner's Sons, 1935.

Swan, Daniel C. *Peyote Religious Art: Symbols of Faith and Belief.* Jackson: University Press of Mississippi, 1999.

Tabeau, Pierre-Antoine. *Tabeau's Narrative of Loisel's Expedition to the Upper Missouri.* Ed. Annie Heloise Abel. Norman: University of Oklahoma Press, 1939.

Talbot, Theodore. *The Journals of Theodore Talbot, 1843 and 1849–52.* Ed. Charles H. Carey. Portland, Ore.: Metropolitan, 1931.

Thorne, Tanis C. *The Many Hands of My Relations: French and Indians on the Lower Missouri.* Columbia: University of Missouri Press, 1996.

Toll, Oliver W. *Arapaho Names and Trails: A Report of a 1914 Pack Trip.* N. p., 1962.

Trennert, Robert A. *The Phoenix Indian School: Forced Assimilation in Arizona, 1891–1935.* Norman: University of Oklahoma Press, 1988.

Trudeau, Jean Baptiste. "Trudeau's Description of the Upper Missouri." *Mississippi Valley Historical Review* 8, nos. 1–2 (1921): 149–79.

————. "Journal of Jean Baptiste Trudeau among the Arikara Indians in 1795." Trans. Mrs. H. T. Beauregard. *Missouri Historical Society Collections* 4, no. 1 (1912): 9–48.

U.S. Bureau of the Census. Washington, D.C.: National Population of the U.S., Archives, 1860 (M653), Indian Population 1900 (T623).

U.S. Congress. House of Representatives. Hearings before a subcommittee of the Committee on Indian Affairs on HR 2614, 67 cong., 2d sess., 1918.

U.S. Congress. Senate. *Report of the Secretary of War on the Sand Creek Massacre.* 39 Cong., 2d sess., 1865, S. Doc. 26.

U.S. Office of Indian Affairs. *Annual Reports of the Commissioner of Indian Affairs.* Washington, D.C.: Government Printing Office, 1846–1906.

Van Kirk, Sylvia. *Many Tender Ties: Women in Fur-Trade Society, 1670–1870.* Norman: University of Oklahoma Press, 1980.

Viola, Herman J. *Diplomats in Buckskins: A History of Indian Delegations in Washington City.* Washington, D.C.: Smithsonian Institution Press, 1981.

Wand, Augustin C. *Jesuits in Territorial Kansas, 1827–1861.* St. Mary's, Kan.: St. Mary's Star, 1962.

Wasson, A. F. Mrs. *One Who Was Strong: Life Story of Mary P. Jayne.* Oklahoma City: Women's Missionary Union of Oklahoma, 1937.

Weist, Katherine M. "Plains Indian Women: An Assessment." In *Anthropology on the Great Plains*, ed. W. Raymond Wood and Margot Liberty, 255–71. Lincoln: University of Nebraska, 1980.

Welter, Barbara. "The Cult of True Womanhood: 1820–1860." *American Quarterly* 18, no. 2 (1966): 151–74.

Wied, Maximilian, Prinz von. *People of the First Man: Life among the Plains Indi-ans in Their Final Days of Glory: The Firsthand Account of Prince Maximilian's Expedition Up the Missouri River, 1833–34.* Eds. Davis Thomas and Karin Ronnefeldt. New York: Dutton, 1976.

Wildman, Thomas G. "Letters of Thomas G. Wildman, 1859." In *Reports from Colorado: The Wildman Letters, 1859–1865,* vol. 13 in The Far West and the Rockies Historical Series, 1820–1875, eds., LeRoy R. Hafen and Ann W. Hafen, 23–85. Glendale, Calif.: Arthur H. Clark, 1961.

Williams, Ezekiel. "Ezekiel Williams' Adventures in Colorado." *Missouri Histori-cal Society Collections* 4, no. 2 (1913): 194–208.

Williams, Walter L. *Spirit and the Flesh: Sexual Diversity in American Indian Culture.* Boston: Beacon Press, 1986.

Women's American Baptist Home Mission Society. *Thirty-Six Years Among Indians.* Chicago, 1914.

INDEX